Introduction
to the
Old Testament

Introduction
to the
Old Testament

A Liberation Perspective

ANTHONY R. CERESKO, O.S.F.S.

Revised and Expanded Edition

ORBIS BOOKS

Maryknoll, New York 10545

The Catholic Foreign Mission Society of America (Maryknoll) recruits and trains people for overseas missionary service. Through Orbis Books, Maryknoll aims to foster the international dialogue that is essential to mission. The books published, however, reflect the opinions of their authors and are not meant to represent the official position of the Society. To obtain more information about Maryknoll and Orbis Books, visit our website at www.maryknoll.org

Unless otherwise indicated, biblical citations are from the New American Bible. Reprinted with permission.
Manufactured in the United States of America

Acknowledgments:
Excerpts from *Psalms* by Ernesto Cardenal copyright © 1969 by Ernesto Cardenal, reprinted by permission of The Crossroad Publishing Company. Illustrations from *Reading the Old Testament: An Introduction* by Lawrence Boadt copyright © 1984 by The Missionary Society of St. Paul the Apostle in the State of New York, reprinted by permission of Paulist Press. Maps from the American Bible Society copyright © 1976 by the United Bible Societies, used by permission of the American Bible Society. Illustration of the prophet Isaiah, fresco from the Sistine Chapel ceiling, used by permission of the Vatican Museum. Photographs of British Museum material reproduced by courtesy of the Trustees of the British Museum. Every attempt was made to locate those who hold copyrights to the material in this book.

Library of Congress Cataloging-in-Publication Data

Ceresko, Anthony R.
    Introduction to the Old Testament : a liberation perspective /
Anthony R. Ceresko.
        p. cm.
    Includes bibliographical references and indexes.
    ISBN 1-57075-348-2
    1. Bible. O.T. — Introductions.   2. Sociology, Biblical.
3. Liberation theology.   I. Title.

Contents

PART V
PROPHECY IN THE PRE-EXILIC PERIOD

List of Illustrations and Maps

Preface

This *Introduction* results from my experience of teaching an Old Testament survey course over a number of years and from my growing appreciation of Norman K. Gottwald's studies on the origins of Israel and Israel's religion. The occasion for the latter was a course entitled "The Bible and Liberation" which I team-taught with Professor Lee F. Cormie during my years at St. Michael's College in Toronto. I owe a special debt of gratitude to Lee. From him I learned much about the role of sociology in the study of religion and the Bible and about the location of Gottwald's work in the larger context of debate within the field of sociology itself.

My primary goal in writing this *Introduction* was to make available to a larger audience the results of Gottwald's work, especially those aspects which help open new theological perspectives on the Bible and which make clearer the possibilities of reading it from a liberation point of view. Thus I had in mind a textbook for a one-semester survey course on the Old Testament for upper-level college or first-year theology students as well as for Bible study or adult education classes.

Thanks are due in a number of quarters: to the administration of the University of St. Michael's College, Toronto, especially Dean Michael A. Fahey, S.J., of the Faculty of Theology, for the semester study-leave in 1989 during which the first draft was written; to my Oblate confreres and to the members of my family for their support and lively interest in the project; to the people at Orbis Books, especially Robert Ellsberg, for their encouragement and careful attention to my work at every stage; finally, to my colleagues both at St. Michael's College and St. Peter's Pontifical Institute in Bangalore, India, and especially to my students at both schools. It is to the latter that I affectionately dedicate this book.

Anthony R. Ceresko

Preface to the Revised and Expanded Edition

In September 1999 I was forced to leave India unexpectedly, after almost nine years of living and teaching at St. Peter's Pontifical Institute, Bangalore. The Central Government in Delhi refused to extend my Residential Permit, but gave no reason for the refusal. The months following that event I spent in Rome and devoted the time to revising and updating my *Introduction to the Old Testament: A Liberation Perspective* (Orbis Books, 1992).

This revised edition reflects the lively interchanges among scholars over the last fifteen years or so concerning the origins of Israel. Chapters four, nine, and ten have been rewritten in light of those discussions. Other additions and revisions take into account recent work on the wisdom writings, the psalter, and the prophets. I have also included brief treatments of Sirach and the Book of Wisdom. The bibliography as well has been updated and expanded.

I am grateful to the various reviewers of the 1992 book. Their helpful comments and suggestions have guided my work of revising. I thank my Superior General, Most Rev. Lewis S. Fiorelli, O.S.F.S., for giving me leave to make use of the months before my move to the Philippines for the revision work. The Superior of the Oblate Generalate in Rome, Rev. Francis J. Blood, O.S.F.S., deserves my gratitude for his support and encouragement during my stay there. The librarians and staff of the Pontifical Biblical Institute Library in Rome were most gracious and helpful. Prof. Norman K. Gottwald deserves a special word of thanks. The bibliographical information he provided proved enormously helpful. Robert Ellsberg, Editor in Chief at Orbis Books, encouraged me to undertake this revision. My own editor at Orbis, Susan Perry, has contributed enormously to this project in terms of her time and energy. To her and to all at Orbis Books, my thanks are due.

Finally, I am grateful to the Philippine Central Province of the Society of the Divine Word for inviting me to join the teaching staff of Divine Word

School of Theology, Tagaytay City. My thanks to the Rector, Rev. Antolin V. Uy, S.V.D., and the Dean of Studies, Rev. Felix S. Ferrer, S.V.D., for their welcome and hospitality.

Anthony R. Ceresko

Books of the Old Testament

Roman Catholic		Protestant
1. Genesis 2. Exodus 3. Leviticus 4. Numbers 5. Deuteronomy	Pentateuch	1. Genesis 2. Exodus 3. Leviticus 4. Numbers 5. Deuteronomy
6. Joshua 7. Judges 8. Ruth 9. 1 Samuel 10. 2 Samuel 11. 1 Kings 12. 2 Kings 13. 1 Chronicles 14. 2 Chronicles 15. Ezra 16. Nehemiah 17. Tobit 18. Judith 19. Esther*	Historical Books	6. Joshua 7. Judges 8. Ruth 9. 1 Samuel 10. 2 Samuel 11. 1 Kings 12. 2 Kings 13. 1 Chronicles 14. 2 Chronicles 15. Ezra 16. Nehemiah *Apocrypha* *Apocrypha* 17. Esther
20. Job 21. Psalms 22. Proverbs 23. Ecclesiastes 24. Song of Solomon 25. Wisdom of Solomon 26. Ecclesiasticus (Ben Sira)	Poetry & Wisdom	18. Job 19. Psalms 20. Proverbs 21. Ecclesiastes 22. Song of Solomon *Apocrypha* *Apocrypha*
27. Isaiah 28. Jeremiah 29. Lamentations 30. Baruch including Letter of Jeremiah 31. Ezekiel 32. Daniel* 33. Hosea 34. Joel 35. Amos 36. Obadiah 37. Jonah 38. Micah 39. Nahum 40. Habakkuk 41. Zephaniah 42. Haggai 43. Zechariah 44. Malachi 45. 1 Maccabees 46. 2 Maccabees	Prophetic Writings	23. Isaiah 24. Jeremiah 25. Lamentations *Apocrypha* 26. Ezekiel 27. Daniel 28. Hosea 29. Joel 30. Amos 31. Obadiah 32. Jonah 33. Micah 34. Nahum 35. Habakkuk 36. Zephaniah 37. Haggai 38. Zechariah 39. Malachi *Apocrypha* *Apocrypha*

*Esther and Daniel in the Roman Catholic canon are larger than their counterparts in the Protestant canon. This surplus material is included in the Protestant Apocrypha as Additions to Esther and Additions to Daniel. The Prayer of Manasseh, also found in the Apocrypha, is not included in the Roman Catholic canon.

Chronological Chart

Events in the Holy Land and in the Wider Ancient World

Holy Land	The Wider Ancient World
9000 B.C.E. Definitive shift from food-gathering to food-producing: first evidence of settled village life in the Fertile Crescent	
	3200 "Dawn of history": first evidence of writing and organized city life in Mesopotamia and Egypt
	2900-2400 Sumerian "Classical" Period
	2900-2200 Egyptian "Old Kingdom" Period (pyramids)
Early Bronze Age Canaan: development of city-states 3000-2000	2500-2200 Kingdom of Ebla (northern Syria)
	2400-2200 Akkadian Empire (Sargon the Great; Central Mesopotamia)
Middle Bronze Age Canaan: city-states 2000-1500	1750-1550 Old Babylonian Empire (e.g., King Hammurabi)
	1400-1300 "Amarna Age" in Egypt
Late Bronze Age Canaan 1500-1200	1290-1224 Pharaoh Ramses II rules Egypt
	1285 Battle of Kadesh and peace treaty between Ramses II and the Hittite Emperor

1220	Memorial Stone of Pharaoh Merneptah: first mention of an "Israel" in Canaan
1182	Ugarit destroyed by the "Sea Peoples"
900-600	Assyrian Empire
612	Fall of Nineveh, the Assyrian capital
605-539	Neo-Babylonian Empire
539	Cyrus of Persia conquers Babylon
539-326	Persian Empire
334-326	Alexander the Great conquers Persian Empire
175-163	Rule of Hellenistic King Antiochus IV Epiphanes

Iron Age	1200-300
Tribal Confederation: Period of the Judges	1200-1020
Israelite army routed by Philistines at Aphek	1050
Saul: "chieftain" over Israel	1020-1000
Kingship of David	1000-962
Kingship of Solomon	962-922
Divided monarchy	922-722
Assyrians destroy Samaria, capital of Northern Kingdom (Israel)	722
Babylonians destroy Jerusalem, capital of Southern Kingdom (Judah)	587
Babylonian Exile	587-539
Dedication of the rebuilt Temple in Jerusalem	515
Hellenistic Period	300-63
Roman army under Pompey takes Jerusalem	63

PART I

INTRODUCTION

1

The Bible in the Modern World

THE BIBLE AND TODAY'S WORLD

The Bible and Politics

You know, I turn back to your ancient prophets in the Old Testament and the signs foretelling Armageddon, and I find myself wondering if—if we're the generation that's going to see that come about. I don't know if you've noted any of those prophecies lately, but believe me, they certainly describe the times we're going through (Ronald Reagan to Tom Dine of the American-Israel Public Affairs Committee; *The Jerusalem Post,* October 28, 1983).

It would be difficult to deny the continuing impact of the Bible in our day and age when confronted with a remark such as this from an American president in the early 1980s. A number of mainline church leaders expressed their alarm at this statement of President Reagan. The statement suggested links between the president and advocates of "nuclear dispensationalist" ideas, and the political and strategic agenda of some of the advocates. Nuclear dispensationalism holds that the present age is under the power of Satan and is rapidly nearing a nuclear war crisis; that such a war has been foretold in the pages of the Bible and constitutes God's plan for human history. The possibility that President Reagan may have been influenced by the beliefs and agenda of these groups and was personally persuaded that the end of the world was near raised some chilling questions about his ability to act rationally in a nuclear crisis.

South Africa provides another example of the role which the Bible has often played in politics. Dutch Reformed theologians for years drew upon the traditions of the Hebrews' Exodus from Egypt as a prototype of the Boer people's experience. Forced to journey to a new land to escape what

3

they saw as the slavery of British colonialism in the Cape Colony, they successfully subdued and subordinated the indigenous populations of what became the Orange Free State. For these pious and Bible-reading Boers, the black population of their new home was the equivalent of the Canaanites whom the people of Israel had encountered and whom God had ordered to be destroyed or subdued. The logic of apartheid for these Afrikaaners was thus partly drawn from and found its justification in the Bible itself. By contrast, these same indigenous peoples found in that same story of the Exodus their own mandate to struggle for a free and better life.

Most recently, both critics and proponents of the so-called "New World Order" have appealed to the Bible to support their positions. Gregory Baum, for example, has expressed his reservations concerning this "New Order" in a post-Gulf War world. He also recalls the stories in the Book of Exodus, but not the ones about the freedom from Egyptian slavery. For Baum, the challenges and difficulties of the wilderness wanderings offer the point of comparison:

> Over a period of some thirty years we lived, prayed and struggled as if the conversion of society to greater justice was an historical possibility in our own generation. This period, I believe, is over. The Gulf War was for me the publicly approved massacre that sealed in blood the new politico-economic orientation, begun over a decade ago, that sought to enhance the material well-being of a privileged minority and assign to the margin the rest of the globe's population. . . .
>
> In my judgment, this "kairos" is over. We now live in the "wilderness". . . . Living in the desert, mourning and lamentation have their place—so the scriptures tell us (Editorial in *The Ecumenist* [Spring 1991]).

In addition to the political sphere, the Bible has an important role in other contexts as well—the church, the university, and popular culture. In each of them, questions of the meaning and role of the Bible, and conflict over that meaning and role, play a part.

The Bible and the Church

Among most Protestant churches, especially of the evangelical and pentecostal variety, the Bible continues to provide the basis of doctrinal expression and worship. For Roman Catholics, the Second Vatican Council (1961-65) gave new importance to the Bible, most noticeably in public worship. Biblical texts are read now in the vernacular, that is, in the language of the people, and congregations hear a much wider selection of passages from both Old and New Testaments at Mass. Catholics, now encouraged to read the Bible, have formed Bible study groups and flock to lectures and courses on the Bible in both parish and school settings. In addition, varieties of prayer groups, especially those inspired by the charismatic movement within Roman Catholicism, usually have the Scriptures as the focus of their reading and reflection.

In 1993 the Roman Catholic Church took another important step with the publication of the document, *The Interpretation of the Bible in the Church*, by the Pontifical Biblical Commission. The document contains a description and evaluation of many of the recent methods and approaches to interpreting the Bible. Authored by a group that includes some of the best Catholic Bible scholars, it provides an authoritative guide to reading and interpreting the church's Scriptures.

Thus the Bible plays a role within all these communities. But it is the communities themselves which determine what that role is. Consequently we often hear reports in the media on the internal conflicts within these churches about "what the Bible means" and how it is to be read and understood.

The Bible and the University

In academic circles the Bible and religion in general have formed the center of a whole growth industry in higher education. Since the 1950s hundreds of colleges and universities have established religious studies departments or departments of religion in which academic study of the Bible has flourished. The number of courses, journals, and books with the Bible as subject has multiplied, and the number of teachers and scholars researching and lecturing on both Old and New Testaments has increased literally thousands-fold. This vast increase in both the number and variety of people, men and women, studying and lecturing on the Bible at both the college and university level has led to the development of a whole array of approaches and methods for reading and analyzing the biblical text.

The Bible's historical and literary value remain high on the agenda in this context. Thanks to new discoveries by archeologists and historians of the Ancient Near East, our knowledge about the history and culture of the biblical world has increased enormously. Scholars have gained many new insights into the grammar and vocabulary of the biblical languages (Hebrew, Greek, Aramaic) and the character and shape of both the Bible's poetry and prose. These approaches in particular offer the possibility of studying the

Bible in a "neutral" or "non-confessional" context, supposedly excluding questions of personal beliefs about the religious demands with which these texts by their very nature confront the reader. Thus this "academic" approach to the Bible sometimes comes into conflict with church authorities. This was especially the case in the nineteenth and early twentieth centuries when the "scientific" study of the biblical text led to interpretations at variance with traditional religious teachings, for example, with regard to the meaning of the Creation stories in Genesis 1-3.

The Bible and Popular Culture

The centrality of the Bible in popular culture remains strong as well. One need only survey briefly the extraordinary variety and popularity (and fall from grace) of the televangelist preachers of recent years. The way of reading the Bible among these people (and among some Catholics) has been strongly influenced by the so-called fundamentalist approach. Basically, this approach understands the biblical text as being able to speak directly to the reader. Its meaning is seen as applying immediately and personally to the life of the individual reader or believer and his or her own context. Having been "saved" and having Jesus as their "personal savior," these individuals consider themselves enlightened and guided by the Holy Spirit in their reading of the text. Theoretically, then, a soldier in battle could decide that the text of Psalm 137:8-9 applies to him. Thus he would presumably justify frightful acts of vengeance against an unbelieving enemy:

> O daughter of Babylon, you destroyer,
> happy the man who shall repay you
> the evil you have done us!
> Happy the man who shall seize and smash
> your little ones against the rock!

Venerated as the "Word of God" and revealing the "Will of God," the Bible has the power to motivate and justify even extreme acts of heroism and/or violence. It has been used both for good and for evil purposes throughout its long history. One need only point out the centuries of persecution endured by the Jewish people, a persecution supported and justified by appeal to the Scriptures. By contrast, some Israeli fundamentalists use the Scriptures to defend their persecution of the Palestinian peoples. Finally, we mentioned above the South African Dutch Reformed theologians' arguments in favor of their government's policy of apartheid based on biblical texts.

The Bible's potential as a political tool or weapon has not been lost on rulers and politicians, whether in the past or in the present. Witness in our own day and age, for example, the frequent election campaign alliances between fundamentalist televangelists and right-wing politicians.

SOCIOLOGY AND THE BIBLE

Consciousness of this "political" potential or role for the Bible has led to a realization that the Bible itself contains evidence of similar processes at work—political, economic, and societal—throughout the long history of the Bible's creation. In an attempt to gain some insight into these processes, recent years have seen the application of the methods and findings of the modern science of sociology in the study of the biblical text.

Those involved in teaching the Scriptures or preaching from them know how often preachers or teachers will take a theme or story from the Bible and attempt to "modernize" it. They try to explain it and put it in terms of issues or problems or people of their community today or of society as a whole. Sometimes they may even be aware that the particular biblical text or story originally had little to do with the situation or issue they are addressing. But somehow the situation or issue seems to "fit" and to help to make the Bible meaningful and relevant to the lives of the congregation or Bible class.

This process of "reapplying" the stories and themes of the Scriptures to contemporary situations is an age-old one as any study of the history of biblical interpretation will readily demonstrate. Jews and Christians have been engaged in it in one form or another for two thousand years, and more. One obvious example, especially among Catholics, is the use of Old Testament texts to laud the example and virtues of Mary, the mother of Jesus. One popular hymn from the Middle Ages ("Tota pulchra es," "You are all beautiful, O Mary"), for instance, uses the words of praise originally meant for the Jewish heroine of the Book of Judith:

> You are the glory of Jerusalem,
>   the surpassing joy of Israel;
>   you are the splendid boast of our people (Jdth 15:9).

The New Testament itself engages in the same reuse of language and themes. For instance, the Gospel of Matthew presents a striking description of the figure of John the Baptist as he emerges from the solitude of the

Judean wilderness and begins his prophetic career: "John wore clothing made of camel's hair and had a leather belt around his waist. His food was locusts and wild honey" (Matt 3:4). When we compare this description with the depiction of Elijah the prophet in 2 Kings 1:7-8, we see that Matthew intended to draw a comparison between the Baptist and this popular Old Testament figure:

> The king [Ahaziah of Israel] asked them, "What was the man like who came up to you and said these things to you?" "Wearing a hairy garment," they replied, "with a leather girdle about his loins." "It is Elijah the Tishbite!" he exclaimed (2 Kings 1:7-8).

Scholars who study the Old Testament know very well what a key role this process of "reapplication" and "reuse" of older stories and themes and texts played in the creation of the Old Testament itself. We know that down through the centuries the Old Testament again and again underwent a "rewriting." Attempts were constantly made to unify and give a single perspective to the diverse materials contained therein. New themes were woven in and new stories added in order to help the Scriptures come alive and speak meaningfully to a new generation in a new historical situation. Much of the work of Old Testament specialists over the last hundred or more years has been to trace back that history of the Bible's creation and/or to try to recover the original context and meaning of a particular story or theme.

One result of this work has been an enormous increase in our understanding and appreciation of the *theology* of the Old Testament. These include the great themes and ideas that have been used to unify and explain the history and experience of the people of Israel, and to show how God has been present and active in that experience and history. The demonstration of the pervasiveness and importance, for example, of the theme of "covenant" all through the Scriptures or of the centrality of "social justice" to the teaching of the prophets provides good examples of this fruitful work.

Recent years, however, have seen new developments in the study of the Old Testament. Among these have been the application of the methods and findings of the modern science of sociology to the biblical text. In other words, scholars in the past have discovered and described the key ideas and themes, that is the *theology* which has been used to unify and give some coherence to the variety of stories and traditions found in the Old Testament. In more recent times they have turned their attention to discovering the social, political, and economic forces which have had an influence on and helped to determine the choice and shape of that theology and those ideas.

The strong emphasis on ritual and sacrifice and temple in the first five books of the Old Testament, the so-called "Pentateuch," for example, betrays the hand of the Jerusalem Temple priesthood in giving those five books their final form. But close study reveals that the "unity" which these five books initially seem to have is a superficial and, at times, an uneasy one. The "gaps" and contradictions which a closer examination of the text uncovers point to some of the conflicts and struggles taking place within the Jewish community of that post-Exilic period (539-400 B.C.E.), the time when these five books reached their final form. The application of the methods and findings of modern sociology has proved helpful in discovering some of the social, economic, and political forces at work in these conflicts and struggles.

One of the key contributors to this new approach in biblical studies has been Norman Gottwald. His monumental work on the origins of Israel and of Israel's religion, *The Tribes of Yahweh,* has become a modern classic. Subtitled *A Sociology of the Religion of Liberated Israel 1250-1050 B.C.E.,* it has been heralded as marking a "paradigm shift" in our study of the Scriptures. Gottwald built on the pioneer work of George Mendenhall in the early 1960s in the use of sociological methods to reconstruct the history of the "Conquest" of Canaan by the Israelite tribes. He has produced a study of Israelite society during the period of the Judges which demonstrates how much of what was considered unique and original in Israel's religion can be linked with an attempt to create a new socio-economic-political order in Canaan of the thirteenth through eleventh centuries B.C.E.

LIBERATION THEOLOGY AND THE BIBLE

Hand in hand with the development of this sociological approach and its attention to social processes in the formation and interpretation of the biblical text have been developments in the Latin American churches. Among other things, the Latin Americans were coming to see the importance of the context in which the Bible is being read. Thus, a biblical text can have one meaning for a church congregation, as part of a religious service, for example, but quite a different meaning for a scholar lecturing on the same text in a university setting. With regard to the Creation stories in Genesis, for instance, the scholar may be more interested in questions of dating, sources, or the precise meaning of certain Hebrew words. The church community, on the other hand, would seek above all the passage's religious meaning and the demands that it makes on their life and beliefs.

These Latin American students of the Bible came to realize that an even more important consideration was the *social location* of those who were reading it. People in different social and political contexts bring to the Bible quite different questions. Thus the meanings they see in the text can vary greatly. The slaveowners in the southern United States, for example, christianized their slaves, believing that this new religion would make the slaves more docile and obedient. Meanwhile, these same slaves found in the stories of the Hebrew people's oppression in Egypt and subsequent liberation a powerful motive for hope in the struggle for their own freedom.

In these Latin American countries a pastoral strategy had developed which drew upon the human resources among the people themselves. Lay leaders were trained to form small communities of the faithful, especially in the remote rural villages and in the sprawling urban *barrios* or slums. These lay leaders organized what came commonly to be called Base Christian Communities, in which reading and reflection on the Bible constituted one of the central activities. The people who formed these Base Communities, uneducated and unsophisticated as they might appear to be, nevertheless needed little encouragement or direction to find so much of their own lives and experience reflected in the stories and songs and the men and women of the Scriptures.

In contrast to the fundamentalist reader of the Bible who also recognized the frequent immediacy of the text, the reading and interpretation of the Scriptures in these Latin American groups was shaped and conditioned by the communal and ecclesial context in which it took place. It was evident to these groups that the people and stories and songs they found in the Bible were relevant to their own social, economic, and political situation. The Bible was proving to be a powerful tool in bringing them to an awareness of their condition as oppressed and exploited people, and for inspiring their initial attempts at organizing and working together for change and reform.

Reform was not seen simply as a political process for the people in the Base Communities. Rather, their reading and reflection together on the stories and personalities of the Scriptures began to affect and shape the nature and character of their religious faith. No longer was God conceived of primarily as one who saves the individual soul. They came more and more to think about the God of the Bible as a God of the people, a God who stands by them when they are oppressed and exploited, a God of the poor who acts on behalf of the poor and the powerless to liberate and free them from their slavery.

A story such as that of the Exodus, the story that stands at the heart of the Old Testament, held great meaning for those who comprised these Base Communities. Theologians in touch with what was happening in the Base Communities gained new insights and perspectives from the astonishing affinity with the Scriptures which these simple "exegetes" possessed. Consequently there began to develop a new way of doing theology during the 1960s. What was happening in Latin America became more widely known throughout other third world countries and in Europe and North America with the publication and then translation of what has become a classic work, *A Theology of Liberation,* by the Peruvian theologian Gustavo Gutiérrez.

One of the key elements in this theology of liberation, then, involves the social location from which it emerged. It does not owe its development so much to scholars and seminaries. Rather, its origins are in the Base Christian Communities drawn from the poor and exploited majority of Latin Americans. Further, those who began to reflect on what was happening came to realize that *any* approach to the Bible will inevitably be affected by the social, economic, and political commitments of the interpreter. The interpreter's context and commitments influence how he or she reads the text as well as what questions they ask of it.

In their study of the Bible these scholars began to realize that the formation of the Scriptures themselves involved the same processes. The various parts of the Bible reflect the economic, political, and social commitments of their authors. Thus one can discern, on closer examination, the conflicts and struggles that determined the shape and content of the Bible as we have it now. This recognition led to the increased use of the methods and findings of the modern science of sociology. In particular it involved the formulation of two important interpretive principles. One of these has been described as "the hermeneutical privilege of the poor"; the second is the so-called "hermeneutic of suspicion."

The Hermeneutical Privilege of the Poor

This "hermeneutical privilege of the poor" counsels us to read the Bible and its history through the eyes of the poor and the powerless. It leads us to understand the meaning and message of the Scriptures as particularly accessible to those "at the bottom" economically and socially. This should not be surprising once we examine and recognize how the Bible itself understands history. We are accustomed to operating with the notion that history involves mainly the important individuals of an ancient society. In the books of Samuel and Kings this indeed seems to be the case. The stories recounted there concern primarily the important personages of the monarchy period—Samuel, Saul, David, Solomon, the kings, warriors, officials, high priests, queens, and queen mothers of both Israel and Judah.

But the stories of the mothers and fathers in Genesis 12-50 are of quite a different type. They are family stories of births and deaths, of marriages and migrations, of the hopes and fears and conflicts of individuals and groups. They seem to have no great stake or part in the larger conflicts between the peoples and nations among whom they live, even though these larger conflicts touch and affect their daily lives. They are stories of individuals and groups who live at the margins, outside the centers of civilization and culture. The importance and centrality given to these stories and memories, the fact that these kinds of people are singled out as Israel's mothers and fathers, give us a clue as to how Israel understood itself, its origins, and its identity. They were a people who had their roots outside the centers where the "important" people lived and effective decision-making presumably took place.

This is all the more true when we remember the central story of the Exodus from Egypt. It is the story of those who were at the very bottom of Egyptian society, effectively non-persons in the greatest empire of the day. It is not an account of a king and his battles or of great alliances and wealth. It is the story of a small group of slaves, their suffering and poverty and struggle, which later Israelites saw as the central moment and source which gave meaning and purpose to their life as a people.

Thus the Scriptures themselves seem to suggest that the angle from which we should read the Bible and its history is "from the bottom," through the eyes of the powerless and the poor, from the point of view of the oppressed. The story that stands at the origins of the biblical tradition, then, is the experience of a group of non-persons miraculously liberated from slavery who journeyed into a new land that offered new opportunities for hope and for freedom. The God whom they encountered in that experience they described as the One who made that liberation possible, who freed them, and who led them to that land, and who gave them new reasons for hope:

> But the LORD said [to Moses], "I have witnessed the affliction of my people in Egypt and have heard their cry of complaint against their slave drivers, so I know well what they are suffering. Therefore I have come down to rescue them from the hands of the Egyptians and lead them out of that land into a good and spacious land, a land flowing with milk and honey. So indeed the cry of the Israelites has reached me, and I have noted that the Egyptians are oppressing them. Come, now! I will send you to Pharaoh to lead my people, the Israelites, out of Egypt" (Ex 3:7-10).

No wonder, then, that among the later generations of those who stand within that biblical tradition, those who also find themselves "at the bottom" can experience and express such astonishing affinity with and insight into the meaning and power the pages of the Bible hold.

A painting in the tomb of Rekhmire from the reign of Thutmose III (15th century B.C.E.) shows the harsh fate of slaves in Egypt.

A painting from the tomb of Puyemre, Thebes, Egypt (15th century B.C.E.) portrays wine making, a bearded Semite driving cattle, and a slave being beaten by an overseer.

The Hermeneutic of Suspicion

It was assumed in the past that theology and interpretation of the Bible were best left in the hands of experts, those trained in philosophy, history, the biblical languages, and so forth. Liberation theologians began to recognize, however, that theology and exegesis done by experts tended to reflect mainly the concerns and questions of such experts. The questions and concerns important to those in the Base Communities, representing the majority of poor and exploited in their countries, usually found no place in exegetical and theological books, journals, and discussions.

These liberation theologians also came to realize the same observation could be made with regard to much of the biblical text itself. It was the product of specific times and places and groups of people at various levels on the social, economic, and political scales, people with a variety of concerns and interests. These liberation theologians formulated what has come to be known as the "hermeneutic of suspicion." This represents the technical term for an approach to the Bible that begins with certain kinds of questions. The word "suspicion" here does not imply a lack of trust in the truth or authority of the Bible. Rather one who follows this approach continually and systematically raises questions. Why was this story told this way, with these personages placed as the central and determining actors? Why are these episodes remembered and narrated rather than others? What biases are implicit in the point of view and relative importance given to certain individuals and events in contrast to other individuals, persons, and events? How does my own "social location" affect the kinds of questions that I ask of the Bible and the kinds of persons and events that attract my attention and interest?

For example, a person reading stories about Israel's ancestors in Genesis 12-50 from a feminist point of view would practice a "hermeneutic of suspicion" by raising the question of why men are seen as the principal, indeed almost exclusive actors in the stories. The women generally stand in the background and are important principally as actors in the men's stories. A feminist "hermeneutic of suspicion" reveals these stories as reflecting not only the patriarchal—male-centered and male-biased—nature of the society out of which the stories came; this "hermeneutic of suspicion" also highlights the patriarchal prejudice of the author or authors who recorded them.

A LIBERATION PERSPECTIVE

The above discussion of these new methods and insights for reading and understanding the Bible suggests that those in the so-called First World are in a position to learn something from their brothers and sisters in Latin America and in other places in the Third World. They can profit from listening closely to the experience of women and blacks in the First World, from native peoples in North America, and from all those in solidarity with these voices and concerns. Many of us recognize a common bond through the biblical faith commitment we share, and as members of the same human family we face together a series of grave crises. The very future of our race, indeed of our planet, is threatened by ecological disaster, the proliferation of nuclear and chemical weapons, and the ever-growing gulf between rich and poor. The imperative for cooperation and solidarity not only among those who stand within the biblical tradition but among all the peoples of the earth has never been stronger.

NEW LANDS AND NEW EYES FOR READING THE BIBLE

Those within the biblical tradition, Christians and Jews alike, are becoming more conscious of the common search for God that they share with peoples of other faiths. Christianity and Judaism sprang from the soil of Asia, a continent that has given birth to other faith traditions as ancient or even more ancient than the Judean-Christian tradition: Hinduism, Buddhism, Islam, Taoism, and so forth. Solidarity with them in the search to build a more human community represents a powerful way to discover what we already share in our common search for God.

Further, Christians in Asia and other locations in the developing world bring new eyes and new experiences to their reading of the Bible. Their contacts with other ancient faith traditions, their different cultural backgrounds, and the fresh questions that they pose enable them to find new meaning and insights in these ancient texts. These Christians have developed new approaches to the Scriptures and demonstrate a growing confidence in the validity of their interpretations.

What follows in this *Introduction to the Old Testament* constitutes an invitation to learn from their experience and insights. They offer us new and important ways of understanding and discovering how the Bible can act as a source of hope and inspiration. And the insights derived from these new approaches to the Bible have been mediated by a growing body of scholarly commentary shaped by the intention of being in solidarity with the world's poor and oppressed.

We saw above some of the ways in which the Bible continues to play a role in life and culture today—in politics, in the church, in the university. The approach we will follow here is an attempt to read and understand the biblical text through the eyes of the poor and oppressed, those "at the bottom."

However, we may find that such an approach is not merely an academic exercise. It may serve to challenge some of our basic economic, social, and political, as well as our theological, ethical, and ecclesial commitments. In that sense it may represent a call to conversion, to a *metanoia,* a change of mind and heart, as well.

REVIEW QUESTIONS

1. Describe some further ways in which the Bible continues to have a place and impact on our world today.

2. How much of the Old Testament have you read? Do you have some favorite books or passages in it? Why are they important for you?

3. Are there parts of the Old Testament you usually avoid or skip over? Why?

4. Can you offer other examples of how the Bible has been used to justify doubtful or even wrong actions by individuals or groups; or examples of how it has been made use of as a political tool or weapon?

5. How would you describe your own "social location"? How might that social location affect the kinds of questions and presuppositions that you bring to the Bible?

6. How would you explain the meaning of the term "a liberation perspective"? Why do you think this approach might be important?

2

A Modern Look at Biblical Times

MODERN DISCOVERIES AND THE HISTORICAL CRITICAL APPROACH TO THE BIBLE

Introduction

Before we begin our discussion of Israel's story as a people and of the body of literature in which the Israelites distilled their memories and reflections on their experience, we need to say a few words about contemporary study and approaches to the Bible. Recent evaluations of liberation theologians have lamented the "sloppy" use of the Scriptures and have challenged those who approach the Bible as well as theology from a liberation perspective to be more careful and critical. Thus it is important to make sure that our reading of the Scriptures is based on the latest advances and methods. The principal direction biblical scholars have taken in the last one hundred fifty years has been the development of what is known as the historical critical approach. This approach acknowledges the *historically conditioned* character of all products of human culture, including the Scriptures; thus it reads and analyzes the Scriptures *critically* as documents reflecting a particular time and place and a specific culture.

The Bible and the Ancient World

Introduction

The enormous advances in human knowledge and technology, especially since the Renaissance, have made available an immense amount of information that is of direct or indirect use in our understanding of the Scriptures. This is not at all to downgrade the inspired character of these books, that is, the recognition of their special status as the Word of God for believing Jews and

Christians. It is rather an acknowledgment of the profoundly human nature of that Word, an ever greater appreciation of the fact that God chose to communicate with human beings through the words and the language of a specific time, place, and culture. Consequently, the more we can learn about that time, place, and culture, the greater will be our understanding of and insight into God's word, which was spoken and which continues to be spoken within a specific context. The Roman Catholic Church officially acknowledged and embraced this approach to the Scriptures beginning with Pope Pius XII's pioneering encyclical *Divino Afflante Spiritu* in 1943, called by some the *magna carta* of modern Catholic biblical studies. The Second Vatican Council reaffirmed and reinforced this direction in its Decree on Divine Revelation (*Dei Verbum*) in 1965 (see especially nos. 12 and 13). In 1993, the Pontifical Biblical Commission's document, *The Interpretation of the Bible in the Church,* summarized and evaluated the new approaches and methods that have taken as their starting point historical critical studies.

To understand the tremendous expansion of human knowledge—for example, just during the past two hundred years—all one need do is imagine a hospital of today in comparison with a hospital in the early 1800s. One quickly becomes aware of the almost unbelievable difference brought about by such discoveries as antibiotics, anesthesia, vaccines, and new operating techniques and procedures. Today's medicine is a whole new world compared to two hundred years ago. Although similar advances have taken place in just about every other area of human knowledge, Raymond Brown has noted how progress in three areas in particular has greatly affected our understanding of the Bible—language studies, history, and archeology.

The Rediscovery of Ancient Languages and the Bible

Prior to the nineteenth century the Bible was the chief source, if not the sole source, for our knowledge of the ancient world before the time of Greece and Rome. All we knew of the civilizations and empires of Egypt, Babylon, Assyria, the Hittites, and the Canaanites, came as background to the main story the Hebrew Scriptures were recounting, the story of the people of Israel. In many cases we knew little beyond the simple fact that these peoples and civilizations existed. All of that changed with a series of discoveries in the last two centuries. First came the discovery in Egypt of the Rosetta stone by French troops under Napoleon Bonaparte in 1799. This inscription had the same text carved in three different languages, one known language, namely Greek, and two unknown languages. These latter both turned out to be forms of ancient Egyptian. With the Greek text providing the necessary key, the French scholar Jean François Champollion was able to decipher the two Egyptian languages. One was written in the *hieroglyphic* script used to record literally thousands of inscriptions found in the ancient tombs and temples of Egypt. Thus the whole panorama of Egypt's three thousand years as one of the central and dominant civilizations in the ancient world was opened up to scholars and historians. Barely a generation later, in the 1830s, a young Englishman named Henry Creswicke Rawlinson began to decipher an inscription in three languages carved high on a rock cliff in what is today Iraq. One of the languages was in cuneiform (wedge-shaped) characters (see illustration on p. 32). It turned out to be the ancient East Semitic tongue spoken by the Assyrians and Babylonians. Thus thousands of texts written in cuneiform—historical annals, treaties, contracts, religious rituals, myths, and epics—became available over the next decades from the massive archeological digs launched in the Middle East. As with Egypt, now the exciting phenomenon of discovery and insight took place for ancient Mesopotamia. The entire sweep of three thousand years unfolded before the historians' eyes—the rise and fall of kingdom and empire, the birth and death of whole civilizations such as the Sumerians, the Babylonians, the Assyrians, and the Hittites.

In this century the discovery of the ruins of the ancient city of Ugarit at Ras Shamra on the northwest coast of Syria in 1928 has yielded thousands of clay tablets written in the Canaanite language. Deciphering these texts has had an enormous impact on our study of the Bible. The matrix out of which Israel emerged was the flourishing Canaanite civilization of Syria-Palestine in the late second millennium B.C.E. The language (Hebrew is the southern dialect of the Canaanite tongue), culture, and many of the customs of this Canaanite civilization are preserved in the Bible. Canaanite poetic style and imagery are reflected in the psalms and in the poetry of the prophets. Thus the texts from ancient Ugarit, especially the myths and epics which deal with the gods and heroes of these people, have greatly illuminated the Hebrew Scriptures and provided us, in one sense, with the equivalent of the "Canaanite Bible."

An important find in Egypt at the end of the last century, to which we will refer in regard to Israel's origins, was the body of the texts known as the Amarna Letters (see illustration on p. 101). This collection contained over three hundred letters inscribed in cuneiform script on clay tablets. The letters came from kings of various Canaanite centers in pre-Israelite Palestine who were pleading with Pharaoh for troops and support. The letters provide a vivid picture of the chaotic decades of struggle and warfare during the fourteenth century B.C.E. in Late Bronze Age Canaan.

Finally, a sensational discovery occurred in 1974 and 1975 at Tell Mardikh in northern Syria: a whole royal archive containing thousands of documents. From these archives it has been established that this was the site of ancient

Ebla. Many of these texts, dating from the latter years of the third millennium (2450-2200 B.C.E.), are written in what some scholars refer to as proto-Canaanite, that is, a not-too-distant ancestor of biblical Hebrew. The implications of the richness of this find will become more and more apparent as study of these texts enlarges our knowledge of the earlier history of the language and culture which eventually gave birth to our Bible.

Archeology and the Bible

Implicit in our discussion of the linguistic advances above are the advances in the science of *archeology,* which made available most of the texts from the ancient world for the linguists to decipher and study, and the resulting enrichment and expansion of our knowledge of the *history* of the pre-Greek and Roman periods. Archeology has matured and developed as a science, especially since the beginning of the nineteenth century. Among the pioneers of archeology in the Holy Land were Sir Flinders Petrie (1853-1942) and William F. Albright (1891-1971).

Petrie was an Englishman who worked principally in Egypt. He pioneered the development of ceramic or pottery chronology in determining the date of artifacts and levels of occupation in the various mounds or tells which abound by the thousands in the Middle East today. In ancient times a favorable site would be inhabited by successive generations or populations, each group or period building its dwellings, temples, administrative structures, and city walls on top of the remains of the earlier settlement. Thus a large mound would form, concealing within itself the evidence of successive generations and levels of habitation over hundreds or even thousands of years. Later layers, for example from the fifth and fourth centuries B.C.E. can be dated by means of coins bearing the names of rulers or kings when such coins are found buried in association with the other remains. But Petrie noticed in his work that the various levels of occupation each contained its own distinctive samples of pottery—fired clay bowls, beakers, cups, storage jars, and so on—which were made and used by the thousands in ancient times. Often

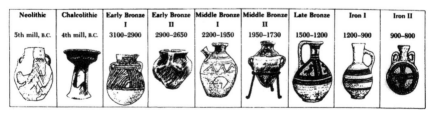

Neolithic	Chalcolithic	Early Bronze I	Early Bronze II	Middle Bronze I	Middle Bronze II	Late Bronze	Iron I	Iron II
5th mill., B.C.	4th mill., B.C.	3100–2900	2900–2650	2200–1950	1950–1730	1500–1200	1200–900	900–800

"Pottery clock" used in dating materials and sites.

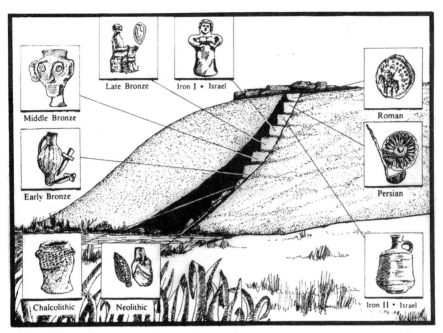

Cross-section of a "tell" preserving evidence of habitation by successive groups.

pottery of the same shape, color, thickness, and decoration was found over a wide area. Thus by keeping track of the layer in which a type of pottery was found and coordinating it with finds in other mounds—especially in those in which other materials such as inscriptions or texts gave an indication for dating—one could create a kind of "pottery clock" to furnish the basis for establishing dates and chronologies of settlements and cultures all over the Ancient Near East.

Following the lead of Petrie, who worked only briefly in Palestine at Tell el-Hesi (possibly the biblical city of Eglon), the American Orientalist William F. Albright directed a series of excavations from 1926 to 1932 at Tell Beit Mirsim (identified by Albright with biblical Debir). From the pottery fragments found in the successive levels of that mound, Albright was able to establish an absolute chronology for Palestinian pottery which has not been substantially modified since.

Archeologists today continue to build on and expand the work of these early pioneers. Earlier exploration focused mainly on great urban centers mentioned in the Old Testament, such as Jericho, Megiddo, Hazor. Today interest has expanded into investigation of the countryside, village life, farming and herding activities, and the evidence of population and settlement patterns. As a result of their excavation and study, archeologists have literally resurrected the history and cultures which flourished for thousands of years in Egypt, in Mesopotamia, and in the Holy Land (Syro-Palestine).

Ancient History and the Bible

In our discussion about the advances in language studies and in archeology, we have already had occasion to mention the great expansion of our knowledge of the *history* of the ancient world in which Israel and its Scriptures came to be. We can now put into a clear historical framework the events of Israel's history and the development of the various books that make up our Bible. In a few cases we can even assign a specific date to a particular event; for example, the first capture of Jerusalem by the armies of the Babylonian king Nebuchadnezzar took place March 16, 597 B.C.E. And scholars can determine whether a particular author intended to write a historical work or is only using historical details as a backdrop for a story or parable. Thus in studying the book of Jonah, for example, this new knowledge about ancient history along with recognition of Jonah's appealing literary qualities—the exaggeration, the irony, the humor—has led scholars to abandon the attempt to read the book as history. Instead, critical interpreters have turned their attention to the work's character and function as story, a story written not simply to entertain but to teach some profound lessons about Israel's God.

THE GEOGRAPHY OF PALESTINE

We turn now to a brief look at the shape and physical characteristics of this small strip of land along the southern third of the eastern shore of the Mediterranean Sea, an area which is conventionally given the geographic name of Palestine. It was on this land that so much of biblical history took place, and the geography and topography of this land has had an enormous influence on the shaping of that history.

This narrow strip of land squeezed between the waters of the Mediterranean to the west and the Great Arabian Desert to the east is divided topographically into four quite distinct zones running north-south: (1) the coastal plain; (2) the central highlands; (3) the Jordan Valley; (4) the Transjordan plateau.

The *coastal plain* has no natural harbors. Thus, in contrast to the Phoenicians farther north, the inhabitants of this southern sector developed no significant maritime trade. It is the most fertile part of the land and was densely populated in biblical days. The gently rolling hills were given to the growing of grains such as wheat and barley.

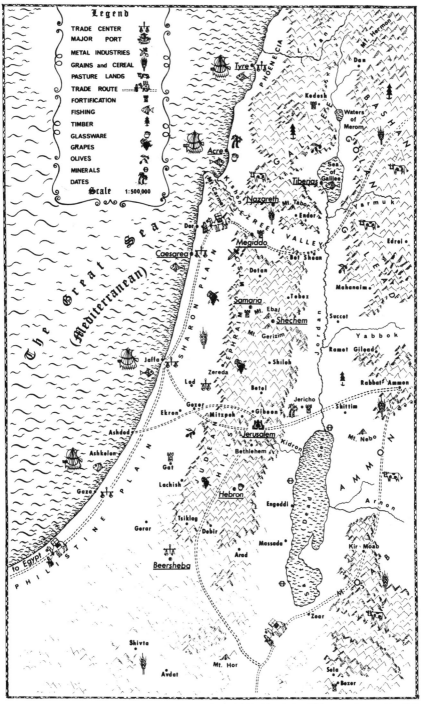

The *central highlands* encompass the long backbone of mountains, hills, and valleys that provided the setting for most of Israel's history. Along the ridges of these highlands runs the watershed of the land: on one side the slope carries west to the Mediterranean and on the other side east to the Jordan Valley. Despite the ruggedness of the terrain, the long season of winter rains enables the inhabitants of this central hill country to reap a decent yield from the olive, fig, and fruit trees of the slopes, and the grain and vineyards on the terraces and in the intervening valleys. These central highlands have been divided historically into three regions: Galilee in the north, Samaria in the center, and Judah in the south. Galilee in turn is separated from Samaria by the Plains of Esdraelon and Jezreel, through which passed a major east-west trade route, the *Via Maris* (Way of the Sea).

Palestine's most characteristic feature is the *Jordan Valley.* It is part of the great geological rift that extends north into Lebanon and Syria and continues south of the Dead Sea into the Wadi Arabah, beneath the Red Sea, and along the eastern coast of Africa. It forms the deepest rift or "wrinkle" on the earth's surface, revealing in certain places some of the oldest layers of the earth's crust. Palestine is parted lengthwise, north to south, by this rift, and through it the Jordan River descends in its snakelike course. The melting snows of Mount Hermon supply the waters of the Jordan River, which eventually empties into the Dead Sea. The latter, because it has no outlet, has become so saturated with salt and mineral deposits that it is unable to support any but a few marginal and somewhat exotic forms of life. The rapid descent of the Jordan's waters may be seen in the contrasting surface levels of its three lakes: (1) the former Lake Huleh, 223 feet above sea level (this lake was drained by Israeli engineers in 1967); (2) the Sea of Galilee, 695 feet below sea level; (3) the Dead Sea, 1,285 feet below sea level and the lowest point on the face of the earth.

Finally, the eastern-most zone, the *Transjordan plateau,* forms the high table-land region which rises abruptly out of the Jordan Valley and is broken into subregions by the Yarmuk, Jabbock, Arnon, and Zered rivers. The Bible says that the central regions were settled by the tribes of Reuben, Gad, and a portion of Manasseh during the Judges period. But Israelite control of this area seems to have been somewhat tenuous and sporadic.

The climate of Palestine comprises two principal periods. The cooler rainy season runs from October to April, at the end of which comes the harvest of the winter crops, mainly the grains such as barley and wheat. The rest of the year, May through September, is dry and hot and provides the growing and ripening season for grapes, figs, olives, and other fruits.

One of the major factors in the history of this land and the various peoples who have inhabited it has been its strategic military and commercial importance. This is due to the conjunction of two major trade routes, east-west and north-south, within its borders. The *Via Maris* or Way of the Sea connecting Egypt on the west with Mesopotamia on the east ran along the coastal plain as far as Mt. Carmel. There it was forced to turn inland through vulnerable mountain passes such as the one protected by the ancient city of Megiddo. It then crossed east through the Jezreel and Esdraelon plains and continued past the Lake of Galilee and on to Damascus. The second major route, the north-south one, was called the King's Highway. It followed the Transjordan plateau and carried the caravans coming from Arabia and the Spice Route from the Far East northward toward Damascus. Control of either of these routes ensured a lucrative income from the tolls imposed on the commerce which traversed them.

REVIEW QUESTIONS

1. Advances in what areas of human knowledge have most affected our current understanding of the Bible?

2. What is a *tell?*

3. How can the pottery found in a mound be of use to an archeologist?

4. How have the contributions of Sir Flinders Petrie and William F. Albright led to an increase in our understanding of the Scriptures?

5. Describe briefly the geography/topography of the four distinct zones running north-south in the Holy Land.

6. What two major trade routes passed through Palestine in ancient times? Why is it important to be attentive to this factor of Palestinian geography and history?

PART II

THE PENTATEUCH

3

The Historical Background
of the Ancient Near East

THE FERTILE CRESCENT AND THE BIRTH OF CIVILIZATION

The story of the people who produced the Bible cannot be told apart from the larger story of the human family. This is especially true for the story of one of that family's principal cultural complexes, known commonly as Western Civilization. Standard histories attempt to present that story from a neutral point of view, but implicit in their discussion is often an emphasis on the benefits of the technological, scientific, and organizational progress produced by the cultures and societies which developed out of this history. Liberation theologies, prompted by their methodological "hermeneutic of suspicion" are not as sanguine in their evaluation of some of the directions this history took. They search the archeological and written records for evidence of other stories and movements whose initiatives and memories were often cut short and expunged by those responsible for the "official" history and record of events. The Hebrew Scriptures in many ways represent the almost miraculous survival of some of these alternative stories and memories. They act as a counterfoil and alternative, a "dangerous memory," in contrast to the standard, implicitly positive, version of a steady and desirable "progress" in the course of Western Civilization.

The setting for the story is what is known today as the Middle East, usually referred to by scholars in this context as the Ancient Near East. It includes the land masses grouped around the eastern end of the Mediterranean Basin, principally western Asia and northeastern Africa. A study of a satellite photo of the region reveals its mainly arid and barren character, except for an arc of green and somewhat fertile land. This arc extends from the mouth of the Tigris and Euphrates rivers where they empty into the Persian Gulf on the east, north along the river valleys, arching west to the

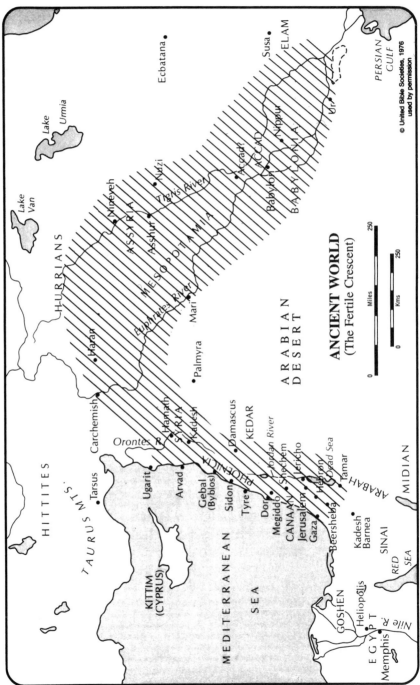

ANCIENT WORLD
(The Fertile Crescent)

© United Bible Societies, 1976
used by permission

Mediterranean, from there swinging south through Syria and Palestine, and on into the Nile River Delta of Egypt. This long extent of arable and relatively level, traversable land is traditionally known as the Fertile Crescent. It was here that Western Civilization and culture had their origins.

As the last ice age began receding around 10,000 B.C.E., weather patterns changed accordingly in the Ancient Near East. Rainfall from the depleted clouds that moved from the North Atlantic across Europe and the Mediterranean was sparse. Much of the interior region was, for all practical purposes, desert. What rain did come watered the eastern coast of the Mediterranean and the foothills of the mountains bordering the north and east of the Fertile Crescent. The Stone-Age population inhabiting these better-watered areas provides evidence of the first major technological revolution in human history, the shift from *food-gathering* to *food-producing,* which took place around 9000 B.C.E. This change may have been sparked by the appearance or discovery of a unique strain of wheat which produced a significantly higher yield than had heretofore been possible. The strain of wheat may have developed by genetic mutation or the coincidental crossing of wild grain varieties in early agricultural experimentation. In any case, the harvest yielded by this strain or combination of strains proved great enough to encourage more ambitious efforts at cultivation. This shift from food-gathering to food-producing was accompanied by the domestication of animals and the beginning of settled village life. Archeological excavations, especially over the last two decades, have revealed the widespread growth and prosperity of village life which began shortly thereafter. These excavations have concentrated in northern and northeastern Mesopotamia, at the foot of the Zagros mountains, and testify to an often astounding degree of organization among the inhabitants of these villages.

Although the Zagros foothills proved hospitable to the development of agriculture and organized village life, the inhabitants of this region gradually moved down into the river valleys, pressured perhaps by population growth and lured by the rich alluvial soil built up by the yearly spring flooding. A similar process was under way at the western end of the Fertile Crescent in the Nile Valley. But in both cases the cultivation along these river banks faced the challenge of developing a *technology* for building the dikes and canals necessary to harness the receding flood waters of the great rivers. The *organization* of human resources and effort on a large enough scale to prove worthwhile offered a second challenge. By the end of the fourth millennium B.C.E., both of these challenges had been met, first in Mesopotamia and shortly thereafter in Egypt.

The organizational needs of these new forms of human social arrangements served as the catalyst for the invention of writing. At first this tool was used to record commercial transactions—bills of sale, inventories, contracts. But soon more complex compositions appeared in the form of administrative documents, tax lists, battle reports, treaties, and finally, literature—the myths and epics, the historical chronicles, and religious texts that preserve the beliefs and fears and hopes of at least the ruling classes in these earliest stages of Western culture.

We thus reach, toward the end of the fourth millennium B.C.E. (that is, around the year 3000 B.C.E.), what is commonly referred to as "the dawn of history." But this phrase has two senses. First of all, "the dawn of history" refers to the appearance of *written records* of human activities, first in Mesopotamia and shortly afterward in Egypt. The *cuneiform* system of writing invented in Mesopotamia was carried out by incising a series of wedge-shaped characters onto wet clay tablets, which were then baked hard for permanent record keeping. The pictorial writing which developed in Egypt around the same time is referred to by scholars as *hieroglyphics*. Both methods were rather cumbersome and complex and required long years of study and application to master. The skill thus remained for the most part in the hands of elite corps of scribes, who mainly served the needs and interests of

Ox	Mountain	Man	Grain	Fish	Bird

The development of cuneiform writing in Mesopotamia. From top to bottom: 1) the earliest pictographic signs, 2) Sumerian signs of 2500 B.C.E., 3) Old Babylonian signs of 1800 B.C.E., 4) Neo-Assyrian signs of 700 B.C.E., and, 5) Neo-Babylonian signs of 600 B.C.E.

the ruling classes: the ruler or king and his commercial, diplomatic, and military activities; and the temple priesthood and administrative apparatus.

Besides the invention of writing and the availability from that point on of a written record of human activity, the term "the dawn of history" also refers to the development of a particular type of social organization known as the state. The human population that had gradually moved into the great river valleys eventually accepted or were cajoled or forced into an authoritarian and socially stratified organizational structure efficient and flexible enough to mobilize work-gangs and to undertake the complex and diversified tasks required by the demands of large-scale cultivating projects. This statist organizational paradigm, and what it implied in the political, social, economic, and religious spheres, began in the great river valleys of southern Mesopotamia (ancient Sumer) and Egypt. But it was imitated and spread and eventually came to dominate life in the ancient world. Politically and socially it meant a hierarchical, socially stratified, and male-dominated society, with elite ruling classes comprising a small minority (1-5%) of the population. This minority inhabited mainly the large walled urban centers and controlled most of the economic surplus the society produced.

The elite ruling classes included the king and nobility, the group of merchants who generally operated as agents of the king and oversaw trade and commerce with neighboring as well as with more distant city-states. There was also the corps of scribes trained in the art of writing and serving the state as bureaucrats. These scribes carried on the correspondence with other state rulers, kept records and copied orders for the state's commercial ventures, and wrote court annals often in the form of proto-historical and usually self-serving accounts of the ruler's exploits. They also ran something of a school to educate the younger members of the ruler's family and to train future scribes and bureaucrats. The ruling classes also included the professional soldiers, who served not only to defend the city-state from outside attack but also to carry on wars of conquest against other city-states and to impose order and submission on those who might challenge the ruling classes' authority from within. Such challenges or threats might include coup attempts from among the nobles or the ruler's own family, or they might take the form of rebellion of the slave or peasant population.

Finally, the ruling classes counted among their number the temple personnel, the priests and scribes charged with providing the ideological justification and legitimation of the existing social and political order through the production of a religious literature—myths, epics, prayers, rituals—and through the conduct of an often elaborate and impressive state-sponsored cult. Cultic activity often included the king in some way, and it affirmed his rule as well as the existing order as the declared will of divine beings. The

Ancient Near Eastern creation myths arose out of such a context; they linked the eternal and unchangeable order of the cosmos to the correspondingly eternal and unchangeable socio-economic and political order— eternal and unchangeable because it too was willed by the gods. Thus a *Weltanschauung,* a world-view, was established and reinforced which attempted to encompass all of reality. To threaten or attempt to change the reigning order was a grievous act of *lèse majesté* not only against the human rulers but also against the divine rulers responsible for the good order and harmony of the universe as a whole.

The artisan class formed a separate group, trained and rewarded for skill in working precious metals and stones, wood, ivory, and so on. They produced luxury items for the upper classes and provided articles for the trade carried on over the vast network of roads and water routes that eventually connected the Ancient Near East with Europe to the north, India and China to the east, Arabia and East Africa to the south, and Italy, Spain, and North Africa to the west.

The lower classes who comprised the vast majority of the population (90% or more) included the peasant farmers and herdsmen, slave laborers (often war captives), and perhaps certain artisan classes. The peasant farmers usually worked plots of land assigned to them by the king, the temple personnel, or the land-holding nobility. The parcels of land may have remained within the same families for a number of generations. Nevertheless, these farmers and herdsmen operated mainly as tenants and often turned over the majority if not all of their *surplus* to the control of the ruling elite classes. (Surplus here means all production over and above the minimum needed to stay alive and remain relatively productive.)

Thus the centralized state with its concomitant social stratification, which had first developed in the great river valleys, soon spread beyond and became the dominant social-political-economic-religious model for thousands of years in the ancient world. Historians and political economists refer to this model as a "tributary mode of production." There certainly must have been challenges to this model, especially from within, as various groups or individuals dreamed of and/or struggled for more just and equitable alternatives. Hints of movements and rebellions are heard, for example in the slave revolts in Greece and later in Italy under Roman rule. But most of these obviously failed and the dominant culture and classes expunged any record or memory of them as far as possible.

One group, however, did succeed. This occurred relatively late in ancient times, beginning shortly after 1250 B.C.E. (that is, two thousand years after "the dawn of history"). The group managed to create an alternative to the statist model, an alternative social, political, and economic order which in many ways represented the very opposite in organization and values to that statist model. This alternative or "mutant" order was supported and sustained by a religio-symbolic or "ideological" system which it had generated, or at least adapted and elaborated, known as *Yahwism.* This novel experiment managed to embody ideals and insights expressed in the collection of traditions, stories, and laws we know as the Bible. It offered an alternative which has served as a model and beacon of hope to peoples and generations and communities ever since.

The setting for that alternative order was a narrow corridor of land that ran along a 150 mile strip at the southern end of the eastern Mediterranean coast and varied in width from 35 miles in the north to 90 miles in the south. This narrow corridor was of crucial military and economic importance because it served as a bridge, a restricted zone of exchange and/or conflict, between the two major river valley centers of Mesopotamia in the east and Egypt in the west. Above we described the geography of this area, known as Palestine. In ancient times it was called Canaan. But before we examine the circumstances which led to the birth of this novel social-economic-religious-political order in this narrow corridor of land, we need to sketch some of the historical picture of the Fertile Crescent which forms the backdrop for that story.

THE HISTORY OF THE ANCIENT NEAR EAST
PRIOR TO THE APPEARANCE OF ISRAEL

Introduction

We noted above that "the dawn of history" was heralded both by the invention of writing and the emergence of the statist form of socio-political and economic organization. The usual date assigned for these two developments is around 3000 B.C.E. The beginning of the widespread use of bronze for weapons and tools throughout this region coincides with this date, and the next two thousand years are subdivided by archeologists into the Early Bronze Age (3000-2000 B.C.E.), Middle Bronze Age (2000-1500 B.C.E.), and Late Bronze Age (1500-1200 B.C.E.). From the extensive written records recovered from palace and temple archives and from the results of a century and a half of archeological exploration, historians have been able to document a good bit of the political history and describe, sometimes in detail, the life and culture of these ancient peoples. The statist form of socio-political and economic organization spread from the focal points of early history, the Nile Valley in Egypt and the Tigris and Euphrates valleys of Mesopotamia, into most areas and became the dominant organizational form. Soon almost every independent region, including the smallest, had its own king, bureaucracy, and army.

In each case an official religious ideology was elaborated to give legitimacy to the resulting socio-economic and political arrangements. Each state claimed that its origins and continued existence were willed by and protected by divine beings. And the often elaborate state-sponsored cult in the local temples seemed to strengthen and facilitate the domination of the ruling elite.

The reconstruction of successive political developments in this ancient world, based as it often is on documents from the official palace and temple archives, presents a sometimes confusing picture of wars of conquest, changes of regime, and the rise and fall of whole empires. Using one's imagination to reconstruct a "view from below," one could picture an even more complex situation of struggle and confrontation not only among the elite and powerful but also between groups of different economic, linguistic, and ethnic backgrounds. The "official" history needs to be complemented and put into perspective by social, economic, religious, and cultural data as well. On the whole, it seems that a common core of intellectual and material culture continued through the history of the major centers in Egypt and Mesopotamia, both of which heavily influenced developments in the "in-between" areas in Syria-Palestine. It is of great interest that the one document which did survive from ancient times and which has had a profound influence on the character and shape of the Western world issued from that "in-between" sector: the Hebrew Scriptures. Much of it represents "official" history in that its final form was shaped by the dominant groups first within Israel and later among the Jewish people. Nevertheless, it preserves, for example, in the stories of Israel's mothers and fathers, the memories and traditions of the outsiders, those who were marginal and unimportant in the eyes of the ones who wrote the "real" histories of the day.

Israel finally appears only at the end of the Late Bronze Age, coincidental with the beginning of the widespread use of iron, around 1200 B.C.E. The people of Israel were relative latecomers on history's stage, arriving well past the midpoint of the whole course of the history of the ancient world. All across the Ancient Near East cultures had arisen, developed their classical expressions, and in some cases declined and disappeared before Israel came on the scene. Before we focus on this people, however, we must set the scene by looking briefly at the political history in the major centers of Egypt, Mesopotamia, and Palestine, as historians have reconstructed it both from archeological as well as from literary remains.

Egypt

The geographic isolation of Egypt, surrounded as it was on three sides by desert and on the fourth by the sea, fostered a relatively continuous political and cultural development in comparison with the other centers. Egypt, even today, is comprised of two quite distinct areas: the Delta region or Lower Egypt in the north, and the valley of the Nile southward (Upper Egypt). Toward the end of the fourth millennium a gradual process of unification took place until finally two kingdoms emerged. Then, at the dawn of the historical period, the first kings or pharaohs claiming to rule a united Egypt appeared on the scene. Pharaoh Narmer, for example, is shown in his portraits wearing a double crown, the white crown of the south (Upper Egypt) and the red crown of the north (the Delta, or Lower Egypt). The assumption of power by Narmer and the first three successive dynasties marks the beginning of Egypt's historical period; from this point on we have written records available. The Third Dynasty of these pharaohs inaugurated what historians refer to as the Old Kingdom, which lasted from the twenty-ninth to the twenty-third centuries B.C.E., that is, through the better part of the third millennium. During this Old Kingdom period Egyptian society and culture assumed the characteristic features that endured relatively unchanged for the next twenty-five hundred years; it is to this period, for example, that the pyramids date. The Middle Kingdom (ca. 2000-1750 B.C.E.) and New Kingdom or Empire periods (ca. 1550-1100 B.C.E.) correspond to the Middle and Late Bronze Ages. During these two periods Egypt's imperial ambitions extended into Asia. Thus, for a good portion of the second millennium, Egypt either ruled or at least dominated Palestine.

Mesopotamia

In the discussion above of "the dawn of history," which was marked by the invention of writing and the creation of the model of societal organization known as the state, we gave the preliminary outlines in the development of the political history of Mesopotamia. It was principally in the southern part of the Tigris and Euphrates valleys that these events took place, in the region called Sumer (equivalent to the land of Shinar mentioned in the Tower of Babel story in Genesis 11:2). The inhabitants of Sumer are credited with many "firsts" in Western culture—the first writing system, the first schools, the first law codes, the first written literature. The so-called classical period of Sumerian culture lasted for the first half of the third millennium, from the twenty-ninth through twenty-sixth centuries B.C.E. Although the various city-states (Uruk, Warka, Ur, Eridu, etc.) were not united politically, they shared a uniform culture in language, literature, religion, art, and their socio-economic and political systems. The second half of the third millennium saw two important developments: (1) the decline of Sumerian dominance; and (2) the appearance of Ebla in north Syria.

Sumerian culture had formed, flowered, and then waned over the years of the early third millennium. At this point dominance passed to the more central part of Mesopotamia, to an East Semitic-speaking people known as the Akkadians, from their chief city, Akkad. Under the leadership of Sargon, this people set the example of *empire* for later history. Sargon led the Akkadians to dominate a large portion of Mesopotamia and thus established the first real empire in human history, that is, the domination by a single group of a wide territory inhabited by diverse populations. Later generations and groups would look back to Sargon as the prototype for imperial aspirations and achievements.

Until 1974 scholars assumed that Syria-Palestine's principal role was that of a bridge for commerce and communication between the two major centers of cultural activity and political power, Egypt and Mesopotamia. The sixteen thousand tablets and portions of tablets discovered in 1974 and 1975 at Tell Mardikh in north Syria, however, reveal Ebla as a major cultural and trading center, which already in the second half of the third millennium rivalled the primary centers in southern Mesopotamia. Although most of the tablets were written in Sumerian and employed the cuneiform writing system, some were composed in or reflected the influence of the language of the local populace, Eblaite. This language has been identified as a West Semitic tongue, which may prove to be an earlier form of Canaanite and thus an ancestor of biblical Hebrew. Early reports claim the presence of both names and cultural features similar to those found later in the Bible.

The second millennium B.C.E. saw the dominance of Assyrian power in northern Mesopotamia. This people, from their main center at Assur, developed an extensive trading network and a reputation as fierce and aggressive fighters. The southern part of the region was called Babylonia after its chief city, Babylon, which enjoyed a period of dominance (1750-1550 B.C.E.) under King Hammurabi (1732-1680 B.C.E.) and his successors. During the latter years of the second millennium (1550-1150 B.C.E.), however, a dynasty of foreign rulers called the Kassites held sway in the region.

Syria-Palestine

Palestine forms the southern part of what was in ancient times called Canaan. The latter term embraced the whole eastern coast of the Mediterranean from Turkey in the north to Egypt in the south, the area presently encompassing northern or coastal Syria, Lebanon, and the modern state of Israel, including the Occupied Territories. This "Greater Canaan," although never a political unity during the third and second millennia B.C.E., formed a cultural and linguistic whole. The picture of Canaanite life and culture has been filled out both by archeology and, especially for the second millennium, in the texts from ancient Ugarit. This city, a port and major trading center on the Syrian coast, was discovered in 1928 and excavations began in 1929. A large number of texts were uncovered there, many of them written in a northern form of the Canaanite language and therefore quite close to biblical Hebrew. Beside many commercial and diplomatic records, these tablets contained myths, epics, and religious rituals that provide insight into the background of much of the religious language, poetic style, and thought-world out of which the Hebrew Scriptures have come.

Ancient Ugarit was one of the largest among the scores of smaller city-states or kingdoms into which Canaan was divided during the two-thousand-year period of the Bronze Age. The people were Semites for the most part, as is evidenced by the place names. They initiated on a smaller scale the statist socio-economic and political organizational model of the great river-valley centers. Because of their strategic position straddling the major trade routes that connected the far corners of the ancient world, these people engaged extensively in trade and commerce. For most of the second millennium they were ruled or dominated by Egypt, their powerful neighbor to the south.

REVIEW QUESTIONS

1. Briefly describe the geographical setting for the birth of Western Civilization.

2. What was the first major technological revolution in human history? How and when did it take place?

3. What are the two senses for the phrase "the dawn of history"? How and when did this take place?

4. Describe briefly the statist organizational paradigm that developed in the two great river valleys in the Ancient Near East.

5. Describe the role and function of official religion within this organizational paradigm.

6. What are the three political-cultural areas into which historians generally divide the Fertile Crescent in the Ancient Near East? Give the highlights of the "official" history of *one* of these three regions.

4

The Ancestors of Israel

Suggested Bible Reading: Genesis 12-50

INTRODUCTION

There have been some modern critical attempts to locate the persons and events mentioned in the stories of Genesis in the second millennium world of the Ancient Near East. But none has proved convincing. Neither the names nor references to places and customs point clearly to one period and setting rather than another. How then are we to read these tales about Abraham and Sarah, Hagar and Ishmael, Isaac and Rebekah, Jacob and Rachel and Leah, Joseph and his brothers and their wives and children? What can they tell us, if anything, about the origins and prehistory of the people of Israel?

Our discussion in the preceding section focused on the *political* history of the ancient world during the Bronze Age. This is history as standard textbooks present it, based on readings and analyses of the historical and other records left by the ancient kings and their allies in the ruling classes. It is thus a political history in two senses. First, it tells the story principally of those who dominated the society politically, the "winners," if you will, in the various struggles for economic and political power. Second, it is political in the sense that it is often meant to serve the purposes of the powerful: to justify their right to rule, to strengthen their hold on power, and to enhance their own reputations and memory.

One of the problems with past attempts to coordinate and link this official historical record as scholars have reconstructed it with the history we find in Genesis 12-50 is that we are dealing with quite a different kind of history. Genesis represents quite a different motivation. It is not the record of individuals and groups who took part in the great power struggles of the day and who were integral members of the dominant social, economic, and political structure. Instead, it records the memories and recollections of various groups who for the most part stood *outside* of these structures, on the margins. These groups, which eventually came together to create Israel in the hill country of thirteenth-century B.C.E. Canaan, attempted by combining their individual stories into a single story to reinforce and cement their newly-won unity as a people. They created this single multicolored tapestry, their "history," to express their common, unifying purpose to create a life together and to take control of their own destiny and future. Thus the history we find in Genesis 12-50 is indeed political (or ideological) in one sense and analogous to the official history of kings and rulers; it was written not only to record the past but to play a definite social and political role in the present.

Not only did that history, that story, play a social and political role, however. It also played a theological one. These peoples shaped their common story to express their experience of the involvement of God in their lives and in their history. Their God was not just another god, like the gods of the other peoples. Their history or their "foundational story" expresses their growing consciousness of a God who stands in solidarity with and who acts on behalf of the poor, the outsider, those on the margins. This powerful God defended the powerless, who were seemingly at the mercy of the decision-makers in the world. As outside individuals and groups, small and large, heard stories of this God, they recognized something of their own experience. Many of them joined with this new people being created in the hill country of Canaan, accepted this God as their own, and added their personal and collective story to that of the others.

THE FORMATION OF THE TRADITIONS IN GENESIS 12-50 AND THE ORIGINS OF EARLY ISRAEL

Recent years have seen enormous progress in our understanding of how and when Israel came into being. The introduction of sociological and anthropological methods and surprising discoveries by archeologists have revolutionized our ways of approaching these texts. The stories about the mothers and fathers of Israel in Genesis 12-50 and the pre-monarchic Israel of the Books of Joshua and Judges now spring vividly to life against the historical and cultural background of ancient Canaan in the Late Bronze (1500-1200 B.C.E.) and Early Iron (1200-1000 B.C.E.) Ages.

The early work of George Mendenhall and especially the ground-breaking books of Norman Gottwald, *The Tribes of Yahweh* (1979) and *The Hebrew Bible* (1985), marked important moments of progress. In the meantime, archeological excavations in the highlands that run from the north through to the south of central Palestine yielded startling new evidence. Archeologists discovered the remains of hundreds of small unwalled villages that suddenly sprang up after 1250 B.C.E. in this central hill country. It is among the settlers who established these villages that historians and Bible scholars now recognize the beginnings of the people of Israel.

We are dealing in these biblical books—Genesis and Exodus through Joshua and Judges—more with "stories" than with what we today would understand as scientific "history." Thus an explanation in story form may constitute the best way to understand the origin and context of these stories in the Bible, and the people who first told these stories.

Who were these people who suddenly appeared in the central hill country of Canaan at the end of the Late Bronze Age? Where did they come from? What had motivated them to settle in this frontier area, establish these villages, and begin the difficult work of clearing and developing the land?

Joseph Callaway is an archeologist who was involved in some of the early work in this region. In 1969, he and his archeological team were uncovering the remains of Raddana, a small settlement in the central hill country, barely twenty kilometers north of Jerusalem. Among the many fragments of pottery found at the site, Callaway discovered the handle of a storage jar fashioned by some ancient potter over three thousand years before. Into the surface of the handle had been carved the name of the owner of the storage jar in archaic Hebrew script, *Ahilud,* a name common in the Hebrew Bible (see 2 Sam 8:16 and 20:24).

The "house" in which the jar handle had been found was one of six such clusters of buildings or "houses" forming a hilltop village surrounded by terraced farmland. The population of the village could not have been more than fifty people. Callaway describes his experience of uncovering the "house" which belonged to the owner of the storage jar:

> Ahilud is important to me because his house is the only one I excavated at Ai or Raddana that can be personalized with a family name. In a special way, he is representative for me of the villagers in scores of nameless settlements that dotted the hilltops of ancient Judea and Samaria during the period of the Judges. When the excavation ended and I was faced with the enormous task of analyzing the results, I thought often of Ahilud. Sometimes I would sit on the hilltop where he had lived. Overlooking a deep valley to the south and surrounded by architectural terraces, Ahilud's hilltop has preserved its ancient appearance. If I could understand Ahilud, I thought, I could understand what it meant to be an Israelite peasant in the days of the Judges.

Callaway provides a vivid description of life in such ancient villages: "In Ahilud's house, there was no furniture of the kind we have. People sat crosslegged on the packed clay and stone floor; there they gathered around a small open fire." If guests came, "A few flat stones placed around the fire pit served as makeshift stools."

Neither did Ahilud's house contain a kitchen. "Small round 'ovens' for cooking bread or boiling foods were located outside the front door or in an adjoining open courtyard that was shared by two or three households." Nor would one find bedrooms in such modest dwellings. Everyone slept on the floor of the large room that also served as the dining area at mealtimes. A modest pad on the floor formed one's bed, and one's outer garments provided covering during sleep.

If the houses in Ahilud's village lacked the kind of "creature comforts" we are accustomed to, Callaway reminds us that "these hill-country settlers were pioneers." They located their dwellings on previously unoccupied hilltops or the unoccupied ruins of ancient cities: "Generally, the new villages were small, less than five acres, and unfortified. The sites were inhospitable and marginal, the kind of places in which people live only to avoid conflict with the owners of more fertile areas."

The immigrants who settled these small villages brought with them considerable knowledge and skills as agriculturalists. They knew how to construct cisterns for collecting and storing fresh water. They introduced the techniques of terrace building to cultivate their wheat and barley crops on the slopes of the hills on which their villages were built. Contrary to the impression given in the stories of the Book of Genesis and especially in the Book of Exodus, these "Proto-Israelites" were not outsiders but "in-migrants" from elsewhere in Canaan itself. They represented the results of a major shift of population within the region from a centralized, urban-based life-style to a decentralized rural and village-based pattern.

Below in chapter nine we will outline the socioeconomic and political factors that lie in the background of the population shift and settlement of the sparsely inhabited and undeveloped hill country region. Suffice it to say that the closing years of Late Bronze Age Canaan were marked by increasing turmoil and conflict. Historians are divided on the causes of the growing breakdown of the established social and political order. But the archives of the Pharaohs in Egypt, who held nominal suzerainty over southern Canaan, provide a vivid picture of that turmoil. These "Amarna Letters," as they are referred to, contain pleas to the Pharaoh for help and accusations of disloyalty and conspiracy against the Pharaoh by various rulers of these Canaanite city-states.

Those who would have suffered the most from these conflicts and turmoil were the peasants and sheepherders in the countryside. Their burden of taxes increased to fund the military expeditions of the rulers. In addition, their crops were often the object of seizure or destructive raids among the various warring parties.

Those who decided to flee this increasingly intolerable situation would account for a large segment of the immigrants into the sparsely settled central highlands. The appearance of hundreds of these unwalled villages coincides with evidence of the abandonment or destruction of a number of large urban centers and the conflicts described in the Amarna Letters. Whatever the cause or causes of the breakdown of Late Bronze Age culture, the archeological record is clear—a major shift of population, or "in"-migration, and the settlement of the central highlands.

We could imagine Ahilud's parents or grandparents as participants in this in-migration. For years they had endured the drudgery and debilitating struggle in an agrarian village close to one of the fortified urban centers. Suddenly word spreads through their village of what was taking place not far from their valley—up there, in the hills. The first reports would have sounded exaggerated: a "Promised Land," fertile and free. These villagers knew only of the wilderness-like state of these highlands—thin, rocky soil covered with thick overgrowth, and water in scarce supply.

Nonetheless, Ahilud's grandparents packed their scarce belongings late one night and, along with a number of other families, fled into those hills and began the difficult process of building not only the new hilltop settlement at Raddana. They also had to develop a new way of organizing their lives together in this new village and in collaboration with other such hilltop settlements in the neighborhood. Free from the domination of the powerful rulers behind their walls and fortifications in the valleys, these people now felt themselves in control of their own lives and futures.

Norman Gottwald describes this group of "proto-Israelites" as originally formed mostly from the indigenous Canaanite population—village-based peasants, sheep and goat herders, itinerant metalworkers (the Kenites), priests renegade from the official urban-based cults, and mercenaries (Hebrews). These various groups had withdrawn from or fled the oppressive economic and social conditions of the coastal plain and fertile valleys of Canaan dominated by the large city-states and their statist mode of political, economic, and social organization. The inhabitants of these frontier villages were intent on making a new home in the sparsely settled hill country. There they sought to escape the reach of the urban enclaves and their ruling elite, who depended on the military with their principal weapon, the war chariot, to maintain control over the populace. Since the war chariot was unable to operate effectively in the rugged hill country, the newly settled inhabitants found themselves free from the strictures of the prevailing social order. Thus they were able to experiment and to create new economic, political, social, and religious models, often consciously the *opposite* of the hierarchically structured and socially stratified situation they had fled. In the statist system, 1% to 5% of the population controlled more than half the goods produced by the society, while 75% to 95% worked the land as tenants and paid heavy taxes in produce and forced labor. But they received only the barest subsistence necessary to remain productive. The hill country settlers consciously worked toward creating this system's *opposite.*

Key factors in forming this new society were an intentional "opening toward equality" in political and economic institutions and a religion based on the worship of a single deity. The story of this single God, and this God's singular involvement in their lives and in their history, served as a powerful force to mold them into a single and singular—"chosen"—people, a community unique in the ancient world in its social, economic, political, and religious character. The shape the community took on and its characterization of the God whom it sensed was standing by them and walking with them emerged chiefly out of the struggles for freedom and liberation in which the various groups were engaged.

The period of the tribal confederation, the period of the Judges (1250-1050 B.C.E.) was a time of a veritable explosion of the traditional material we find in Genesis 12-50. Stories were composed and combined and woven together. Some of the stories and memories date from the decades or even centuries before 1250 B.C.E. and reflect the experiences of the various groups before they began joining to form Israel. The experience of ancestor groups reflects the attempts of individuals, families, and clans to make their way along the margins and survive in situations in which they could be relatively free and able to control and determine their own destiny. Early relations and contacts with other groups who eventually leagued with them are reflected in the tentative attempts at cooperation and solidarity.

Rejecting the temptation to read these stories naively as straightforward historical accounts frees us to "read between the lines." Although they do not offer us the kind of historical data we are used to dealing with—dates and rulers and battles—they do have much to tell us in an *indirect* way about the hopes and ideals, the struggles and failures of these groups, and above all, about the unique character of the God Yahweh, whom they worshipped. The stories hint at the diversity of the groups involved and the separate paths along which they travelled in eventually creating that unique phenomenon known as Israel.

READING BETWEEN THE LINES OF GENESIS 12-50

First of all, declining to read these stories as straightforward history allows us to examine more closely the *functions* they served. One obvious role was to serve as a means of unifying the diverse groups. They linked and combined their various stories. In this way they were able both to embody and to symbolize the unity they had or hoped to achieve and to strengthen and ensure that unity. For example, recent anthropological research has demonstrated that the exchange of genealogies continues to function among certain Bedouin tribes to symbolize and strengthen newly created social, political, or economic ties. One tribe or clan finds that it is to its advantage to establish links with another, for example, for mutual defense or for cooperative trade ventures. Those links are formalized by the merging of their separate genealogies or family trees. The socio-economic and political function of the genealogy is thus more relevant and more to the point than any historical value it might have. Indeed, interpreting it as a straightforward historical document would be to misinterpret and be misled by it. The early linking of Isaac with Abraham thus reflects the union of at least two of the groups that eventually formed the tribe of Judah. And the realization of the cultural and linguistic ties these groups in the south had with neighboring peoples such as the Ammonites, Moabites, and Edomites, is embodied in the stories about the relations between Abraham and Lot. Chapter 13 of Genesis, for example, tells the story of how and why Abram and Lot, and thus their respective descendants, came to inhabit different parts of the land:

> From Egypt Abram went up to the Negeb with his wife and all that belonged to him, and Lot accompanied him. . . .
> Lot, who went with Abram, also had flocks and herds and tents, so that the land could not support them if they stayed together. . . . There were quarrels between the herdsmen of Abram's livestock and those of Lot's. . . .
> So Abram said to Lot: ". . . Is not the whole land at your disposal? Please separate from me. If you prefer the left, I will go to the right; if you prefer the right, I will go to the left." . . . Lot, therefore, chose for himself the whole Jordan Plain and set out eastward. Thus they separated from each other; Abram stayed in the land of Canaan, while Lot settled among the cities of the Plain, pitching his tents near Sodom (Gn 13:1, 5-7, 9, 11-12).

Thus the respective "descendants" of each of these ancestor figures, Abram's descendants on the one hand (Israel), and Lot's descendants on the other (the peoples of Moab and Ammon), handed on this story. It reflects their vague memories of those earlier ties and explains the many things which they had in common such as similar languages and culture.

A second function these stories and traditions in Genesis 12-50 served as they took shape over the years was to express the ideals and aspirations of the various groups that are their source. Abraham's welcome of the three strangers into his camp in Genesis 18:1-21 reflects the kind of mutual aid and generosity even toward strangers that the groups living in the frontier conditions of the newly opened hill country realized was vital to their survival:

> Looking up, he saw three men standing nearby. When he saw them, he ran from the entrance of the tent to greet them; and bowing to the ground, he said: "Sir, if I may ask you this favor, please do not go on past your servant. Let some water be brought, that you may bathe your feet, and then rest yourselves under the tree. Now that you have come this close to your servant, let me bring a little food, that you may refresh yourselves; and afterward you may go on your way" (Gn 18:2-5).

As we shall see in Chapter 5, one of the strangers turns out to be Yahweh himself. Thus Abraham's hospitality to strangers is rewarded. As the author of the Letter to the Hebrews reminds us: "Do not neglect hospitality, for through it some have unknowingly entertained angels" (Heb 13:2). Through this story we gain insight into the powerful sense this people had of the closeness, indeed daily involvement of their God in their everyday lives. Yahweh is a God who walks with and occasionally even shares a meal with his people.

In Genesis 30-31, Jacob demonstrates skill, cunning, and resourcefulness in dealing with those more advantaged economically, in this case, his father-in-law, Laban:

> Jacob replied: "You know what work I did for you and how well your livestock fared under my care; the little you had before I came has grown into very much, since the LORD's blessings came upon you in my company. . . . "What should I pay you?" Laban asked. Jacob answered: "You do not have to pay me anything outright. I will again pasture and tend your flock, if you do this one thing for me: go through your whole flock today and remove from it every dark animal from among the sheep and every spotted or speckled one from among the goats. Only such animals shall be my wages. . . .

So Jacob sent for Rachel and Leah . . . [and] said to them: "You well know what effort I put into serving your father; yet your father cheated me and changed my wages time after time" (Gn 30:29-30, 31-32; 31:4-7).

Through his cunning, however, the success of which he attributes to God's assistance and sanction, Jacob was able to secure his just wages and head for home with his new wives and family:

[Jacob said:] "God, however, did not let him [Laban] do me any harm. . . . Once, in the breeding season, I had a dream. . . . In the dream God's messenger called to me, 'Jacob!' 'Here!' I replied. Then he said, 'Note well. All the he-goats in the flock, as they mate, are streaked, speckled and mottled, for I have seen all the things that Laban has been doing to you. I am the God who appeared to you at Bethel, where you anointed a memorial stone and made a vow to me. Up, then! Leave this land and return to the land of your birth.' . . ."
Rachel and Leah answered him [Jacob]: "Have we still an heir's portion in our father's house? . . . He not only sold us; he has even used up the money that he got for us! All the wealth that God reclaimed from our father really belongs to us and our children. Therefore, do just as God has told you." Jacob proceeded to put his children and wives on camels, and he drove off with all his livestock and all the property he had acquired in Paddan-aram, to go to his father Isaac in the land of Canaan (Gn 31:7, 10-18).

One thing this story reflects is the realization by the various groups of settlers of the need for similar self-reliance and resourcefulness in the face of the precariousness of their own economic and military situations.

Some actions or experiments proved unhelpful or even harmful to the process of building a life together. Memories of these setbacks, mistakes, and failures served as reminders and cautions against such actions in the future. The incestuous activity of Reuben, for example, posed a threat to family stability and could create problems of inheritance and property rights:

While Israel [Jacob] was encamped in that region, Reuben went and lay with Bilhah, his father's concubine. When Israel heard of it, he was greatly offended (Gn 35:22).

Reuben's action comes under particularly strong condemnation and sanction:

"You, Reuben, my first-born,
    my strength and the first fruit of my manhood,
    excelling in rank and excelling in power!
Unruly as water, you shall no longer excel,
    for you climbed into your father's bed
    and defiled my couch to my sorrow" (Gn 49:3-4).

Clearly these stories can give us insight into the life and the processes by which these peoples of different origins found ways to live and work together in their common project.

Reading between the lines can also help us understand some of the conditions the settlers faced and obstacles they had to overcome during this crucial period in their formation and the formation of their traditions. In other words, we can intuit from the probable function these stories served how this grouping of tribes formed. We can also gain access to a certain *content* of information. For example, we can reconstruct some of the contexts within which and conditions under which these traditions took shape the way they did.

The principal context, as we said earlier, was the formative process of the tribal confederation, the weaving of a unity out of diverse groups by weaving together their stories and traditions. It was a unity they at least implicitly realized they had to achieve if they were going to survive and maintain control over their own social and economic relationships. It was a unity they had to forge and work at preserving if they wished to take hold of and be able to live their *own* story, their *own* history, and not be simply a part of someone else's history.

The stories are set in two groups of sites: (1) the highlands of Samaria around Bethel and Shechem, and Gilead across the Jordan around Penuel and Succoth; (2) the highlands of Judah around Hebron, and the Negeb (the southern wilderness area) of Judah around Gezer and Beersheba. The stories set in the first group of sites, in Samaria and Gilead, mainly concern the patriarch Jacob. The stories recounted in connection with the second group of sites, the highlands and Negeb of Judah, are linked with Abraham and Isaac. These were, in fact, the areas of the earliest strongholds of the tribal confederation. Jacob seems to have been the first ancestor figure to have played a central role in the tribal league traditions, and he thus came to have the place of progenitor or "father" of the whole people; his twelve "sons" stand at the head of each of the twelve tribes that formed the confederation.

This principal role assigned to Jacob points to the earliest center of the formation of the tribal league in the more northern area, the location of many of the Jacob stories. Although the southern tribe, Judah, came on the scene

DIVISION OF CANAAN

© United Bible Societies, 1976
used by permission

later, in the closing years of the confederation, it assumed more and more prominence. Because the place of the northern patriarch, Jacob, was already so secure, the growing prominence of Judah was indicated by making the southern ancestor figures, Abraham and Isaac, the grandfather and father, respectively, of Jacob.

These stories indirectly yield information on the contexts, both political and geographical. They also indicate some of the conditions and concerns that were a part of life for these peoples who eventually joined together into the tribal league. For one thing, the diversity of the groups that eventually came together into the tribal league is seen in the diversity of activities, occupations, and economic conditions in which the various ancestor figures are set. In other words, the Genesis stories often tell us as much, if not more, about a later period, and the diversity of the groups that wove these stories together, than they do about the people and period in which the stories had their origins. Abraham, for example, is presented as a man of relative wealth: "Now Abraham was very rich in livestock, silver, and gold" (Gn 13:2). But Jacob had to work for some length of time to earn the dowry for his two wives, Rachel and Leah:

After Jacob had stayed with him a full month, Laban said to him: "Should you serve me for nothing just because you are a relative of mine? Tell me what your wages should be." . . . Since Jacob had fallen in love with Rachel, he answered Laban, "I will serve you seven years for your younger daughter Rachel" (Gn 29:14b-15, 18).

Both Abraham and Isaac are also pictured as acting in the role of leaders of mercenaries for a time in the hire of city-state rulers. For example,

When Abram returned from his victory over Chedorlaomer and the kings who were allied with him, the king of Sodom went out to greet him in the Valley of Shaveh (that is, the King's valley). . . .
The king of Sodom said to Abram, "Give me the people; the goods you may keep." But Abram replied to the king of Sodom, "I have sworn to the LORD, God Most High, the creator of heaven and earth, that I would not take so much as a thread or a sandal strap from anything that is yours, lest you should say, 'I made Abram rich.' Nothing for me except what my servants have used up and the share that is due to the men who joined me" (Gn 14:17, 21-24).

The one thing which stands out in the stories about all of the ancestor figures, however, is their marginality. They live near and have some associations with larger population centers. But it is clear that they consciously and purposefully shunned integration into or submission to the established political, social, and economic structure.

These ancestor traditions in Genesis 12-50 allow us to gain access, although indirectly, to some of the concerns of these varied groups who wove them together. One clear set of concerns involved the obstacles that needed to be overcome in the building of a life and community together. This concern for community-building expresses itself in two concrete ways: concern about offspring, and the attempt to secure productive land both for agriculture and pasturage.

Especially in the frontier context of the newly opening central hill country, the desire for children, for more "hands" to help with the various necessary tasks, is understandable. Thus we read often of concerns about female sterility—Sarah (Gn 16:1), Rebekah (Gn 25:21), and Rachel (Gn 30:1).

The desire to escape the control of the dominant city-state rule also meant a search for adequate productive land in more marginal areas and in areas which needed to be cleared and cultivated. In the areas controlled by the city-state regimes the king was considered sole possessor of all property and whatever it produced—by divine right. He could give or take away land at will and demand as much as he wanted of its fruit and crops. In other words, he and his family and retainers could and did control the land's "surplus production." They usually demanded a good portion of it, up to 50% or more, for military purposes as well as to support a luxurious lifestyle. Early Israel was thus composed of many who had fled this oppressive and exploitative system. As people close to the land they appreciated and valued its richness and fertility, as well as its fragility. Many of the stories thus reflect their hopes and struggles for adequate and productive land and for access to and control over all that it could yield to provide a relatively satisfying and productive life for them and for their families. In such a context the key role "the land" played even early in Israel's history is reflected in the hope for and gift of land to the patriarch by God. Note the centrality of "the land" in the passages about covenant in Genesis 13 and 28:

> The LORD said to Abram: "Look about you, and from where you are, gaze to the north and south, east and west; all the land that you see I will give to you and your descendants forever. . . . Set forth and walk about in the land, through its length and breadth, for to you I will give it" (Gn 13:14-15, 17).

> Then he [Jacob] had a dream: a stairway rested on the ground, with its top reaching to the heavens; and God's messengers were going up

and down on it. And there was the LORD standing beside him and saying: "I, the LORD, am the God of your forefather Abraham and the God of Isaac; the land on which you are lying I will give to you and your descendants. . . . Know that I am with you; I will protect you wherever you go, and bring you back to this land. I will never leave you until I have done what I promised you" (Gn 28:12-13, 15).

Life outside the accepted patterns of the dominant society meant that these various groups of people had to develop defenses and strategies to offset the pressures to become absorbed into that larger society. Again, the picture of Abraham and Isaac as mercenaries in the service of but not subservient to city-state rulers represents one such strategy to retain a degree of independence (Gn 14, 26). Accommodation with settled groups and cities are reflected in Abraham's covenant with Abimelech (Gn 21), and his purchase of the cave at Machpelah from the Hittites for family burials (Gn 23):

Thus Ephron's field at Machpelah, facing Mamre, together with its cave and all the trees anywhere within its limits, was conveyed to Abraham by purchase in the presence of all the Hittites who sat on Ephron's town council. After this transaction, Abraham buried his wife Sarah in the cave of the field of Machpelah, facing Mamre (that is, Hebron) in the land of Canaan. Thus the field with its cave was transferred from the Hittites to Abraham as a burial place (Gn 23: 17-20).

We observed the dispute over fresh water wells and pasturage between the shepherds of Abraham and those of his "nephew" Lot in Genesis 13: 7-12. Therein is also preserved evidence of the various strategies adopted to reduce or eliminate such friction. In the case of Abraham's people and Lot's people, the strategy chosen was negotiation and mutual agreement to separate and set off in different directions.

One of the striking things about the ancestor stories in Genesis 12-50 is the prominence of women in them. The society is clearly patriarchal in structure, that is, it is marked by a system of relationships that institutionalize male dominance. Nevertheless, in the context within which the events take place—for the most part within and between *family* groups—the women play a prominent role. Sarah, Hagar, Rebekah, Rachel, Leah, Tamar, all demonstrate initiative, strength of will, intelligence, wisdom, self-possession, and a degree of independence in their actions and in their dealings with the male figure. Sarah (Sarai), for example, does not hesitate in enlisting her husband's cooperation in dealing with her sterility:

Abram's wife Sarai had borne him no children. She had, however, an Egyptian maidservant named Hagar. Sarai said to Abram: "The LORD has kept me from bearing children. Have intercourse, then, with my maid; perhaps I shall have sons through her." Abram heeded Sarai's request. Thus, after Abram had lived ten years in the land of Canaan, his wife took her maid, Hagar the Egyptian, and gave her to her husband Abram to be his concubine. He had intercourse with her, and she became pregnant. . . .

Hagar bore Abram a son, and Abram named the son whom Hagar bore him Ishmael. Abram was eighty-six years old when Hagar bore him Ishmael (Gn 16:1-4, 15).

This prominence of women, which continues in the later history of the tribal league (for example, Miriam, Rahab, Deborah) and monarchy (for example, Hannah, Bathsheba, Jezebel, Huldah) is possibly due to two factors. First, in the context of the frontier conditions of the opening up of the central highlands, women's participation in activities outside the immediate context of household duties was necessary. These activities included clearing the land and raising and harvesting the crops. Even more essential in a situation of restricted population was their role as childbearers. Both their necessary involvement in duties outside the household and their crucial contribution to the increase in numbers led to an enhancement of their value and status within the community as a whole. A second factor in this unusual prominence of women is the "opening toward equality" toward which these groups were moving in their ethos and in the shape their political, economic, and social structures were assuming. This "opening toward equality" eventually became embodied and rooted in the constitution of the tribal league when at last the league came into being. Such an "opening toward equality" also favored a place for women within that society higher than what might normally be expected in the world of the Ancient Near East.

The picture that emerges from this approach to the stories of the ancestors of Israel—male and female—thus resembles a mosaic made up of separate and diverse panels. Each panel represents the cherished memories of one of the groups out of which a single people was eventually forged. But the period represented by these stories in Genesis 12-60 is, in general, *before* the tribal league was formed. In other words, the picture is one of a whole complex of small groups sometimes cooperating, sometimes competing, sometimes even in conflict in their struggle for existence on the margins of a larger world. It is no wonder, then, that the names or events mentioned in these chapters find no place in the official records and accounts of the royal courts and temple administrations of the city-states of contemporary Canaan. It is no wonder that the attempt to coordinate these people and their experience with the larger historical record has largely proved unsuccessful. The most we can say at this point is that these individuals and their stories fit broadly into the patterns and context of the second millennium B.C.E.

These individual complexes of tradition and memories were precious and valued because they gave a sense of identity to each of the separate groups. They preserved the stories of the individual struggles and failures and successes in securing land and offspring and in maintaining distance from the city-state network, which constantly threatened to catch them up and submerge them in its consuming thirst for control and power. Despite the diversity of the groups and the memories of their frictions and conflicts, two threads run through this tapestry, two complementary strands of color that give it unity and coherence. One of these threads consists in the conscious move to marginality. Each story in its own way embodies a group's overriding concern to maintain an autonomy and to retain control of its life and future in spite of the hardships its members had to endure and the problems such marginality inevitably entailed. The second thread weaving its way among these separate tradition complexes is the overriding swell toward and pressure in the direction of unity.

Despite the intergroup tensions and frictions, which continued even after the tribal league was formed (see Jgs 5:15-18; Jgs 20), a unity did emerge and a sense of common purpose and identity was forged. One of the principal elements of that unity was loyalty to the one unique God, Yahweh. They came to recognize this God as the source of and symbol of that unity, that necessity, indeed that desire to transcend their differences and overcome the obstacles to cooperation and recognition of their common interests. Their understanding of and description of that unique God emerged from their sense of God's involvement in their common struggle to create a just and peaceful community, a community free from domination and oppression by the powerful.

REVIEW QUESTIONS

1. Why have attempts to coordinate and link these stories and individuals (e.g., Abraham, Sarah, Isaac, Rebekah, etc.) in Genesis 12-50 to the wider "official" history of the Ancient Near East in the second millennium proved largely unsuccessful?

2. According to the archeological record, where did most of the "Proto-Israelites" who settled the central hill country come from? According to historical records, what are some of the reasons why this population shift took place?

3. Describe life in one of these pioneer villages of the hill country during the Early Iron Age when Israel was born.

4. Find other examples among these stories in Genesis 12-50 that reflect the following:
   — recognition of the need to act with cunning and indirectness in dealing with the more powerful;
   — the characteristics of their God, especially as a God particularly close to the poor, the outsider, those on the margins;
   — the prominence of women in these stories;
   — "virtues" to be cultivated and/or unhelpful strategies to be avoided.

5. Name two factors that help explain the unusual prominence of women in these stories in Genesis 12-50.

6. Give one or more examples of situations in today's world where people need to discover sources of unity and solidarity in order to overcome the superficial differences and conflicts that divide them.

5

The Documentary Hypothesis

INTRODUCTION

Before we continue with the story of Israel's origins, we need to take a closer look at one of the major sources for our knowledge about those origins, the Pentateuch. *Pentateuch* is a common name for what the Jews call the *Torah,* that is, the *Law* or the *Law of Moses.* It encompasses the first five books of the Old Testament: Genesis, Exodus, Numbers, Leviticus, and Deuteronomy. The name *Pentateuch* comes from the Greek word that means "the fivefold book," a name which reflects two of its aspects, its unity and its division into five parts. Its inner unity was given it by its final authors or editors shortly before 400 B.C.E. This unity reflects its function as the fundamental law, constitution, or charter for what had by that time become the Jewish people (the term *Jew* comes out of the Babylonian Exile [587-539 B.C.E.]; before that time the people were known as the "children of Israel" or "Israelites"). And the Pentateuch is a *fivefold* book because it is divided into five parts.

There are at least two reasons for this fivefold division. First, the scrolls upon which ancient books were written could contain only a limited amount. The Pentateuch in its entirety could not be copied onto a single scroll; it needed five scrolls. Second, although the convenience of dividing it into five manageable scrolls played a part, each of the five sections or "books" has a certain unity and completeness by itself.

The names in Christian Bibles for these five parts of the Pentateuch— Genesis, Exodus, Leviticus, Numbers, Deuteronomy—are taken from the names assigned to them in the first translation of the Pentateuch from its original Hebrew into Greek by Jews living in Alexandria, Egypt, in the third century B.C.E. The names are based to a certain degree on the content of each book. Thus *Genesis* ("origin") recounts the origins of the world, the human race, and the people of Israel in the person of their ancestors, Abraham,

Sarah, Isaac, Rebekah, Jacob, Rachel, Leah, and Joseph and his brothers. *Exodus* relates the "going out" of a group of slaves, later identified with the whole people of Israel, under the leadership of Moses. *Leviticus* contains in large part material concerned with ritual and sacrificial practice, the domain of the priests, who were from the tribe of *Levi*. The Book of *Numbers* begins with a census or "numbering" of the people during their time of sojourn in the wilderness before entering the Promised Land. Finally, *Deuteronomy* seems to be a *second* rehearsal of the Law (from *deuteros nomos,* the Greek for "the second law") by Moses on the Plains of Moab just prior to the entry into the Promised Land under Joshua.

THE DOCUMENTARY HYPOTHESIS OR FOUR-SOURCE THEORY

The Pentateuch was one of the first parts of the Old Testament to benefit from modern approaches to biblical study. Chapter 2 discussed the archeological finds of the 1800s and the resulting advances in the understanding of the languages, cultures, and history of the Ancient Near East, the world within which Israel and its Scriptures came to be. Previous to these discoveries, however, another movement began, which had its more immediate roots in the Renaissance, that is, in the revival or rebirth of Greek and Roman classical learning and art which began in Italy in the fourteenth century. The rediscovery of Greek and Roman culture brought with it a growing appreciation of the human mind's independence and ability to arrive at truth through its powers of reason and investigation. Coupled with this renewed sense of security in intellectual research was the development of an historical consciousness, that is, the realization of the historically conditioned nature of human life and culture. Past ages were *different* in so many ways, from each other and from the present. Thus documents from the past, in order properly to be understood, must be understood as past, that is, as belonging to a different age and culture. Only when one can study the document as part of the human past can one truly grasp its sense and meaning. This was the beginning of the "critical" approach to the Bible.

The approach is critical in the sense that it brackets the inspired character of the documents and attempts to use the critical or discerning power of the human intellect in order to investigate and grasp their meaning and significance. Also, the growing importance of the Bible as a result of the Protestant Reformation gave further impetus to the application of critical learning to the study of the Bible. The principal focus of interest in these early years was the Pentateuch, in many ways the original and foundational part of the Hebrew Scriptures. A whole series of scholars contributed to the development and refining of what came to be known as the Documentary Hypothesis for the formation of the Pentateuch.

Richard Simon (d. 1712), a French Catholic priest, was one of the first to question the sole authorship of the Pentateuch by Moses and to argue that it is in fact a compilation of diverse documents. He based his argument on his studies of the creation stories in chapters 1-3 of Genesis and of the Flood Story in Genesis 6-8. Along with other early critics he noted inconsistencies that required explanation if one held to the traditional Jewish and Christian tradition of the Mosaic authorship of the Pentateuch. Moses' description of his own death and burial in Deuteronomy 34:1-8 represents an example of one such anomaly.

The internal discrepancies in the creation and flood accounts are also perplexing. The account of creation in Genesis 2:4b-25 has human beings created first, while Genesis 1:1-2:4a placed them last, the summit of God's creative activity:

At the time when the LORD God made the earth and the heavens— while as yet there was no field shrub on earth and no grass of the field had sprouted . . . the LORD God formed man out of the clay of the ground and blew into his nostrils the breath of life (Gn 2:4, 7).

Then God said: "Let us make man in our image, after our likeness. Let them have dominion over the fish of the sea, the birds of the air, and the cattle, and over all the wild animals and all the creatures that crawl on the ground."
 God created man in his image;
  in the divine image he created him;
  male and female he created them (Gn 1:26-27).

We now understand that these differences in detail between the two creation accounts reflect two sources that have been woven together in these chapters. Each source stems from a different time period in Israel's history, and each represents a different theology of creation.

The account in chapter 2 has its origins in the early days of the monarchy. In this source God is closer to and more directly involved in the everyday lives of human beings. Thus the first human is depicted as a partner in God's work of creation: he is told to till the soil to make it bear fruit:

The LORD God then took the man and settled him in the garden of Eden, to cultivate and care for it (Gn 2:15).

He is also invited to give names to the creatures God subsequently fashions:

So the LORD God formed out of the ground various wild animals and various birds of the air, and he brought them to the man to see what he would call them; whatever the man called each of them would be its name (Gn 2:19).

The source used for the creation account in Genesis 1:1-2:4a stems from a later period and reflects its origin among priestly circles particularly concerned with ritual and legal matters. Thus, the fact that God "rested" on the seventh day after working for six days provides the example and source for the law concerning the sabbath rest for human beings:

Since on the seventh day God was finished with the work he had been doing, he rested on the seventh day. . . . So God blessed the seventh day and made it holy, because on it he rested from all the work he had done in creation (Gn 2:2-3).

We are coming to understand more clearly the introductory or preparatory function of these first eleven chapters of Genesis. The authors who wove these two sources into a larger whole were not so much intent on telling a story for its own sake, that is, simply to entertain or to satisfy an idle curiosity about the origins of this world in which we live. Rather, for Israel, nature and creation served as the backdrop, the stage, for the more important drama of the creation of the human community, the family of humankind in all its diversity. Central, indeed in some ways crucial, to that drama was the origin of the people of Israel. Chapters 1-11 of Genesis lead us to that origin in the persons of Abraham, Sarah, and their family, beginning in chapter 12. Chapters 1-11 thus describe the origin of the physical universe and of the wider human family. With chapter 12, however, Israel's story as such begins with the call of Abraham.

The high-water mark of these early stages of modern biblical research came with German biblicist Julius Wellhausen (d. 1918) and his *Prolegomena to the History of Israel* (1878). He presented the results of historical criticism of the Pentateuch in a clear and forceful way and established the definitive formulation of the Documentary Hypothesis for the composition of the Pentateuch. Wellhausen's work continues to be a reference point for the contemporary study of these first five books of the Bible.

One of the starting points for early literary critics was the variation in the name used to designate Israel's God. Some passages, especially in Genesis, used the generic term *'elohim* (Hebrew for "god" or "gods"), usually translated simply as "God." Other passages employed what seemed to be the proper name for Israel's God, *Yahweh,* represented by "LORD" in most modern translations, or *Yahweh God,* "LORD God." Other clues included the diverse names for the sacred mountain in Exodus (Sinai and Horeb), the two different names for Moses' father-in-law (Reuel and Jethro), and clear differences in literary style and theological outlook from one chapter or one part of a chapter to another. These clues led scholars to isolate two, then three, and finally four separate strands or sources, which seem to have been woven together into the composition we now know as the Pentateuch.

During the years in which this Documentary Hypothesis was taking shape, scholars were thinking very much in literary, almost library-like terms, and thus they wrote of the four strands as if they were four separate *written* "documents." Serious doubt has been cast on this way of conceptualizing the four strands, because it seems that at least some, if not a good part, of the four sources was still in oral form when it was finally incorporated into what became the Pentateuch. Today scholars speak more in terms of "strands," "layers," "traditions," or "sources."

In summary form, these four sources can be reduced to a combination of two *dualities,* a duality involving the *kind* of material represented in the sources and a duality involving their milieu or geographical *origin.* The four sources contain basically two kinds of material, narrative and legislative, and generally stem from two separate geographic regions, north and south. Thus we have the narrative source that took shape among the various groups living in the northern part of Palestine. This narrative, which uses the generic term for designating Israel's God throughout Genesis, *'elohim,* is called the *Elohist* or *E* source. Besides reflecting the source's preferred name for God, *E* can also recall Ephraim, one of the principal tribes of the north in the early days of Israel.

The southern narrative of Israel's origins is represented in the *J* or *Yahwist* source (the *J* comes from the German spelling of Yahweh—*Jahve*), with Yahweh being the personal name of Israel's God. This source employs the personal name for God right from the opening pages of Genesis. The *J* cipher also recalls the name of the principal southern tribe, Judah.

These two narrative versions of Israel's origins offer answers to questions such as *Who are we?* and *Where did we come from?* They represent attempts to give a sense of identity and purpose and to communicate to newcomers as well as to new generations the particular world-view, approach to life, and important values this community of peoples treasured.

The second kind of material answers a consequent question, *If this is who we say we are, then how should we live, how should we act so as to reflect who we say we are?* This second kind of material is thus concerned primarily with *legislation,* that is, collections of social, economic, organizational, and religious laws and customs. The legislative materials, which have their origin in circles in the *south,* are known collectively as the *Priestly* source or *P.* This source reflects in large part the language, outlook, and ritual concerns of the levitical priesthood, whose locus was in the south and especially in the Temple in Jerusalem.

The people in the north developed their own set of customs and legal traditions parallel to the southern *P* source. For example, just as the list in Exodus 20:1-17 represents the southern or *P* version of the Ten Commandments, Deuteronomy 5:6-21 gives the northern version of that same list. This body of laws and customs developed in the north is known as the Deuteronomist or *D* source, since much of that material is gathered into the fifth book of the Pentateuch, the Book of Deuteronomy.

We can thus summarize this preliminary overview of the Documentary Hypothesis or, as it is currently referred to, the Four-Source Theory for the origin and composition of the Pentateuch in terms of the two dualities, a duality of the *kind* of material involved and a duality of *geographic* origin.

Sources of the Pentateuch

	Narrative	Legislative
North	*E* (Elohist)	*D* (Deuteronomist)
South	*J* (Yahwist)	*P* (Priestly)

AN EXAMPLE OF SOURCE CRITICISM

The story of Joseph's betrayal by his brothers in Genesis 37:14-36 serves as a good example of how source analysis or source criticism can be helpful in understanding and gaining insight into the biblical text. In the *New American Bible* version of the story below, the Yahwist source appears in regular print and the Elohist source in italics. The division is based on the analysis of Bruce Vawter (see bibliography).

When Joseph reached Shechem, a man met him as he was wandering about in the fields. "What are you looking for?" the man asked him. "I am looking for my brothers," he answered. "Could you please tell me where they are tending the flocks?" The man told him, "They have moved on from here; in fact, I heard them say, 'Let us go on to Dothan.'" So Joseph went after his brothers and caught up with them in Dothan. *They noticed him from a distance,* and before he came up to them, they plotted to kill him. *They said to one another: "Here comes that master dreamer! Come on, let us kill him and throw him into one of the cisterns here; we could say that a wild beast devoured him. We shall then see what becomes of his dreams." When Reuben heard this, he tried to save him from their hands, saying, "We must not take his life. Instead of shedding blood," he continued, "just throw him into that cistern there in the desert; but don't kill him outright." His purpose was to rescue him from their hands and restore him to his father.* So when Joseph came up to them, they stripped him of the long tunic he had on; *then they took him and threw him into the cistern which was empty and dry.* They then sat down to their meal. Looking up, they saw a caravan of Ishmaelites coming from Gilead, their camels laden with gum, balm, and resin to be taken down to Egypt. Judah said to his brothers: "What is to be gained by killing our brother and concealing his blood? Rather, let us sell him to these Ishmaelites, instead of doing away with him ourselves. After all, he is our brother, our own flesh." His brothers agreed. They sold Joseph to the Ishmaelites for twenty pieces of silver. *Some Midianite traders passed by and they pulled Joseph up out of the cistern and took him to Egypt. When Reuben went back to the cistern and saw that Joseph was not in it, he tore his clothes, and returning to his brothers, he exclaimed: "The boy is gone! And I—where can I turn?"* They took Joseph's tunic, and after slaughtering a goat, dipped the tunic in its blood. They then sent someone to bring the long tunic to their father, with the message: "We found this. See whether it is your son's tunic or not." He recognized it and exclaimed: "My son's tunic! *A wild beast has devoured him!* Joseph has been torn to pieces!" *Then Jacob rent his clothes, put sackcloth on his loins,* and mourned his son many days. Though his sons and daughters tried to console him, he refused all consolation, saying, "No, I will go down mourning to my son in the netherworld." *Thus did his father lament him. The Midianites, meanwhile, sold Joseph in Egypt to Potiphar, a courtier of Pharaoh and his chief steward* (Gn 37:14-36).

Reading the verses assigned to each of the two sources separately provides in sketch form two almost complete versions of the same story, but with significant differences in the details. In the Yahwist version of the story, for example, Judah, the ancestor of the major southern tribe of the same name, is the one responsible for saving Joseph's life. But the Elohist, in the northern version, presents Reuben, the ancestor of the important northern tribe bearing his name, as the one who had compassion on Joseph. In the case of the Yahwist, a caravan of Ishmaelites takes Joseph down to Egypt. In the Elohist version, however, it is Midianite traders who bring him there. The one responsible for weaving together the two stories has done the job so skillfully that we scarcely notice the discrepancies. This editor has managed to recount the story, preserving the main elements of the two versions of that story, and along with these elements, the valued memories, perspective, and theological emphasis of both sets of traditions. Only if we read closely do these inconsistencies begin to appear, and we see the value of the Four-Source Theory in explaining these discrepancies.

THE CONTEXT FOR THE PENTATEUCH'S FOUNDATIONAL STORY

Both kinds of material we find in the Pentateuch, the *narrative* and the *legislative,* have their origins in the long years before and during the formation of the tribal confederacy that took the name Israel and that came into existence formally between 1250 and 1220 B.C.E.

As the various groups scattered throughout the hill country of Canaan overcame their differences, they recognized their common interests. They gradually formed a network of peoples bound together by their common hope and ideal to maintain a territory free from the control of the city-state network. They formed a social, economic, political, and religious system unique in the ancient world. An important element in their community-building process was the creation of a common story and a common ethos. They created this common story and ethos by blending and weaving together their separate stories and by forming a body of laws and customs which embodied both the wisdom they had inherited from their own separate pasts and their experiences in creating this new community. The context for this tradition-building process was the regular pilgrimage festivals. Groups from a particular area or sometimes the whole assembly of tribes would gather at fixed intervals for a whole host of community-building activities: exchange of news, settling of disputes, recognition of new leadership, incorporation of new groups, and so forth. A central component of these regular pilgrimage festivals was the specifically religious element, the worship of their common God, Yahweh. In this worship their common story would be recounted and their common commitment to live by certain laws and values reaffirmed. Thus over the years a common pool of narrative and legislative material accumulated, more or less unified but not yet rigidly fixed. Some of it may have been reduced to written form, but a certain flexibility and openness were necessary, especially in those early years. New groups, each with its own stories and memories, would join this growing movement. As social, political, economic, and religious conditions changed, it became necessary to modify or adapt the traditions.

It is important to point out here that the shape and focus of these traditions is on the already-formed tribal league. It was only in the context of this unity that the process of combining the separate traditions makes sense. The traditions about the ancestor figures and Moses were the earlier, separate stories and traditions of the smaller, distinct groups that eventually came together to form Israel. Only in the process of tradition-building were these various stories and traditions gradually combined into a single, coherent, unified whole and accepted by the full body of the combined tribes as its own story.

German Old Testament scholar Martin Noth has identified five principal sets of traditions or themes that were gradually linked together into the standard narrative recital. Each seems to have been contributed by a *different* group. These five themes include: (1) the Exodus from Egypt; (2) the entry into the Promised Land; (3) the ancestor stories, especially the promises (children and land); (4) the wilderness wanderings; and (5) Sinai and the covenant. The stories revolving around the promise of land to the ancestors may represent an almost defiant way of laying rightful claim to land that urban rulers may have unjustly extorted or seized from one or more of the groups who joined the tribal league. The stories associated with the wilderness wanderings seem to represent the contributions of groups especially in the south. Their retreat from the more fertile settled areas into the more arid and harsher regions in search of refuge from urban control involved many wanderings and obstacles before they were able to discover ways of living and working together under these more difficult conditions. These five themes or sets of traditions were gradually joined and woven together into the larger, unified foundational story of the unified tribal league.

We are thus removed to a considerable degree from these stories and traditions. They have been reworked and combined for the purpose of creating a single story meant to function as a symbolic and identity-bestowing expression to unify previously heterogeneous and sometimes antagonistic groups. Thus they serve as historical sources only *indirectly,* and then only as the sources for the history of the pre-Israelite groups *before* they formed or joined the united tribal league. Since the Exodus from Egypt and the subsequent entry into the Promised Land provided the basic outline around which the edifice of the Pentateuch was built, even the sequence of events cannot be read as if it were a direct witness of an actual historical chronology. What the stories and traditions preserved in the Pentateuch do give us access to, and then only indirectly, is the formation of the united tribal league—the obstacles the peoples faced, the hopes they shared, and their various means of forging and maintaining unity.

REVIEW QUESTIONS

1. The name *Pentateuch* is the Greek name for "the Torah" or "the Law of Moses," and means "the fivefold book." What two aspects of this collection of books are reflected in the name?

2. What is the difference between the terms *Israelite* and *Jew?*

3. What are the four sources that were gradually woven together to form the Pentateuch? How were they first identified as distinct sources?

4. Explain briefly the two *dualities,* of which the four sources are combinations.

5. What was the original *context* for the development of these sources and the *dynamic* that lay behind their creation and eventual combination?

6. What five main sets of traditions or themes (identified by Martin Noth) were gradually linked to form the standard *narrative* recital that lies behind the Yahwist and Elohist sources? Were these sets of traditions or themes the property of the same group or of separate groups?

7. How are we to understand and use the material we find in the Pentateuch to reconstruct the history of the origins and growth of early Israel?

6

The Four Sources

Suggested Bible Reading: Genesis 12-50, especially 18:1-15

CREATION OF THE PENTATEUCH

During the years of the tribal league the stories and traditions of the distinct tribes were gradually combined and woven together into a single story. Parts of that story may have been written down, while other elements in it remained mainly in oral form. The main outlines of the story eventually became relatively fixed and unchanged from one recital to the next. A common context for this recital was the periodic pilgrimage festivals when groups of clans or tribes came together at one of the shrines where Yahweh was worshipped. Central to every recital of the story was the rescue by Yahweh of the group of slaves (their "going out" from Egypt), their eventual entry into the land of Canaan, and, in between, Yahweh's forging of a covenant with them in the wilderness. Exactly how that rescue from Egypt was effected, however, and how that entry into Canaan took place probably varied somewhat from group to group, from shrine to shrine, and from one generation to the next. The importance and character of the other themes, for example, the wilderness wanderings and the promises to the ancestors, were also relatively flexible. But early on, the main thrust of the narrative and movement of events from Egypt to the wilderness to the "land of promise" had become clear and established.

The first to put this story into a fixed written form was the writer responsible for the *J* or Yahwist source. Scholars refer to this individual as the Yahwist or *J* because of his preference for the personal name of Israel's God, Yahweh, right from the beginning of the narrative. The Yahwist worked chiefly with the form the story took among the clans and groups that made up the southern tribe of Judah. He included mainly those traditions and elements of the basic themes that were more specific to the south.

In order to understand the Yahwist's purpose in putting into a written form this story of Israel's origins, we need to jump ahead a few generations to the days when the tribal league evolved into a monarchy. As we shall see in Chapters 13-15, by around the year 1050 B.C.E. a series of crises threatened the very existence of Israel. The apparent need for strong internal leadership in order to survive these crises led to the formation of a monarchy, first under David (ca. 1000-961 B.C.E.) and then under his son and successor, Solomon (ca. 961-922 B.C.E.). These first two kings of Israel were able to hold the tribes together in a fragile unity for approximately two generations. But with the death of Solomon the united kingdom broke apart into two smaller kingdoms. The northern tribes made up one kingdom, which retained the name of the united tribal league, Israel. The southern tribes continued to be ruled by the heirs of David and Solomon (the House of David), and went by the name of Judah, the name of the principal tribal group in the south. This southern kingdom had its center and capital in Jerusalem, the city of David, which David had seized from the Jebusites and in which Solomon had built his famous palace and Temple.

The Yahwist, or *J,* who wrote between 960 and 930 B.C.E. was most likely a member of Solomon's court. He was presumably part of the corps of bureaucrats which Solomon had formed as he enlarged and developed the royal administrative apparatus established by his father David. *J* may have been a scribe and/or advisor to the king. *J*'s association with the royal court can be perceived in what appears to be the purpose for which these stories and traditions of the people of Israel were reduced to written form. That purpose differed from the original purpose of this complex of stories and traditions, that is, to provide the sense of identity and focus of unity for the tribal league. Instead, *J*'s purpose was to put this story into such a form as to act as a kind of national epic for the recently created monarchy.

J's attempt to link that novel development of the Israelite state or monarchy with its predecessor, the united tribal league, can be discerned easily. In the story of Abraham, for example, God's covenant with the patriarch includes the promise of "the land," that is, the territory of the Canaanites. The dimensions of that land "promised" to Abraham and his descendants are described as extending "from the Wadi [border] of Egypt to the Great River [the Euphrates]" (Gn 15:18). These dimensions encompass, in fact, the furthest extent of David's modest empire by the time of his death and were looked upon by later generations as the ideal borders of the land of Israel. Again, in Genesis 17:6, God tells Abraham, "I will render you exceedingly fertile; I will make nations of you; kings shall stem from you." These last two references, to "nations" and "kings" stemming from Abraham, are clearly meant as a foreshadowing of the creation of the nation-state and monarchy under David and Solomon.

The Yahwist was a gifted storyteller and possessed profound theological insight. The Patriarch Joseph's words in Genesis 45:5-8 provide a good example of this kind of insight. Up to this moment in the story Joseph's brothers had failed to recognize him. He was clothed in Egyptian garments and his brothers presumed that he had died through their cruel treachery many years before. The brothers are now terrified that Joseph will seek revenge on them and treat them in a similarly cruel way. But Joseph attempts to calm their fears and says:

"But now do not be distressed, and do not reproach yourselves for having sold me here. It was really for the sake of saving lives that God sent me here ahead of you. For two years now the famine has been in the land, and for five more years tillage will yield no harvest. God, therefore, sent me on ahead of you to ensure for you a remnant on earth and to save your lives in an extraordinary deliverance. So it was not really you but God who had me come here; and he has made me a father to Pharaoh, lord of all his household, and ruler over the whole land of Egypt" (Gn 45:5-8).

The Yahwist here alerts us to the fact that God cannot be thwarted even by human sin. God is capable of accomplishing good, even in spite of human perversity. Here God has taken the opportunity of the brothers' cruel betrayal of Joseph to effect the eventual rescue and survival of the whole of Jacob/Israel's family.

Shortly after the Yahwist's work was completed, the fragile unity of the Davidic-Solomonic kingdom dissolved into two kingdoms, Israel and Judah. The northern kingdom, Israel, was now in need of its own version of the national epic, because the Yahwist work was so explicitly focused on the south and the Davidic monarchy. Thus, somewhere between 900 and 850 B.C.E., a writer in the northern kingdom paralleled the work of the Yahwist by creating the northern narrative of the peoples' origins. This writer is known by scholars as the Elohist or *E* because of the use of the word '*elohim* for Israel's God. The Elohist avoided using the deity's proper name, Yahweh, until it was revealed to Moses in Exodus 3:14. The Elohist tends to downplay the monarchic institutions then governing the people in both north and south. He emphasizes instead the older focus on Israel as a people, a community covenanted with Yahweh, and the attendant ethical and religious obligations.

There are indications that *E* wished to serve as a corrective to some of the enthusiasm for and optimism about the institution of monarchy.

The Elohist shared similar concerns with northern prophetic circles; in fact, the Elohist lived during the time when the early prophets, Elijah and Elisha, were active. In the emphasis on the religious and covenantal aspects of Israel's traditions, *E* focuses on fear of God as a key attitude of the members of this covenant community. In other words, closer reading of and attention to detail in the *J* and *E* stories in Genesis reveal diverse pictures of God and ways of understanding human relationship with the divine. Besides the primary picture of a God who stands by the poor and the oppressed in their struggle for freedom and a better life, the Yahwist and the Elohist sources put us in touch with two quite different ways of relating to the divine.

The Yahwist offers us a sense of the nearness of God, indeed the involvement of God in our daily lives to the point of walking with and sharing a meal with his creatures (Gn 18). A different experience of the deity emerged in the north among what later evolved into the prophetic movement. Groups and individuals in the north sensed in particular the power and transcendence of God—distance and awesomeness. The proper attitude toward such a God is reverence and fear, in the sense of obedience, and devoted filial love. God seemed more father than friend. The proper response is to obey God's commands. The Elohist preserves the story of Abraham's obedience to the seemingly impossible demand from God that he sacrifice his son and heir, Isaac. The story offers a striking example, perhaps to a degree exaggerated, of such obedience on the part of the patriarch. Abraham is stopped at the last moment from actually carrying out the order, but the authentic and profound nature of his fear of God has been proven.

> When they came to the place of which God had told him, Abraham built an altar there and arranged the wood on it. Next he tied up his son Isaac, and put him on top of the wood on the altar. Then he reached out and took the knife to slaughter his son. But the LORD's messenger called to him from heaven, "Abraham, Abraham!" "Yes, Lord," he answered. "Do not lay your hand on the boy," said the messenger. "Do not do the least thing to him. I know now how devoted you are to God [literally, 'How great is your fear of God'], since you did not withhold from me your own beloved son" (Gn 22:9-12).

The northern kingdom, Israel, lasted approximately two hundred years. It was brought to an end by the invasion and conquest of the Assyrians from central Mesopotamia in 722 B.C.E. and by the subsequent population deportations carried out by the Assyrians. With its homeland destroyed, this *E* version of Israel's origins made its way south to Judah, and somewhere between the demise of the northern kingdom in 722 B.C.E. and the death of the Davidic king Josiah in the south in 609 B.C.E., a redactor in the south joined the two sources, *J* and *E*. The *J* or Yahwist epic served as the framework, and elements of the Elohist were used to supplement it, especially where the Elohist preserved traditions not found in *J*, or where the Elohist version was quite different in details from its southern counterpart. The apparent sparseness of the *E* source in comparison with the dominant *J* narrative has led some scholars to deny that *E* was ever a full epic in and of itself. They hold, rather, that it represents a pool of northern traditions from which anecdotes and episodes were drawn and used to complement *J*. In any event, the enthusiasm and optimism of the Yahwist, especially for the political institution of the monarchy, were now tempered and supplemented by the religious, ethical, and prophetic concerns embodied in the *E* materials. The fusion of the two sources also served as a symbol of and hope for the eventual restoration of the unity of the whole people of Israel now that the division of the kingdoms had been brought to an end by the destruction of the north.

Another effect of the destruction of the northern kingdom in 722 B.C.E. was the migration south of the northern legal traditions. These included the northern version of the Ten Commandments in Deuteronomy 5:6-21. Circles settled in or even indigenous to the south were responsible for preserving these northern traditions. Since the bulk of this northern legislation and custom is found in the Book of Deuteronomy, scholars have designated it the Deuteronomist source, or *D*. The document that formed the heart of this book, chapters 12-26, played an important role in the reform inaugurated by King Josiah of Judah in 622 B.C.E.

The final element in the creation of the Pentateuch was the work of the Priestly or *P* source. This source dates from the latter years of the Babylonian Exile and/or the first years of the post-Exilic period, that is, 550-450 B.C.E. *P* represents the legal traditions preserved and developed in the south. Their reduction to a definitive written form came relatively late in comparison with the other three sources. But material dating back even to the days of the tribal league before the monarchy is believed to be preserved therein. The Babylonian Exile in 587-539 B.C.E. saw the effective end of political independence for the people of Israel. Henceforth they would not write their own history but became a part of the other histories, the histories of the powerful imperial systems that dominated the Ancient Near East. The focus of Israelite identity thus shifted from a national identity to identity as a community, a unique and recognizable religious culture with two main focuses: (1) the family; and (2) the Temple, with its priesthood and ritual. It is the latter, the priesthood and the sacrificial ritual of the Temple, which particularly stamped and shaped the traditional materials that had been accumulating and from which the *P* traditionist would finally create what we know as the Pentateuch.

The bulk of the material and the final shape of the Pentateuch is thus attributed to the priestly groups originally associated with the Jerusalem Temple. Eighty-seven of its 187 chapters come from the *P* source, in contrast to the 65 chapters credited to the combined *JE* narrative and the 34 belonging to the Deuteronomist. The focus on the Temple and on priestly ritual and sacrifice is clear. The intent of the Priestly source is to preserve the older traditions but cast them in a form and framework that would emphasize Israel's new identity as a *religious* community, unique among the other peoples of the earth and clearly set apart from them through God's special blessing and choice.

The great collection of law and ritual practice which comes from this Priestly source takes up most of the latter part of the Book of Exodus and the entire Book of Leviticus. Little narrative as such is found among the *P* materials. Instead, by means of genealogies and chronological notes, the Priestly writers created a literary frame of ten panels or sections into which the combined *JE* narrative was worked. The result is a rich tapestry of story and law, of tradition and traditional practices, that could serve a community shattered by the Exile and help it rebuild and create a new identity based on and founded on the rich heritage from the past.

By 400 B.C.E. the work was finished, as we know from Nehemiah 8:1-8. This account tells how, in approximately that year, the priest/scribe Ezra brought "the Book of the Law of Moses" from Babylon. Along with a cadre of Levites, Ezra read and explained the contents of that Law of Moses to the people of Jerusalem as they assembled in one of the city's squares. Scholars identify the by-now completed Pentateuch with that "Book of the Law of Moses" from which Ezra read.

The present Pentateuch is thus a weaving together of these four strands—the northern and southern narratives of Israel's origins (Elohist and Yahwist sources, respectively) and the northern and southern legal materials (Deuteronomist and Priestly sources). At each stage along its eight hundred year history, a crisis or major change in Israel's context and situation served as the catalyst for a reformulation and precipitation into written form of Israel's traditions. Thus the transition from the tribal league to the monarchy around 1000 B.C.E. led to the eventual creation of the two national epics, *J* and *E,* and the destruction of the northern kingdom of Israel in 722 B.C.E. formed the context for the emergence of the central core, chapters 12-26, of the Book of Deuteronomy. Finally, the destruction of Jerusalem in 587 B.C.E. and the ensuing Exile in

Development of the Pentateuch

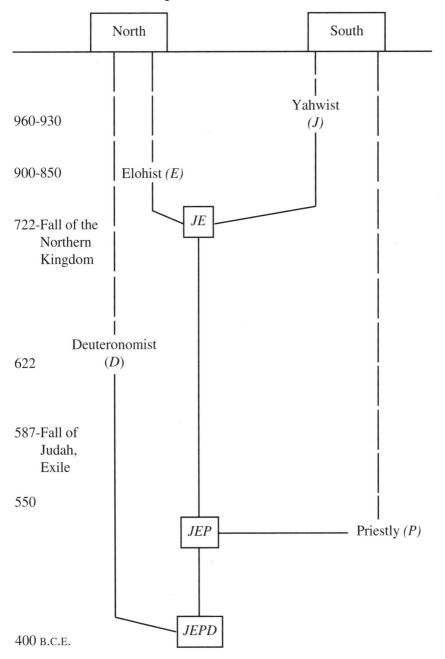

Tradition, stories, laws, customs, worship, and practice gradually were linked together to form one continuous common story and body of traditions.

Babylon were the crises which initiated the work of the Priestly circles. They completed the Pentateuch by around the year 400 B.C.E. This story of the composition of the Pentateuch is summarized in the chart on page 73.

ISRAEL'S SCRIPTURES: A LIBERATING WORD

Study of the formation of the Pentateuch and ultimately of Israel's Scriptures as a whole gives us insight into this people's understanding of the living and dynamic character of those scriptures. The originally oral form of many of the stories and traditions in those Scriptures meant that each retelling or recital of the stories would result in some changes and adaptations for new audiences and new historical situations and circumstances. Even after some of the stories were put into written form, the process of combining and rewriting and adapting continued.

Israel thus conceived of their Scriptures as a *living* word. In order for that word to continue to live, and to give life and inspiration, it had to grow and adapt. It is in this sense that Israel's Scriptures can be called a life-giving and *liberating* word. To fix that word in written form and to try to fix its meaning and interpretation for all time is a potentially oppressive and enslaving action. Even when the Scriptures reached their final written form, the ways of reading and interpreting that written word could and did change, thus ensuring that its meaning and interpretation could develop and adapt. It could continue to speak in a living and life-giving way to new audiences or new generations, or to new peoples and cultures.

A study of the formation of Israel's Bible can teach us a liberating lesson. In this sense, the Bible itself acts as a model and paradigm for a liberative reading and interpretation of it.

A PRACTICAL APPLICATION OF SOURCE CRITICISM:
A STORY FROM THE YAHWIST

One of the ways of coming to appreciate the value and helpfulness of source criticism is to study one passage in detail, examining it in the light of our knowledge of both its source and its function in the larger and later composition of which it is now a part, the Pentateuch. We will focus on the story of Abraham's hospitality to the three strangers who happen on his camp at the *terebinth* (oak) of Mamre near Hebron.

The LORD appeared to Abraham by the terebinth of Mamre, as he sat in the entrance of his tent, while the day was growing hot. Looking up, he saw three men standing nearby. When he saw them, he ran from the entrance of the tent to greet them; and bowing to the ground, he said, "Sir, if I may ask you this favor, please do not go on past your servant. Let some water be brought, that you may bathe your feet, and then rest yourselves under the tree. Now that you have come this close to your servant, let me bring you a little food, that you may refresh yourselves; and afterward you may go on your way." "Very well," they replied, "do as you have said."

Abraham hastened into the tent and told Sarah, "Quick, three measures of fine flour! Knead it and make rolls." He ran to the herd, picked out a tender, choice steer, and gave it to a servant, who prepared it. Then he got some curds and milk, as well as the steer that had been prepared, and set these before them; and he waited on them under the tree while they ate.

"Where is your wife Sarah?" they asked him. "There in the tent," he replied. One of them said, "I will surely return to you about this time next year, and Sarah will then have a son." Sarah was listening at the entrance of the tent, just behind him. Now Abraham and Sarah were old, advanced in years, and Sarah had stopped having her womanly periods. So Sarah laughed to herself and said, "Now that I am so withered and my husband is so old, am I still to have sexual pleasure?" But the LORD said to Abraham: "Why did Sarah laugh and say, 'Shall I really bear a child, old as I am?' Is anything too marvelous for the LORD to do? At the appointed time, about this time next year, I will return to you, and Sarah will have a son." Because she was afraid, Sarah dissembled, saying, "I didn't laugh." But he said, "Yes you did" (Gn 18:1-15).

First of all, an entire scene is set in the single opening sentence. Abraham's camp is pitched in the midst of the dry, hot wilderness near Hebron. It is early afternoon, the hottest part of the day. The camp is quiet as both people and animals seek shade and rest away from the burning sun. The landscape turns hazy as the heat rises from the scorched ground. As Abraham sits in the opening of his tent and gazes out across the landscape, the scene has an almost dreamlike quality. Suddenly Abraham is startled from his repose by three figures who seem to materialize out of the desert heat.

The author skillfully employs suspense and irony. While the reader knows from verse 1 that one of the strangers is Yahweh himself, Abraham does not. It only gradually dawns on Abraham who these strangers are. Finally, when the one announces unhesitatingly that Abraham's wife Sarah will give birth to a son scarcely a year hence, his identity becomes clear. We have been kept in suspense also, since, although we know that one of the strangers is Yahweh, we do not know which one until the moment Abraham and we discover together from the prophecy about the child. We also wonder when and if Abraham will discover their identity. The irony comes from Sarah's disbelief and laughter at the seeming absurdity of the prophecy. In her very laughter (the Hebrew is *tizaq*) she foreshadows the name of the son of promise, Isaac (*yizaq* in Hebrew), and she thus implicitly affirms the prophecy's truthfulness.

Insight into Abraham's character is provided skillfully but only indirectly. His almost unparalleled hospitality to the three strangers unfolds not in direct description but in action and dialogue. When Abraham first catches sight of the three travelers, he *rushes* to greet them and to press them to accept his welcome. Abraham's generosity is emphasized again not by direct description but in the contrast between his words and his actions. Although his invitation is simply to share "a morsel of bread," the meal he puts out is a rich feast: "three measures of fine meal" for the bread, a calf from the herd, "tender and good," as well as "curds and milk."

The picture of the deity presented in this story is typical of the Yahwist. God is reduced almost to human scale. In the Yahwist's world, the inhabitants are so natural and candid that even their relations with God have a note of intimacy and familiarity, to the point that God even appears here in human form. This parallels other pictures of the deity presented by *J*: God "molds" the first human out of the clay of the earth, like a potter making a vessel (Gn 2:7); God "plants" a garden like a farmer (Gn 2:8); God "strolls" in the garden in the cool of the evening (Gn 3:8); God "grieves" over humanity's wickedness like a disappointed parent (Gn 6:6).

Three elements in this story indirectly give us insight into the context of the tribal confederation and earlier, when this story and others like it were first taking shape. The first element is the concern for progeny, for children, especially sons. One of the needs the pre-Israelite and the Israelite groups faced in the sparsely settled wilderness of the central hill country was hands to help with the work of clearing and planting. The sometimes meager diet as well as disease may also have contributed to conditions of sterility in the women and a high infant mortality rate. In his visit to Abraham in Abraham's very own tent, God assures him that he will have a son and heir. Abraham believes, and his faith parallels the faith of this people in their common project and the transcending hope in its eventual success. There *will* be children; there *will* be sons; there *will* be a new generation to carry on and see to fruition the hopes and dreams they shared. Besides giving insight into the earlier context of the united tribal league and the prehistory of the groups that formed it, the story also tells us something about the context and purpose of the Yahwist. In the optimism and success of the days of David and Solomon, the expansion of Israel to embrace the whole of the land and its inhabitants seems indeed a fulfillment and affirmation of the hope and faith the story originally expressed. As well, it served to affirm God's continued benevolence.

Another important aspect of this story is its intimate family setting. This contrasts with the kind of history more common in the Ancient Near East (and today) involving kings and warriors with their armies and conquests, whose exploits are legitimated and supported by their patron deities. In the story of Abraham and Sarah we have instead an affirmation of the value and worth of ordinary human beings, their families, and their everyday struggles and hopes and dreams. These are the memories of people outside the centers of power, people whose concern was to survive in a context in which their lives and activities were important as well as self-determined. In the days of the Yahwist writer, such a message could serve as an implicit caution and critique of the pretensions of the royal court and the ruling classes. In the heady days of kings and imperial ambitions, Israel's origins were not to be forgotten.

We see also in the story how the ancestor figures came to function as models and embodiments of values and virtues both for the united tribal league as well as the later Davidic-Solomonic monarchy. Abraham as the paragon of generosity and hospitality served as an example and model of the virtues that Israelites from both periods—the tribal league and the monarchy—saw as necessary for individual as well as for community well-being. There is an essential link between the character and commitment of the individual members of the covenanted community and the character and well-being of that community itself. Neither aspect is neglected in Israel's traditions.

Finally, the person and actions of Sarah are important for gaining insight into the place and role of women in ancient Israel, again in both periods. The patriarchal character of the society is clear; the men eat while the women stay out of sight. But Sarah refuses to be left out of the picture and has no hesitation about intruding on the scene. She listens in on the conversation at the door of the tent, and she laughs aloud at the thought of bearing a child at her advanced age.

REVIEW QUESTIONS

1. Why is the older Pentateuchal narrative source called *J* or the Yahwist? Discuss briefly the date, the context, and the purpose behind the origin of this source.

2. Why is the other Pentateuchal narrative source called *E* or the Elohist? Discuss briefly the date, the context, and the purpose behind the origin of this source.

3. When and why were *J* and *E* combined into a single narrative?

4. What is the origin of the *D* or Deuteronomist legislative source of the Pentateuch?

5. Why is the other Pentateuchal legislative source called the Priestly source or *P*? Discuss briefly the date and context of its origins.

6. Discuss briefly the date and intent of the work of the Priestly groups originally associated with the Jerusalem Temple in shaping the present Pentateuch.

7. What crises or major changes in Israel's context and situation served as catalysts for the reformulation and precipitation into written form of Israel's traditions as reflected in the formation and eventual combination of the four Pentateuchal sources?

8. What liberating lesson can a study of the formation of the Pentateuch teach us?

7

The Exodus

Suggested Bible Reading: Exodus 1-15

HISTORICAL BACKGROUND

The Moses Group

The formation of the united tribal league of Israel in the hill country of central Canaan was a long and complex process, one in which a number of different and even antagonistic groups discovered the need to join together in a common effort. That common effort was to create and protect a fragile zone of life free from the reigning political, social, economic, and religious order of the day. The unique society these groups managed to create and the values that it embodied often had their origin as *antitheses* to the society they had fled, such as the Canaanite city-state network with its hierarchical and socially stratified character.

One of the components that went into the creation of Israel was the Moses group or Exodus group. The present shape of their story of rescue from Egypt identifies this group as *Israel*. The Moses group was *not* Israel. Israel came into being *only later* in the hill country of Canaan. The great majority of those who eventually became Israel were indigenous and diverse groups of *Canaanites,* each of which brought separate experiences and separate stories to what eventually would be woven into a single common fabric. Much of what was to go into the creation of Israel, both in terms of human subjects and in terms of stories and traditions, was already *in* Canaan and already taking on its singular shape and pattern. It only needed a catalyst, some key element or "glue," to crystallize and give the decisive and unified shape and character to this new people with their new common story in the already ancient land of Canaan. It was the small but decisive Exodus group or Moses group that provided that "glue." This group was the element around which other groups and stories could gather; its story became the appropriate vehicle for forging and expressing their new identity and common project.

Egypt under Pharaoh Ramses II (1290-1224 B.C.E.)

Does the Exodus story contain any information that allows us, even tentatively, to locate it in the wider history of the Ancient Near East? We present here a summary of the arguments of those who would venture a date for the escape of the Moses group of slaves from Egypt, conscious of the tentativeness of such a proposal. The evidence used by these scholars is ambiguous. Thus any combining of the elements is hypothetical and open to serious questioning.

The thirteenth century B.C.E., the last century of the Late Bronze Age, coincided in Egypt with what historians label the New Kingdom or Empire Period. A new dynasty, the Nineteenth, came to power in 1305 B.C.E. The first pharaoh of this dynasty, Ramses I, reigned only a few months. His son and successor, Seti I (1305-1290 B.C.E.) transferred the capital from Thebes, in central Egypt, north to the delta city of Avaris. He and his son, Ramses II, who renamed Avaris "the House of Ramses," both conducted ambitious building programs there. Exodus 1:11, although it does not name the pharaoh of the Exodus, speaks of the pharaoh who "built the store cities, Pithom and Ramses," using slave labor. Thus these building projects of Seti I and Ramses II form one of the pieces of evidence scholars seize upon for assigning a date to the Exodus.

Ramses II enjoyed a successful reign of nearly seventy years, 1290-1224 B.C.E. Under him Egypt's empire reached one of its zeniths. Ramses carried his imperial adventures so far into Asia in the first years of his reign that he came into conflict with the Hittite Empire centered in Anatolia (present-day Turkey). The conflict between these rival imperial powers reached a climax in the confrontation at Kadesh, in what is today southern Lebanon, in 1285 B.C.E. The fact that both sides claimed victory indicates the inconclusive nature of the struggle. A few more years of further skirmishing ended with a peace treaty that set the Orontes River in central Canaan (present-day Lebanon) as the border between the two spheres of influence. After reaching this limit on the possibilities of further imperial expansion, Ramses turned his efforts to projects at home, such as the rebuilding of the new capital at Avaris (Ramses) mentioned above.

Ramses II was succeeded by his son Merneptah (1224-1211 B.C.E.). It is Merneptah who some claim gives us the first extra-biblical witness to events in the Bible. After one of his military excursions into Canaan to collect tribute and receive the homage of his vassal kings there, Merneptah raised a *stele* or stone memorial, with a lengthy inscription. He describes the campaign and boasts of his success in subduing and punishing rebellious kings and peoples. At one point he mentions a people whom he calls Israel:

> Plundered is Canaan. . . .
> Carried off is Ashkelon; seized upon in Gezer;
> Yanoam is made as that which does not exist;
> *Israel* is laid waste; his seed is not;
> Hurru has become a widow on account of Egypt!
> (*ANET*, p. 378)

This stone inscription celebrating Merneptah's victories is dated by scholars to around 1220 B.C.E. and is claimed as the first historical mention of Israel in Canaan. For those scholars who venture to assign a date to the escape of the Moses group from Egypt, these two events—the building projects of Seti I and Ramses II employing slave labor in the late fourteenth and early thirteenth centuries B.C.E. and this mention of an Israel in Canaan by Merneptah in 1220 B.C.E.—are key pieces of evidence. Around 1280 B.C.E. is the date most often mentioned by these scholars.

THE EXODUS ITSELF

Although later Jewish and Christian traditions presume a relatively straightforward account of the Exodus, a closer study of the texts themselves raises a number of questions and reveals a number of gaps and inconsistencies. One major question is the definition of the Exodus itself. Later tradition tends to follow the Priestly writer, who has shaped the final form of the account so that the Exodus is identified with the escape of the slaves and defeat of Pharaoh's army through the sea. But earlier tradition, which speaks of the Exodus in terms of "the going out from" or Yahweh "bringing Israel out from" Egypt, seems to identify the Exodus as the flight from Egypt following the death of the firstborn, *before* the rescue at the sea. The second question, *What actually happened at the sea?*, arises once we become aware of the gaps and inconsistencies in the

A painting reproduced from the tomb of Tutankhamen (14th century B.C.E.) showing the Pharaoh in his chariot leading Egyptian troops.

account. Source analysis reveals that we have in the Book of Exodus elements of at least three and possibly four different versions of the event (chaps. 14-15).

Chapter 14, the prose account of the rescue at the sea, consists in a weaving together of the Yahwist and Priestly stories. The Yahwist version begins with the Moses group leaving Egypt. It is unclear whether they simply fled or whether they were given leave to go by Pharaoh. In any case, Pharaoh decides to pursue them with his chariot force. When he reaches them encamped by the sea, the cloud that had been leading the Israelites turns into darkness and conceals them. That night a strong east wind springs up and lays bare a dry sea bed. Yahweh causes a panic among the Egyptian chariot force. When they attempt to flee, the returning waters drown them. Note that this version carries no actual description of a crossing of the dry seabed by the Moses group:

> The LORD swept the sea with a strong east wind throughout the night and so it turned into dry land. When the water was thus divided . . . just before dawn the LORD cast through the column of the fiery cloud upon the Egyptian force a glance that threw it into a panic; and he so clogged their chariot wheels that they could hardly drive. With that the Egyptians sounded the retreat before Israel, because the LORD was fighting for them against the Egyptians. The Egyptians were fleeing head on toward the sea, when the LORD hurled them into its midst.

Thus the LORD saved Israel on that day from the power of the Egyptians. When Israel saw the Egyptians lying dead on the seashore and the great power that the LORD had shown against the Egyptians, they feared the LORD and believed in him and in his servant Moses (Ex 14:21b, 24, 25, 27b, 30, 31).

The Priestly account also finds the fleeing slaves trapped by Pharaoh's chariot force at the waters of the sea. When the people cry to God, God commands Moses to raise his staff over the waters. As Moses obeys, the waters divide and reveal a path through the sea with the waters standing as a wall on either side. The fleeing slaves pass through followed by the Egyptians. But once the slaves have crossed, Moses again stretches out his arm and staff and the waters return, drowning the Egyptian charioteers and their horses. Israel then proceeds in safety into the wilderness:

> Then Moses stretched out his hand over the sea. The Israelites marched into the midst of the sea on dry land, with the water like a wall to their right and to their left. The Egyptians followed in pursuit; all Pharaoh's horses and chariots and charioteers went after them right into the midst of the sea. Then the LORD told Moses, "Stretch out your hand over the sea, that the waters may flow back upon the Egyptians, upon their chariots and their charioteers." So Moses stretched out his hand over the sea, and . . . the sea flowed back to its normal depth. As the water flowed back, it covered the chariots and the charioteers of Pharaoh's whole army which had followed the Israelites into the sea. Not a single one of them escaped. But the Israelites had marched on dry land through the midst of the sea, with the water like a wall to their right and to their left (Ex 14:21a, 22, 23, 26, 27a, 28, 29).

The third version of the rescue at the sea occurs in the ancient victory poem, the "Song of the Sea" in Exodus 15:1-21. It has some similarities with the Yahwist version and is probably the most ancient of these three accounts. In fact, it may represent the oldest specifically Israelite piece in the Bible. This ancient song's recounting of the story implies that a detachment of Egyptian soldiers attempted to follow the fleeing slaves in one or more boats across one of the lakes along the Sinai frontier. A storm came up and sank the boat or boats, thus drowning the Egyptian soldiers. This seems to be the implication in, for example, Exodus 15:5, where the Egyptians are described as "sinking like stones into the water." Also, in Exodus 14:30 in the Yahwist account, the rescued slaves observe the bodies of the drowned Egyptians washed up on the seashore the next morning.

Finally, in what may also be a more ancient version of the Exodus (or *an* Exodus), there are scattered references to a "plundering" or a "despoiling" of the Egyptians by the fleeing slaves. The references to this tradition (Ex 3:21-22; 11:2-3a; 12:35-36; Ps 105:37) may have been preserved by the Elohist writer. They describe the Exodus from Egypt as a clandestine escape by a group of slaves who took with them a quantity of goods and valuables stolen from their masters.

THE PARADIGMATIC NATURE OF THE EXODUS TRADITIONS

The sources differ among themselves as to what actually constituted the Exodus— the escape from Egypt or the rescue at the sea. Even with regard to the rescue at the sea, none of the sources gives a complete and coherent account of what happened. Nor has any attempt to reconstruct the event from the fragments preserved in the sources proved convincing. We may, in fact, be faced with the combined memories of more than one group, involving several successful escapes at various times.

One way to answer the question concerning the meaning of the event or revelatory moment is to focus on the canonical text, the final version of the story created by and for the believing community and accepted by that community as its Scripture. It is in this final version that we could choose to locate the "revelation" contained in the story, that is, the proclamation of God's saving love and power on behalf of this people.

Another way to approach the question, however, is to emphasize the *paradigmatic* nature of the story. We noted that this group of slaves who escaped from Egypt under Moses was not, in fact, what we ordinarily identify as Israel. They most likely contributed only a fraction of the number of people who eventually formed Israel. Their role, however, in providing two catalytic elements was key in the creation of this "Israel." The first of these catalytic elements was, of course, their story, the story of an oppressed and powerless group who managed to escape from oppressive conditions. They told this story over and over, celebrating their God's liberating power in ritual and song:

Then Moses and the Israelites sang this song to the Lord:
I will sing to the Lord, for he is gloriously triumphant;
horse and chariot he has cast into the sea.
My strength and my courage is the Lord,
and he has been my savior.

He is my God, I praise him;
 the God of my father, I extol him. . . .
Pharaoh's chariots and army he hurled into the sea;
 the elite of his officers were submerged in the Red Sea.
The flood waters covered them,
 they sank into the depths like a stone. . . .
The enemy boasted, "I will pursue and overtake them;
 I will divide the spoils and have my fill of them;
 I will draw my sword; my hand shall despoil them!"
When your wind blew, the sea covered them;
 like lead they sank in the mighty waters.
Who is like to you among the gods, O LORD?
Who is like to you, magnificent in holiness?
O terrible in renown, worker of wonders. . . .
In your mercy you led the people you redeemed;
 in your strength you guided them to your holy dwelling.
(Ex 15:1-2, 4-5, 9-10, 11b-13)

The escape, then, they attributed to a god they called Yahweh, and they managed to forge in the wilderness a new community, united and determined by a covenant with this god. It was the entry of this group and their story into the context of thirteenth-century Canaan that marked the beginning of the Israel we know from the Bible. The desperate and sometimes antagonistic groups seeking refuge from a dominating and oppressive network of socially stratified city-states found in this story a root metaphor for their diverse experiences of liberation. This dramatic narrative became the symbolic vehicle for bringing together and unifying a variety of groups and peoples, each of whom could see reflected in that narrative something of its own experience of oppression and liberation. Thus the story was *one* of the key elements contributed by this Moses group. The *other* key element this group contributed was the notion of a covenant with that god, with Yahweh. It is to that notion of covenant that we now turn.

REVIEW QUESTIONS

1. In what sense can the "Exodus event" be called "historical"?

2. Can we identify the "Moses group" who escaped from Egypt as "Israel"? When and where did "Israel" as such (= the Tribal Confederation) come into existence?

3. What is one plausible date arrived at by scholars for the escape of the "Moses group" from Egypt? Describe briefly some of the historical data which can be read as pointing to this date.

4. Describe briefly the four older versions of the Exodus from Egypt, elements of which have been combined to form the account as it now stands in the Book of Exodus.
   —Yahwist
   —Priestly
   —"Song of the Sea" (Ex 15)
   —Plundering of the Egyptians (e.g. Ps 105:37).

5. What do we mean when we speak of the "paradigmatic" nature of the Exodus story, or its function as "root metaphor" for early Israel?

8

Covenant

Suggested Bible Readings: Exodus 16-24; Numbers 21-25; Joshua 24

The Moses group contributed two key elements to the process by which the growing number of disaffected groups and families settling in the central hill country of Canaan finally were able to come together as Israel. The first element, as we saw in the last chapter, was the story of their liberation, which they attributed to the action and graciousness of a god whom they called Yahweh. A second key element they apparently contributed was the idea for an instrument that would serve to unify and preserve in a community the individuals now united by that common experience and freed from bondage. That instrument seems to have been some form of covenant with that liberating god, Yahweh. The introduction of these two key elements united the refugee population in the hill country of Canaan, and Israel was born. We have already examined the first of these elements, the story of the liberation of the Moses group. Now we shall look more closely at the second element, that of the covenant with Yahweh.

The idea and instrument seem to have been born out of two complementary sets of circumstances. First, these slaves from Egypt now found themselves suddenly free from their situation of slavery. But they were threatened by new circumstances and challenges to life in the wilderness and in need of a whole array of social instruments—political, economic, religious—with which to deal successfully with those challenges. In other words, they faced a situation in which they would either find ways to work together and survive or fail to find those ways and means and perish.

The second set of circumstances, which complemented the first, was the extraordinary room for flexibility and creativity they found they possessed. Having, in effect, rejected a previous form of social organization in Egypt, which they had experienced as detrimental, indeed death-dealing, they were now free to build anew; they had the opportunity to create something life-giving. It seems that one of the means they employed was to take the social setting they had just rejected as a kind of *foil,* that is, a model embodying those things which they especially wished to *avoid.* Both the need to create an effective instrument for their survival as a group and the opportunity and flexibility they now enjoyed to create that instrument enabled them to draw upon the experiences of the society or societies of which they had been a part. Having learned from both the successes and the failures of those older societies, they forged the instrument of a covenant with the God who had rescued them from Egypt. The Egypt they had fled was a patriarchal, hierarchical, and socially stratified society, on the bottom rung of which these slaves had suffered. Thus one of the foundational elements in the new social instrument was an "opening toward equality." In other words, they created institutions and legal provisions, especially in the economic and political spheres, that would inhibit the accumulation of the communal resources and political and social power into the hands of individuals or small groups.

The notion of covenant pervades the Bible. Even the names that have often been used by Christians for its two components, the Old and New Testaments (or Covenants), attest to that. The idea persists even into the New Testament texts, for example, in the words of Jesus in blessing the cup at the Last Supper: "This is my blood of the new covenant, which is poured out for the many" (Mk 14:24). The Priestly tradition projects back a series of individual covenants with Israel's ancestors: God's covenant with Abraham, Isaac, and Jacob, foreshadowed in the earlier covenants with Adam and Noah. For the Priestly writers all of these earlier covenants are struck with individuals; they point toward and prepare for what in their minds is the central event, *the* covenant with the whole people at Sinai. Much of the complex of ideas and language that has sprung up around covenant and enriched the concept is the result of later reflection, theologizing, and spiritualizing of the notion. One must be careful not to project all of this back onto the Moses group in the wilderness and the subsequent tribal confederation in Canaan. It is important to remember that, although the religious aspect was also central in these earlier contexts, the covenant served principally a social and political function. It formed the basis of the entire life of the community in *all* of its aspects. In fact, the main source of information about covenant in the ancient world comes from the political arena. Analogous phenomena such as binding agreements between individuals and/or groups, legal contracts, and so on, abound. However, two examples from the arena of international relations seem to provide the most helpful parallels for understanding the function and language of covenant in the Bible.

International covenants or treaties in the ancient world were of at least two kinds: the parity treaty and the suzerainty treaty. The parity treaty constituted an agreement between two equals, usually two kings or overlords. An example would be the covenant or treaty mentioned above between Ramses II of Egypt and the Hittite emperor, Hattusilis III, a few years after their inconclusive confrontation at Kadesh. Copies of both the Hittite and the Egyptian versions of this treaty are known.

The second type of covenant or treaty was the suzerainty treaty, an agreement between a suzerain or overlord and a vassal or subject king. Examples of the suzerainty treaty came to light during excavations of the ancient Hittite capital of Hattusa in what is now central Turkey. When the texts were finally published in the early 1950s, biblical scholars immediately noticed striking similarities between this ancient covenant or treaty form and the language, terminology, and formal elements in the description of Israel's covenant with Yahweh.

Some of the formal elements found in the Hittite suzerainty treaty include: (1) a *preamble* that identifies the suzerain or overlord and gives his titles; (2) a *historical prologue* detailing the series of events by which links have been established between the suzerain and the vassal, especially the acts of beneficence by the suzerain toward the vassal which call forth the vassal's gratitude to the suzerain; (3) *stipulations* imposed upon the vassal by the suzerain as a way for the vassal to show his gratitude; (4) *provision for the preservation of the treaty* and for its periodic public reading as a reminder of the obligations accepted by the vassal; (5) a *list of the gods as witnesses and enforcers* of the treaty's stipulations; (6) *curses and blessings* for the violation or fulfillment of the treaty. Excerpts illustrating these formal elements from one of the Hittite treaties follow.

1. *Preamble*
   These are the words of the Sun, Mursilis, the great king, the king of the Hatti land, the valiant, the favorite of the storm god, the son of Suppiluliumas, the great king, the king of Hatti land, the valiant.

2. *Historical prologue*
   When your father died, in accordance with your father's word, I did not abandon you. Since your father had mentioned to me your name, I sought after you. To be sure, you were sick and ailing, but although you were ailing, I, the Sun, put you in the place of your father and took your brothers and sisters and the Amurru land in oath for you.

3. *Stipulations imposed on the vassal*
But you, Duppi-Teshub, remain loyal toward the king of Hatti land (and toward) my sons and grandsons forever! The tribute which was imposed upon your grandfather and your father—they presented 300 shekels of good, refined, first-class gold weighed with the standard weights—you shall present likewise. Do not turn your eyes to anyone else! Your fathers presented tribute to Egypt. You shall not do that!

(The following quotations have been supplied from a similar treaty.)

4. *Provisions for the preservation of the treaty*
In the Mitanni land, a duplicate [of the treaty] has been deposited before Teshub. . . . At regular intervals they shall read it in the presence of the king of the Mitanni land and in the presence of the sons of the Hurri country.

5. *The list of the gods as witnesses and enforcers*
At the conclusion of this treaty we have called the gods . . . to be present, to listen and serve as witnesses: the Son goddess of Arinna . . . the Sun-god, the lord of heaven, the Storm god . . . Seris and Huris, the mountains Nanni and Hazzi . . . (the names of almost 100 deities follow).

6. *Curses and blessings*
Should Duppi-Teshub not honor the words of the treaty and the oath, may these gods of the oath destroy Duppi-Teshub together with his person, his wife, his son, his grandson, his house, his land, and together with everything he owns.
But if Duppi-Teshub honors the words of this treaty and the oath that are inscribed in this tablet, may these gods of the oath protect him together with his person, his wife, his son, his grandson, his house and his country (Hillers, chap. 2; *ANET,* pp. 203-6).

Other treaty texts that are helpful as background to formulation of covenant and covenant language come from a later period, the early first millennium, contemporary with Israel's monarchic period. These texts stem from Assyria and, although related in format to the Hittite treaties, clearly differ at certain points. The Assyrian treaties, for example, generally omit the historical prologue but greatly lengthen and elaborate the curses and blessings section.

Although scholars agree that these treaty texts are important for understanding covenant in the Bible, they differ in their evaluation of how they can be helpful. Some scholars hold that the international treaty forms, especially the Hittite suzerainty treaties, were crucial in the development of the covenant idea and language in Israel, even from the time of Moses or shortly after. These scholars point out parallels, for example, between the Hittite treaty form and the Sinai covenant in Exodus 20 or the covenant renewal account in Joshua 24. Compare the preamble of the Hittite treaty above with Joshua 24:2a: "Joshua addressed all the people: 'Thus says the LORD, the God of Israel . . .'" (see also Exodus 20:2a). Or compare the Hittite treaty's historical prologue with Exodus 20:2b: ". . . who brought you out of the land of Egypt" (see also Joshua 24:2b-13). The stipulations of the Hittite form possibly find correspondence in the so-called Ten Commandments in Exodus 20:3-17 (compare also Joshua 24:14). The provisions for the preservation of the treaty seem to parallel Joshua 24:25-26: "So Joshua made a covenant with the people that day and made statutes and ordinances for them at Shechem, which he recorded in the book of the law of God." Further, we have the mention of the witness (compare with list of gods) in Joshua 24:26-27: "Then he [Joshua] took a large stone and set it up there under the oak that was in the sanctuary of the LORD. And Joshua said to all the people, 'This stone shall be our witness, for it has heard all the words which the LORD spoke to us.'"

Other scholars argue that the international treaty form exerted an influence only much later. They hold that it was chiefly the Deuteronomist circles in the seventh century B.C.E. that elaborated the metaphor of covenant for describing and expressing Israel's relationship with Yahweh.

Debate continues on the relationship between the theme of covenant in the Bible and the international treaty forms. What does seem clear is that, in addition to the story of a liberating God named Yahweh, the other key contribution from the Moses group to the rise of Israel in Canaan was that of a binding agreement between that deity and the people liberated. This notion of a binding agreement or covenant with the liberating God served two functions in the formation of Israel in Canaan. First, it provided the mechanism by which these diverse groups could transcend their differences or even antagonisms in forming a common bond with the single deity. Second, this covenant, with a liberating God acting in the place of a human suzerain or king, became the means by which these peoples could assert and affirm their claim to self-determination. They owed allegiance to no human sovereign. Their destiny, their future, was not in the hands of one or another human being, but in the sovereign care of their covenant God. In other words, within the context of obedience to the covenant stipulations, they were in effect free to determine their own conduct and control their own history.

It is important to keep in mind that later reflection and theologizing on both the liberation from Egypt and the covenant formulations and language have greatly elaborated and given depth, color, and dimension to both of these foundational notions. "Liberation" and "covenant" have been broadened and deepened to include personal, spiritual, and existential dimensions. For example, the New Testament has extended the language of Exodus to include liberation from sin and death and has applied the language of covenant to the marriage bond. Indeed, the spiritual and personal applications have taken such a prominent place in Christian thought that they tend to obscure and crowd out the social and political dimensions of both the Exodus and covenant. Nonetheless, for the Exodus, the language of liberation is so deeply imbedded and woven into the tradition that it has not been difficult, for example, for the proponents of liberation theology to recover again this aspect of the biblical tradition. That the covenant with the deity at Sinai was not restricted to the religious sphere alone is clear from the inclusion within it of Israel's entire body of legislation covering almost every aspect of its social and economic life.

Finally, recent study of covenant has located its origins in kinship relations. In other words, covenant originated as a legal means by which the duties and privileges of kinship could be extended to another individual or group. This resulted in the creation of a kinship-in-law relationship, as opposed to a kinship-in-flesh. Frank Cross has recently explained Israel's covenant with Yahweh in these terms. Through its covenant with God, Israel becomes the "kindred of Yahweh." Yahweh, in effect, adopts the people of Israel, and mutual obligations are thereby created. Cross thus proposes that the phrase in Hebrew, *'am yhwh,* usually translated "people of Yahweh" (see Jgs 5:13; 1 Sm 2:24; and so forth), would be more accurately rendered "kindred of Yahweh." Thus God was considered Israel's "divine Kinsman" who redeemed them from slavery, loved them, and shared the land of his divine heritage (*nahala*) with them. He provides for and protects them.

REVIEW QUESTIONS

1. What were the two key elements the Moses group supplied in the formation of Israel?

2. What two complementary sets of circumstances for the Moses group contributed to their ability to forge the social, political, economic, and religious instrument of a covenant with Yahweh?

3. How did the social setting the "Moses group" had just left behind in Egypt act as a kind of *foil* in their attempt to build a life together and survive as a community?

4. How was an "opening toward equality" a key foundational element for the early Israelite community?

5. What are the six formal elements usually found in a suzerainty treaty?

6. In what ways have the two key notions of liberation (the Exodus event) and covenant been broadened and deepened among subsequent generations of those who stand within the biblical tradition?

PART III

THE RISE OF ISRAEL
IN CANAAN

9

The "Conquest" of Canaan

Suggested Bible Readings: Joshua 1-12; Judges 1-21; Ruth

INTRODUCTION

Descriptions of the origins of Israel vary greatly in their starting point. Some commentators locate these origins in the ancestor figures of Abraham and Sarah, setting the story of these Ur-parents against the wider background of the origins of the human race and the cosmos. The Book of Genesis does this. Others begin Israel's story with the Exodus from Egypt, seeing the creation of Israel in all its essential elements as having taken place in connection with the group who was led out of Egypt by Moses. At Mt. Sinai these people covenanted with a god called Yahweh, to whom they credited their deliverance from Egypt and whom they identified with the god of their ancestors. But close study of these texts in Genesis through Judges reveals a complex and complicated weaving together of traditions. The stories and traditions of a *number* of diverse groups have fed into this uneasily unified and, from a contemporary historical perspective, artificially constructed narrative.

In fact, the tradents who put these traditions into the form in which they have come to us lived and worked six hundred years and more after the events being described. Their version of those events reflects more about their own situations and concerns in the sixth and fifth centuries than the period of Israel's origins in the thirteenth and twelfth centuries B.C.E. The vision that they projected back on their past was that of an Israel already unified and confirmed in their commitment to Yahweh, their covenant God. When we put together the archeological record and the carefully unravelled complex of traditions in the biblical text, we find a somewhat different picture.

Behind the stories of conquest and settlement of Canaan by Israel, found principally in the Books of Joshua and Judges, lies the story of social revolution by a large segment of the indigenous population of Canaan. Until recently, this story of the "conquest" has been interpreted based on two major reconstructions advanced by Martin Noth and William F. Albright.

CONQUEST OR GRADUAL SETTLEMENT?

The Bible contradicts itself in offering two quite different accounts of the origins of Israel in Canaan. The Book of Joshua presents the dramatic picture that is inevitably conjured up in our minds by the word *conquest,* and indeed it gives the impression of a full-scale invasion that eventually engulfed the whole country. The vast multitude of Israelites under Joshua marches in from the east across the Jordan River. The "Holy War" described in Joshua 1-11 has the aura of a religious ritual, with processions, for example, around the walls of Jericho (Jos 6), the sounding of trumpets and ram's horns, and the accompaniment of the troops by the sacred ark of the covenant. In three swift and decisive campaigns—into the center, then north, then south—the whole land is brought under Israelite control and most of the indigenous Canaanite population either driven out or exterminated.

Book of Judges, on the other hand, implies that the Canaanites were slow in yielding their territory to the incoming Israelites. Indeed it seems to describe the "conquest" more in terms of a gradual settlement, with the individual tribes or groups of tribes acting independently in securing a foothold in the land. Only gradually did Israelite numbers and strength increase to the point that, under Saul and then David, the "conquest" of the land was complete.

Archeological evidence is ambiguous and does not fully support either version. Despite the colorful picture of the conquest and destruction of Jericho in Joshua 6, for example, archeological investigation reveals no signs of such a destruction. Present evidence points to only a sparse occupation of the site during the thirteenth century B.C.E., and that settlement, ironically, was without walls.

On the other hand, there *are* some cities that give evidence of violent destruction. Bethel, for instance, was destroyed by a terrific conflagration in the latter part of the thirteenth century B.C.E., as attested by a thick layer of ash and debris. The same is true of other towns mentioned in Joshua: Lachish, Eglon, and Debir in the south, and the great city of Hazor in the north. All give evidence of destruction followed by the first signs of what may be Israelite occupation.

In the last fifty years two prominent biblical scholars have lent their names to two conflicting readings of the evidence concerning the Israelite conquest of Canaan. German scholar Martin Noth (d. 1971), basing his opinion on a detailed examination of the biblical text, weighs in heavily against the conquest model. His study of the relevant texts downplays the historical value of the accounts of a conquest and the evidence of archeology. He prefers to describe the origins of Israel in terms of a gradual settlement over a number of generations by different groups entering Canaan from different directions and at different times.

A second approach is associated with the renowned American Orientalist William F. Albright, who was involved in much of the archeological work in the Holy Land between the two World Wars. He took part in the excavations at Bethel and directed the dig at Tell Beit Mirsim (biblical Debir). Both cities give evidence of a destruction during the latter part of the thirteenth century B.C.E. His familiarity with the archeological evidence inclined him to credit the historical basis of the conquest accounts in Joshua. Thus he upheld the view that Israel's origins in Canaan were due to an invasion by the tribes following the Exodus from Egypt and the sojourn in the wilderness.

A THIRD WAY: THE SOCIAL REVOLUTION MODEL

Introduction

In contrast to the Albright school's picture of Israel seizing Canaan in a massive, unified military conquest and Noth's description of a more gradual process over generations of infiltration and settlement, a recent third model has been advanced. This third model of Israel's origins takes elements from both prior reconstructions and rearranges them into what has come to be called the social revolution model. This model was first advanced by George Mendenhall in 1962 and later taken up and elaborated by Norman Gottwald in his 1979 volume, *The Tribes of Yahweh: A Sociology of the Religion of Liberated Israel, 1250-1050 B.C.E.* The social revolution model draws on the immigration and infiltration model of Noth, for example, in its affirmation that most of the elements that made up early Israel were indigenous peoples. They were Canaanites who migrated from the coastal plains and the valleys to escape the oppressive rule of the city-state system. They settled in the sparsely inhabited hill country and gradually formed more unified groupings and developed networks of mutual aid and self-defense.

And that brings us back to the story of Ahilud and his family that we began back in chapter four. Ahilud's parents or grandparents were among those Canaanite farmers and sheepherders who had migrated to the central hill country. When they arrived on the hilltop of Raddana with a few other families, their first priority would have been to clean away some of the thick brush and begin farming and herding. They needed to work together and develop modes of interaction that would foster cooperation and mutual support rather than competition. They brought with them the skills for survival: farming, terrace-building, construction of cisterns to collect and store fresh water, the ability to manufacture and repair tools and implements. For the latter, they continued to use mainly bronze, although some iron was coming into wider use.

Besides the basic material assets for struggling to build a life and community in this highland wilderness, they also brought their traditional religious beliefs and practices. These beliefs and practices gave meaning and texture to their daily life and had developed through many generations of close contact with the rhythms of nature and the challenges of survival. We come very close to the warp and woof of the religious dimensions of the life of Ahilud's grandparents in the stories of Genesis 12-50. Therein we find religious practices and ideas that relate to the central questions of survival for the families of the time: for example, land, descendants, and freedom from domination.

The Context of the Social Revolution

Late Bronze Age Canaan (1500-1200 B.C.E.) was divided into scores of small city-states. This mode of social organization mirrored on a small scale the larger state and imperial systems that dominated the Near East in ancient times.

The seeds for social revolution grew from the turmoil in Egypt in the fourteenth and thirteenth centuries B.C.E.—troubles over novelties and changes introduced by Pharaoh Akhenaton (1364–1347 B.C.E.) as well as struggles over succession to the throne. This period is referred to as the Amarna Age, from the extensive correspondence between the Egyptian court and various Canaanite rulers discovered during the last century in Egypt at Tell el Amarna. These letters give a vivid picture of the chaotic situation in Canaan. Egypt, preoccupied with internal problems, was unable to exert a strong hand or presence there.

It was not only Canaan that witnessed turmoil at this time. The entire eastern Mediterranean region saw a disruption of trade, mass migration of peoples, and the destruction of large cities as the Late Bronze Age came

Amarna Letter No. 68 speaks of the lack of military preparedness in the Canaanite city of Hebron in the mid-14th century B.C.E. The Amarna Tablets are in cuneiform script, written in the Babylonian language, evidently the *lingua franca* of the day.

to a close. We will discuss this phenomenon in detail below in chapter twelve on the origin of the Philistines.

This critical moment in history, the collapse of the Late Bronze Age civilization and culture, witnessed the birth of new movements and peoples. Among them were the various groups from the margins and anonymous underclasses of ancient Canaan who would join together to create something unique and decisive for the future of humankind—a compelling vision of what human life and community can and should be like under the rule of a just and loving God.

With the lack of a strong Egyptian presence, competition for regional dominance among the various city-states in Canaan increased. The Amarna correspondence alludes to wars and sedition, with the various kings asking for help from the pharaoh and accusing one another of being a *Habiru*, a term that in this context means something like "outlaw." Political and social turmoil increased. The ones who suffered most in the midst of all of this, of course, were the underclasses. Their burden of taxes was increased to fund the military expeditions of their rulers against each other. In addition, their crops were often the objects of destructive raids among the various warring parties.

This atmosphere of political and social turmoil provides the background for the social revolution model of the origins of Israel. Most of the hundreds of unwalled villages discovered by archeologists in the central hill country date from this period, the end of the Late Bronze Age (the late 1300s B.C.E.), and especially in the early years of the Iron Age (1200s B.C.E.). The material remains of these villages, particularly the pottery, link the inhabitants with the peoples of Bronze Age Canaan. In other words, the inhabitants of these new settlements were not outsiders. They had not migrated nor invaded from some other region, outside Canaan. They were "in-migrants," that is, Canaanite peasant farmers and sheepherders who had come there from some other part of Canaan, especially from the rich agricultural lands of the plains and valleys controlled by the city-states.

The archeological record is clear that they were "in-migrants." They brought with them farming methods and skills that reflected long experience with the soil and climate of their native Canaan—hillside terracing and the contruction of cisterns to store rainwater, for example. But this agricultural technology had to be adapted to the new challenges of a life in the highland frontier.

There were other disaffected groups on the margin of and at the mercy of the dominant socio-political and economic order of Canaan. One such group was the *Habiru.* The term appears in extra-biblical texts throughout the second millennium, including the Amarna correspondence. It may be the same as the Hebrew term *'ibri,* usually translated into English as "Hebrew." It was often applied to Israelites by non-Israelites, especially in the early period. In Exodus 1:16, for example, Pharaoh tells the midwives of the Israelite slaves, "When you act as midwives for the Hebrew women and see them giving birth, if it is a boy, kill him; but if it is a girl, she may live" (see also Gn 14:13; 39:14, 17; 41:12; Ex 1:19; 2:7). The term *'ibri* is possibly related to the Hebrew root *'br,* "to cross over," and a definition recently proposed for *Habiru/'ibri* would then be "one who has crossed over," that is, crossed over the social and legal boundaries to become an "outlaw" or "renegade." In other words, especially in the turmoil and unrest of the Amarna period in Canaan, certain groups formed outlaw bands and operated as mercenaries for the warring kings or took up raiding and looting on their own. In the midst of the social and political confusion they managed to survive on the fringes of and in symbiosis with the dominant socio-political system. Groups of these *Habiru* or Hebrews, it seems, also

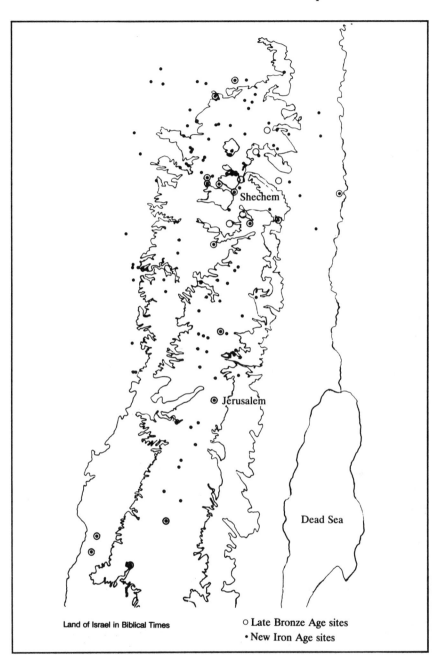

Land of Israel in Biblical Times

○ Late Bronze Age sites
• New Iron Age sites

Canaan between 1200 and 1150 B.C.E. The sudden appearance of over 200 new settlements in the previously sparsely settled central hill country of Palestine. Open circles represent the Late Bronze Age sites and dots represent the new Iron Age sites.

took advantage of the opening up of the hill country to pursue a more peaceful and independent existence, thereby making available to the accumulating mixture of groups in that hill country their military expertise for defense against the encroachment of city-state control.

The "El-Federation" and the Entry of the Moses Group

For Ahilud's grandparents and the other residents of Raddana, new factors soon entered the picture. Both internal and external pressures moved them to forge links with neighboring settlements. Internally they recognized the advantages, indeed the necessity of cooperation and mutual support in their struggle against the harsh environment in which they had settled. They also had to cooperate in defending themselves against external dangers. City-state rulers sought to extend their rule over the hill country region and once again dominate the people's life and economy. The religious symbols associated with this networking among inhabitants of the central highlands built on family piety with its notion of a god who attaches himself to the group and offers unconditional guidance and protection. Thus, this expanding network invented a name for itself to reflect that unity and that divine protection— "Israel," a name that probably means "God (or El) rules" or "may God show himself as ruler."

The name "Israel" first appears in an historical record just around this time, in the stone inscription celebrating the Egyptian pharaoh Merneptah's victories in Canaan (1220 B.C.E.). Rainer Albertz comments:

Such a name sounds almost like a confession: God should rule and not any human ruler, whether coming from outside or within. The option of this society to oppose domination finds its religious expression in the name which it had given itself.

As a people free now from domination and exercising control over their lives and future, they began to experiment with and institutionalize ways of interacting that would insure their survival as a community.

But it seems that ideological factors were not quite adequate and were not able to provide a sufficiently strong motivating force to overcome the rivalries and antagonisms among these people of such diverse origins who were scattered up and down the length of Canaan's central highlands. For one thing, the name "El" was the same as the chief god of the city-state rulers. This new federation of families and clans required a stronger "glue" to unify them. They required a more adequate way to express in symbolic form their experience as a people struggling to meet the challenges of their pioneer life and to create a zone of freedom far from the domination of the powerful ruling elite in the city-states.

The path toward greater unity opened with the arrival of a small group of refugees from Egypt under the leadership of a man named Moses. These refugees told stories about a god named Yahweh, whom they credited with their miraculous escape from slavery and forced labor under the pharaoh. The struggling Canaanite peasants, herders, and others who had escaped from similar situations of domination or virtual slavery adopted the Egyptian refugees' story as their own. They also began to worship Yahweh as their patron deity. Thus, the common allegiance of these various disaffected groups to Yahweh, who stands by the poor and frees the oppressed, became a powerful force for unifying these disparate and sometimes desperate peoples.

The coincidental analogies between the experience of those former Egyptian forced laborers under the leadership of Moses and that of the marginal and lower-class groups of Canaanite society were remarkable. The story told by these Egyptian slaves was able to crystallize and express in the powerful symbol of a dramatic narrative the diverse experiences and hopes of the different groups already settled or settling in the central highland areas. Further, the name and character of the Egyptian group's deity, "Yahweh," provided a clear contrast with the "El" worshipped in the Canaanite city-states. Yahweh was a God who proved his divinity specifically in the liberation from oppression.

These groups in Canaan had also fled from situations of oppression, situations in which they had had no say in how leadership was exercised or resources were distributed. Now they enjoyed the freedom and flexibility to build "from scratch." Thus the socio-political and economic structures that they began to build moved in the opposite direction from the city-states model toward a definite egalitarianism or, at least, with openings toward equality. In other words, these new structures and institutions were meant to impede the accumulation of economic and political power by a few individuals or groups.

In this situation, with more opening toward equality, the question of the activity and even leadership role of women surfaced and had to be dealt with. This can be seen, for example, in the prominent place Miriam had within the Moses group during the desert wanderings. The later Israelite prophet, Micah, preserves a memory of this leadership role exercised by Miriam when he mentions her in the same breath as Moses and Aaron, when God says to the people: "I brought you up from the land of Egypt, from the place of slavery I released you, and I sent before you Moses, Aaron, and Miriam" (Mi 6:4; see Ex 15:20; Num 12). Note also the crucial role that the Hebrew midwives played in the story of the liberation from Egypt as recounted in Exodus 1:15-22.

Finally, the religious factor was crucial. The Moses group, in rejecting both the physical and psychic bondage of the Egyptian socio-political and economic system, had also abandoned the religious ideology that legitimated and reinforced that system. In replacing the Egyptian gods, whose son the pharaoh claimed to be, they chose, or claim to have been chosen by Yahweh, the god of the oppressed, a god who stands by the poor and frees those enslaved.

In his almost thousand-page volume, *The Tribes of Yahweh* (1979), Norman Gottwald provides a thorough and detailed argument for this social revolution model. His book stimulated much discussion and debate and opened the way for new directions in the study of Israel's origins. Since its publication in 1979, new data from historical studies and archeological excavations, plus the increasing application of the methods and results of the modern social sciences, have prompted scholars to propose modifications in Gottwald's description of Israel's origins, or even alternatives. Many of these scholars rightly stress Israel's cultural continuity with predecessor societies. They emphasize Israel's origins from among Canaan's indigenous population.

Gradually, a specifically "Israelite" culture and identity, including the religious ideology that explained and motivated their efforts, emerged. It evolved out of the struggle to survive and find ways of interacting and working together to build a new life in the difficult frontier area of the central highlands. Most of the basic elements of that new culture were already available from the preceding Late Bronze Age Canaanite culture. But new circumstances and new challenges led them to reconstellate in new and innovative ways these elements of Canaanite culture, including its religious components, to forge a new culture and new identity—"Israelite." In other words, it constituted what Gottwald now refers to as a "communitarian social revolution." And an inextricable part of this new culture and identity was the religious ideology that gave meaning and purpose to their project. This included the worship of Yahweh and a covenant with their new, *divine* Sovereign. Henceforth, no human power would dominate them and demand their loyalty and obedience. They saw themselves now as masters of their own destiny and future.

REVIEW QUESTIONS

1. Summarize the model of the "conquest" of Canaan according to Martin Noth. What evidence does he draw on to support his model? Which biblical book corresponds most closely to his model?

2. Summarize the model of the "conquest" of Canaan associated with William F. Albright. What evidence does he draw on to support his model? Which biblical book corresponds most closely to his model?

3. Outline the main features of the Mendenhall-Gottwald reconstruction of the "conquest" of Canaan. How does it draw on elements of both the "conquest" and "gradual settlement" models of Albright and Noth?

4. Why is this period of the Late Bronze Age in Canaan called the Amarna Age, and what effect did Egypt's internal problems have on life in Canaan?

5. Where did the majority of those who formed early Israel come from? What caused them to migrate and settle in the central highland region?

6. Who were the *Habiru?*

7. An intermediate step in the creation of Israel was, according to Gottwald, the formation of an "El-confederation." Explain.

8. Where did the name "Israel" come from? What does the word itself mean?

9. How and why did the story and experience of the Moses group come to play such a pivotal role in the origins of Israel in Canaan?

10

Israel in the Period of the Judges

Suggested Bible Readings: Ruth 1-4; Exodus 23:14-17; Deuteronomy 16:1-20; Joshua 2, 9; Judges 6-9; 1 Kings 21; Isaiah 5:8; Micah 2:2

LIFE IN THE CENTRAL HIGHLANDS

The social structure within these early Iron Age villages was basically an egalitarian one. Several extended families constituted the population of one village. They consumed or bartered what they produced by agriculture, the pasturing of flocks, and essential crafts and small industry (the production of pottery, the making and repair of tools, etc.). Decisions were made and disputes settled by consensus in a council formed by the heads and older members of the extended families.

Anthropologists have a standard description of the phases of movement through which a human community proceeds as the population grows and the need for more complex organizational structure arises. This movement is from band to tribe to chiefdom to state. The band society comprises hunting and gathering groups who wander in a particular territory but have not settled into a village pattern to produce their own food by agriculture and herding. Tribal society, by contrast, characterizes the social structure of self-supporting families in an agricultural village setting. The chiefdom and state emerge when and if one individual or group finally manages to centralize and monopolize economic and political power under its own control. Then a specialized ruling elite emerges, able to coerce and channel human resources toward its own economic and military purposes.

Local village social structure in the Ancient Near East, basically tribal in organization, was usually incorporated into a larger statist complex ruled from urban or imperial centers. These centers imposed a secondary system of control on top of and often in conflict with local practices. The purpose of this secondary system of control was to siphon off as much of the production of the villages as possible in agricultural products and to conscript male inhabitants of the villages for military service and large work projects. This superimposed system was enforced by agents of the urban elite—tax collectors, district governors, and others who had military and/or police units at their disposal. The tendency was to extract as much as possible from the village production system for use and control by the urban elites, leaving the minimum necessary to keep the population reasonably productive. This system for centralizing control over a society's surplus production is called a "tributary economy."

The diverse groups in the central hill country had fled from this oppressive tributary system that had drained off most of their surplus production. They developed instead a "communitarian economy" in which they could freely dispose of all of their resources. The extended families in a village grouped with extended families in neighboring villages to form clans (*mispaha* in Hebrew). Annual festivals, apparently obligatory for all the clan members, were held regularly. We see this reflected, for example, in this conversation between Saul and his son Jonathan:

> Saul inquired of his son Jonathan, "Why has the son of Jesse not come to table yesterday or today?" Jonathan answered Saul: "David urgently asked me to let him go to his city, Bethlehem. 'Please let me go,' he begged, 'for we are to have a clan sacrifice in our city, and my brothers insist on my presence. Now, therefore, if you think well of me, give me leave to visit my brothers.' That is why he has not come to the king's table" (1 Sm 20:27-29).

These clan festivals fulfilled important religious, social, political, and economic functions. Clans gathered at a local shrine, exchanged news, arranged marriages, settled disputes, planned military strategy if danger seemed imminent, and shared genealogies, stories, and traditions. The religious dimension was crucial and pervasive. Common rites were observed in the public assembly's worship of Yahweh, and the local priests and Levites expounded and explained Yahweh's covenant law.

The economic factor was also central. The covenant law demanded accessibility to the basic resources for survival for each extended family group. This clan system provided the first link in an important network for mutual aid and defense among the various groups that formed "the Tribes of Yahweh." If a family or village, for example, suffered the loss of a crop due to bad weather or raids by outsiders, other members of the clan were obliged to come to its aid by donations or non-interest loans. Such economic mechanisms were not considered voluntary or supererogatory. There was a note of pragmatism and necessity in this arrangement. Things *had* to be this way; such structures were absolutely necessary if the people as a whole were to survive. The economic institutions and structures contained built-in levelling mechanisms to *discourage* the accumulation of economic resources and power in the hands of a few individuals or groups. Key to the success of the system was the control and access of each extended family to its own basic resources—thus the covenant stipulation we know as the tenth commandment (Ex 20:17; Dt 5:21; see also Is 5:8; Mi 2:2). "You shall not covet your neighbor's house" was meant chiefly to *discourage* the accumulation of "houses" by a single individual or group. "You shall not covet your neighbor's house." In other words, you shall not even harbor in your heart the desire to appropriate and accumulate properties for the sake of property, over and above what is needed to provide you and your family with the basic necessities for a satisfying and productive life. Despite its negative formulation, the *prohibition* of the accumulation of property, the commandment affirmed a positive value—the protection of the right of every Israelite family to the necessary basics, especially the possession of a "house." This house included not only the dwelling place but also the productive land that went with it.

The periodic assemblies also played an important political role. The leadership of groups of extended families lay in the hands of a council of elders. The periodic assemblies provided the opportunity for a council to meet with other councils of the clan and reach decisions, judge disputes, and choose delegates to the larger assembly of an entire tribe. Political power was thus widely diffused, and the institutions and structures were designed to provide levelling mechanisms that inhibited the accumulation of power in the hands of a few individuals or groups. Temporary individual leadership was allowed to emerge for specific circumstances and crises. However, as the stories of Gideon (Jgs 6-8) and Abimelech (Jgs 9) demonstrate, the attempt to establish or institutionalize more permanent leadership roles met strong opposition.

Above all, the periodic pilgrimage festivals offered the context for this people to affirm, strengthen, and celebrate their unity and identity as Yahweh's "chosen" people. For they were a people who, in adverse and trying circumstances, had found a way to come together and as a people seize control of their destiny, their future, their history.

The clans were, in turn, part of a larger network, the tribe, which included all the villages/extended families in a geographically defined region. Finally, this tribal network, spread up and down the central hill country of Canaan from the hills of Galilee in the north to the Negeb wilderness in the south, was organized into a loose federation embracing the entire people, "the people/tribes of Israel/Yahweh." The regular assemblies at the clan level were paralleled in turn by assemblies or "pilgrimage festivals" on the tribal and confederation level. Such assemblies on the confederation level were mandated three times a year: the Passover (spring equinox), Feast of Weeks or Pentecost (summer solstice), and Feast of Tabernacles (autumn equinox) (Ex 23:14-17; Dt 16:1-20). All three occurred when respite from the necessary work in the fields was available to undertake the required journeys.

The movement spread rapidly and the Canaanite leaders quickly realized the threat this new movement posed. Reactions to this so-called Israel varied. In some cases, such as Jerusalem, the Canaanite royal/military establishment managed to retain control of its cities and countryside populations. These were not brought into Israel until the time of David. Other cities, as the story of the taking of Jericho suggests, found themselves at the mercy of individuals or groups who sympathized with the revolt and destroyed the city-state from within. Rahab offers a paradigm of this scenario in the story of her collaboration with the Israelite spies in the second chapter of Joshua. Others, like the Gibeonites (Jos 9), reached a compromise with Israel and became quasi-partners in the confederation. In still other cases, such as Shechem, the countryside population allied itself with the fledgling federation while the urban center remained formally outside it. The variety of responses by the urban centers to the Israelite revolution helps make sense of the confusing image archeology presents of this period—the destruction of some of the fortified cities, but the lack of any evidence of destruction with others. The cities that suffered destruction such as Lachish, Debir, and Hazor, did so not at the hands of invaders from outside Israel necessarily, but rather as attacks by the alienated members of the indigenous population. Those cities that did not suffer destruction had either reached an accommodation with the tribal league or had managed to hold on to their grip on power, at least within their own walls.

This social revolution took hold and initially spread quickly, especially in the central hill country. But its extension into the rest of Canaan, the plains and valleys, was slower and spread over generations. This we can gather especially from the episodes related in the Book of Judges. The confederation gained complete control of the land only in the time of David. But with David a new stage was reached. Not only was there an external threat to the confederation from the Philistines. There emerged within Israel economically and politically powerful individuals and families competing for leadership and control.

From this discussion of Israel's origins in terms of a social revolution and retribalization process, we can see that the understanding of the terms

Canaanite and *Israelite* as two opposed racial, ethnic, and cultural groups is a later development and projection back onto the earlier stage. From this reconstruction it is obvious that the terms *Israelite* and *Canaanite* represented opposed systems of a social, economic, and political organization. Each system was explained and legitimated by its own appropriate religious ideology. "Canaanite" referred, then, to the hierarchically organized and socially stratified system that continued to hold sway over parts of the plains and valleys, and even some hill country centers, such as Jerusalem. It was supported and legitimated by a religious system known as Baalism. Israel, on the other hand, designated that system and those within it who formed the network of villages and groups (and some allied urban centers) mainly in the hill country. It was characterized by its decentralized structures and institutions that fostered a levelling process both economically and politically toward more egalitarian configurations. This system was supported and legitimated in the worship of the one God, Yahweh, and by the common covenant into which each Israelite had entered with him.

YAHWISM: THE RELIGION OF THE SOCIAL REVOLUTION

Revelation

One might legitimately ask after the foregoing discussion, Where was God in all of this? The biblical text seems to present the story of Israel's origins—the Exodus, Sinai, the desert wanderings, the entry into the Promised Land—as if Israel's God, Yahweh, had a direct and decisive role to play in the course of these events. Yet *our* description of these originating events has taken a different approach. It presents Israel's origin as a successful movement by groups of oppressed peoples to free themselves from their former bondage and establish themselves in a situation in which they could maintain that freedom.

The two approaches do not exclude each other; they are not necessarily in contradiction. A combination of the two would see the hand of Israel's God working in and through the desire for and struggle for freedom from oppression. That same God was with them, guiding the process of constructing a new community in such a way as to ensure as far as possible the maintenance of that freedom. In other words, our view has been that the origins of Israel are most authentically read not as the result of an arbitrary choice by a God who intervenes into the history of an ethnically and racially homogeneous people by miraculous works in a "top-down" model of divine action. Rather, our view sees how Israel emerged as one of the many movements within human history of groups of people at the bottom or on the margins struggling to achieve and maintain a more just, peaceful, and free human community. Israel was one of the few groups successful in its efforts, and part of that success is the written record of the struggle. They have left it as a heritage for future generations, a sign and beacon of hope to all those who long for liberation. In this struggle, the people were responding to the call of the Spirit of God in their midst, a Spirit who invites all human beings to free themselves from every kind of bondage.

The literature of this people, which we have fallen heir to as our Bible, was not produced in a vacuum. The authors and poets did not compose or write for the purpose of communicating "revelation." Often the poetry, stories, and literature, especially of the earliest periods, had the specific purpose of supporting and furthering the struggle for liberation. In that sense the writings were an intimate part of that struggle, forged in its midst. As Israel's religious literature, they give expression to the sense of the transcendent dimensions of that struggle. It was a struggle and a process that did not end with the period of Judges, but continued all through Israel's history. Sometimes collectively and often through the voices of gifted individuals, this people drew on the language, conceptual models, and literary tools of their time and culture. Indeed, often they expanded, developed, and created new ones. They sang of their successes, lamented their failures and shortcomings, and above all recounted and affirmed in astonishingly rich and profuse ways the story of their seizing of their future. They told of their formation into a people, and of the guidance and benevolence of their God, Yahweh, who, they confessed, made all this possible.

The Uniqueness of Israel's Religion

Our discussion of Israel's religion and faith involves two factors. First, we will see how what are often pointed to as the distinctive and unique features of Israelite religion do not in fact represent such clear innovations in the world of which they were a part. With regard to its religious expression, Israel did not somehow stand in total opposition to and in clear separation from that Ancient Near Eastern culture in which it found itself. Israel was, in fact, unique in the ancient world, but that uniqueness must be understood as involving the totality of Israel's life as a people, that is the economic, political, and social as well as the religious dimensions of that life. Second, with regard to Israel's religion and faith, we will develop the description of Israel's specifically religious component as having evolved its distinctive features, along with the other aspects of its social organization, in the midst of a struggle to achieve liberation and to build a new and a more just social order. In other words, Israel's religion was not a conceptual whole, communicated from on high, that had simply to be implemented in order to be effective and life-giving. Rather, the shape, pattern, and character of Israel's faith arose from the midst of struggle, of experiment, of successes and failures, of confrontation and compromise. In short, it expressed the joys and hopes and efforts of a people striving to achieve and maintain a just and life-giving community.

In reading the Scriptures, one cannot help but be struck by the sense this people expressed of their own uniqueness, their own distinctiveness among the variety of peoples who shared the world of which they were a part. One of the tasks modern biblical research has set for itself is to discover and describe the basis for that distinctiveness. This quest for Israel's uniqueness or specialness has tended in the past to focus mainly on Israel's religion. For example, some have pointed to Israel's monotheism, in contrast to the polytheism of the surrounding peoples and cultures as the source of that sense of uniqueness. Others have pointed to Israel's concern for social justice, the protection offered, for example, to the weakest and most vulnerable members of society. Still others have highlighted the covenant with Yahweh as the defining feature of Israel. Finally, one very influential and widespread approach has stressed Israel's unique understanding of history. This people saw their God, Yahweh, as having a direct hand in the course of their history, guiding it in accord with his gracious yet often mysterious plan. Israel's so-called linear view of world events was contrasted with the cyclical view of the surrounding "pagan" nature religions.

A more balanced and accurate approach recognizes that Israel was very much in continuity with the ancient world and its various cultures. With regard to Israel's monotheism, for example, we know that most of the other religions of the Ancient Near East had "high god" tendencies; that is, almost inevitably one deity emerged as the chief god, the major and focal divinity, more powerful and more important than the other gods. Israel represents the carrying of this tendency to its logical conclusion. Most of the other cultures and religions of Israel's world also spoke of justice and of the respect for and protection of the weaker members of the society such as "the orphan, the widow, and the stranger." Israel's uniqueness did not lie in having such concerns, but in the prominence that it gave to them.

Finally, scholars have recently begun to recognize that the notion of Israel having a linear view of history in contrast to the cyclical, nature-oriented view of neighboring peoples is much oversimplified. Israel did not possess a historical consciousness, the way we in the twenty-first century do, but a kind of proto-historical approach. Any historical information in Israel's narrative has been subordinated to the more prominent political, social, economic, or religious purposes of the writer or writers. In this, Israel's history writing had much in common with similar annals of kings in other contemporary cultures and these kings' accounts of their heroic deeds. Israel's history writing was different, however, in the *prominence* given to the linear or historical perspective, that is, the chronological sequence of events which seeks the causal links between those events. Israel's history writing was different also in telling the story not just of kings and armies but of a people and their struggle for a freer, better life.

Thus the uniqueness or distinctiveness of Israel and of its religion does not lie necessarily or exclusively in its monotheism or concern for justice or understanding of history. Rather, the distinctiveness of Israel and thus of its religion lies in the particular combination of these elements. Israel carried the "high god" tendency latent in the other religions to its full extent in finally eliminating all other deities and focusing divine attributes and activities in a single god-figure. Israel gave particular prominence to the concern for justice already present in the laws and ethos of other peoples. Israel gave the linear perspective of the purposefulness of divine activity in historical events a much greater place and development in its literature. This new combination of elements was possible because of Israel's situation as a newly emerged people made up of "outsiders," people from the margins of the older civilizations who had no great stake in the present order. They were thus able to take existing ideas and values and build them into a new configuration as they struggled to build a new society. They were able to create a community and a way of life unique in the ancient world. But this involved *all* the dimensions of human life and community—economics, law, politics, social organization, as well as religion. It was in this wider, fuller sense that Israel was unique, special, chosen, and not in some exclusively religious sense.

Israel developed its characteristic and defining features in the midst of a struggle to achieve liberation and to build a new social order. Thus individual or isolated features of Israel's total life—the specifically religious element, for example—are puzzling and ultimately inexplicable unless we place them within this wider context. Otherwise we are forced to resort to mystifying and *deus ex machina* understandings of those religious elements and also of how revelation takes place.

The affirmation of God's uniqueness played an important role in the struggle to create a new social order. That social order, as we have seen, was characterized by its egalitarian nature. Yahweh was the one God of this one and equal people. Each individual was linked with this God and with one another through the one covenant. Canaanite society, on the other hand, was hierarchically structured. Accordingly, it had a hierarchically structured and stratified pantheon. In their affirmation of the uniqueness of Yahweh the people of Israel were expressing their sense of the transcendent dimension involved in the single-mindedness of their efforts to overcome their differences and antagonisms to become a single people. They were unique in the ancient world in terms of the organization of their society. Thus their God was unique, unlike and distanced from the array of gods of other peoples. In emphasizing this uniqueness and exclusivity of their God, Israel expressed at the same time its own sense of uniqueness, its sense of being different from the others, and the necessity to exclude other systems of communal organization from its midst.

Here lie the roots of the notion of a "Chosen People," their self-consciousness as being different, as standing out from and in contrast to the other peoples of the ancient world. They *were* different insofar as their way of organizing their life together was different. They were conscious of having created something new, something special, as if their struggle had been blessed in a unique way by their unique God. Also, Israel's *covenant* with this God was a religiously grounded and sanctioned mechanism that went far beyond its religious meaning and role. The covenant served as the basis and ordering force for the whole complex of society in ancient Israel, regulating political, economic, and social relations as well as the religious dimension. Thus the biblical notion of covenant is only incompletely understood when it is examined solely in its religious aspects. Crucial as well were the economic, social, and political dimensions to which the religious aspects were intimately connected and from which the religious aspects took their particular shape and concrete expression.

Unanswered Questions

Among the questions currently occupying Bible scholars' attention are the nature of Israelite monotheism and the contrast between "official" and "popular" religion. For example, did the ancient Israelites worship and acknowledge the existence of only *one* God (monotheism)? Or did they practice what is called "monolatry," that is, the acknowledgement of the existence of many gods, but loyalty to the *worship* as a people of only one (chief) God? Recent archeological discoveries suggest that, up until the time of the Babylonian Exile (587-539 B.C.E.) Israel practiced more a form of monolatry, A variety of excavation sites in Israelite villages and cities have yielded numerous "mother goddess" figurines dating from the eighth and seventh centuries B.C.E. These small statuettes, usually depicting naked pregnant women with exaggerated breasts, appear both in domestic settings and in shrines. They possibly represent "Asherah," a female deity venerated by women for protection and assistance in conception and childbirth (see Jgs 3:7; 1 Kgs 15:13; 18:19; 2 Kgs 21:7; 23:4).

The obviously widespread nature of this practice among Israelite women has opened the eyes of scholars to the existence of a "popular religion" practiced alongside the "official" or normative Yahwism. In other words, future studies of Israel's religion must take into account how Israelite religion was practiced and expressed on at least two levels, the "official" and the "popular." Other evidence of such "popular piety" includes the veneration of the dead (Is 65:4) or of ancestors (the "teraphim" of Gn 31:19, 30-35 and 1 Sm 19:13,16), and the worship of the sun as a symbol of Yahweh (see 2 Kgs 23:11; Ps 84:12, Ezek 8: 16).

The Bible contains principally the "official" or normative version. It represents a description of Israel's faith as it had crystallized by the sixth and fifth centuries B.C.E. By this time, Yahwism had developed its explicitly monotheistic character. Thus the final redactors of Israel's scriptures either modified evidence of the earlier monolatry and "folk piety," or stigmatized such beliefs and practices as "heretical."

This new focus on "popular piety" raises the question of women's role in the development and expression of Israel's religious beliefs. The Hebrew Bible is a document written by men and embodying the official and public (male) version of Israelite religion. Further, the principal interpreters and commentators on this document through the years have been men. In recent years, however, new archeological evidence and growing numbers of women trained to study and interpret the Bible have opened our eyes to this whole new field of Israel's religion as it found expression among the common people and especially in the home. In such contexts the role and influence of women would have been greater, if not dominant. The relationship between this "popular piety" and the "normative" monotheism needs more study and reflection, as does the role of women in the organization and formulation of ancient Israel's beliefs and worship. Such study and research promises to expand and deepen our knowledge and appreciation of this ancient faith.

Other Aspects of Early Israel's Faith

Israel also developed an eschatology, a sense that there was a goal, a purpose, toward which its history was moving. The people's hope, as they looked to and envisioned that future, was grounded in their confidence and determination that what they were about was indeed possible and achievable despite the numerous obstacles they had to overcome.

Other religious cults of the Ancient Near East revolved around idols who were housed in temples and who had to be fed and clothed as a part of the regular worship. This usually involved a quantity of goods brought to the temple by the people out of their surplus production of grain, wine, oil, fruits—plus textiles and garments. In these socially stratified societies, the cult served to siphon off a quantity of the surplus production of the lower classes into the control and use of the ruling class, especially of the priesthood and temple personnel. With Yahwism, there was no idol to clothe and feed. The role of the priesthood was important, especially in the area of teaching, inculcating, and interpreting the covenant law. But it was also a role sharply circumscribed, and the place of sacrifice in the cultic celebration of the pre-monarchic period appears to have been a relatively small one. Thus the contrast between the idolatry that characterized the Canaanite cult and the "aniconic" or imageless cult of Israel was not simply a contrast of religious ideas and practices. It represented a contrast even more of competing political and especially economic systems. This contrast between the Canaanite cult with its idols, on the one hand, and the imageless cult of Israel, on the other, represented the emergence at the symbolic level of a sharp differentiation between two contrasting notions of how a human community can and should be organized. The exploitative socio-economic and political structures of Canaanite society were justified and abetted by the exploitative cultic practices. The cult served as the occasion, religiously justified, for the transfer of large quantities of goods from the producers to the ruling elites. Israel's cult, however, legitimated and facilitated a socio-economic system in which control over surplus production was maintained by the producers themselves, that is, by the extended family units.

The multitude of and complexity of early Israel's wealth of historical traditions testify to Israel's sense of God working in and through the whole people, not just a few elite leaders or heroes. Israel's story is the story of a people intent on and initially successful at retaining control over its history, giving it direction and having a say in the future. Yahweh represents in some ways the transcendent dimension of the people's sense of their own power to shape events and indeed to change and transform themselves and their situation. The way of bringing about and of giving expression to that sense of their power as a people was in the production of the whole variety and complexity of their story as they told, retold, and expanded it, as they wove together the various individual stories of the groups that formed that new people.

Perhaps the easiest way into that story, the way that best puts us in touch with its dynamics and fundamental concerns, is the perspective of contemporary struggles for liberation. This is where the real history of the peoples of this earth is taking place. Israel's God was a liberating God, one who was "revealed" in the midst of a struggle for liberation and in the efforts of a people to build a more just and peaceful human community. Perhaps it is in the midst of these same kinds of struggles and efforts taking place throughout our contemporary world, and in solidarity with those engaged in them, that we can most adequately and authentically discover the God of Israel's Scriptures today.

REVIEW QUESTIONS

1. What is meant by a "communitarian economy," such as the one which developed among the Iron Age villages of early Israel? How does it differ from a "tributary economy"?

2. In the regular festivals/assemblies of clans and tribes in early Israel, how was the economic factor a particularly important one? Within this context, how would you interpret the tenth commandment?

3. How was political power exercised in Israel during the period of the tribal confederation (the Period of the Judges, 1250-1050 B.C.E.)? What place did leadership roles hold?

4. In the context of social revolution, what did the terms *Israelite* and *Canaanite* come to mean?

5. In this description of the origins of Israel and of biblical faith, how would you describe what is traditionally called revelation?

6. If the uniqueness or distinctiveness of Israel did not lie necessarily or exclusively in its monotheism or in its concern for justice or in its understanding of history, in what did that distinctiveness or uniqueness lie? What was it about the people who formed ancient Israel that enabled them to create something so unique and new?

7. How are we to understand the notion of Israel as a "Chosen People"?

8. Discuss some of the "unanswered questions" currently occupying Bible scholars attention. What impact might answers to these questions have on our understanding of biblical faith today?

9. What contemporary perspective allows easiest access to our understanding of what was happening in the development of Israel and the Yahwism that lies at the origins of our biblical tradition and biblical faith?

PART IV

THE PERIOD
OF THE
MONARCHY

11

The Book of Deuteronomy and the Deuteronomistic History

Suggested Bible Readings: Deuteronomy 1-11, 15-18, 26, 28-32, 34; Leviticus 25; 2 Kings 22

The Period of the Judges (1250-1050 B.C.E.), which we have just seen in chapter 10, comes to an end with the movement toward a monarchy. The movement began with Saul and the Philistine crisis, and especially with the story of David, Israel's first real king. The history of the monarchy itself encompasses the 430 or so years from Saul's days as leader (1020-1000 B.C.E.) to the Fall of Jerusalem in 587 B.C.E. and the Babylonian Exile. The Deuteronomistic History (DH) provides most of what we know about this story of the monarchy. The Book of Deuteronomy serves as an introduction, and the Deuteronomistic History itself includes, besides Deuteronomy, the Books of Joshua, Judges, 1 and 2 Samuel, and 1 and 2 Kings. It is to that Book of Deuteronomy, and the Deuteronomistic History which it heads, that we now turn.

THE BOOK OF DEUTERONOMY

The Origins of the Book of Deuteronomy and the Deuteronomic Reform

In our discussion of the Pentateuchal traditions, we described the relationships among those traditions in terms of two dualities: (1) a duality of geography, that is, north and south; and (2) a duality of kinds of material, that is, narrative (Who are we and where did we come from?) and legislative (How shall we live if this is who we say we are?). The Yahwist represents the synthesis of the southern narrative traditions. The Elohist followed his lead in creating a parallel northern narrative. The Priestly tradition forms the southern exemplar of Israel's *legislative* traditions. It is now time to treat the northern version of Israel's legal materials, as embodied in the Book of Deuteronomy.

After the division of Solomon's kingdom in 922 B.C.E., the Elohist brought together the northern narrative traditions. At about the same time there was another group or groups in the north, who were engaged in preserving, teaching, and explaining to the people Israel's covenant with Yahweh. This group began to develop its own particular style of preaching and exhortation. They were most likely Levites, descendants of the very ones who had performed a similar role during Israel's formative years. The style is highly exhortative and is characterized by series of subordinate clauses, often quite stereotyped in expression. The focus is on encouraging and instructing the people in their obligations and duties under their covenant with Yahweh and on warning them of the consequences if they fail to obey. Note, for example, the three lengthy verses that introduce the so-called Great Commandment in Deuteronomy 6:5 ("Therefore you shall love the LORD, your God, with all your heart, and with all your soul, and with all your strength"):

> These then are the commandments, the statutes and decrees which the LORD, your God, has ordered that you be taught to observe in the land into which you are crossing for conquest, so that you and your son and your grandson may fear the LORD, your God, and keep, throughout the days of your lives, all his statutes and commandments which I enjoin on you, and thus have a long life. Hear, O Israel, and be careful to observe them, that you may grow and prosper the more, in keeping with the promise of the LORD, the God of your fathers, to give you a land flowing with milk and honey (Dt 6:1-3).

This peculiar style was probably developed and the traditions elaborated in the centers of worship in the north, especially during the periodic covenant renewal celebrations. The principal synthesis and collection of these traditions is found in the Book of Deuteronomy; thus scholars have named the group the Deuteronomists or Deuteronomic circle/school. Sometimes the group is referred to in the singular as the Deuteronomist.

Since the context for the development of much of this material was the periodic covenant renewal ceremonies, the collection and synthesis of these traditions in the Book of Deuteronomy follows the broad outline of a covenant document. There is the *historical prologue,* for example, in chapters 1-11, which recalls the events at Sinai, including the northern version of the Ten Commandments in Deuteronomy 5:6-21; the *stipulations* in the form of the Law Code itself in chapters 12-26; and the *curses and blessings* of chapters 27-28.

When the northern kingdom, Israel, was destroyed by the Assyrians in 722 B.C.E., circles or groups sympathetic to the Deuteronomic outlook in the south preserved and continued its traditions. Members of these circles may have included Levites, prophets, and others who fled south after the destruction of the northern kingdom. It is possible that King Hezekiah of Judah (715-686 B.C.E.) was influenced by these circles in his efforts at religious and social reform. However, the long reign of Manasseh ensued (686-642 B.C.E.), during which the devotion to and influence of Yahwism reached an all-time low and social and economic injustices were widespread. At this point these Deuteronomic circles went underground until more favorable conditions allowed them to continue their activity.

Following the brief reign of Manasseh's son Amon (642-640 B.C.E.), young Josiah took the throne, and Judah's fortunes appeared to brighten. First of all, Assyria's power was on the wane, threatened by the growing strength of Babylon to the south and the Medes and Persians to the east. Second, the new leadership in Judah reversed some of the policies of Manasseh's regime and began to promote Yahwism. A religious and social reform was underway, supported and urged on by Josiah as he reached his majority and began to govern on his own. With the decline of Assyrian power, Josiah extended Judean control over a good bit of what had been the northern kingdom of Israel. As part of his political program of regaining the fuller extent of the kingdom of his ancestors David and Solomon, he highlighted the religious and social reforms that were underway in a bid to attract the loyalty and support of the groups of Yahwist Israelites remaining in the north. Their numbers were probably not inconsiderable, and it could very well be that they found this notion of a revived Davidic kingdom an attractive one.

It is at this point that the Deuteronomic circles and their traditions emerged from the "underground" and entered the picture. 2 Kings 22 relates how, in the year 622 B.C.E., a program of restoration, repairs, and renovations was carried out on the Jerusalem Temple at Josiah's orders. In the course of the work, a document called "The Book of the Law" was "discovered" and brought by the high priest to the young king Josiah. Upon hearing the words of this book, Josiah "rent his garments" in sorrow and frustration when he realized how far he and his people had strayed from the Law of Moses represented in the book:

> When the king heard the contents of the book of the law, he tore his garments and issued this command to Hilkiah the priest, Ahikam, son

of Shaphan, Achbor, son of Micaiah, the scribe Shaphan, and the king's servant Asaiah: "Go, consult the LORD for me, for the people, for all Judah, about the stipulations of this book that has been found, for the anger of the LORD has been set furiously ablaze against us, because our fathers did not obey the stipulations of this book, nor fulfill our written obligations" (2 Kgs 22:11-13).

This group of officials, with Hilkiah, the high priest, at their head, followed the orders of the king to "consult the LORD . . . about the stipulations of this book." They sought out a woman prophet living in Jerusalem, Huldah, the wife of Shallum, a member of the royal court. Huldah affirmed the authenticity of the document and issued a warning: if the people of Judah and their king fail to observe the covenant stipulations found therein, "Thus says the LORD: I will bring upon this place and upon its inhabitants all the evil that is threatened in this book which the king of Judah has read" (2 Kgs 22:16).

Scholars generally agree that the book "discovered" in the Temple was the Law Code section of our present Book of Deuteronomy, at least chapters 12-26. Whether this Book of the Law had actually been lost at some point and then found during the Temple restoration work is a matter of speculation. The more likely scenario is that the circles who had preserved and carried on the Deuteronomic traditions realized that the moment was opportune for them to come forward now that the religious and social reform was well underway and had the strong support of the young king. Whatever the story behind the "discovery" of the Book of the Law in the Temple, the Deuteronomic tradition and its chief collection and synthesis of Israel's ancient covenant laws and customs in Deuteronomy 12-26 became the blueprint for Josiah's religious and social reform in Judah.

The prior decades of reflection and development in the south had introduced a number of important southern elements into the Deuteronomic tradition, for example, the centrality of Jerusalem as a place of worship and the importance given to the Ark of the Covenant. But the roots of the tradition and the bulk of its material had its origins in the north. This can be seen especially in the tradition's strong prophetic quality, in its ambivalent attitude toward the monarchy, and in the central place Moses occupies. Consequently, the use of this Book of the Law as the blueprint for religious and social reform would have been another way of attracting the loyalty and support of the Israelites living in the lands of the former northern kingdom, now brought under the control of the Judaite king as Assyrian strength declined.

The Socio-economic Elements in the Deuteronomic Reform

An overlay of a state apparatus had been introduced into Israel with the rise of the monarchy. This had resulted in a hierarchically organized and socially stratified political and socio-economic order. However, recollections and enduring elements of the more egalitarian order of the tribal confederation period remained alive at the village/clan level and were preserved and affirmed in various ways in the narrative and legal traditions. These elements and recollections continued to exercise a powerful and influential hold on Israel both at the grassroots level and in the more formal traditional circles, such as that of the Deuteronomists.

The temptation in reading the Book of Deuteronomy is to adopt the perspective of its authors uncritically and to focus almost exclusively on the religious and theological aspects of the reform, downplaying or ignoring the social and political aspects, which were intimately connected with its theological aspects. One cannot talk about the beliefs or character of the religious doctrine of the Deuteronomistic writers divorced from the way they saw those beliefs expressed in *action,* that is, in the provisions for a just and humane political, social, and economic order.

This is reflected in a number of ways in the kinds of laws we find in the Deuteronomic Code itself. It is observable, first of all, in the impassioned and repeated exhortation to faithfulness to the covenant with Yahweh. Only through fidelity to the provisions of that covenant, the great charter which served as the organizational foundation of Israel's distinctive society, would Israel continue to prosper and possess the land. It was not merely a matter of an extrinsic link between commandment and consequence. The commandments represented and distilled distinctive aspects of Israel's social, economic, and political order, at base an egalitarian order. Thus the violation of these commandments could bring about the eventual dissolution and disappearance of Israel as the unique and distinctive society that it was. The jubilee provisions for the relaxation of debts found in Deuteronomy 15 (see also Leviticus 25), for example, were aimed at preventing the accumulation of land in the hands of a small number of individuals or groups. This would result in the impoverishment and disempowerment of those who had been dispossessed. The opening verses of the chapter set forth the rationale:

> At the end of every seven-year period you shall have a relaxation of debts, which shall be observed as follows. Every creditor shall relax his claim on what he has loaned his neighbor; he must not press his neighbor, his kinsman, because a relaxation in honor of the LORD has

been proclaimed. . . . Since the LORD, your God, will bless you abundantly in the land he will give you to occupy as your heritage, there should be no one of you in need (Dt 15:1-2, 4).

Provisions for the political organization of the society are also included, for instance, strict limits on the rights and powers of the kings:

He shall not have a great number of horses. . . . Neither shall he have a great number of wives, lest his heart be estranged, nor shall he accumulate a vast amount of silver and gold. . . . He shall have a copy of this law made from the scroll that is in the custody of the levitical priests. He shall keep it with him and read it all the days of his life that he may learn to fear the LORD, his God, and to heed and fulfill all the words of this law and these statutes (Dt 17:16-19).

Finally, the custom of leaving the gleanings of field and vine for the poor—"the widow, the orphan, and the stranger"—is but one example of a number of specific measures designed to institutionalize protection for the economically vulnerable:

When you reap the harvest in your field and overlook a sheaf there, you shall not go back to get it; let it be for the alien, the orphan or the widow, that the LORD may bless your undertakings. When you knock down the fruit of your olive trees, you shall not go over the branches a second time; let what remains be for the alien, the orphan, and the widow. When you pick your grapes, you shall not go over the vineyard a second time; let what remains be for the alien, the orphan, and the widow. For remember that you were once slaves in Egypt; that is why I command you to observe this rule (Dt 24:19-22).

These examples show the intimate link Israel presumed between its relationship with Yahweh and the organization of its political, economic, and social life.

THE DEUTERONOMISTIC HISTORY (DH)

The Origins of the Deuteronomistic History

The social and religious reforms initiated under King Josiah were rudely interrupted by the premature death of the young king in a battle at Megiddo Pass with the army of Pharaoh Neco of Egypt in 609 B.C.E. The death of

Josiah put the brake on the reform movement undertaken by him and inspired and guided by those associated with the Deuteronomic circles. Consequently, the Deuteronomists turned their interests and energies to another project, the creation of the second major component of the collection we know as the Hebrew Scriptures. In the Hebrew Bible it is called the *Former Prophets.* Scholars generally refer to it today, however, as the Deuteronomistic History (DH). This document embraces the biblical books of Deuteronomy, Joshua, Judges, 1 and 2 Samuel, and 1 and 2 Kings. Even though the present arrangement in the Bible gives the impression of seven separate books, in fact we have a single work made up of seven parts (each perhaps conforming to the convenient length of one scroll).

This Deuteronomistic History picks up the story line of the Pentateuch and carries it down to the Deuteronomists' own day. In other words, it recounts the history of the people of Israel beginning with their entry into the Promised Land from the Plains of Moab across the Jordan River through the period of the tribal confederation, the rise of the monarchy under Saul, the united monarchy under David and Solomon, and the separate histories of the northern (Israel) and southern (Judah) kingdoms.

One of the primary purposes for the creation of this literary work seems to have been to provide an answer to the question that had apparently haunted Deuteronomic circles for generations: Why had the northern kingdom suffered the fate it had? Why had God allowed the Assyrians to overrun the kingdom, destroy its capital, Samaria, and carry off large numbers of its inhabitants into exile and slavery? The answer provided by the Deuteronomistic historians centered on the Mosaic covenant and traditions. They saw the lack of fidelity to that covenant by the people, and especially by the kings, as the root cause of the disaster which their land had met. Their fate would now serve as a salutary lesson for the inhabitants of Judah, and for their leaders, the Davidic kings. Only loyalty and fidelity to Israel's covenant with Yahweh would ensure their survival as a people and as a nation. If they failed in that loyalty and fidelity, their fate would be the same as that suffered by the northern kingdom—destruction and exile and an end to their existence as a people and as a nation.

Key Themes of the Deuteronomistic History

Even though these books are often referred to as the Historical Books of the Old Testament or even the Deuteronomistic History, a more accurate description of their contents is probably found in the Hebrew Bible's designation of them as the Former Prophets. Indeed, the books contain much history-like writing as well as material that can serve as a source for a history of this period in our modern sense of history.

But that is not the intent of the DH. The purpose was nothing less than to explain how God acts in the world, as revealed particularly in the life of the people of Israel. In carrying out this purpose, the DH reflects in its traditions and outlook the strong prophetic influence of its northern origins. One of the main themes of the work is prophecy and fulfillment. Fulfillment demonstrates in particular the faithfulness of God to his promises. A promise or prophecy is enunciated through a prophet and inevitably that prophetic word proves effective. God declares to David through the prophet Nathan that David must not build a "house" for God. Rather, God will build a "house," that is, a lasting dynasty for David (2 Sm 7). That prophecy is fulfilled in David's son Solomon, who takes possession of the throne and builds a "house" for God, the Jerusalem Temple (1 Kgs 5-8).

The central place occupied by the stories about the great preaching prophets, Elijah and Elisha, in the DH is another example of the important role prophecy and the theme of prophecy-fulfillment had in the minds of the Deuteronomists. For instance, the prophet Elijah predicts of Jezebel, wife of King Ahab of the northern kingdom, that "dogs shall devour Jezebel in the district of Jezreel" (1 Kgs 21:23). He also foretells the death of a northern king, Ahaziah (2 Kgs 1:1-8, 16). In both cases the word of Yahweh through the prophet proves effective. 2 Kings 9:30-37 tells of the gruesome death of Jezebel. 2 Kings 1:17 likewise notes the death of King Ahaziah, "according to the word of the LORD that Elijah had spoken."

The writers of the DH employ this prophecy-fulfillment theme as a structuring and interpretive pattern by which they attempt to make sense of and bring some order into the sequence of events over the six hundred year span of Israel's existence. This prophecy-fulfillment pattern, seen from the perspective of Israel's God, highlights Yahweh's faithfulness to his promises and constant loyalty to his covenanted people. The same pattern, seen from the perspective of the people, brings to the fore their failure in covenant loyalty and thus helps to provide an explanation for the sad train of events that led finally to the destruction of the northern kingdom. Judah, the southern kingdom, now seemed headed in the same direction. But the affirmation of Yahweh's constant fidelity to his covenant promises continued to offer a reason for hope.

The pattern that emerged from the interplay between these two poles—God's constant loyalty and Israel's consistent failure—took the form of a continual cycle, which provided the Deuteronomistic writers with an interpretive key for elucidating Israel's history and giving it purpose and explanation. Scholars have characterized that cycle as a recurring pattern involving four stages: (1) Israel's failure in covenant loyalty, its "sin"; (2) Israel's consequent punishment or suffering, such as falling into the hands of and under the power of its enemies; (3) the cry to God for deliverance; and (4) the intervention of God, ever faithful, on Israel's behalf. This pattern sets out in all its simplicity the two poles between which Israel's history oscillates. From the very beginning of Israel's story in the Land of Promise (Jgs 2) that pattern is set forth by the Deuteronomistic writers: the people served Yahweh all the days that Joshua was alive (v. 7), but after Joshua's death a "later generation arose . . . that did not know the LORD, or what he had done for Israel" (v. 10); "and the Israelites offended the LORD by serving the Baals" (v. 11); "because they had thus abandoned him and served Baal and Ashtaroth, the anger of the LORD flared up against Israel, and he delivered them over to plunderers who despoiled them" (vv. 13-14); but then God would raise up judges "to deliver them from the power of their despoilers" (v. 16); "it was thus the LORD took pity on their distressful cries of affliction" (v. 18).

Finally, the theological insightfulness and genius of the Deuteronomists is perhaps best seen in the theme of "the heart," a term that appears forty-one times in the book of Deuteronomy alone. It occurs, for example, in the passage on "the Great Commandment," quoted by Jesus in the Gospels: "Therefore, you shall love the LORD, your God, with all your *heart,* and with all your soul, and with all your strength" (Dt 6:5; see Mt 22:34-40; Mk 12:28-31; Lk 10:25-28).

With this theme of "the heart" we have, perhaps for the first time in human history, the recognition of the centrality of *motivation* in the God-human relationship. The Deuteronomists take us below the level of action and behavior to a deeper level. The external aspects of religion—words and actions—are not sufficient. Even more important is the internal: a mind and a will that are aware of and acknowledge the sovereignty of God; a *heart,* in other words, that accepts and commits itself to the loyalty and obedience that the covenant commands.

The Sources for the Deuteronomistic History

In composing their account of this six hundred year period of their people's history, the Deuteronomistic writers drew upon a number of sources. They began with the fundamental charter of Israel as a people as distilled in the Deuteronomic Code (Dt 12-26). They added a preface, which sets the historical scene on the Plains of Moab as Israel is encamped, awaiting instructions for entry into the Promised Land. The Law Code itself is presented in the context of a speech by Moses to the assembled Israelites in which he rehearses the events at Mt. Sinai (Horeb) and repeats the Covenant Law "a second time" (hence the name of the book in Greek, *deuteros nomos,* "the *second* law").

The authors also had available a number of stories and traditions handed down among the various tribes about their settlement in ancestral lands and the continuing struggles of the tribes, both individually and collectively, in the face of the constant encroachment by alien elements—Canaanite kings, Midianite raiders, Philistines. The Deuteronomistic historians used two devices in bringing together and reworking these diverse stories from various tribes and groups. The first of these devices was "periodization." In other words, they grouped the stories into two "periods." They set some of the stories in the lifetime of Joshua and presented the stories as if they had to do with the so-called *conquest* of the land (the Book of Joshua). They placed the remaining stories after the death of Joshua as having to do with Israel's *keeping* of the land (the Book of Judges). Second, the Deuteronomistic historians set these stories, originally concerned with individual clans or tribes for the most part, into an "all Israel" context, as if the whole people were involved in each of the events recounted. Close reading shows, however, that most of the episodes concerned only one or two tribes or groups, the largest single gathering being for the war against the Canaanite king of Hazor. This latter is reported to have involved only six tribes under the leadership of the woman judge and prophetess Deborah (Jgs 4-5).

For the rise of the monarchy, as rehearsed in what is now 1 and 2 Samuel, the DH had stories about Samuel and Saul, and two works concerning the life of David. One David story told of his rise to kingship (1 Sm 16-2 Sm 5). The second, the so-called Throne Succession Narrative (2 Sm 9-20; 1 Kgs 1-2), recounted how Solomon, even though not the eldest son and obvious heir of David, managed to succeed David on the throne. Further, the Deuteronomistic writers had access to administrative documents from the period of the united monarchy as well as excerpts from the chronicles of the courts of both Israelite and Judaite kings. Finally, the DH also used tales and legends about various prophets, especially the great northern figures of Elijah and Elisha.

The immense task of bringing together and imposing some measure of unity on this vast array of diverse materials was accomplished through an interpretive framework constructed around the two poles mentioned above: (1) God's faithfulness as demonstrated in the promise-fulfillment theme, and (2) Israel's failure as proved by the lack of covenant loyalty.

The authoring/editing process for the DH included careful choice and arrangement of material (including omissions) and the addition at key points of speeches and prayers by major figures. For example, Deuteronomy 1-4 represents a major speech by Moses couched in Deuteronomic language (see also Joshua in Jos 23; Samuel in 1 Sm 12; Nathan in 2 Sm 7:4-17). Likewise, David utters a lengthy prayer in 2 Sm 7:18-29 (see also Solomon in 1 Kgs. 8):

> Great are you, LORD God! There is none like you and there is no God but you, just as we have been told. What other nation on earth is there like your people Israel, which God has led, redeeming it as his people; so that you have made yourself renowned by doing this magnificent deed, and by doing awe-inspiring things as you cleared nations and their gods out of the way of your people, which you redeemed for yourself from Egypt? You have established for yourself your people Israel as yours forever, and you LORD, have become their God. And now LORD God, confirm for all time the prophecy you have made concerning your servant and his house, and do as you have promised. Your name will be forever great, when men say, "The LORD of hosts is God of Israel," and the house of your servant David stands firm before you (2 Sm 7:22-26).

These speeches and prayers by major figures were couched in the style of the Deuteronomistic writers and were filled with Deuteronomic themes and theology. Note, for example, the allusion to the prophecy-fulfillment theme (the promise of a dynasty for David) in the prayer quoted above. In addition to these speeches and prayers by major figures, the authors/editors themselves provided reflective comments (see Jgs 2:11-23; 2 Kgs 17:7-18).

This arranging and supplementing created a framework that acted as a lens through which the course of Israel's life and history were to be viewed. The framework provides the reader with a ready-made interpretive key for understanding why the northern kingdom collapsed (and later, as we shall see, why the southern kingdom collapsed as well). The principal reason given by the DH is the failure in covenant loyalty, especially by the northern kings. But the framework also includes a note of hope in its affirmation of the pole opposite to Israel's lack of loyalty. That pole was, of course, *God's* unfailing loyalty and fidelity. If the people repent and return to observing the covenant obligation, God may yet reestablish them as a people.

The Two Editions of the Deuteronomistic History

Popular opinion among scholars who have studied the DH sees it as having gone through two editions. The first edition, the actual creation and composition of this immense work, took place after the premature death of Josiah in 609 B.C.E. interrupted his reform. His death prompted the Deuteronomistic writers to turn to their writing of this great historical work. The main purpose of this work seems to have been an attempt to explain the disaster that had overtaken the northern kingdom in 722 B.C.E. Why had God allowed the Assyrian armies to overwhelm the northern kingdom, destroy its capital, Samaria, and carry off into exile and slavery large numbers of its population?

The answer seemed to lie in the people's lack of fidelity to the covenant with God, their failure to follow its stipulations as enumerated and explained in the Law of Moses. Not only had the nation as a whole failed, but especially the kings of that northern kingdom, beginning with the very first one, Jeroboam, had proven unfaithful. Had not Jeroboam turned against the Law by ignoring one of its most important provisions, that of the single sanctuary for Yahweh? Indeed, he had set up the sanctuaries at Dan and Bethel, at the northern and southern extremes of his kingdom, as rival shrines to the Temple of Solomon in Jerusalem. The Deuteronomistic historians looked upon this action of Jeroboam as a direct and fateful violation of the "single sanctuary" command of the Deuteronomic Code and as an opening for contamination of the Yahwistic cult by "pagan" (Canaanite) elements. Every northern king after Jeroboam was thus seen as tainted by Jeroboam's "original sin," and the eventual downfall of the north at the hands of Assyria was seen as inevitable.

The southern kingdom, Judah, where these Deuteronomistic writers now found themselves, seemed to be headed in the same direction. Thus, as they rehearsed the story of the people of Israel during the years following the "arrival" of the people of Israel in the Promised Land, the Deuteronomistic historians stressed the need for loyalty and fidelity to the Mosaic covenant and its traditions and laws. But the premonition of these historians proved accurate when the Babylonian armies under Nebuchadnezzar brought an end to the independent existence of Judah as a political state. This took place with the destruction of Jerusalem and its Temple in 587 B.C.E. and the beginning of the Babylonian Exile (587-539 B.C.E.).

The stage was now set for the second, or Exilic, edition of the DH. Additions were made at key points containing forewarnings of the fate of the southern kingdom and the Exile:

> I call heaven and earth this day to witness against you, that you shall all quickly perish from the land which you will occupy when you cross the Jordan. You shall not live in it for any length of time but shall be promptly wiped out. The LORD will scatter you among the nations, and there shall remain but a handful of you among the nations to which the LORD will lead you (Dt 4:26-27; see also Dt 30:1-10; 1 Kgs 8:46-53).

The stark account of the decline and fall of Judah and the destruction of Jerusalem was added in 2 Kings 23:26-25:30. The final episode in this account tells of the release from prison of King Jehoiachin and the invitation issued him by the Babylonian king, Evil-merodach, to join his court:

In the thirty-seventh year of the exile of Jehoiachin, king of Judah, on the twenty-seventh day of the twelfth month, Evil-merodach, king of Babylon, in the inaugural year of his own reign, raised up Jehoiachin, king of Judah, from prison. He spoke kindly to him and gave him a throne higher than that of the other kings who were with him in Babylon. Jehoiachin took off his prison garb and ate at the king's table as long as he lived (2 Kgs 25:27-30).

This turn for the better in the fortunes of the heir to David's throne seems to have been interpreted by the Deuteronomistic historians as a sign of hope. The date of this event, determined from Babylonian court records, was 561 B.C.E. Groups of Jews, some in Babylon and others left behind in Judah, a "faithful remnant," continued to believe and trust in Yahweh despite the catastrophes that had befallen their people. The lessons from their past of Yahweh's continued fidelity toward his people provided a basis for this hope. Thus the release of the young Judaite king, Jehoiachin, from his Babylonian prison and the favor shown him by the Babylonian king may have been interpreted by them as a sign that Yahweh was once more about to intervene in their lives and in their history. In this context renewed loyalty and obedience to the covenant law were now called for above everything else. Yahweh might once more be coming to save his people.

REVIEW QUESTIONS

1. Discuss briefly the origins of the Book of Deuteronomy, its contents, structure, and how it assumed a prominent place in the so-called Deuteronomic Reform movement under King Josiah of Judah.

2. Describe the origins and contents of the Deuteronomistic History. Why is Former Prophets probably a more accurate description of its contents than Historical Books?

3. What was the purpose of the first version of the Deuteronomistic History; that is, what question was it meant to answer and what was that answer?

4. What two principal devices did the writers of the Deuteronomistic History use to structure and rework their diverse materials?

5. How are theology and political, social, and economic practice related in the Book of Deuteronomy and in the Deuteronomistic History?

6. By what two means did the Deuteronomistic historians bring order into the diverse stories from various groups and tribes about their settlement of and struggle to hold their ancestral lands?

7. How do the Deuteronomistic historians make use of the theme of "prophecy-fulfillment"?

8. What are the four stages in the recurring cycle which the Deuteronomistic historians make use of as an interpretive key for elucidating Israel's history?

9. What is the significance of the theme of "the heart" in the book of Deuteronomy and in the Deuteronomistic History?

10. Name some of the sources on which the Deuteronomistic historians drew in writing their "history."

11. What was the context and purpose of the second edition of the Deuteronomistic History? How is it possible to assign a date to this second edition?

12

The Philistines and Saul

Suggested Bible Readings: Judges 13-16; 1 Samuel 1-15

THE ORIGINS OF THE PHILISTINES

The major external factor in the move of Israel from a socially and economically egalitarian tribal-based confederation to a hierarchically organized and socially stratified monarchy was the pressure on the tribal confederation from the Philistines. There were significant internal factors at work as well.

Who were these Philistines and where did they come from? Why did they pose such a threat to the tribal confederation? To find an answer to these questions we need to go back in history a bit to the years of the Late Bronze Age, 1500-1200 B.C.E. During this period something of a balance was maintained among the major centers of power in the Ancient Near East. There seems to have been relatively free movement and interchange of trade, commerce, and cultural contacts. A good example of the widespread trade is the diffusion of Mycenean ware, a delicate and highly prized type of pottery produced in Mycenean Greece. Numerous pieces of this type of pottery have been found at sites all over the Ancient Near East and beyond, as well as a number of locally produced but poorer quality imitations.

Egypt was enjoying its Empire Age and had reached one of the zeniths of its power and influence in Syro-Palestine. The flourishing Hittite Empire dominated most of Anatolia. The Mycenean culture in Greece and its cousin the Minoan culture in Crete enjoyed the Golden Age later celebrated in legend and song by the poets and dramatists of classical Greece. A group of Indo-Aryan warriors, the *maryannu,* had moved into northern Mesopotamia and had established control over the indigenous Hurrian peoples. The territory these Indo-Aryan warriors ruled came to be known as the kingdom of Mitanni. This kingdom was wedged among the three great power centers of the Ancient Near East—Syro-Palestine (under Egyptian control) to the southwest, Mesopotamia to the southeast, and the Hittite Empire to the west—blocking further expansion by any of the three. (See map on p. 30.) Thus it was one of the factors that helped to establish the semblance of equilibrium which characterized the international politics of this period. These Indo-Aryan *maryannu* introduced the horse into the Ancient Near East and with it, the war chariot, revolutionizing the waging of battle. They also popularized the use of the composite bow. This weapon was constructed of layers of wood, metal, and bone, greatly increasing the effective distance and force of impact.

The Late Bronze Age came to an end toward the latter years of the thirteenth and early years of the twelfth centuries B.C.E. These years were characterized by massive changes and disruptions in the way of life of the previous three or four centuries. Numerous large urban centers were abandoned and/or destroyed; population declined; international trade was disrupted or brought to a virtual standstill; and movements and migrations of peoples, some appearing on the historical scene for the first time, took place. Whether these new groups had in fact entered the Ancient Near East for the first time or had been there all along is difficult if not impossible to tell. It is during this period, of course, that Israel emerged onto the stage of history. Because neither of the major river-based cultures, Egypt or Mesopotamia, was able to exert strong control over Syro-Palestine, David and then Solomon were able to create a small empire for a short eighty-year period.

A number of factors may have been responsible for the eclipse of the urban-based socio-economic and political order of the Late Bronze Age. Previous historical treatments of this era placed responsibility for the apparent turmoil on invasions of the Ancient Near East by peoples from outside the region. However, now historians are beginning to note a whole complex of contributing factors.

The sudden spread of some plague-like disease or complex of diseases may have been a factor. Hints of this may be detected in the seemingly excessive concern with primitive hygienic problems among the Moses group: reluctance to eat certain foods (cf. Lv 11; Dt 14:3-21); special care in the cleaning of cooking and eating utensils (Dt 14:21b); strict rules about contact with bodies of the deceased; and avoidance of certain population groups (see the story of Phineas and the Midianite woman in Numbers 25). The origin of the practice of the *herem*, "the ban," which is so central in the stories in Joshua and Judges may be linked to this serious concern about contagion (e.g. Dt 7; Jos 6:21-27; 7).

Another factor may have been widespread crop failures and famine caused by severe changes in the weather patterns in areas outside the Eastern Mediterranean Basin. Movement of peoples from those areas into the Eastern Mediterranean Basin would have dislodged groups already settled there. The migrations may have overburdened the trading systems and networks built up during the Late Bronze Age. The collapse of these systems and networks, in turn, would have provoked widespread economic chaos and decline.

Finally, social unrest and rebellion among the oppressed lower classes and subject peoples, such as those in Canaan resulting in the emergence of Israel, may have been a factor.

Whatever the reasons, two things are clear: the effects on the major urban centers and imperial powers, and the appearance on the scene of various migrating groups along the coastline of the Eastern Mediterranean referred to collectively in the written records as the Sea Peoples. The capital of the Hittites, Hattusas, in central Anatolia (Turkey) was destroyed and its empire all but disappeared during the latter decades of the thirteenth century B.C.E.; it was one of the victims of a Sea Peoples' coalition. Also destroyed at the hands of the latter was the major north Canaanite trade and cultural center, the city of Ugarit on the Syrian coast. This city, which was the hub of a vast commercial network in the Eastern Mediterranean, was sacked and burned in 1182 B.C.E. In Greece the Mycenean civilization came to an end with the burning of the large palace structures at Pylos, Tiryns, and Sparta, and the destruction of the citadel at Mycenae itself. The stories preserved in the *Iliad* and *Odyssey* of wars, of destructions of major urban centers such as Troy, and of the wanderings of individuals like Odysseus

Battle of the Sea People against Egypt about 1150 B.C.E. Defeated by the Egyptians, many settled in southern Palestine and became known as Philistines.

find their origin in the events of this period. The Sea Peoples seem to have come from places in and around Greece. Perhaps displaced by new populations moving into their former homeland or forced to migrate by economic or population pressures, they took to the sea in ships, invading, attacking, and generally taking advantage of and adding to the disruptions already underway.

Groups of Sea Peoples mounted a series of invasions of Egypt, one during the reign of the Pharaoh Merneptah (1224-11 B.C.E.) and another during the time of Ramses III (1183-52 B.C.E.). The Egyptians were ultimately successful in driving them off, but the effort significantly weakened Egypt and led to a further decline in its ability to control its vassal states in Canaan.

One of the groups that took part in the Sea Peoples' invasions of Egypt was called, in the Egyptian historical documents, the *pi-las-tu*. Scholars have identified this group with the biblical Philistines. Their cultural remains indicate some association with Crete. Either they had originated in Crete or at least had spent some time there before arriving on the borders of Egypt. After initial conflicts with the Philistines, the Egyptians appear to have reached a kind of accommodation with them. They established them as semi-autonomous vassals over the southern coastal plain of Canaan, including what is today known as the Gaza Strip. It represents something of an extension of Egypt north-eastward along the coastline. Both by geography and by its character as a communications and trade linkage between Egypt and Asia this strip of land formed a "toehold" for Egypt in Palestine and, ultimately, on the Asian mainland. Thus, by around 1150 B.C.E. the group of Sea Peoples known as the Philistines was established under the patronage of Egypt as the semi-autonomous rulers of the southern coastal plain in Canaan. They formed the ruling class in the five major fortified urban centers which controlled this plain: Gaza, Gath, Ashkelon, Ashdod, and Ekron. Their interlocking leadership and their access to the newly-developing iron technology (note the iron-tipped spear of the Philistine hero Goliath in 1 Samuel 17:7) gave their confederacy a unity and potential superiority unparalleled among the other groups of Canaanite city-states. It also made them an obvious threat to the growing Israelite tribal confederation of the central hill country.

The Philistines seemed content at first to secure and strengthen their position on the southern coastal plain and to profit from their control of the traffic on the Way of the Sea, the major international trade route that ran directly through their territory. During the period between 1150 and 1050 B.C.E. an uneasy truce prevailed between the Philistines and Israelites, as the Samson stories in the Book of Judges give witness (Jgs 13-16). There appears to have been a relatively fluid border and even a certain free interchange between the Philistines and the groups who made up the tribal confederation.

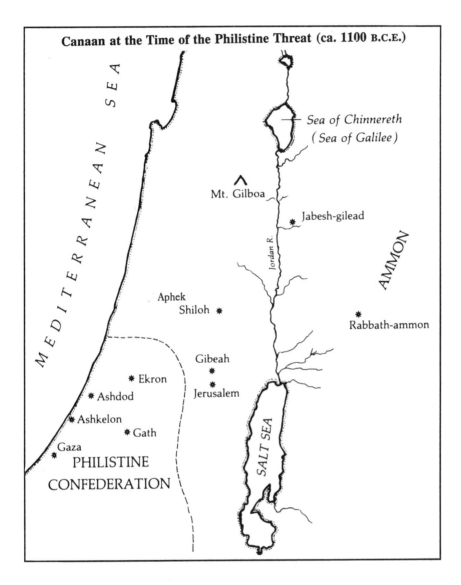

Canaan at the Time of the Philistine Threat (ca. 1100 B.C.E.)

By the time of Saul, however, the imperial ambitions of the Philistines were on the rise, and the expanding and vigorous Israelite confederation in the hill country posed a potential threat to Philistine hegemony over the peoples of the southern coastal plain. A major clash occurred in the battle of Aphek (near modern Tel-Aviv; see 1 Sm 4) in 1050 B.C.E., and the Philistines scored a decisive victory. The Israelites had brought the Ark of the Covenant from the pilgrimage center at Shiloh, hoping that its presence would ensure success. But along with the Israelite defeat came the capture of the Ark and the subsequent destruction of the shrine at Shiloh, which was never rebuilt. According to the events recounted in 1 Samuel 5-7, the Israelites eventually regained possession of the Ark. But the fact that it lay neglected at Kiriath-Jearim (1 Sm 7:1-2) until David brought it up to Jerusalem a generation later (2 Sm 6), along with the failure to rebuild the pilgrimage center at Shiloh, were signals that major changes were unfolding in the life of the tribal confederation. New forms of cooperation, a new political and social strategy, were essential if Israel was to survive and keep alive its vision of a people's life in common.

Just as Pharaoh and his imperial apparatus had been the major source of the oppression and slavery in the paradigmatic story of liberation which served to give identity and unity to the tribal confederation, so now that same confederation faced a new life-threatening challenge from these agents of Egypt's power in Canaan, the Philistines. After their victory at Aphek, the Philistines were obviously intent on extending their control beyond the southern coastal plain into the hill country, and especially along the lucrative trade routes straddled by the various components of the Israelite league. Pressure was mounting within the league for a more unified and effective military response to the Philistine threat. This external pressure combined with internal pressures hinted at in the opening chapters of the First Book of Samuel led to the rise of the monarchy in Israel.

THE PHILISTINES AND THE EXTERNAL THREAT TO EARLY ISRAEL

The rise of the monarchy in Israel is still only partially understood. Yet recent study, especially with the help of the social sciences, has greatly illumined the period and the process. One difficulty comes from the biblical sources themselves. Although they preserve pre-monarchic elements and even bits of anti-monarchic polemic, for the most part they were written from a later point of view. They were put together after the monarchy was an established fact and accepted as an inevitable development, indeed one willed and blessed by God.

Still, many questions remain unresolved. How did a society that created a culture and a socio-economic and political system based on values opposed to a hierarchical and stratified society such as a monarchical state allow itself to evolve so rapidly into that very phenomenon? What were the internal and external dynamics that led to such a profound change?

The obvious major external factor was the Philistine threat. The dual identification of the Philistines both with the Canaanite city-state system and with the Egyptian pharaoh clearly identified them to the Israelites as the embodiment of imperial ambitions and values directly contradictory to and threatening to the Israelite way of life. It would have been a relatively easy task to adapt much of the ideological power of the confederation's religious and social self-expression and use it to rally large segments of the confederation to oppose its legendary enemy, the Egyptian pharaoh, in his latest incarnation as the Philistine princes.

It is not clear what prompted the Philistine coalition to move suddenly against the tribal confederacy. One factor may have been increasing friction or competition for land between the two peoples. The pressures of population growth had prompted Israelite expansion into the western slopes of the hill country. This region was the most rugged and least fertile in the highlands and thus the last to be settled. Here the Israelite groups found themselves beginning to encroach more directly on Philistine-controlled territory.

In addition, the Israelites had succeeded in making this sparsely inhabited region of the central highlands productive by using innovative agricultural techniques and by entering into the cooperative arrangements. The Philistines seemed intent on incorporating this relatively thriving territory into their empire and expropriating its surplus production, which for the moment was under the direct control and use of the producers themselves. This is especially true if the Philistines were experiencing declining production in the coastal plains already under their control, or if they needed additional food and revenue sources to support their commercial and territorial expansion. Imposing their control, for the Philistines, would have meant extending their tax and forced-labor gathering apparatus into this region which, up until now, had not been exploited.

The Philistines moved against the tribal confederation; their intent was obvious—bring these former peasants and herdsmen with their unexploited surplus production under their control. One of the first major military confrontations took place at Aphek around the year 1050 B.C.E., an event narrated in the opening chapters of the First Book of Samuel (1 Sm 4). The battle proved to be a disastrous defeat for Israel, which suffered a large number of casualties (1 Sm 4:2, 10), including two key but corrupt religious leaders, Hophni and Phinehas, sons of Eli, the priest of the Shiloh shrine. As disastrous were the capture of the Ark of the Covenant by the Philistines and their destruction of the pilgrimage center at Shiloh. The loosely organized militia units of the tribal confederation, so dependent on *ad hoc* leadership and on the good will and cooperation of the participating tribes and clans, were clearly no match for the unified and disciplined Philistine forces. Hitherto able to take advantage of the hill country terrain to frustrate the Canaanite armies, which were dependent on chariots and cavalry, the Israelite militia was now the underdog in the face of the trained Philistine infantry, which was able to adapt successfully to Israel's home ground. With Israelite resistance initially broken at Aphek, the Philistines moved to follow up their victory and to establish control over Israelite territory.

All that the Israelites had struggled for generations to develop, their unique social-economic-political system, undergirded and legitimated by a religious ideology just as unique, was in danger of disappearing. This would mean a return to the former days of slavery or near slavery on which their ancestors had turned their backs. The only way open seemed to be through some drastic changes and realignment in their organizational structures. But that would require a delicate balance between the need for concerted and unified action against the Philistine aggressor, who would impose a hierarchical and socially stratified governing apparatus from without, and the danger that the centralization needed for such unity and action would evolve into a similar hierarchy and social stratification from within.

SAUL AND THE INITIAL ATTEMPT TO MEET THE PHILISTINE CRISIS

The stories associated with the rise of Saul as king in 1 Samuel 8-12 are ambiguous as to the desirability of the institution of monarchy. Some passages do not seem favorable to the appointment of a king (1 Sm 8; 10:17-27; 12; 15). Such passages probably reflect an awareness of both the advantages and dangers involved in moves toward a greater degree of centralization in face of the Philistine threat.

Recent studies in comparative anthropology have demonstrated that societies, and ancient societies in particular, usually pass through a somewhat predictable series of steps as the various factors such as population growth, external threat, and economic prosperity ensue. The first of these is the period of segmentation, which includes societies still at the level of the band (smaller groups dependent on hunting and gathering) and tribal (village-based communities dependent on agriculture and herding) organization. This segmentation stage is marked by its decidedly egalitarian character and local control of the means and products of labor.

A second stage involves the emergence of a chieftain; it is marked by the first steps in centralization and the resulting social ranking. The chief emerges and bases his authority on his skill in warfare, in winning and solidifying allegiance, and in effecting a balance in the distribution of the society's resources. Besides a certain presumption and hope that the chief will be able to pass his leadership gifts to his sons, there is no fixed pattern for transfer of authority. Thus the death of the chief usually results in a protracted struggle for power among potential successors both within and outside the chief's family.

The final stage is reached when the society clearly stratifies into "rulers" and "ruled." The rulers assume the decision-making power for the entire society and are able to impose those decisions by force on the whole of the society.

The present form of the Saul stories in the first part of 1 Samuel speaks of Saul having been chosen and anointed as "king" (*melek* in Hebrew) over Israel (1 Sm 10:24; 11:15; 13:1). However, another word intrudes in the texts that suggests that the tribal confederation had not yet evolved to the point of exhibiting the stratification and centralized monopoly of force that characterizes an archaic civilization or state organization such as a monarchy. These texts speak of Saul (and, initially of David as well, see 1 Samuel 25:30) as a *nagîd*, usually translated "prince," "leader," "commander":

The day before Saul's arrival, the LORD had given Samuel the revelation: "At this time tomorrow I will send you a man from the land of Benjamin whom you are to anoint as commander (*nagîd*) of my people Israel. He shall save my people from the clutches of the Philistines" (1 Sm 9:15-16; see also 10:1).

This probably points to the fact that Saul (and initially David) was not considered a king in the full sense of the word, but rather functioned as a chieftain, a leader whose duties concerned mainly military matters. In fact, Saul's emergence came largely in response to a military crisis and the need to mount a more unified and effective military effort against the Philistine encroachment. Saul's leadership did not involve the building of a capital and palace. Gibeah, Saul's family home, served as his military headquarters. No bureaucratic apparatus was put in place for the collecting of taxes or the conscripting of manpower for military duty or work projects. Instead, Saul headed a detachment of experienced warriors from his own Benjaminite clan around which were gathered the various militia levies from the other tribes. His emergence seems to have been based on a number of factors including his own impressive appearance and military skill: "There was a stalwart man from Benjamin named Kish. . . . He had a son named Saul, who was a handsome young man. There was no other Israelite handsomer than Saul; he stood head and shoulders above the people" (1 Sm 9:1-2). Also, Saul came from a prosperous and influential family (1 Sm 9:1) which had the resources to arm and supply him and probably some of his close associates, for example, the detachment of Benjaminite warriors he led. This gave him a certain autonomy in action and decision-making and provided him with a basis for his emergence as a leading figure.

Saul was initially successful in rallying the tribes and in mounting a campaign to drive the Philistines from the hill country. He was able to thwart incursions from other sources as well—Edomites, Moabites, Amalekites, and Arameans (1 Sm 14:47-48). However, his "chieftainship" suffered handicaps right from the beginning. For one thing, Israel was still at a technological disadvantage because the Philistines were able to maintain a control on metal weapons (bronze, and especially iron):

> Not a single smith was to be found in the whole land of Israel, for the Philistines had said, "otherwise the Hebrews will make swords and spears." All Israel, therefore, had to go down to the Philistines to sharpen their plow shares, mattocks, axes, and sickles . . . . And so on the day of battle neither sword nor spear could be found in the possession of any of the soldiers with Saul or Jonathan. Only Saul and his son Jonathan had them (1 Sm 13:19-22).

In addition, Saul exhibited a streak of depression and jealousy that significantly hampered his leadership (1 Sm 16:14-23; 18:8-9). There is some confusion about how long he actually exercised his leadership and thus how long the "breathing spell" from Philistine pressure lasted (see 1 Samuel 13:1, which is variously read as two, twelve, or twenty-two years). Finally, in a desperate attempt, Saul sought to halt a renewed bid by the Philistines to seize control of the Jezreel valley and the main east-west caravan route, the Way of the Sea. But Saul's army suffered a terrible defeat on the slopes of Mount Gilboa. Saul died in the encounter—or committed suicide rather than face probable torture, humiliation, and execution—along with three of his sons, including his favorite and heir apparent, Jonathan (1 Sm 31).

REVIEW QUESTIONS

1. Describe the historical situation that enabled David and then Solomon to create a small empire.

2. Name some of the factors that may have been responsible for the collapse of the urban-based socio-economic and political order of the Late Bronze Age (1500-1200 B.C.E.) in the Ancient Near East.

3. Who were the Sea Peoples? What is the relationship of the Philistines of the Bible to these groups?

4. What may have prompted the Philistine coalition to move suddenly against the tribal confederation?

5. Explain the significance of the victory of the Philistines over Israel in the battle at Aphek around 1050 B.C.E.

6. Why did the Philistines pose a threat to the existence of the Israelite tribal confederation?

7. What is the significance of the Hebrew word *nagîd,* "chieftain," being used of Saul in a number of passages?

8. Name two factors that led to the fall of Saul.

13

From Chieftain to King

Suggested Bible Readings: 1 Samuel 16-19, 25, 28-31; 2 Samuel 1-2, 5-7, 9-12, 15-19; 1 Kings 1-3, 5, 8:1-9:9, 10-12

INTERNAL FACTORS IN THE RISE OF THE MONARCHY

After David became king and alleviated the external pressure by subduing the Philistines and confining them to the southern coastal plain, he continued to build on the momentum toward centralization. The result was a full-blown kingship, either by the end of his reign or at least under his successor Solomon. There must have been factors within Israel itself which allowed or even abetted the move toward statehood that went hand in hand with the external pressure of the Philistine threat.

The earlier description of the organization of society under the tribal confederation represents an "ideal type." In other words, it describes the ideal or goal toward which the various efforts, mechanisms, and institutions of the tribal confederacy moved. How far Israelite society had actually moved toward this ideal type and successfully embodied it is open to question. There were undoubtedly anomalies, imbalances, failures, and weak points in the actual realization of these goals. For one thing, the ideal type presupposes that all the members of the society understand, take seriously, and are committed to the covenant or fundamental organizational charter to which they have pledged themselves. Also, it presupposes that the various clans and tribes have approximately equal resources and proportionate amounts of fertile land at their disposal. Finally, it presumes that all covenant partners will abide by the expectations and obligations of mutual aid and support in times of difficulty caused by crop failure, drought, population depletion due to disease, or loss from military raids and destruction. In fact, the biblical record suggests that there were problems in all of these areas.

For one thing, the various regions of the central hill country were not all equally fertile and productive. Some clans and tribes thus enjoyed advantages over others right from the start in having more economic autonomy and being less dependent on the cooperation of other clans or tribes for the smooth functioning of the mutual aid system. Some clans and tribes prospered and became more influential and powerful than others. The tribes of Ephraim and Benjamin in the north and the later emergence of Judah in the south are clear evidence of this. The importance of Benjamin from the earliest days of the confederation is witnessed to by the importance of one of the earliest leaders and organizers of the confederation, Joshua. Samuel, another important figure, is from the tribe of Ephraim, and the fact that his father, Elkanah, was able to support two wives (1 Sm 1:2) indicates that he must have been fairly well to do. Another Benjaminite, Saul, who is said to have come from a "wealthy" Benjaminite family (1 Sm 9:1), emerged as the first chieftain in the initial steps toward monarchy.

There were also failures in the system of mutual aid. For example, when David fled from Saul's jealousy, he was able to gather around himself four hundred men who had experienced economic difficulties and were "embittered" because they were victims of the failures of the system: "David left Gath and escaped to the cave of Adullam. . . . He was joined by all those who were in difficulties or in debt, or who were embittered, and he became their leader" (1 Sm 22:12). The attitude of the "harsh and ungenerous" Nabal, a wealthy sheepherder, in disdainfully refusing help to David and his followers may have been typical of certain Israelites who felt comfortable and secure enough to ignore the covenant requirements of mutual aid:

> But Nabal answered the servants of David: "Who is David? Who is the son of Jesse? Nowadays there are many servants who run away from their masters. Must I take my bread, my wine, my meat that I have slaughtered for my own shearers, and give them to men who come from I know not where?" (1 Sm 25:10-11).

Recent excavations by Israeli archeologist Israel Finkelstein provide more information. His work documents a shift of population toward the end of the premonarchic period from the eastern side of the central highlands to the more rugged and less fertile western slopes. This indicates a growth of population of the Israelite tribes and the need to bring more land under cultivation. The challenges of settling these less hospitable areas in the highlands demanded greater collaboration among larger groups, sometimes transcending family and clan boundaries. Wider networks of trade began developing.

Conditions were thus in place for a move to greater centralization and the possibility of social and economic stratification typical of a chiefdom or monarchy.

THE RISE OF DAVID

With the death of Saul, the chief southern tribe of Judah chose David as its *nagîd* or "prince/commander/chieftain" (2 Sm 2:4). The northern tribes experimented with successors to Saul from among Saul's own family. In the ensuing seven-year struggle for leadership over the full confederacy, David's family gradually won the upper hand. With the Philistine pressure still bearing down, the elders representing the northern tribes came to David at his capital in Hebron and invited him to assume the "chieftainship" (*nagîd*) of the northern tribes as well:

> When all the elders of Israel came to David in Hebron, King David made an agreement with them there before the LORD, and they anointed him king of Israel. David was thirty years old when he became king, and he reigned for forty years (2 Sm 5:3-4).

One of David's first moves as chieftain over all Israel was to attack and capture the Jebusite citadel of Jerusalem (see 2 Sm 5:6-9). Although centered in the heart of the hill country, it had remained a part of the Canaanite city-state system. With its position on the border between the northern and southern tribal territories, it offered David a neutral ground from which to rule the two entities, thus undercutting the jealousies or suspicions that would have arisen if he had kept his capital at Hebron in the south or moved it to one of the major northern centers.

With a broadened base of support from a now united tribal confederation, David moved against the Philistines and in a series of decisive battles quickly broke their power. He assumed suzerainty over them and confined them to the territory around their five home cities in the southern coastal plain.

FACTORS THAT FACILITATED CENTRALIZATION
AND MONARCHY

David had learned from some of Saul's mistakes. He undercut potential jealousies between north and south by moving his headquarters to the centrally located Jerusalem. Saul had apparently been too eager to usurp religious elements of the tribal league, such as dictating policy in cultic/sacrificial matters (1 Sm 13:8-15). Consequently he had alienated Samuel and lost his support. David was careful to maintain and strengthen the continuity between the new political structure he was in the process of creating and the religious traditions of the tribal confederation. The Ark of the Covenant, for example, the ancient cultic symbol of the tribal confederation (see 1 Sm 3:3), had lain neglected following the Philistine destruction of its shrine at Shiloh. David brought the Ark to Jerusalem with much fanfare and celebration:

> David went to bring the ark of God from the house of Obed-edom into the City of David amid festivities. As soon as the bearers of the ark of the LORD had advanced six steps, he sacrificed an ox and a fatling. Then David, girt with a linen apron, came dancing before the LORD with abandon, as he and all the Israelites were bringing up the ark of the LORD with shouts of joy and to the sound of the horn (2 Sm 6:12-15).

David installed the Ark in what was apparently the former Canaanite high place, now transformed into a Yahwist shrine under David's own protection and patronage (see 2 Sm 24:16-25). Zadok, the high priest of the Jerusalem Canaanite cult, was now appointed priest of Yahweh in partnership with Abiathar, the representative of the tribal cultic traditions (2 Sm 8:17). David thus attempted to balance the two social and cultural elements that coexisted under his rule, Israelite and Canaanite, and somehow blend or at least balance the two.

Although at first glance the duality which David faced was that of north/south or Israelite/Judaite, in fact it was more decisively this new duality of Israelite/Canaanite. After his defeat of the Philistines we hear no more about wars or battles within the boundaries of David's kingdom itself. Rather, David turned his energies and ambitions to foreign wars, mainly across the Jordan, against Ammon, Moab, Edom, and Damascus (the Arameans). No further mention is made of fighting in Canaan, this suggests that the remaining Canaanite city-states, who had previously been vassals of the Philistines, simply transferred their allegiance to David once he had broken the Philistine power. Besides being *nagîd* over the Israelite tribal confederation, David was now also suzerain over a sizable Canaanite population as well. The territory he controlled thus embraced two contrasting socio-economic, political, and religious systems, Canaanite and Israelite.

Yahwism was installed as the official religion of the new political entity, but the way was now open for two quite distinct developments in the understanding of Yahwism, two quite distinctive theologies or at least theological tendencies. The original village- and tribal-based Yahwism continued

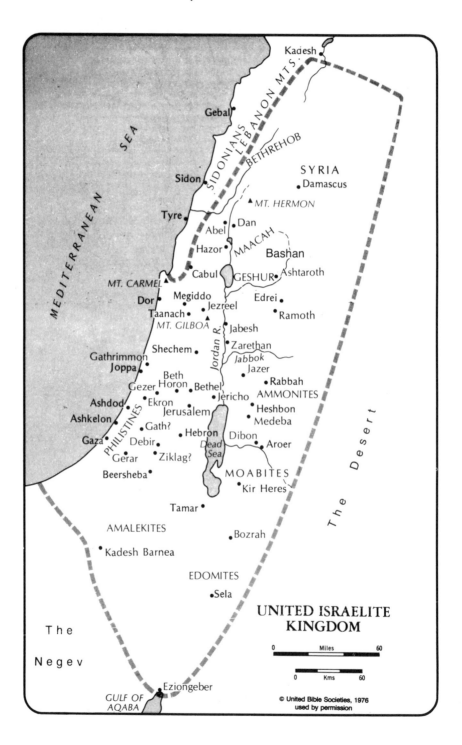

Kadesh

Gebal

SIDONIANS
LEBANON MTS.
BETHREHOB

SEA

Sidon

SYRIA
● Damascus

▲ MT. HERMON

Tyre ●

Abel

● Dan

MEDITERRANEAN

Hazor ●

MAACAH

Bashan

Cabul ●

GESHUR ● Ashtaroth

MT. CARMEL ▲

Dor ●

Megiddo ●

Edrei ●

Taanach ●

Jezreel

Ramoth

MT. GILBOA ▲

Jabesh

Jordan R.

Shechem ●

Zarethan
Jabbok

Gathrimmon

Jazer

Joppa

Beth
Horon

Gezer ●

Bethel ●

● Rabbah

Jericho ●

AMMONITES

Ashdod

Ekron ●

Heshbon ●

Jerusalem

Medeba ●

Ashkelon

PHILISTINES

Gath? ●

Hebron ●

Dibon ●

Gaza ●

Debir ●

Dead
Sea

Aroer ●

Gerar ●

Ziklag? ●

The   Desert

Beersheba ●

MOABITES

● Kir Heres

Tamar ●

The   Desert

AMALEKITES

● Bozrah

● Kadesh Barnea

EDOMITES

● Sela

UNITED ISRAELITE
KINGDOM

The

0   Miles   60

N e g e v

0   Kms   60

Eziongeber

GULF OF
AQABA

© United Bible Societies, 1976
used by permission

to be closely linked with a particular vision of human community and embodied its own socio-economic and political arrangements. However, a new current of Yahwism took into account and was linked to the new political, social, and economic realities that the territorial state founded under David implied. Both currents had potential to and did in fact expand and enrich the development of Yahwism. Both, however, also had their limitations. David's preservation of and respect for the Yahwist faith ensured his continued support among the confederacy. On the other hand, his association of the Yahwist tradition in a new way with the official Canaanite religious system—the state shrine, cult, and high priesthood in Jerusalem— was a way of seeking support as well from the new specifically Canaanite elements under his control.

KINGSHIP AND ZION

The association of the older tribal league religion, Yahwism, with the new political, social, and economic arrangements established by David, had a potential both to enrich and deepen the Yahwist faith as well as to distort and manipulate it. The positive side, the enrichment of it, drew from two sources. One of these was the Ancient Near Eastern concept of kingship and the special relationship between king and deity. The second source was the so-called Zion tradition, the complex of Canaanite mythological and cosmological language and imagery inherited from the religious traditions of pre-Davidic Jerusalem. Elements from both of these sources are seen especially in the poetry of the Psalms, for example, Psalms 89 and 132, and in the prophets, particularly Isaiah.

In the Ancient Near Eastern concept of kingship we can trace, especially in the prophets and the Psalms, the language which speaks about the special relationship between Yahweh and the king:

> I will proclaim the decree of the LORD:
>   The LORD said to me, "You are my son;
>   this day have I begotten you.
> Ask of me and I will give you
>   the nations for an inheritance
>   and the ends of the earth for your possession."
>   (Ps 2:7-8)

The king is seen as an intermediary between Yahweh and the people, one who carries out Yahweh's will for justice and especially for the protection of the poor and vulnerable members of the society. The king's administration of justice and righteousness within the kingdom must mirror the righteousness and justice evident in Yahweh's rule over the cosmos.

> O God, with your judgment endow the king,
>   and with your justice, the king's son;
> He shall govern your people with justice
>   and your afflicted ones with judgment.
> The mountains shall yield peace for the people,
>   and the hills justice.
> He shall defend the afflicted among the people,
>   save the children of the poor,
>   and crush the oppressor (Ps 72:1-4).

Language and imagery such as this could serve as the basis for a critique of a king's abuse of power to exploit and oppress the weak and vulnerable. But it could also serve as the basis for an optimistic assessment of kingship. Deuteronomistic historians later employed this image of the ideal just king to express their confidence and hope in the possibilities of a continued monarchy under a descendant of David. This language eventually developed into the language of messianism, associated with the Davidic dynasty, which plays such a central role in some of the New Testament traditions.

Pre-Davidic Jerusalem seems to have developed a whole complex of religious traditions associating the city and Mt. Zion on which it was built with the "cosmic mountain" and other similar motifs in Canaanite and Near Eastern myths. The tradition of the city's invulnerability, its role as a source of fertility and prosperity, and its destiny to hold a unique place among the cities and peoples of the earth were blended into the traditions of the tribal league. These themes helped provide a richer and more universal mode of religious language and expression for the Yahwist faith.

> Great is the LORD and wholly to be praised
>   in the city of our God.
> His holy mountain, fairest of heights,
>   is the joy of all the earth;
> Mount Zion, "the recesses of the North,"
>   is the city of the great King.
> God is with her castles;
>   renowned is he as a stronghold. . . .
> As we have heard, so have we seen
>   in the city of the LORD of hosts.

In the city of our God;
God makes it firm forever (Ps 48:2-4, 9-10).

Isaiah 2:1-5, 26:6-8, 60:1-22, and Psalm 46 are further examples of the Yahwistic adaptation and development of these Canaanite motifs. Ben Ollenberger argues for a connection between this Zion imagery and Yahweh's kingship over creation. It was through his conquest of chaos that Yahweh established his kingship and fashioned a world order that is good (see Genesis 1) and just (Psalm 99). He has made Zion, his seat and stronghold, into a refuge and place of protection for the poor and oppressed. The popular Christian hymn based on Psalm 46, "A Mighty Fortress Is Our God," echos this same theme. The role of the Davidic king, as Yahweh's representative, was to maintain that world order of God's good and just creation, and thus to shelter the weak and persecuted in Yahweh's sacred city. Seen from this perspective, the royal theology was supposed to act as a brake against monarchical abuse of power.

As with any religious tradition, there is a double edge to its expressive potential. On the one hand, the Second Isaiah (see chap. 20) took up the motif of God's unconditional promise of loyalty and faithfulness to the dynasty of David and to the city of Jerusalem. In his preaching, these promises provided a powerful basis for hope among the suffering and bewildered group of Jewish exiles in Babylon (see Isa 49:14-18, 52:1-9). On the other hand, this same theme of Zion's (Jerusalem's) invulnerability became a stumbling block to the inhabitants and rulers of Jerusalem when they failed to heed the warning of Jeremiah about the impending doom (see Jer 7).

SOLOMON: THE TRIUMPH OF THE COUNTER-REVOLUTION

The developments that had been set in motion by the external threat of Philistine domination and the internal factors favoring centralization picked up momentum during the latter years of David's reign and culminated in a full hierarchic and socially stratified state under the Solomonic monarchy. By the end of David's reign the line had been crossed between a community in which an egalitarian ideal dominated, and a full-blown state in which a ruling elite imposed its will on the majority. David's astute balancing act had allowed the effects of the older tribal organization to continue. But David had also set in place a new organizational structure that could, and eventually under Solomon did, override the older order. David did not need lavish sums of money for building projects since those he carried out were relatively modest. What revenues he did need came not from taxes on the

A reconstruction of Jerusalem (1st century C.E.). The Temple is in the upper right corner.

surplus production of his citizens but from the incomes of the estates in the coastal plain and valleys he had acquired after his defeat of the Philistines. David also had access to tribute revenues from the newly conquered foreign states such as Edom, Moab, Ammon, and Damascus. All that changed under Solomon. With the death of David, Solomon moved swiftly and ruthlessly to consolidate his power and establish a firm grip on the apparatus of government. He ordered the assassination of at least three of his principal opponents in the struggle for the throne: his brother Adonijah (1 Kgs 2:19-25); David's military commander Joab (1 Kgs 2:28-34); and Shimei, the man who had cursed David as David fled from Absalom (1 Kgs 2:36-46; see 2 Sm 16:5-13). Solomon also banished the high priest Abiathar (1 Kgs 2:26-27). These steps seem to have given Solomon enough security and confidence to pursue the full development of a typical Ancient Near Eastern monarchical state.

Since no major power during this period (1200-750 B.C.E.) was strong enough to extend its control over a significant portion of the Ancient Near East, the various peoples inhabiting the Syro-Palestinian corridor had something of a "breathing space" before the rise of Assyria in the eighth century B.C.E. It was this "breathing space" that allowed the Israelite tribal league to develop and subsequently enabled David and then Solomon to establish modest empires.

At various moments during his reign Solomon moved to secure adequate sources of income for his various endeavors. Early in his reign he took advantage of his country's strategic position along the major international trade routes to collect tolls from the caravans plying those routes. For example, he developed a lucrative trade involving Egyptian chariots and Anatolian horses:

Solomon's horses were imported from Cilicia, where the king's agents purchased them. A chariot imported from Egypt cost six hundred shekels, a horse one hundred and fifty shekels; they were exported at these rates to all the Hittite and Aramean kings (1 Kgs 10:28-29).

To further supplement revenues and carry out his extensive building projects, he enforced a corvée on his subjects equivalent to two months of service every year:

King Solomon conscripted thirty thousand workmen from all Israel. He sent them to the Lebanon each month in relays of ten thousand, so that they spent one month in the Lebanon and two months at home (1 Kgs 5:27-28).

Finally, both to undercut the influence of the older tribal organization and to centralize further the tax-gathering apparatus, he replaced the tribal administrative districts set up by David with a more efficient redistricting plan (1 Kgs 4:7-19).

With the new wealth available from these various sources, plus the corvée gangs, Solomon began an ambitious building program to enhance and beautify his capital. With the help of Phoenician architects and artisans he constructed the famous Temple and, for himself, a luxurious palace. This enhancement of his capital city formed part and parcel of the consolidation of monarchic power; it represented a concrete visual statement of the shape and strength of the new socio-economic, political, and religious order. What had started out as a loose federation of extended family clusters pledged to mutual aid and defense and grouped into larger units called tribes had now evolved into a hierarchic, socially stratified, and centralized territorial state ruled by an hereditary monarchy. With the new lavish Temple structure rising in the heart of the capital and adjacent to the palace, the message was that this new order had been willed by and enjoyed the blessing of the deity.

To consolidate the "monopoly of force" available to him through the state apparatus, Solomon created and maintained large contingents of chariots. He fortified strategic cities throughout the kingdom and on the borders, and he stationed units of the chariot force in each (1 Kgs 9:15-22). This military build-up had a twofold purpose: to strengthen his hold internally on power, for example, over the potentially troublesome northern tribes; and to protect his lucrative foreign trade.

Solomon's house, however, had been built on sand. Despite the initial success and influx of wealth, his policies and projects carried the seeds of eventual failure. The wealth and prosperity were enjoyed only by the privileged few. The expansion, both commercial and military, had spread available resources too thin. When Edom and Damascus revolted, Solomon was unable to stop them. He thus lost control of a significant part of the trading network and the crucial revenue that had been accruing from that source (1 Kgs 11:14-25). Weaknesses developed internally as well, especially from the loss of support and alienation of a large portion of the population. The increased prosperity had not affected the ordinary citizens; instead, it had been gained at their expense. The increased burden of taxes plus the annual two-month turn at forced labor had made life harder. Added to this was the resentment of a people whose traditions carried the memories of a different way of life, a different vision of human community in the simpler and more egalitarian order of the tribal confederation. Now they found themselves once again part of a system in which their ability to use and control the product of their own labor and to determine their own direction and future no longer lay in their hands.

When Solomon died, a delegation from the northern tribes attempted to extract from his son and successor, Rehoboam, a commitment to a mitigation of his father's harsh rule. Urged by his younger councillors to display a strong hand, Rehoboam rebuffed the plea of the northern tribal elders for redress of their grievances against Solomon's policies. Ignoring the advice the elders had given him, the king gave the people a harsh answer. He said to them, as the young men had advised: "My father put on you a heavy yoke, but I will make it heavier. My father beat you with whips, but I will beat you with scorpions" (1 Kgs 12:11).

The northern leaders then simply refused to acknowledge Rehoboam's succession and chose Jeroboam as king. The fragile empire of Solomon fell apart almost overnight. The unified territorial state David had established had lasted less than two generations. For the next two hundred years the history of this people would be the history of two separate kingdoms, Israel in the north ruled by a succession of dynasties, and Judah in the south with its capital at Jerusalem and a ruler from the lineage of David.

CHANGES IN ISRAEL'S WAY OF LIFE

We have dwelt at some length on this period of Israel's history because it represents a crucial stage in that history and in the development of Israelite society and religious traditions. With the rise of the monarchy major structural changes came about, which we will attempt to summarize.

Political Changes

From the emergence of Saul as a chieftain, through David, and into Solomon's time, Israel moved quickly from a loose federation of tribes united by their commitment to a particular vision of human community to a full-blown unified territorial state which encompassed both the older tribal confederacy and a new Canaanite population. Under the tribal confederation political and social decision-making was in the hands of the village, clan, and tribal elders. These elders attempted to represent and form consensus among this people of whom they were a part and with whom they had frequent and face-to-face contacts. Now, under the monarchy, a small body of ruling elite held the decision-making power and could impose their decisions on the majority, even by force.

Military Changes

Under the tribal confederation the *decision* to use force either for internal order or external security was in the hands of the assemblies of elders at the various levels—family, clan, tribal, inter-tribal. The *ability* to use force was in the hands of militia units made up of levies from the various families, clans, tribes, and groups of tribes in moments of internal or external crisis. Under the monarchy, however, the ruling elite had at its beck and call a standing army of professional soldiers, including foreign mercenaries, to impose its will and enforce its decisions.

Socio-economic Changes

The move to a territorial state opened the path to social and economic stratification. The question now arose that would serve as the source of confrontation and dispute between Israel's kings and prophets, the question of how Yahweh would feed and protect his people. Would it be through a centralized economy, controlled and regulated by the king and his bureaucrats (tributary economy)? Or would it be through a decentralized economy as had been the practice among the highland towns and villages in premonarchic times (communitarian economy)? Under the tribal confederation, structures and institutions were designed to inhibit and discourage the accumulation both of land and resources as well as decision-making power in the hands of individuals or groups. The Canaanite city-state system was the *opposite* of what the tribal confederacy was designed to be. Now the way lay open to a return to the Canaanite city-state model of hierarchy and social stratification. The elite ruling class of the Davidic and Solomonic state held the decision-making power and the ability to impose those decisions, even by force.

Economic inequality increased as the ruling elite influenced and even controlled the society's resources by tax collection and forced labor, effectively siphoning off the surplus production of the farmer and herdsman majority. This "surplus" revenue allowed members of the ruling class to pursue an extravagant lifestyle and provided them with the resources to increase even further their social, political, and economic power. Thus two quite contrasting socio-economic and political systems grew and uneasily operated side by side. On the one hand, the older tribal organization with its economic and legal structures continued, principally in the rural countryside at the village level. This system was ideologically reinforced and supported by the older Yahwist traditions. It was presupposed that the land belonged to Yahweh, Israel's unique King, who granted to his covenant partners parcels large enough to provide satisfying and productive lives for them and their families. On the other hand, this traditional system at the village level was overlaid with and penetrated by the statist structure imposed from the centralized state government with its ruling elite, its bureaucracy, and its professional army. This system presumed that the land was the property of the king (along with the members of the ruling class), who distributed parcels of it to his subjects and who could, and did, demand payment of rent and who could, and did, expropriate the land and evict its tenants at will.

With the older system of land tenure under the tribal confederation, each extended family held its parcel of land, its "house" (see Ex 20:17), in perpetuity. In addition, the obligatory mutual aid provision of the federation provided protection against loss of that property in times of economic crisis. This system, however, was now subject to erosion both in practice and in ideology. Under the recently imposed statist model, the perpetual right of the family to its patrimonial inheritance had no standing. The way was opened for purchase, sale, and accumulation of property. Failures in the mutual aid system forced individuals and families to go into debt, mortgage their ancestral lands, and eventually lose them. This flouting of the traditional egalitarian economic arrangements of the old tribal order became one of the principal targets of the preaching and denunciation of the prophets (see 1 Kgs 21; Is 5:8-10; Mi 2:1-5). Isaiah, for example, decried the creation of large estates by the seizure of smaller family holdings:

> Woe to you who join house to house,
>   who connect field with field,
> Till no room remains, and you are left to dwell
>   alone in the midst of the land (Is 5:8).

Religious Changes

The older Yahwist faith remained strong in the countryside at the village level, nourished and passed on in the context of the family and local shrine. It served to support and legitimate the socio-economic and political arrangements continuing from the days of the tribal confederation. However, a new element was now entering Yahwism. Yahweh was now also the patron deity of a national state with a royal shrine located in the capital and under the control and protection of the king. A professional priestly caste, assisted by a corps of musicians, singers, and attendants, presided over an expensive and lavish cult. In addition, there were scribes attached to the Temple whose task it was to compose, sing, and write the ritual texts.

Thus, a whole new body of religious language, concepts, and imagery was added to the older tribal traditions which enriched and enlarged the expressive possibilities for Israel's faith and traditions. The Mosaic covenant themes were now supplemented by and aligned with a royal theology based on God's special relationship with his king, "whom he had chosen" (Ps 89:4-5). In addition, there was the promise of an enduring dynasty for the monarch and an assurance by the deity of his lasting presence in the royal shrine:

> The LORD swore to David
> a firm promise from which he will not withdraw:
> "Your own offspring
> I will set upon your throne;
> If your sons keep my covenant
> and the decrees which I shall teach them,
> Their sons, too, forever
> shall sit upon your throne."
> For the LORD has chosen Zion;
> he prefers her for his dwelling.
> "Zion is my resting place forever;
> in her will I dwell, for I prefer her" (Ps 132:11-14).

REVIEW QUESTIONS

1. Discuss some of the *internal* factors that could have fostered the movement toward greater centralization and eventually the monarchy in Israel.

2. How was the capture of the Jebusite citadel of Jerusalem a part of David's strategy?

3. Describe the background and development of the two distinct understandings of and theological tendencies within Yahwism that came about under David, especially with his establishment of Jerusalem as the capital.

4. Describe the Ancient Near Eastern concept of kingship. What effect did this concept have on Yahwism beginning with David's rule?

5. What is meant by the "Zion tradition"? What effect did this have on Yahwism beginning with David's reign?

6. What "critical line" had the Israelite community crossed by the end of David's reign? What were some of the implications of Israel's having crossed over this line?

7. Describe some of the manifestations of the typical Ancient Near Eastern monarchical state that Solomon displayed during his reign. Why could it be said that his house was built on sand?

8. What crucial political and military changes occurred in the development of Israelite society and religious traditions under David and Solomon?

9. Describe the important changes in the socio-economic sphere during this period.

10. What decisive religious changes came about during this era?

14

The Divided Monarchy

Suggested Bible Readings: 1 Kings 12, 17-21; 2 Kings 1-2, 9-10, 17-25

THE SHIFT FROM TRIBAL LEAGUE TO MONARCHY

It would be a mistake to take an overly simplistic view of the shift from tribal league to monarchy under David and treat this shift as a kind of fall from grace or return to paganism or betrayal of the revolution. On the other hand, a naive acceptance of the view garnered from a superficial reading of the Bible—that the move to a monarchy was somehow willed by God—does not do justice to the ambiguity and nuances of the biblical text itself. The Bible both juxtaposes and weaves together texts favorable to and texts unfavorable to the monarchy (cf. Jgs 9:7-15 or 1 Sm 8 with 2 Sm 7). The complexity of the situation, of the factors involved, and of the final results demands a more careful and nuanced evaluation. It may be best simply to discuss briefly both the advantages and disadvantages this novel development brought to Israel as a whole and to the average Israelite in particular.

First of all, the most obvious advantage was the survival of the Israelite culture and tradition from possible dismemberment and destruction at the hands of the Philistines. The ability to mount a more centralized and stronger military response not only against the Philistines but against other similar future aggressors may have eventually become a necessity for Israel. David was able not only to mount a more effective response and save Israel from the Philistine threat, but also to do so in such a way as to leave relatively intact the major features of Israel's traditional tribal organization. It is even possible that David had reached some kind of understanding with the tribal elders when they made him king, whereby his role within the tribal confederation and his rights and powers, were strictly circumscribed and defined. In other words, it was a kind of constitutional monarchy designed to provide the advantages of a king, with a stronger hand, for example, in military matters, while at the same time safeguarding and respecting the principal features and operation of the older tribal structures in other spheres. Evidence for such a formal agreement is hinted at, for example, when Samuel anointed Israel's first king, Saul:

> Samuel said to all the people, "Do you see the man whom the LORD has chosen? There is none like him among all the people!" Then all the people shouted, "Long live the king!" Samuel next explained to the people the law of royalty and wrote it in a book, which he placed in the presence of the LORD (1 Sm 10:24-25).

Deuteronomy 17:14-20 also seems to presuppose such a document.

David, however, and many others, apparently did not recognize immediately the implications and potential of some of these new structures or forces which had been set in motion.

Another advantage of the monarchy was the substantial enrichment in the religious expressivity of Yahwism. Under David and Solomon the adaptation and appropriation of the religious traditions of pre-Davidic Jerusalem took place. These traditions included the Canaanite cosmological and mythic language and imagery. This language and imagery now made possible the development of both the royal and Zion theology which have such a prominent role, especially in the psalmic and prophetic literature. The royal patronage of the Temple supported a staff of scribes and musicians. This initiated and fostered the growth of an artistic tradition, which, among other things, issued in the unsurpassed collection of religious hymns in our present Book of Psalms.

Despite these advantages, the disadvantages probably outweighed the benefits, especially from the point of view of the average Israelite. Under David the line had been crossed from the older order in which an egalitarian ideal, or at least an opening toward equality, had been the principal and determinative factor in policy and decision-making. Under David the newly established ruling elite of the state apparatus reserved that policy and decision-making power to themselves, and they possessed the necessary means to impose that policy and those decisions. Especially under Solomon the ruling elite used this power to ensure an extravagant and privileged lifestyle for themselves. The legendary wealth and prosperity of Solomon's reign (1 Kgs 10:14-25) were in fact enjoyed by a tiny minority of the population. The rest suffered under the burden of taxes and enforced labor imposed by Solomon's misguided economic and social policies. The resentment and discontent of the bulk of the population resulted in the quick collapse of Solomon's modest empire at his death.

Nevertheless, the new reality of kingship in Israel and its accompanying structures and implications would dominate the history of this people over the next four hundred years. Further, it provides important lessons for us as we study this story of the struggle of a people to balance the vision of a just and peaceful human community with the realities of a changing socio-economic, political, and religious situation. We can see how Israel as a people and as individuals met their challenges, where they succeeded, and how they failed insofar as we can judge success and failure from the privileged distance and perspective of three thousand years.

No clear answer is forthcoming on what was or what might have been the right or wrong course of action. David's ability to balance the need for a more unified military response to the Philistine threat with a respect for the main features of the tribal organizational structures is rendered ambiguous by some of the steps he took, steps which set the stage for the eventual eclipse of the old order. Nevertheless, the older ideals and vision remained alive as a kind of "dangerous memory," which continued to inspire and guide the struggle of future generations. We see this vision and these ideals kept before the eyes of the people during the next four hundred years of monarchy in north and south, especially in the powerful voice of Israel's prophets. Prophets continued to articulate and nuance and to deepen and broaden those ideals of justice and that powerful sense of the presence and activity of the divine in the life of a people and in the lives of individuals. Before we turn to this movement and the body of texts central to the biblical tradition and without parallel in the world's religious literature and history, we will briefly summarize the course of history of the two monarchies, a history that forms the background to this unique movement.

A BRIEF HISTORY OF THE DIVIDED MONARCHY

Introduction

The Bible itself provides two sources for the remaining period of the monarchy (922-587 B.C.E.). One of these is the Former Prophets, especially the First and Second Books of Kings (plus some supplementary material from the Books of Chronicles). Along with archeological evidence and extra-biblical texts, mostly from Moab and Assyria, this source gives us the history of the power struggles, the coups and assassinations, in short, the successes and failures of the ruling classes. Another important source, mostly indirect, is the texts associated with the prophetic movement which arose and flowered during this period. These include the accounts in the Books of Kings about such figures as Ahijah of Shiloh (1 Kgs 11:26-40; 14:1-17), Jehu ben Hanani (1 Kgs 16:1-4), and especially Elijah the Tishbite (1 Kgs 17-2 Kgs 2:12) and Elisha ben Shaphat (1 Kgs 19:12-21; 2 Kgs 2-10; 13:14-21). We also have the Latter Prophets, the records of the preaching and activity of prophetic figures such as Amos, Hosea, Isaiah, Jeremiah, and Ezekiel. From the prophetic literature of this period, which preserves some historical memories and traditions, we glimpse what must have been the experience and condition of the vast majority of the people of Israel during this time.

In contrast to the prosperity and luxury enjoyed by the kings and ruling classes, the life of the average Israelite was generally harsh and precarious. The older traditions and structures of the tribal confederation continued at the clan and village level—the protection of extended families' patrimonial lands and the mutual aid mechanisms. But these became more and more hampered and seriously eroded by the overlay of the state structure, which weakened these older structures by drawing off "surplus production" in taxes and forced labor. There was also the massive shift in land tenure, witnessed especially in the Book of Amos, whereby "latifundization" (the appropriation and accumulation of patrimonial lands into larger and larger estates) dispossessed increasing numbers of extended families of their ancestral properties. The conflicts between prophet and king are described in the biblical record as mainly religious conflicts between Baalism and Yahwism. But in fact they represent a much broader and more pervasive conflict involving two contrasting visions of how to organize and maintain human community and society. Thus most of the kings of both Israel and Judah were criticized for "failing to walk in the ways of Yahweh." They were presented in the Deuteronomistic historical sources as erring principally by theological failures, for example, in cultic matters such as the proper sanctuary where worship of Yahweh was supposed to take place.

But this conflict of theologies represents only the tip of the iceberg. Baalism and Yahwism constituted, in fact, the ideological elements of much broader visions and practices. Baalism favored and promoted a community and society based on hierarchy and social stratification, and a centralized or "tributary" economy. Yahwism, by contrast, represented the more egalitarian ideals of the older tribal confederation with its decentralized or "communitarian" economic arrangements. The majority of Israelites in the villages and countryside still clung to and practiced these traditions.

The biblical record itself represents something of a paradox in its preservation of both of these traditions side by side. The memories and values of the tribal organization and practices are preserved and handed on by the scribes and bureaucrats who served the centralized monarchic state. Frith Lambert has studied this puzzling phenomenon and concluded:

Israel's religious and political pluralism was largely the outcome of an early tribal history, which left a legacy (within a centralized state) of a tribal ideology, of the tribe as symbol, as a major component of state religion and, in practical terms, an effective underpinning for the political activity of the Yahweh prophets, who were a significant power class in themselves. ("The Tribe/State Paradox," p. 40)

These prophets were the most eloquent and aggressive defenders and promoters of the older ideals of the tribal confederation. They were innovative and creative in the new ways they promoted and expressed these ideals and adapted them to new circumstances. At the same time, they were radically conservative in their challenge to return to the ideals of justice and egalitarian communal practices of former days.

In this section we will focus briefly on the data from the first source for this period of the monarchy, the history in terms of the monarchic states of Israel and Judah. We already began this story with the break-up of Solomon's kingdom. This collapse had been provoked by the refusal of Solomon's son Rehoboam to accede to the pleas of the elders from the northern tribes to mitigate his father's harsh economic policies. Jeroboam, one of Solomon's officials and a director of the corvée gangs in Ephraimite territory, had organized a revolt. With the failure of the revolt, he had fled to Egypt where the pharaoh had given him political asylum. The seceding northern tribes invited him to return from Egypt and assume the kingship over them.

The Northern Kingdom (Israel), 922-722 B.C.E.

The establishment of the northern kingdom of Israel resulted from the harsh economic policies of Solomon's reign, but it also had roots in the older rivalry and antagonisms between the two major power centers of the Israelite confederation, Ephraim-Benjamin-Manasseh in the north and Judah in the south. This rivalry and antagonism went back to the days of the tribal confederation. The duality in geography, culture, and tradition eventually manifested itself in the political duality of the two kingdoms.

Although Israel was the larger of the two both in territory and population, it suffered under distinctive handicaps which probably determined its shorter independent existence. Its larger population was also more diverse, encompassing land and groups east and west of the Jordan and north and south of the Plains of Esdraelon and Jezreel. These groups possessed different interests and agenda, which had to be carefully balanced and negotiated if any centralized governing authority was to be successful. In addition, its geopolitical position was more vulnerable. The northern kingdom's larger territory included trade routes and rich agricultural lands, and both were tempting objects for conquest and control by foreign powers with imperial ambitions. In the south, the dynasty established by David and Solomon ruled through twenty kings (including one queen) for the entire 355-year history of the kingdom. But the less politically stable north saw five dynasties and nineteen kings come and go in its briefer two-hundred-year span.

1 Kings tells us that the first northern king, Jeroboam, established two pilgrimage centers at the ancient Yahwist shrines of Dan and Bethel (1 Kgs 12:26-30). The purpose of these pilgrimage centers, at the northern and southern extremities of his kingdom, was to counteract the attraction of the Jerusalem Temple with its Ark of the Covenant, the ancient cult object from the days of the tribal confederation:

> Jeroboam thought to himself: "The kingdom will return to David's house. If now this people go up to offer sacrifices in the temple of the LORD in Jerusalem, the hearts of this people will return to their master, Rehoboam, king of Judah, and they will kill me" (1 Kgs 12:26-27).

In place of the Ark, over whose "mercy seat" Yahweh's invisible presence was believed to dwell, Jeroboam installed a golden calf in each shrine, meant also to be a symbolic throne for the invisible presence of the deity. The Deuteronomistic historians, however, interpreted the golden calves as idolatrous:

> After taking counsel, the king [Jeroboam] made two calves of gold and said to the people: "You have been going up to Jerusalem long enough. Here is your God, O Israel, who brought you up from the land of Egypt" (1 Kgs 12:28).

The Deuteronomistic historians thus brand this action of Jeroboam in establishing rival shrines to the Jerusalem Temple as a kind of "original sin," which lay at the root of all the evils perpetrated by the northern kings. In the eyes of the Deuteronomistic writers, it constituted an abomination that would lead eventually to the kingdom's downfall at the hands of Assyria some two hundred years later.

Two dynasties in the northern kingdom enjoyed some degree of permanency, that established by Omri and the one founded by Jehu. In 876 B.C.E., Omri, a military commander in the Israelite army, managed to consolidate his hold on power after a four-year-long civil war. He established a dynasty that lasted through four kings. Omri may have been a non-Israelite; thus he had no qualms about ruling in the typical Ancient Near Eastern kingly style. He built an elaborate new capital and palace at Samaria, for example, and engaged in both military and commercial ventures with neighboring states. He and his son Ahab enjoyed considerable success in their efforts to make a name and place for their kingdom among the nation-states of the time. Under their rule Israel may have reached a position equal to or even greater than that attained by the united monarchy under Solomon. The first extra-biblical records to mention individuals in Israel's history are Assyrian inscriptions that refer to Omri and Ahab, and Assyrian records continued for decades to refer to Israel as "the land of Omri."

It was under these two kings, however, that the chorus of prophetic criticism began to swell, offering evidence of how their imperial ambitions affected the vast majority of the inhabitants of their kingdom. The degree to which both felt comfortable in ignoring, or at least in compromising, the traditional Yahwist religion of their kingdom is evidenced by Ahab's taking of a Phoenician princess, Jezebel of Tyre, as his wife. Jezebel's ability to prevail on Ahab to construct a temple to Baal of Tyre in the new capital of Samaria witnesses to her zeal for her Canaanite religion. That zeal was matched by her enthusiasm for the accompanying economic presuppositions of Canaanite Baalism in her role in the Naboth affair recounted in 1 Kings 21.

Next to Ahab's palace was a vineyard belonging to a man named Naboth. Ahab had been eyeing the property and eventually approached Naboth, offering to purchase it:

> Some time after this, as Naboth the Jezreelite had a vineyard in Jezreel next to the palace of Ahab, king of Samaria, Ahab said to Naboth, "Give me your vineyard to be my vegetable garden, since it is close by, next to my house. I will give you a better vineyard in exchange, or, if you prefer, I will give you its value in money" (1 Kgs 21:1-2).

Naboth refused: "'The LORD forbid,' Naboth answered him, 'that I should give you my ancestral inheritance'" (1 Kgs 21:3). The property, a section of his "ancestral inheritance," belonged not so much to Naboth personally as to his family—past, present, and future. It was a part of the covenantal grant made by Yahweh to the people of Israel and was to remain within the family so as to ensure both present and future generations guaranteed access to the family members' most fundamental source of life and livelihood—*land*. To sell permanently this parcel of land would have betrayed one of the most important elements of Israel's basic socio-economic structure and religious ethos. Ahab at least vaguely understood the implications of Naboth's reply; he realized it would prove impossible to satisfy the royal whim. His frustration drove him into a depression: "Lying down on his bed, he turned away from food and would not eat" (1 Kgs 21:4).

At this point Jezebel, Ahab's queen, entered the picture. As a Canaanite princess and an ardent devotee of Baalism, she viewed the question of the vineyard from an entirely different perspective. As far as she was concerned, Ahab, as king, owned all the land in the kingdom as a grant from the gods. For Naboth to refuse to surrender the plot of land to the king was tantamount to treason in her eyes and a crime deserving of death:

> "A fine ruler over Israel you are indeed!" his wife Jezebel said to him. "Get up. Eat and be cheerful. I will obtain the vineyard of Naboth the Jezreelite for you" (1 Kgs 21:7).

Jezebel had Naboth convicted of blasphemy on the basis of false testimony by men in her pay. Naboth was stoned to death and his property reverted to the crown:

> When Jezebel learned that Naboth had been stoned to death, she said to Ahab, "Go on, take possession of the vineyard of Naboth the Jezreelite which he refused to sell you, because Naboth is not alive, but dead" (1 Kgs 21:15).

Ahab thus obtained his vegetable garden and Jezebel's socio-economic and religious program prevailed.

Omri's dynasty was replaced by that of Jehu in 842 B.C.E. in a coup apparently sparked by and supported by prophetic critics of the Omride abuses. 2 Kings 9 reports that Elisha had Jehu anointed as king and urged him to rebel and overthrow the reigning Omride ruler, Joram:

> The prophet Elisha called one of the guild prophets and said to him: "Gird your loins, take this flask of oil with you, and go to Ramoth-gilead. When you get there, look for Jehu, son of Jehoshaphat, son of Nimshi. Enter and take him away from his companions into an inner chamber. From the flask you have, pour oil on his head, and say, 'Thus says the LORD: I anoint you king over Israel.' Then open the door and flee without delay" (2 Kgs 9:1-3).

Jehu was successful in the coup and founded the third dynasty to rule the north, a dynasty that lasted through five kings and almost one hundred years. Especially during the long reign of the fourth king of the dynasty, Jeroboam II (786-746 B.C.E.), the northern kingdom enjoyed a period of growth and prosperity. The voice of the prophet Amos, however, gave witness to the sometimes desperate situation of large numbers of the population, who were suffering from the highhanded and oppressive policies of the ruling elite.

A relief from the Black Obelisk of Shalmaneser III (857-824 B.C.E.) of Assyria. The inscription above the second panel reads, "The tribute of Jehu, son of Omri." Jehu wears western Semitic dress, a turban and long over-garment. This representation of Jehu is the only known portrayal of an Israelite king.

With the assassination of the fifth and last member of Jehu's dynasty, Zechariah, in 745 B.C.E., the northern kingdom began a rapid decline. The main source of its problems was Assyria, whose growing strength and imperial ambitions carried it farther and farther west toward the Mediterranean. The Assyrian rulers coveted the cedar and other wood from the abundant forests of Syria and Lebanon as well as the lucrative trade from the Syro-Palestinian caravan routes and the Phoenician port cities.

Israel lay directly in the path of Assyrian expansion. In 722 B.C.E., the Assyrian king, Shalmaneser V, laid siege to and captured Samaria, the capital city (see 2 Kings 17 for the biblical version of these events). Shalmaneser's successor, Sargon II, carried through the Assyrian policy on conquered peoples. Most of the ruling classes were deported and resettled in other parts of the empire, while foreigners were brought from these lands and resettled in turn in Israel. Samaria was rebuilt and served as the administrative center of the newly erected Assyrian province of Samerina. Significant portions of the Israelite population remained in the territory, however, and presumably continued to worship Yahweh and follow the ancestral customs. Some apparently fled south, taking up residence in Judah. They brought with them considerable elements of their traditions and literature, such as the cycles of Elijah and Elisha stories, the court annals, the Elohist epic, and the earlier form of the legal traditions preserved in the Book of Deuteronomy. But the independent political existence of the northern kingdom as a state came to an end. The "history-making" ruling classes of Judah continued the story for another four generations.

The Southern Kingdom (Judah), 922-587 B.C.E.

The southern kingdom of Judah enjoyed a greater degree of stability as a political state than did the north for a number of reasons. Unlike the northern kingdom, with its access to trade routes and rich agricultural lands, Judah was smaller and more isolated. It thus did not present as tempting an object for conquest and control. Another factor in Judah's greater longevity was the dynasty of David and Solomon, a dynasty with a record that would be difficult for any newcomer to match. Also, in the monarchy the kings of Judah instituted early the practice of co-regency, whereby the heir apparent joined in the ruling responsibilities during the latter years of his predecessor's reign. This not only gave the incoming king a good deal of practical experience before he himself took power, but it also gave him the opportunity to consolidate and strengthen his hold on the throne ahead of time.

Sporadic warfare was carried on between the two monarchies in the first few years after the split of Solomon's kingdom. Peace finally came during

The Kings of Northern Israel and of Judah (922-586 B.C.E.)

Northern Israel		Judah	
Jeroboam I	922-901	Rehoboam	922-915
Nadab	901-900	Abijah	915-913
Baasha	900-877	Asa	913-873
Elah	877-876	Jehoshaphat	873-849
Zimri	876	Jehoram	849-842
Omri	876-869	Ahaziah	842
Ahab	869-850	(Athaliah)	842-837
Ahaziah	850-849	Joash	837-800
Jehoram	849-842	Amaziah	800-783
Jehu	842-815	Uzziah (Azariah)	783-742
Jehoahaz	815-801	Jotham	742-732
Jehoash	801-786	Ahaz	732-715
Jeroboam II	786-746	Hezekiah	715-686
Zechariah	746-745	Manasseh	686-642
Shallum	745	Amon	642-640
Menahem	745-738	Josiah	640-609
Pekahiah	738-737	Jehoahaz	609
Pekah	737-732	Jehoiakim	609-598
Hoshea	732-722	Jehoiachin	598-562(?)
		Zedekiah	597-586

the Omride dynasty in the north. Under the Davidic kings Amaziah (800-783 B.C.E.) and Uzziah (783-742 B.C.E.), Judah seems to have enjoyed the same relatively tranquil and prosperous conditions as the north did under Jeroboam II (786-746 B.C.E.). This was, at least in part, the result of the weakened condition of Assyria during the first half of the eighth century.

Three kings of the seventh century deserve mention. Hezekiah (715-686 B.C.E.) reversed the pro-Assyrian policies of his father, Ahaz (732-715 B.C.E.). As a part of this anti-Assyrian and pro-nationalist campaign Hezekiah strengthened the official standing of Yahwism by purging Assyrian elements that had encroached on the Jerusalem Temple worship and by suppressing Yahwist and other shrines outside of Jerusalem. For this he received high praise from the Deuteronomistic historians:

He pleased the LORD, just as his forefather David had done. . . . He put his trust in the LORD, the God of Israel; and neither before him nor after him was there anyone like him among all the kings of Judah. Loyal to the LORD, Hezekiah never turned away from him, but observed the commandments which the LORD had given Moses. The LORD was with him, and he prospered in all that he set out to do (1 Kgs 18:3, 5-7).

The reverse is true for Hezekiah's successor, Manasseh. Of his long reign (686-642 B.C.E.) we know very little other than the report of the DH that "he did what was evil in the sight of Yahweh" (2 Kgs 21:2). Apparently he played his role as loyal Assyrian vassal to the hilt, unabashedly flaunting the royal lifestyle with its accompanying harsh and oppressive policies toward the vast majority of the population. These policies would have included a generally cool attitude toward Yahwism, even to the extent of an attempted persecution and suppression of Judah's traditional religion. The installment of his grandson Josiah on the throne by anti-Assyrian forces in 640 B.C.E. after Manasseh's forty-four year reign was hailed by the Deuteronomistic historians as a welcome relief. Josiah appears as a real hero and savior in the Deuteronomistic History (see 2 Kgs 22-23). The pro-Assyrian stance of Manasseh was quickly reversed and a period of both socio-economic and religious reform was undertaken according to the guidelines and program of the Deuteronomic circles. It was under Josiah that the Book of the Law, probably an earlier version of the core of the Book of Deuteronomy, was "found" in the Temple. Because Assyria's power was on the wane, threatened and eroded by the rise of Babylon, Josiah enjoyed a degree of freedom. He was able to extend Judean influence northward to encompass a good bit of the territories and inhabitants of the former kingdom of Israel. Josiah's adoption of the Deuteronomic reform, based on northern traditions, helped him secure a friendly reception from the descendants of the inhabitants of that northern kingdom.

The hopes raised by Josiah and the Deuteronomistic circles were quickly shattered, however. Babylon overwhelmed Assyria and in 612 B.C.E. destroyed the legendary Assyrian capital at Nineveh. Babylon then began its push westward. A period of chaos and turbulence ensued. Josiah himself was killed in a battle at Megiddo in 609 B.C.E. The four kings who followed him in quick succession were, for all practical purposes, pawns in the larger conflict between Babylon and Egypt. Finally, the Babylonian king Nebuchadnezzar sent his army to deal with this troublesome vassal, Judah. In 587 B.C.E. Judah was devastated and Jerusalem taken. The Babylonians pulled down the city's walls, burned the Temple and royal palace to the ground, and marched off the ruling classes and leading citizens into exile in Babylon. Thus the independent existence of the political state of Judah ended. It suffered the same fate as had its sister kingdom, Israel, some 135 years earlier.

A six-sided clay prism inscribed in cuneiform with an account of the early campaigns of Sennacherib of Assyria, including his attack on Hezekiah of Judah in 701 B.C.E. Nineveh, 691 B.C.E. This attack marked the end of Isaiah's carer as a prophet (see pp. 209, 218-20).

Reflections on the Monarchy

As we look back over the history of Israel under the monarchy, a number of questions emerge. Perhaps the most crucial is whether Israel erred in accepting the chieftainship first of Saul and then of David. This acceptance of a more centralized rule resulted in what seems to have been an inevitable slide into a monarchical state under David and Solomon. Did Israel have any other choice, given the historical situation? Was the monarchy indeed a betrayal of the ideals Israel had originally embraced? Or were the benefits enough to justify the apparent compromise with the hopes and dreams of the tribal confederation?

There are no easy answers to these questions. On the one hand, one could argue that Israel had no choice but to accept the leadership of David, even if it meant starting down the road toward a centralized monarchic state. The alternative, some would argue, would have been subjection to the Philistines and the inevitable dissolution and disappearance of all for which they had worked and suffered. It was a question of life or death. Besides this most fundamental element in the decision—the issue of their very survival as a people, there were other, positive elements on the monarchy's side. We have already mentioned the enrichment of Israel's religious language. This resulted in the expansion of that language's expressive possibilities with the development of the royal and Zion theologies, especially under the Judaite monarchy. Also, Israel under David and Solomon, and then for a time both the northern and southern kingdoms, enjoyed brief periods of prestige and standing within the international community of states. Nevertheless, that prosperity and success were enjoyed by a quite small and privileged minority.

On the other hand, a quick glance at the price paid by the average Israelite for these gains and successes places a question mark over them. And there is the key issue of whether Israel could have survived even if it had declined the Davidic option. Looking back from the historical distance of three thousand years, we are able to see a little more clearly the factors that made the slide toward monarchy inevitable, once David was accepted as chief. The implications of that step were probably not as clear to those involved in the actual decision. And even if they had realized the danger involved, the immediacy of the Philistine threat may have led them to see no alternative. At least with the monarchy they had a "fighting chance." They would have the possibility and opportunities to reach some kind of accommodation.

Indeed there were ambiguities involved in attempting to combine the social organization of a *state* and its inevitable social stratification with the vision of a *community* in which all the members are guaranteed a relative equality. But living with that ambiguity and surviving was apparently deemed better than declining to cross the line into statehood and eventually disappearing from history along with all their hopes and dreams. Could Israel have survived if it had not crossed over that line into statehood? Looking back in time that question may appear at this point merely an academic one. And yet, the answer consistently given by a significant number of voices preserved in the biblical text is yes, it could have survived, even if it had not finally opted for the monarchy. This seems to be the answer implied in the preaching of a number of the prophets, and it is raised as a possibility by the Deuteronomistic historians.

REVIEW QUESTIONS

1. What were some of the advantages to the Israelite community of the move to a monarchical state? What were some of the disadvantages?

2. Compare and contrast the two kingdoms into which Solomon's kingdom divided at his death in 922 B.C.E.

3. What was the "original sin" attributed to the first northern king, Jeroboam, by the Deuteronomistic historians? Explain.

4. Describe briefly the reign and importance of the northern king Omri.

5. How does the story of Naboth and his vineyard in 1 Kings 21 highlight the differences between Canaanite religion and Yahwism?

6. Outline the events that led up to the fall of the northern kingdom at the hands of the Assyrian army in 722 B.C.E. What were some of the consequences of that event for the people of the northern kingdom?

7. Why was Judah more stable than Israel as a political state during the period of the divided monarchy?

8. Explain briefly the importance of Hezekiah (715-686 B.C.E), Manasseh (686-642 B.C.E), and Josiah (640-609 B.C.E).

9. Is the biblical text unanimous in judging that the movement from tribal confederation to monarchy was initiated and willed by God? Explain.

PART V

PROPHECY
IN THE
PRE-EXILIC PERIOD

15

The Origins and Definition
of Prophecy

BACKGROUND

The Word *Prophet*

Prophecy and the prophetic movement are central to any discussion of the Hebrew Scriptures. We have already seen how the Deuteronomistic History, the major literary complex following the foundational Torah or Law (the Pentateuch) in the Hebrew Bible, goes under the name Former Prophets and not Historical Books. And in the Latter Prophets (Isaiah, Jeremiah, Ezekiel, Daniel, Book of the Twelve) we have the complement to the Former Prophets. The books of the Latter Prophets contain writings of both the prophets themselves and the reflections and redactional activity of their disciples and the schools that cherished and handed on their teachings. (See chart of Old Testament books on p. xix.)

The word *prophet* itself is a potential source of confusion as to the nature of the office and the movement. In popular parlance the word is usually associated almost exclusively with a kind of clairvoyance, an ability to predict future events and happenings. Also, within Christian circles there is a long tradition of interpreting the prophets almost completely in Christological terms. The liturgy unfortunately continues this practice, too often not reading texts from the prophets for their own sake but in conjunction with the New Testament texts that have interpreted the passages Christologically. This tendency to focus almost exclusively on the tradition of Christological interpretation has the danger of reducing the prophets to one-dimensional figures whose value is restricted to their "predictions" about Christ. To do so ignores the central importance of the role of the prophets both in Israel's history and in the development and expression of Israelite thought and tradition.

Focusing for a moment on the word *prophet* itself, however, can be helpful in gaining some insight into the role and function of these important figures from Israel's past. Various terms from the earlier days of prophecy, for example, *rō'eh,* "seer" (1 Sm 9:9) or *hōzeh,* "discerner" (2 Sm 24:11; Am 7:12), stress the more clairvoyant element of prophecy.

But the most common term for prophet in the Old Testament is *nabī',* from the Semitic root *nb'* "to call." Some scholars argue that the active sense, "to call, name, invoke," best represents the earlier usage of this term. Thus the *nabī'* was one who called or invoked God or the gods. In 1 Kings 18:24, the prophet Elijah tells the prophets of Baal, "You shall call on your gods, and I will call on the LORD."

Other commentators point to the related Akkadian root *nabū,* meaning "to call, commission." In this understanding of the word's etymology, the noun in Hebrew would belong to vocational terminology. It would thus imply the official standing of the one who carries the title as a spokesperson chosen or "called" by God to deliver a message in God's name. Our English word *prophet* is derived from the Greek *prophetes,* with which the Septuagint, the early Greek version of the Hebrew Scriptures, translated *nabī'*. The word *prophetes* in Greek means "spokesperson," reflecting this sense of *nabī'* as "one called, commissioned" to speak God's word.

The More Remote Background of Israelite Prophecy

Communication with and consultation of the gods was an important element in almost all religions in the ancient world. In order to eliminate the possibility of any arbitrary human element entering into the consultation process, various techniques were developed. These involved the observation and use of natural phenomena that presumably could not be manipulated and controlled by human agents. Texts from the Ancient Near East attest to the development of divining techniques centuries before Israel came on the scene. These techniques included the observation of the flight patterns of birds, designs created by oil on the surface of still water, the interpretation of dreams, and the shape of the inner organs of sacrificed animals. The reading of the livers of sacrificed animals, with the technical name of "hepatoscopy," was apparently a favorite in ancient Mesopotamia, both in Assyria and in Babylonia. A specially trained group of priests called *baru* ("seers," "inspectors," "diviners") were charged with performing this consultation. Archeologists have discovered whole collections of clay models of sheep livers, many of them covered with cuneiform texts. The livers of sacrificed sheep were compared with these models. The inscription on the model corresponding in shape and size to that of the sacrificed sheep was considered to be a message or communication from the gods.

The social sciences, especially sociology and anthropology, have provided another direction for studies concerning the background of Israelite prophecy. In many societies even today "prophetic" or "charismatic" individuals play roles similar to the prophets of Israel in leading, inspiring, and giving direction to movements that have greater or lesser impact on society as a whole. Revivalist, millenarian, and reformist movements challenge certain elements or directions in a community.

Study of these contemporary cross-cultural phenomena reveals parallels and patterns which are then helpful in illuminating what we know of similar movements in ancient Israel, especially those associated with the prophets. Thomas Overholt, for example, has documented many illuminating parallels with Old Testament prophecy provided by cultural anthropology studies. Among the figures Overholt has studied are prominent Native American "prophets" or intermediaries such as Handsome Lake (d. 1815) and Wovoka (also known as Jack Wilson, d. 1932).

The More Immediate Background of Israelite Prophecy

The claim of Israelite prophets to be in privileged communication with the deity was thus not an exclusive or unique phenomenon in the ancient world of which Israel was so clearly a part. The Scriptures themselves recognize the existence of prophets outside the confines of Israel. The Moabite prophet Balaam, who appears in Numbers 22-24, is a good example. According to the story, Balak, king of Moab, offered a rich reward to Balaam to curse this people of Israel who were making their way through his country toward Canaan. But Balaam received a revelation from Yahweh and ended up blessing Israel instead, thus frustrating and angering the king.

Scholars have focused on two examples of the wider Ancient Near Eastern phenomena that seem to form a more immediate background for Israelite prophecy. One of these is the phenomenon of Canaanite "ecstatic" prophecy. We have a record of this type of prophecy both from outside the Scriptures and within them. An Egyptian text from the eleventh century B.C.E., the Tale of Wen-Amun (*ANET,* pp. 25-29), tells the story of an Egyptian official who visits the court of the king of Byblos in Phoenicia. While the official is there, a young servant boy in the temple of Byblos falls into an ecstatic trance and utters what apparently is to be taken as a communication from a Canaanite god. The message the boy delivers from the god urges the king to welcome the Egyptian official and accede to his request.

This Canaanite-type ecstatic prophecy appears in the Bible as well in the famous story of the confrontation of the prophet Elijah with the prophets of Baal and the prophets of Asherah on Mt. Carmel. In 1 Kings 18 we read that the Canaanite prophets (the so-called prophets of Baal) achieved a state of collective hypnosis by engaging in a frenzied "limping" dance until they began to rave and slash themselves with knives. Less extravagant examples of this mode of prophesying are mentioned in the Bible in connection with some of the earlier prophets. Incidents associating both Samuel and Saul with this kind of prophesying are found in 1 Samuel 10:5-13 and 19:18-24; 2 Kings records that Elisha used music to induce a prophetic trance:

> Then Elisha said, ". . . Now get me a minstrel." When the minstrel played, the power of the LORD came upon Elisha and he announced: "Thus says the LORD, 'Provide many catch basins in this wadi.' For the LORD says, 'Though you see neither wind nor rain, yet this wadi will be filled with water'" (2 Kgs 3:14-17).

Even though there seems to be some relationship between Canaanite ecstatic prophecy and early Israelite prophecy, it certainly could not be called a *characteristic* of Israelite prophecy in general. Therefore, scholars turned from this avenue of research when early second millennium texts from the northern Mesopotamian city of Mari revealed what promised to be a more fruitful avenue of comparison. These texts mention people who performed functions similar to those of the Old Testament prophets. Letters from persons who bear the title *apilu* (female *apiltu*) contained messages from a god to the king, for example, criticizing his lack of attention to the gods. An *assinnu,* either a male cult prostitute or eunuch, warned a king of plots against his life. A member of the temple personnel called a *muhhu* ("ecstatic, madman") delivered messages dealing principally with cultic matters, for instance, about funerary offerings to a former king. The designations *nabû* (paralleling the Hebrew title *nabī'*) and *qam(m)ātum* have now been added to the list. But their functions are not clear. Even though these individuals generally claimed divine authority for their prophecies, it seems at least in some instances that their messages had to be corroborated and confirmed by more traditional divining techniques.

This research into the Ancient Near Eastern background of Israelite prophecy is important for at least two reasons. First, it provides another example of the *continuity* between the people of Israel and the wider culture and history of the ancient world of which they were a part. Israel was not alone in possessing the phenomenon of prophecy. Rather, Israelite prophecy demonstrates how very much a part of the life and culture of the ancient world Israel was. Second, this research also helps us to clarify and understand more fully the form and expression of Israelite prophecy. We have a wider range of forms and a fuller history of the development of the phenomenon of prophecy into which we can place Israelite prophecy and more easily highlight its distinctive characteristics and features.

THE PROPHET IN ISRAEL: MESSENGER
OF THE DIVINE ASSEMBLY

Out of this research and comparison, one thing has become clear: in conceiving of and describing their role, Israel's prophets, from Samuel onwards, consistently used a distinctively *political* metaphor. The discussion above concerning the meaning of the most frequently used word for prophet, *nabī'*, provides the clue. The prophets saw themselves as "called" or "appointed," commissioned to speak on behalf of Yahweh. And their commissioning was most frequently described in terms of the role of messenger of the divine assembly. The background of this notion is provided by a common element in Ancient Near Eastern, and particularly Canaanite, mythology. In the mythological texts the high god or chief deity was usually pictured as an Ancient Near Eastern monarch or emperor seated upon his throne and surrounded by his officials and advisors. When a subject came up for discussion—some situation or development that needed the attention and decision of the king—he sought the advice and counsel of his officials and advisors. A decision was reached and one from among the council was designated as the messenger of the king to proclaim the decision or decree of the king and thus put it into effect.

A good example of this type of imagery drawn from Canaanite mythology is the divine assembly described by the prophet Micaiah ben Imlah:

Micaiah continued: "Therefore hear the word of the LORD: I saw the LORD seated on his throne, with the whole host of heaven standing by to his right and to his left. The LORD asked, 'Who will deceive Ahab, so that he will go up and fall at Ramoth-gilead?' And one said this, another that, until one of the spirits came forth and presented himself to the LORD, saying, 'I will deceive him.' The LORD asked, 'How?' He answered, 'I will put a lying spirit in the mouths of his prophets.' The LORD replied, 'You shall succeed in deceiving him. Go forth and do this'" (1 Kgs 22:19-22).

Chapters 1 and 2 of the Book of Job also describe a divine assembly wherein discussion and debate take place, a decision is reached, and a member of the assembly is designated to carry out the assembly's will.

In general, the prophets of Israel seem to have understood and described their role in these terms. They saw themselves as the messengers or agents of the divine council, commissioned or deputed by God to announce and thus to put into effect the divine decree or decision. One of the clearest examples of this way of conceiving the prophetic role is found in Isaiah's vocation narrative or description of his prophetic call in Isaiah 6. The scene is a solemn liturgy in the Jerusalem Temple, possibly the celebration of the enthronement of the king, or the anniversary of his enthronement. Isaiah is present, perhaps taking part in some official capacity in the ritual. He suddenly finds himself no longer in the earthly Temple in Jerusalem but in the celestial throne room of Yahweh himself. There is Yahweh, "sitting upon a throne, high and lifted up" (v. 1). Yahweh is surrounded by the heavenly court, made up not of other lesser gods as in the Canaanite mythological texts, but of "seraphim" (heavenly beings and precursors of the "angels" of late Jewish and Christian lore). Isaiah is overcome by the awesomeness of the scene and by a sense of his own powerlessness and unworthiness to be a witness of, much less a participant in, this divine council: "Woe is me, I am doomed! For I am a man of unclean lips, living among a people of unclean lips; yet my eyes have seen the King, the LORD of hosts!" (Is 6:5). But after one of the seraphs purifies Isaiah's lips with a burning coal, his courage returns. Hence, when Yahweh asks for someone from the divine assembly to act as its messenger, its agent, to announce its decrees and thus put into effect its decisions, Isaiah readily volunteers: "Here I am. . . . Send me!"

Thus does Isaiah describe his mission as a prophet. He has been privy to the deliberations of the divine council and been deputed to announce and put into effect its decisions and decrees. But he will not necessarily find it a pleasing and easy task that he has been designated to undertake, as we see in the words that follow. He must proclaim the impending demise of the northern kingdom, the kingdom of Israel: they will refuse to heed God's warning and thus their houses and cities will lie empty and desolate, for the people will have been carried off into exile (Is 6:10-13).

Thus we see in this call narrative of Isaiah the image or metaphor the prophets adopted and developed for describing the role they saw themselves playing. In addition, this passage clearly presents us with two other important characteristics of prophetic speech. The first is the prophet's overwhelming sense of an *encounter with God*. The experience has made a powerful impact on the mind of the prophet. So seized and transformed does he feel himself to have been by this encounter that from this very moment on he carried out his mission of proclaiming God's message with supreme confidence and almost obsessive impulse. A second characteristic is the inevitably *political or socio-economic character of the message* from God the prophets felt impelled to proclaim. Almost invariably, whether the messages are words of consolation and comfort, or words of challenge, warning, and doom, they do not involve purely personal or exclusively religious matters. Rather, they concern the life of the entire people and the shape and character of Israelite society, whether the messages are delivered to an individual such as the king or proclaimed to the people as a whole. Isaiah, for example, is made to confirm the unwillingness of the people to heed Yahweh's words of warning. He must thus proclaim the imminence of the resulting disaster, the northern kingdom's destruction:

Go and say to this people:

Listen carefully, but you shall not understand!
Look intently, but you shall know nothing! . . .

"How long, O Lord?" I asked. And he replied:

Until the cities are desolate,
   without inhabitants,
Houses, without a man,
   and the earth is a desolate waste.
Until the LORD removes men far away,
   and the land is abandoned more and more.
(Is 6:9, 11-12)

THE DISPUTE BETWEEN PROPHETS AND KINGS

A little background knowledge can help one better understand the frequent clashes between the prophets and the kings of Israel or Judah. Their sharp disagreements often centered on the different answers they proposed for a key question: what was the best way to provide food and protection for God's people? The kings tried to impose a "tributary economy," while the prophets called for a return to Israel's traditional "communitarian economy." Victor Matthews and Don Benjamin summarize the issues involved this way:

Monarchs and prophets were both committed to fulfilling Yahweh's covenant with Israel. They shared the traditions which stressed that ultimately only Yahweh fed and protected Israel. They disagreed, however, on which social system best reflected that conviction.

Monarchs argued for the surplus, centralized economic and military system of a state. Prophets, on the other hand, argued for the subsistence, decentralized system attempted by the villages of early Israel. . . . For the prophets, diplomatic policies providing economic security and military preparedness did not lead to peace for Israel and Judah but to disaster.

FROM PREACHING PROPHETS TO WRITING PROPHETS

Before we look at some of the individual prophets in detail, we should also say a few words about the obvious shift that takes place when we reach Amos. With the prophets prior to Amos—Samuel, Nathan, Ahijah of Shiloh, Elijah, Micaiah, Elisha—we have chiefly the record and stories of their *deeds,* their preaching, their active involvement in the life and often the politics of their times. Very little is heard about the *content* of their preaching. From Amos on, however, the equation is reversed. We have very little record of the prophets' lives and activities. Instead we are confronted with a whole collection of their messages and oracles to the people. Scholars in the past have thus contrasted the "preaching prophets" (for example, Nathan, Elijah, Elisha) with the "writing prophets" (Amos, Hosea, Isaiah, and so on), or the "early prophets" and the "classical prophets." What accounts for this shift from recording the activities and stories about the prophets to a preservation of and elaboration or reflection on their words?

One popular theory traces the shift to a corresponding shift in the political policies of Assyria, the major imperial power of those years. Prior to the eighth century B.C.E., treaty arrangements between nation-states were usually in the form of ruler-to-ruler agreements. These could follow the model of a parity treaty between more or less equally powerful states, or the suzerainty treaty model that involved a suzerain and his vassal. Thus it was mainly the individual kings and rulers who were held responsible for the obligations and infractions of the treaty's terms. The missions and messages of the prophets of this earlier time were directed primarily to the rulers and kings of Israel. Samuel, for example, often dealt with Saul and David, and in fact anointed each of them. Nathan and Gad (2 Sm 24:11) functioned similarly as messengers of God to David. Elijah's dealings were with King Ahab, while Elisha anointed Jehu as king to replace the dynasty of Omri. In other words, following the *political* metaphor of a covenant between a suzerain and his vassal, Yahweh, the Suzerain, commissioned a messenger to proclaim a decree of his council to one of his vassals, that is, to one of the rulers or kings.

With the eighth century, however, there was a clear shift in Assyrian foreign policy. This shift apparently had a corresponding effect on the political image or metaphor that provided the prophets of Israel with the model for their self-understanding. In the eighth century the Assyrians began to make treaties or covenants with whole peoples, not just with individual rulers or kings. Thus it was no longer the individual ruler who was held responsible for the obligations or infractions against a treaty or covenant, but the people as a whole. This was obviously a purposeful move with a clear political intent on the part of Assyria. The people as a whole were now responsible for the obligations of the treaties and thus were liable to punishment and reprisals for infractions. This put pressure on the vassal kings not only from the outside, from Assyria, but from within as well, from their own people. For the people were aware that they would bear the brunt of Assyrian wrath for obduracy or rebellion. It was around this same period that Assyria first began to employ the terror tactics of population massacres and deportations. No longer were just the king of a conquered people and the members of his court murdered or carted off into exile; now a policy of large-scale massacres and deportations of whole cities and peoples began. The practice did not simply arise from a particularly cruel and sadistic streak in the Assyrians; it was clearly intended as a propaganda technique to terrorize and frighten other cities and peoples into compliance and submission.

This shift in the foreign policy and practice of the major imperial power of the day seems reflected in the imagery and metaphor Israel's prophets used to describe their role and function. From Amos on, the recipients of their messages, the ones to whom they were sent, were no longer individual rulers and kings, but the people of Israel as a whole. Thus, we do not have extensive information about the words of the earlier so-called preaching prophets. These words were spoken mainly in private, in the presence of the king and possibly his court, and preserved, if at all, in the royal archives. Instead, we have stories *about* these prophets. By contrast, once prophets such as Amos begin to address the people as a whole, their messages were spoken in public for all to hear. They were preserved and published, especially if, as often proved to be the case, the warnings and announcements of impending doom and disaster proved accurate.

THE PREACHING PROPHETS

Scholars used to identify the rise of prophecy in Israel as coincidental with the move to the monarchy, as if the newly established institution of kingship needed some kind of corresponding charismatic office to challenge and

A group of three deportees—two men and a boy—from a relief
from the palace of Ashurbanipal (668-630 B.C.E.) in Nineveh.
Note that the Assyrians first introduced systematic mass deportations as a matter of policy.

critique it. Now, however, it is more widely recognized that the history and
antecedents of prophecy during the monarchy stretch back possibly to the
earliest days of Israel. It may not be simply an anachronism that the title of
prophet is applied to figures such as Moses (Dt 34:10), Aaron (Ex 7:1),
Miriam (Ex 15:20), and Deborah (Jgs 4:4), for example. It is also clear that
prophecy developed different forms and functioned in different ways at various points in Israel's history, down to the time that it seems to have disappeared early in the post-Exilic period.

During the later years of the tribal confederation, especially during the
Philistine crisis, groups appeared on the scene called the *bene nebi'im,* literally "sons of the prophets." A better translation is "members of
prophetic guilds" or "professional prophets" or "prophetic disciples." The
prophet-judge figure Samuel is described as exercising a kind of supervi-
sory role over various groups of these *bene nebi'im* (see 1 Sm 19:20), and
Saul also had some contacts with them (1 Sm 10:5-12; 19:18-24). The

function of these prophetic groups during this period may well have been to encourage and rally the tribes to continue their resistance against the Philistines. With the destruction of the major pilgrimage center at Shiloh, the poor example of some elements of the Levitical priesthood, such as the sons of Eli (see 1 Sm 2:12-36) and other anomalies caused strains within the tribal confederation. A revivalist movement such as these groups may represent would have served to counteract the disillusionment and discouragement brought on by the Philistine threat.

Note, for example, the role of Deborah "the prophetess" in rallying the northern tribes against Jabin and Sisera in Judges 4-5, or Gideon, who also received divine communication and used divining techniques (Jgs 6-7). He played a key role in organizing resistance against the Midianites.

With the coming of the monarchy the function of these groups appears to have changed. For one thing, the popular stories told of Elijah (1 Kgs 17-2 Kgs 2:12) and Elisha (1 Kgs 19; 2 Kgs 2-10, 13) reveal situations of fairly widespread suffering and distress among the majority of the population as a result of the worsening socio-economic conditions under the monarchy. The concrete instances of individuals suffering from famine, disease, and poverty may well be representative of more pervasive conditions among the majority of Israelites. 2 Kings 4:1-7, for instance, tells the story of the miraculous increase of oil by Elisha on behalf of the wife of one of the prophetic guild members. She is able to sell the oil and save her two children from being seized and sold as slaves by an unscrupulous creditor. 2 Kings 6:1-6 recounts how Elisha miraculously recovered a metal axe head for use among his prophetic guild. In the straitened economic conditions of the time, the loss of such a valuable item could have proven crucial for the ability to survive. The stories associated with these prophets and the prophetic groups with which they were associated may be typical of the situations faced by large numbers of Israelites under the monarchy. The stories also illustrate one of the roles these prophetic guilds could play. They acted as agents and catalysts in building solidarity and providing *ad hoc* structures for self-help, cooperation, and relief to offset the erosion of the older institutions created for these purposes.

A second function of these prophetic groups during the earlier days of the monarchy would have been to offer support and encouragement to members such as Elijah and Elisha who engaged in political action and criticism. There was clearly no hesitancy on the part of these personages to involve themselves actively or even to intervene in a decisive and directive role in the political life of Israel. We see, for example, that Elijah intervened in the story of the unlawful seizure of Naboth's vineyard by Ahab and Jezebel, fearlessly condemning Ahab's action (1 Kgs 21). And Elisha engaged in what could be considered an implicitly treasonous act. He sent a member of his prophetic group to anoint the Israelite general Jehu as king, announcing in the process the overthrow of King Joram and the extinction of the Omride dynasty. Such a gesture might not have been simply an announcement but an instigation to and support of a revolt against the Omrides (2 Kgs 9).

REVIEW QUESTIONS

1. What tendency in Christian tradition contributed to the reduction of the prophets to one-dimensional figures? How has this been corrected in recent decades?

2. What is the most common term in the Old Testament for "prophet"? What seems to be its primary meaning?

3. Describe hepatoscopy and the various roles of charismatic personalities in a society.

4. Who was Balaam? Why is he important for understanding Israelite prophecy?

5. Discuss briefly Canaanite ecstatic prophecy and the prophecy roles revealed in the texts discovered at Mari.

6. Why is research into the Ancient Near Eastern background of Israelite prophecy important?

7. The Israelite prophets understood and described their role as "a messenger of the divine assembly." What *kind* of language is this? What is its mythological background?

8. How does Isaiah describe his mission as a prophet (Is 6)?

9. What two important characteristics of Israelite prophecy are evident as well in Isaiah 6?

10. What question was often central to the frequent clashes between prophets and kings? How did prophets and kings differ in their answer to this question?

11. What shift in Israelite prophecy had taken place by the time of the prophet Amos in the eighth century B.C.E.? How might this shift reflect a corresponding shift in the political policies of Assyria?

12. Who were the *benē nebī'īm* ("sons of the prophets")? What role did they play during the later years of the tribal confederation? What two functions did they have with the coming of the monarchy?

16

The Eighth-Century B.C.E. Prophets: Amos and Hosea

Suggested Bible Readings: Amos 2-4; 6-9; Hosea 1-6; 9; 11-14

INTRODUCTION

A variety of contexts and institutions provided the setting within which prophecy functioned and developed in Israel. The roles the prophets played within these institutions and settings also varied with the times and within the historical circumstances. Two early and influential institutional settings for the development of prophetic speech included the Temple or shrine and the royal court. The massive amount of legislation in the Pentateuch suggests that the principal function at the Temple or shrine was the offering of sacrificial gifts. But a much greater variety of activity was, in fact, carried on there. Among other things, the Temple or shrine served as an important center for teaching and instruction. Both within and alongside public worship, extensive instruction in the law and traditions of Israel took place. During the days of the divided monarchy, for example, the shrines in the northern kingdom formed the setting for the development and elaboration of the instructional and exhortative style of Levitical preaching so typical of the Book of Deuteronomy.

People came to the shrines and the Jerusalem Temple for worship and instruction, and they also came at times seeking guidance and help from Yahweh. As persons in privileged communication with God, there seems to have been a regular and accepted role for the prophet to play in both a public and a private capacity as announcer of God's word, especially to individuals or to the assembled community who came to the shrines or Temple. The people came to hear the word God was addressing directly to them, whether a word of comfort and encouragement or one of challenge and warning.

Besides the shrine or Temple, another early setting for prophetic activity was the royal court. Israel's kings had prophets attached to their court whom they consulted regularly for advice and for direction from Yahweh on what courses of action they should follow. The prophet Nathan, for example, played a key role in the life of David's court. He advised against the building of a temple and delivered the crucial "dynastic oracle" assuring the stability of the House of David's rule over Judah:

The LORD also reveals to you that he will establish a house for you. And when your time comes and you rest with your ancestors, I will raise up your heir after you, sprung from your loins, and I will make his kingdom firm. It is he who shall build a house for my name. And I will make his royal throne firm forever. I will be a father to him, and he shall be a son to me. . . . I will not withdraw my favor from him as I withdrew it from your predecessor Saul, whom I removed from my presence. Your house and your kingdom shall endure forever before me; your throne shall stand firm forever (2 Sm 7:11-16).

Nathan also accused David and condemned his double sin of adultery and murder in the Bathsheba episode (2 Sm 11-12, especially 2 Sm 12:1-15). Nathan's words of judgment and condemnation here are in sharp contrast to the words of the "dynastic oracle":

Then Nathan said to David: ". . . Thus says the LORD God of Israel: 'I anointed you king of Israel. I rescued you from the hand of Saul. . . . Why have you spurned the Lord and done evil in his sight? You have cut down Uriah the Hittite with your own sword; you took his wife as your own, and him you killed with the sword of the Ammonites. Now, therefore, the sword shall never depart from your house, because you have despised me and taken the wife of Uriah to be your wife'" (2 Sm 12:7, 9-10).

Early in Israel's life, however, it appears that in addition to these two institutional settings, prophecy took on an independent role as an institution in its own right within Israelite society. It achieved an identity and played a key role of criticism and of opposition to abuses and to the often arrogant and oppressive measures of the monarchical establishment. To engage in this important role within Israelite society, prophecy developed a whole range of speech forms and, later, literary forms. In addition, it borrowed and adapted forms from other contexts and institutional settings. From Israel's public worship, for example, it borrowed and adapted the hymn or song of praise, as we see in this passage from Isaiah:

> Sing to the LORD a new song,
>   his praise from the end of the earth:
> Let the sea and what fills it resound,
>   the coastlands, and those who dwell in them.
> Let the steppe and its cities cry out,
>   the villages where Kedar dwells;
> Let the inhabitants of Sela exult,
>   and shout from the top of the mountains.
> Let them give glory to the LORD,
>   and utter his praise in the coastlands (Is 42:10-12).

To accuse Israel of violations of the covenant law, the prophets borrowed and adapted the language of the courtroom. Chapter 6 of Micah, for example, begins with the words:

> Hear, then, what the LORD says:
> Arise, present your plea before the mountains,
>   and let the hills hear your voice!
> Hear, O mountains, the plea of the LORD,
>   pay attention, O foundations of the earth!
> For the LORD has a plea against his people,
>   and he enters into trial with Israel.

But Israelite prophecy also had its own unique speech forms, the basic and most characteristic of which was the *prophetic oracle*. The prophetic oracle was a short utterance in poetic form, usually preceded or followed by the formula, "Thus says Yahweh," or "It is Yahweh who speaks." It thus represented a message or communication directly from God, which the prophet had been commissioned to deliver. Examples from the preaching prophets include Samuel's rebuke of Saul in 1 Samuel 15:22-23:

> "Does the LORD so delight in holocausts and sacrifices
>   as in obedience to the command of the LORD?
> Obedience is better than sacrifice,
>   and submission than the fat of rams. . . .
> Because you have rejected the command of the LORD,
>   he, too, has rejected you as ruler."

Another example is provided by the passage quoted above, Nathan's "dynastic oracle."

The prophetic oracle was meant to be delivered orally and addressed to contemporaries. In the case of the preaching prophets the recipients of these oracles were generally the king or leaders of the people. But once we reach the time of Amos, the intended object of the prophets' preaching was the people as a whole. Thus the prophetic oracles were delivered publicly, and the practice of preserving and collecting them began. The intention behind their preservation was at least twofold. First, publishing the collection could be a way to reach a wider audience. Second, the warnings of imminent doom or the announcement of future salvation warranted the preservation of these words until the time they would prove accurate and thus would testify to the authenticity of the prophet's mission from God.

The practice of collecting and preserving the words of the prophets was an established practice for later generations of prophets such as Isaiah, who ordered his disciples to write down and preserve his words:

> The record is to be folded and the sealed instruction kept among my disciples. For I will trust in the LORD, who is hiding his face from the house of Jacob; yes, I will wait for him (Is 8:16-17).

Jeremiah also dictated his oracles to his disciples and to his amanuensis, Baruch, so that they could record his words for posterity (Jer 36).

This much we can say, then, with regard to the genesis and production of the prophetic books that have the names of prophets attached to them. Early in his career either the prophet himself or one or more of his disciples or collaborators began writing down his oracles, which had originally been proclaimed orally to a live audience. The question becomes more complex, however, once we move beyond this initial stage. Scholars are only beginning to unravel the complicated compositional process and to understand some of the techniques in the production of the prophetic books now found in the Hebrew Scriptures. We are dealing with a genre of literature and a process of composition quite unfamiliar to modern, and especially Western, understanding and tastes. There are a few things we can say, however, with a certain amount of confidence.

First, scholars have recognized the importance of the role of disciples (or collaborators) in the collection and preservation of a prophet's words. For major figures such as Isaiah, for example, it seems that a "school" formed around him which lasted at least two hundred years into the Exilic and post-Exilic periods. Besides editing and handing on Isaiah's oracles, the members of his school added the words of at least two later prophets (Is 40-55;

Is 56-66) who, though they lived more than 150 years after the great Isaiah, wrote very much in his spirit.

Besides the recognition of the importance of prophetic disciples and schools, scholars have learned much about some of the techniques and principles followed in composing and editing the prophetic books. One obvious technique was collecting material on the basis of common subject matter, for example, the series of oracles against Tyre in Ezekiel 26-28 or the oracles against Egypt in Ezekiel 29-32. Another technique was grouping sayings on the basis of a "catchword," for example, the sayings containing the word "idol" in Ezekiel 6 (vv. 4, 6, 9, 13).

Using these and similar techniques and following principles we are only beginning to understand, later generations added to, reworked, and even rewrote the earlier prophetic materials so that they would continue to speak in fresh, new, and relevant ways. In the years after the Babylonian Exile, after the Pentateuch or the Law had reached its final form, the second major collection of Israel's religious heritage, the Prophets, was added to the Law. The Prophets included the Former Prophets, that is, the Deuteronomistic History, and the Latter Prophets, that is, the prophetic books as such. First among these Latter Prophets come the three longest books, the Book of the Prophet Isaiah, the Book of the Prophet Jeremiah, and the Book of the Prophet Ezekiel. Following these three longer books credited to individual prophets are twelve shorter prophetic works gathered into a collection known as the Book of the Twelve or the Minor Prophets.

AMOS

The Book of Amos provides a good example of the way in which our present prophetic books were formed. At its origin lies the eighth-century prophet Amos himself, a towering figure whose life, words, and activity had a profound impact on the people of his day. Amos launched a new and vigorous movement in Israel that lasted for hundreds of years. This movement resulted in a whole series of prophetic texts produced both by individual prophets and by the groups of disciples that came after them.

In the case of the prophet Amos, scholars have been able to discern up to six stages in the formation of the book attributed to him. The prophet's own words, spoken in the mid-eighth century B.C.E., constitute the first of these stages. The post-Exilic period, some three or four hundred years later, forms the final stage. The stages have been simplified and focused by one recent commentator into three periods of composition or editing. These include (1) the prophet Amos himself addressing the people of the northern kingdom of Israel in the mid-eighth century B.C.E.; (2) a reworking and expansion of Amos's words, now edited and arranged to address the southern kingdom of Judah in the late seventh century B.C.E.; and (3) a final revision of the book during the late Exilic or post-Exilic period. This third stage has the Jews in the Exile or recently returned from the Exile in Babylon as the intended audience.

A key to understanding Amos is found in the socio-economic situation to which he addressed himself. True, his message was couched in religious terms and arises out of a profound religious experience and consequent moral outrage. But that moral outrage was provoked by the suffering and hardship he saw around him. Further, that outrage was compounded by the heartbreaking realization that the injustice in Israelite society had already doomed his world to extinction. Thus, despite the religious nature and foundation of his preaching, Amos's message is inextricably bound up with and directed at the socio-economic and, by implication, the political situation of the community in which he lived.

What exactly was the nature of that suffering and hardship with which Amos was confronted, and what was the nature of the injustice that lay at its roots and was so harshly condemned by him? We have already described the socio-economic and political situation in the northern kingdom during the days of Jeroboam II (786-746 B.C.E.). The threat from the imperial ambitions of Assyria was temporarily in retreat and the monarchic state of Israel was enjoying a time of expansion and prosperity equal to if not greater than in the days of Solomon. However, the profound changes introduced into Israelite society with the full-scale monarchical apparatus under David and Solomon paved the way for a stratification of the Israelite social order. These changes were reaching their logical issue by the time of Amos. Wealth and resources, as well as social and political power, were being concentrated in the hands of an ever smaller, wealthier, and more arrogant ruling class.

One practice that particularly irked Amos was the accumulation of properties into large estates by wealthy individuals and families. One of the foundation stones of the socio-economic order under the tribal confederation had been the possession by each extended family of its own dwelling and plot of land sufficient to provide the basic necessities of life to its members. In addition to this were the provisions for mutual aid and support among the extended families of a clan, among the clans which formed each of the tribes, and finally among the tribes themselves within the larger confederation. Israel's foundational vision had been that of a people joined together in the common project of building a just and peaceful community guided by and animated by their covenant loyalty to their common God, Yahweh. That vision had been grounded on the right of access to the sources of life's basic necessities and the provisions for mutual aid. Both of these foundation stones were being crushed and thrown by the wayside. Motivated by greed and a lust for power, and intent on aping the elegant and arrogant trappings of the court and ruling classes of imperial powers like Assyria, the nobility and rich merchant classes of the northern kingdom ignored the covenant obligations toward their fellow Israelites. Instead of low or no-interest loans to help a family through a period of economic hardship brought on by drought, for example, they charged exorbitant interest rates, often 50 percent or more. When people could not pay, they seized the land and either evicted the occupants or reduced them to a state of near slavery as tenant farmers. This is the background of an oracle such as that found in chapter 2:6-7 of the Book of Amos:

> Thus says the LORD:
> For three crimes of Israel, and for four,
>   I will not revoke my word;
> Because they sell the just man for silver,
>   and the poor man for a pair of sandals.
> They trample the heads of the weak
>   into the dust of the earth,
>   and force the lowly out of the way.

Added to the sharp and questionable economic practices were also the outright unjust and extortionist tactics Amos exposes:

> Hear this, you who trample upon the needy
>   and destroy the poor of the land!
> "When will the new moon be over," you ask,
>   "that we may sell our grain,
>   and the sabbath, that we may display the wheat?
> We will diminish the ephah,
>   add to the shekel,
>   and fix our scales for cheating!
> We will buy the lowly man for silver,
>   and the poor man for a pair of sandals;
>   even the refuse of the wheat we will sell!" (Am 8:4-6).

The landowners also added to the hardships of the population by shifting the way the land was used. When controlled by the extended families, the properties were devoted to crops which they themselves ultimately used and consumed, especially grains such as wheat and barley. As the land came under the control of the large estate owners, however, tenants were forced to turn the land over more and more to the growing of crops such as grapes and olives for the production of luxury commodities like wine and oil. These luxury commodities were destined for the ruling groups themselves and for export and sale in exchange for imported luxury items such as carved ivory furniture, jewelry, perfumes, and so on.

As they increased their land holdings and wealth, the ruling classes also increased their social and political power. They were eventually able to enforce the levying of taxes in order to siphon off even more wealth from the larger population, and thus added further to their burdens. During these "prosperous" and "peaceful" years of Jeroboam II's reign in Israel, it was a small number, perhaps 5 percent at the most, who enjoyed this "prosperity" and "peace." As more and more of the surplus production of the society came under their control, they used it to support the wasteful and luxurious lifestyle so vividly described and condemned by Amos:

> Lying upon beds of ivory,
> stretched comfortably on their couches,
> They eat lambs taken from the flock,
> and calves from the stall!
> Improvising to the music of the harp,
> like David, they devise their own accompaniment.
> They drink wine from bowls
> and anoint themselves with the best oils. . . .
> Therefore, now they shall be the first to go into exile,
> and their wanton revelry shall be done away with.
> (Am 6:4-7; see also 3:15; 4:1)

The surplus production which had come under their control was also used to finance a military to maintain the necessary internal control over the subservient population and to carry on external wars in a game of make-believe imperialism:

> Proclaim this in the castles of Ashdod,
> in the castles of the land of Egypt:
> "Gather about the mountain of Samaria,
> and see the great disorders within her,
> the oppression in her midst."
> For they know not how to do what is right,
> says the LORD,
> Storing up in their castles
> what they have extorted and robbed.
> Therefore, thus says the Lord GOD:

> An enemy shall surround the land,
> and strip you of your strength,
> and pillage your castles (Am 3:9-11; see also 2:14-16).

Finally, the surplus wealth extorted from the larger population went into lavish liturgical displays intended to hide under the legitimating cloak of Yahwistic ritual the unjust order these ruling groups were responsible for creating:

> On that day, says the Lord GOD . . . I will turn your feasts
>   into mourning
> and all your songs into lamentations (Am 8:9-10).

Unlike the earlier prophets such as Elijah and Elisha, about whom we have some biographical information, we know practically nothing about Amos other than the approximate dates of his preaching (Jeroboam II's reign, 786-746 B.C.E.; see Am 7:11); his origin in Tekoa, a little village some twelve miles south of Jerusalem (Am 1:1); and his earlier occupation as a shepherd and agricultural worker (Am 7:14-15). Only one actual incident from Amos's life is recorded in the book, the confrontation between Amos and the priest Amaziah in the royal shrine at Bethel which is narrated in Amos 7:10-17.

A careful reading of Amos's words, however, reveals two important insights into his character. First, it is clear that he had experienced an encounter with God so overwhelming that it empowered him courageously to challenge and condemn the injustices he saw around him and to proclaim the imminent and inevitable end of the little world of which he was a part. Second, he had been born and brought up in the rural village of Tekoa, where the traditions and practices of the tribal confederation days were still alive and practiced insofar as the structural institutions of the monarchy had not eroded or destroyed them. He was deeply imbued with the old ideals of the just and egalitarian social order that those traditions and practices attempted to embody. His life among the villagers as a shepherd and agricultural worker had given him firsthand experience of the destructive pressures and deep suffering his people were undergoing as a result of the injustices fostered and carried out by the elite ruling classes. The "peace" the ruling elite was enjoying was a result of the war they were carrying on against the large majority of their fellow Israelites, and the "prosperity" they enjoyed came at the expense of the destitution and suffering of the many. Amos's encounter with God was thus an experience that issued in a call to denounce these injustices and to proclaim the imminent end of that society.

We do not know what finally became of Amos. But his words were remembered, perhaps recorded by a collaborator or disciple, and later, during the period of the Deuteronomic reform under Josiah (640-609 B.C.E.), they were reworked and added to in order to speak to a new situation. This time the editor addresses Amos's words to the southern kingdom, to Judah, where conditions and injustices paralleled the situation of the northern kingdom a century earlier. But the message of unrelenting doom is mitigated, apparently because the editor/author harbored a hope that the Deuteronomic reform would result in changes that would alleviate some of the injustices. Such was not to be the case, however. The southern kingdom was also swept away by the tide of imperial conquests that engulfed again and again this vulnerable land.

Finally, yet another generation would find inspiration and meaning in the words of Amos. This time, humbled and renewed by the disastrous destruction of the old order, the exiles returning from Babylon in 539 B.C.E. and thereafter found comfort and hope in the clear proclamation of God's justice that the words of Amos contained. This third and final reworking and expansion of the book made that hope explicit. The message of unrelenting doom in the original words of Amos was thus softened. But the proclamation of Yahweh as a just God, who stands by and rescues the suffering and oppressed, again and again speeding to their aid, comes through as forcefully and explicitly as ever.

HOSEA

Hosea's prophetic career also took place in the northern kingdom of Israel. He was a younger contemporary of Amos, perhaps inspired by and following the model of Amos's forthright and courageous public preaching. The political situation Hosea faced, however, had evolved from the days of Amos. Assyria's ominous shadow loomed over Israel. Political turmoil marked these closing years of the northern kingdom, from the death of Jeroboam II in 745 B.C.E. until the end of the kingdom in 722 B.C.E. Six different kings sat on Israel's throne during these twenty-three years, four of their reigns ending by assassination. It was within this context of turmoil and uncertainty that Hosea preached, and his words suggest a widespread attitude of disillusionment and self-interest, especially among the ruling elite. While his career seems to coincide mainly with these final years of the northern kingdom, Hosea may have survived the collapse of 722 B.C.E. Although a contemporary of Amos, facing a similar but evolving political and socio-economic situation, Hosea's preaching has its own qualities and distinctiveness. Amos, as we have seen, was sharply critical of the injustices of the contemporary social order and especially of the injustices perpetrated by the ruling classes:

> Woe to those who turn judgment to wormwood
> and cast justice to the ground!
> They hate him who reproves at the gate
> and abhor him who speaks the truth.
> Therefore, because you have trampled upon the weak
> and exacted of them levies of grain,
> Though you have built houses of hewn stone,
> you shall not live in them!
> Though you have planted choice vineyards,
> you shall not drink their wine!
> (Am 5:7, 10-11; see also 5:12-13)

Hosea likewise spoke out against these injustices (see Hos 4:1-2; 12:8), but unlike Amos, there is a note of hope with Hosea. The demise of the present order is inevitable, according to this prophet. In this he agrees with Amos. However, Hosea looks beyond the collapse and sees new possibilities on the horizon. The period following the collapse holds out the hope of rebirth. It will be in some ways a return to the wilderness, to the desert, but a wilderness and desert like the wilderness and desert in which Israel was born. It will be an opportunity for repentance and rebirth. Hosea's hope is founded on his firm conviction and trust in the mercy and love of Yahweh. It was that mercy and love that brought Israel into being in the first place, when Yahweh took pity on the people crying out in their misery in the slavery of Egypt.

> When Israel was a child I loved him,
> out of Egypt I called my son. . . .
> It was I who taught Ephraim to walk,
> who took them in my arms;
> I drew them with human cords,
> with bands of love;
> I fostered them like one
> who raises an infant to his cheeks.
> (Hos 11:1, 3-4)

If Israel repents, there is the hope that Yahweh will once again renew that mercy and love. But such a renewal will take place only *after* the inevitable demise of the present order and only *if* Israel repents.

Amos's focus was on nature imagery as a vehicle for his message. His experience as a shepherd and agricultural worker had provided him with a whole stock of analogies and comparisons to illumine the historical experience and social injustices that were the target of his condemnations: the lion's roar of triumph over its quarry (Am 3:4), the bird caught in the trap (Am 3:5), the realities and hardships of drought (Am 4:7-8). Hosea also employed metaphors and similes derived from agriculture and nature:

> For I am like a lion to Ephraim,
>   like a young lion to the house of Judah;
> It is I who rend the prey and depart,
>   I carry it away and no one can save it from me.
>   (Hos 5:14; see also 7:11-12)

But more prominent in Hosea are images involving human relationships, especially as those relationships mirror God's relationship with Israel and with each Israelite. Perhaps the most well-known and distinctive aspect of Hosea is his use of the marriage metaphor in chapters 1-3 to illumine and add new dimensions to Israel's covenant relationship with God:

> Therefore I will hedge in her way with thorns
>   and erect a wall against her,
>   so that she cannot find her paths.
> If she runs after her lovers, she shall not overtake them;
>   if she looks for them she shall not find them.
> Then she shall say,
>   "I will go back to my first husband,
>   for it was better with me than now. . . ."
> So I will allure her;
>   I will lead her into the desert
>   and speak to her heart. . . .
> I will espouse you to me forever:
>   I will espouse you in right and in justice,
>   in love and in mercy;
> I will espouse you in fidelity,
>   and you shall know the LORD (Hos 2:8-9, 16, 21-22).

The father-son imagery of chapter 11 is also a powerful and popular description of God's love and concern for his people.

Hosea stresses images and language involving human relationships to mirror God's relationship with Israel. This may represent an implicit move by the prophet to counteract the frantic and self-centered attitude of so many in Israel during the confusion and disorientation of the closing years of the monarchy. This stress by Hosea may also have served to strengthen and recommend those older traditional family, clan, and tribal ties that were an important part of the institutional infrastructure from the days of the tribal confederacy; these family ties were the vehicles for mutual aid and support in times of hardships. With the imminent collapse of the state apparatus, what remained of these older institutions and networks would be important if not essential to those who would manage to survive the storm.

The powerful language of God's love and mercy in the covenant relationship with Israel (see Hos 2:18-20) is easily transferable to the personal level of the individual's relationship with God:

> I will espouse you to me forever:
> I will espouse you in right and in justice,
> in love and in mercy;
> I will espouse you in fidelity,
> and you shall know the LORD (Hos 2:21-22).

Hosea began to develop that dimension of biblical tradition as the necessary correlate and support of the social dimensions of the people of Israel's relationship and obligations to their God.

Finally, passages such as Hosea 1-3 clearly reveal the obviously patriarchal nature of Israelite society. On the one hand, the introduction by Hosea of the marriage metaphor as an image for God's relationship with Israel was a great enrichment for the biblical tradition. It would be taken up and developed by later generations. On the other hand, the patriarchal form of that marriage metaphor, with its clear subordination of the woman, has too often itself become the message and been used to justify and legitimate the subordination and oppression of women.

Repentance and Return

The book of Hosea received its final form at the hands of an editor during the Babylonian Exile. He gave the book its present three-fold structure by adding chapters three, eleven, and fourteen. Each of the chapters concludes one part of the book by emphasizing a different aspect of human repentance and divine forgiveness. The first part of the book, chapters 1 through 3, presents a story about the God/Israel relationship through the metaphor of husband (God)/wife (Israel). The wife's (Israel's) return to her husband (God) in chapter 3 symbolizes Israel's repentance or return to God: "Then the people of Israel shall turn back and seek the LORD, their God, and David, their king. They shall come trembling to the LORD and to his bounty, in the last days" (Hos 3:5).

The second part of the book, chapters 4 through 11, makes use of the parent/child metaphor in describing Israel's relationship with God. In chapter 11, the wayward son is welcomed back by the parents, symbolically representing God's mercy and forgiveness in welcoming back Israel:

> How could I give you up, O Ephraim,
> or deliver you up, O Israel?
> How could I treat you as Admah,
> or make you like Zeboiim?
> My heart is overwhelmed,
> my pity is stirred (Hos 11:8).

The third and final section, chapters 12 through 14, weaves together both the child/parent and husband/wife metaphors. The section concludes with chapter 14's celebration of a repentant Israel's renewed abundance in a restored land following the return from exile in Babylon:

> I will be like the dew for Israel:
> he shall blossom like the lily;
> He shall strike root like the Lebanon cedar,
> and put forth his shoots.
> His splendor shall be like the olive tree
> and his fragrance like the Lebanon cedar.
> Again they shall dwell in his shade
> and raise grain;
> They shall blossom like the vine,
> and his fame shall be like the wine of Lebanon.
> (Hos 14:6-8)

In fact, the theme of repentance/return to God in all three sections of the book evokes and highlights the hopes for an actual *physical* return journey home from exile:

> Out of Egypt they shall come trembling, like sparrows,
> from the land of Assyria, like doves;
> And I will resettle them in their homes,
> says the LORD (Hos 11:11).

REVIEW QUESTIONS

1. Describe the basic speech form of the Israelite prophets. How was it meant to be delivered, and to whom was it addressed?

2. Give two possible motivations for writing down the oracles of the "writing prophets."

3. Discuss the stages in the formation of the Book of Amos.

4. What is the key element in coming to understand the message of Amos?

5. What practice particularly irked Amos? What two aspects of Israel's originating vision did this practice attack?

6. List three ways the ruling classes in Israel made use of the surplus production that came under their control.

7. What two important insights into Amos's character are revealed by a study of his words?

8. Describe briefly the historical context of Hosea's prophetic career.

9. How did Hosea's message differ from that of Amos?

10. Describe the images and language that appear especially prominent in the preaching of Hosea. In what way might the historical situation have influenced his choice of images and language?

11. What metaphors dominate the three parts of the book of Hosea in its final (exilic) form? Explain the author's play on the double meaning of return/ repentance.

17

Isaiah

Suggested Bible Readings: 2 Kings 16-20; Isaiah 1-12; 28-32

ISAIAH AND HIS SUCCESSORS

The importance of Isaiah as a person and as a prophet is witnessed by the forty-year duration of his prophetic career. It is obvious also from the fact that, with its sixty-six chapters, the Book of the Prophet Isaiah is the largest compendium of prophetic texts in the Hebrew Bible. Finally, the prophet's stature and reputation gave impetus and inspiration to a two-hundred-year (700-500 B.C.E.) tradition of reflection, writing, and preaching that was associated with his name and spirit.

Isaiah's life as a prophet began with his call from Yahweh; "in the year King Uzziah died," he tells us in his unforgettable narrative of that experience (Is 6). It continued through the reigns of Jotham (742-732 B.C.E.) and Ahaz (732-715 B.C.E.). His career as a prophet lasted until the punitive invasion of Judah and siege of Jerusalem by the Assyrian king, Sennacherib, in 701 B.C.E. under King Hezekiah (715-686 B.C.E.). Although Isaiah's own activity as a prophet concluded in 701 B.C.E., his spirit and influence continued in a circle or school which preserved, added to, and reworked his prophecies down into the post-Exilic period. Historical-critical scholarship has been able to determine that the words of the great prophet are found principally in the first thirty-nine chapters of the book that bears his name.

Chapters 40-55 come from the hand of an anonymous prophet who stood in the tradition of the "historical" Isaiah and who brought a message of hope and deliverance to the Jews in Exile in Babylon somewhere between 551 and 539 B.C.E. Since we do not know this anonymous figure's name, scholars have traditionally referred to him as Deutero-Isaiah (or the Second Isaiah). We will say more about these chapters when we discuss the Babylonian Exile.

Finally, the last ten chapters of the book are the work of an anonymous prophet or prophets from the early post-Exilic period (after 539 B.C.E.). This section is often called Trito-Isaiah (Third Isaiah). We will focus at this point on the words and activity of the "historical" Isaiah, especially those words and actions associated with two key moments in Israel's history during Isaiah's lifetime: the Syro-Ephraimite Crisis (735 B.C.E.), and the invasion of Sennacherib (701 B.C.E.).

THE POWER AND SUBTLETY OF ISAIAH'S POETRY

The stature and influence that Isaiah had as a human being and as a prophet among his contemporaries and disciples and the profound impact he was to have on future generations is borne out by an examination of his poetry. These texts are characterized by their power, subtlety, complexity, and breadth of vision. Complexity can be seen, first of all, in his poetry's often biting irony. We find a good example of this irony in the beautiful poem in chapter 9:1-6, written perhaps on the occasion of the coronation of Hezekiah. Isaiah gives us a moving description of the possibilities for a just, peaceful, and life-giving society under the rule of a righteous king:

> The people who walked in darkness
>   have seen a great light;
> Upon those who dwelt in the land of gloom
>   a light has shown.
> You have brought them abundant joy
>   and great rejoicing,
> As they rejoice before you as at the harvest,
>   as men make merry when dividing spoils.
> For the yoke that burdened them,
>   the pole on their shoulder,
> And the rod of their taskmaster
>   you have smashed, as on the day of Midian. . . .
> For a child is born to us, a son is given us;
>   upon his shoulder dominion rests.
> They name him Wonder-Counselor, God-Hero,
>   Father-Forever, Prince of Peace.
> His dominion is vast
>   and forever peaceful,
> From David's throne, and over his kingdom,
>   which he confirms and sustains

By judgment and justice,
    both now and forever.
The zeal of the LORD of hosts will do this! (Is 9:1-3, 5-6).

The vision of such a society, however, only partially conceals the cutting edge of irony the passage contains. Judean society and the rule of Davidic royalty was greatly at odds with the vision Isaiah proclaims. Far from celebrating the accession of the new monarch, the poem functions as an indictment and condemnation of royal rule until that moment:

The LORD enters into judgment
    with his people's elders and princes:
It is you who have devoured the vineyard;
    the loot wrested from the poor is in your houses.
What do you mean by crushing my people,
    and grinding down the poor when they look to you?
    (Is 3:14-15; see also 1:12-17; 5:1-7, 8-10)

Isaiah's mention of a "remnant" that will survive the coming debacle (for example, Is 4:3-4; 5:13) served in his day as a dire warning of the imminent destruction. So great would be the disaster that it would almost totally annihilate the kingdom of Judah, the city of Jerusalem, and the house of David. It would be so total as to almost completely destroy life in the land. Yet later generations were able to seize upon that "almost" and Isaiah's words about "only a remnant" and see in them a reason for hope. They built around this phrase a message of consolation and mercy for the Jews in Exile and in the difficult days of the post-Exilic period.

The staggering breadth of Isaiah's vision forms another element that gives his poetry its power. He offers penetrating insights into both the implications of the decisions and policies of the Assyrian and Judean kings in the international arena. He also exposes, at the same time, the attitudes and decisions of the king and people in the depths of their own hearts. Further, he is able to show the links between the two. Isaiah's encounter with Ahaz is a good example of this (Is 7). Isaiah denounces the king's foreign policy decision of calling on Assyria for help and blames the *political* error on Ahaz's *personal* lack of trust in God. These elements of complexity, irony, dialectical thought, and breadth of vision gave example and direction to the later disciples, editors, and prophets who followed in Isaiah's footsteps. It was they who would eventually produce the final monumental work that stands at the head of the collection of the Latter Prophets in the Hebrew Bible.

THE UNRELENTING DOOM IN HIS MESSAGE

Isaiah's own oracles were understandably judgmental. He preached a message of imminent doom and disaster for both the northern and southern kingdoms and then, after the fall of the northern kingdom, he continued his warnings to Judah and Jerusalem. The power politics the king of Judah and ruling classes were engaged in, their futile attempt to gain advantages for themselves by playing off Egypt, Assyria, and Babylon against one another, were doomed to failure. This game they so obsessively took part in revealed their own inner attitudes of pride, selfishness, and greed. Their lust for power and wealth undermined the very foundations of the community's life and resulted in the exploitation and suffering of the majority of the people of the country. A society built on equality, with institutions encouraging and enforcing mutual aid and social justice, seemed farther and farther from realization. The outcome could only be failure and disaster for the nation as a whole.

Isaiah could see no hope for a change of heart within the leadership. Therefore his message was one of imminent doom. If there was any reason for the least hope, for example, the survival of a "remnant," it would only be possible *after* the debacle and *if* there proved to be a change of heart as a result of the disaster.

ISAIAH AND THE ROYAL/DAVIDIC
AND JERUSALEM/ZION TRADITIONS

We mentioned above that David's establishment of a capital in Jerusalem led to a coopting of the Canaanite elements of the city's religious traditions. This resulted in a greatly expanded range of imagery and motifs and expressive power in Yahwism. This imagery and these motifs included mythological elements such as the "garden of God" and "divine mountain" (see Gn 2-3; Ez 28, 31), motifs about creation in terms of the victory of the creator God over chaos (e.g., Is 51:9-10; Ps 19:9-11; Jb 9:13; 26:12-13); the centrality and permanence of Mt. Zion/Jerusalem as the abode of God on earth and the source of life and prosperity (e.g., Ps 46; 48). To these was added the covenant with David promising an unending dynasty (2 Sm 7). Isaiah draws extensively on this language and imagery, probably because of his close association with Jerusalem and its royal and cultic traditions. He does this in preference to the Mosaic/Sinai themes dominant in the earlier northern prophets, Amos and Hosea. We have already pointed to Isaiah's "coronation hymn," which heralded the possibilities for a society promised by a just and righteous ruler. Elsewhere

Jerusalem/Zion is hailed as a potential model and a source of prosperity and peace for all nations of the earth:

> In the days to come,
> The mountain of the LORD's house
>> shall be established as the highest mountain
>> and raised above the hills.
> All nations shall stream toward it;
>> many peoples shall come and say:
> "Come, let us climb the LORD's mountain,
>> to the house of the God of Jacob,
> That he may instruct us in his ways,
>> and we may walk in his paths."

Michelangelo's depiction of Isaiah from the Sistine Chapel.

> For from Zion shall go forth instruction,
>   and the word of the LORD from Jerusalem.
> He shall judge between the nations,
>   and impose terms on many peoples.
> They shall beat their swords into plowshares
>   and their spears into pruning hooks;
> One nation shall not raise the sword against another,
>   nor shall they train for war again.
>
> O house of Jacob, come,
>   let us walk in the light of the LORD! (Is 2:2-5)

Again, the duties of a righteous ruler are described:

> But a shoot shall sprout from the stump of Jesse,
>   and from his roots a bud shall blossom.
> The spirit of the LORD shall rest upon him:
>   a spirit of wisdom and understanding,
> A spirit of counsel and of strength,
>   a spirit of knowledge and of fear of the LORD,
>   and his delight shall be the fear of the LORD.
> Not by appearance shall he judge,
>   nor by hearsay shall he decide,
> But he shall judge the poor with justice,
>   and decide aright for the land's afflicted.
> He shall strike the ruthless with the rod of his mouth,
>   and with the breath of his lips he shall slay the wicked.
> Justice shall be the band around his waist,
>   and faithfulness a belt upon his hips (Is 11:1-5).

The passage goes on to proclaim a utopian vision of the peaceful and harmonious society which will result from such a righteous rule. Nature itself will mirror the harmony and concord of human society:

> Then the wolf shall be the guest of the lamb
>   and the leopard shall lie down with the kid;
> The calf and the young lion shall browse together,
>   with a little child to guide them.
> The cow and the bear shall be neighbors,
>   together their young shall rest;
>   the lion shall eat hay like the ox.

The baby shall play by the cobra's den,
  and the child lay his hand on the adder's lair.
There shall be no harm or ruin on all my holy mountain;
  for the earth shall be filled with knowledge of the LORD,
  as water covers the sea (Is 11:6-9).

As we pointed out above, for Isaiah these themes were played upon and employed with a profound and subtle sense of irony. They offer a utopian vision of a harmonious and peaceful and prosperous society centered upon Jerusalem and upon the Davidic king. These were juxtaposed with the actual situation, one of disharmony and of constant warfare resulting from the imperial ambitions of the ruling elite. Added to this was the glaring gulf between the life of luxury of the privileged few and the suffering, misery, and uncertainty of the vast majority. One must read between the lines of the present shape of the texts to catch this irony at work in the Isaian material.

Later generations employed these utopian elements in Isaiah in a different mode. For example, the Jews in exile in Babylon or the struggling community attempting to rebuild its society after the Exile in a devastated Judah and Jerusalem found in these texts a basis of hope and encouragement. They saw in these visions of a harmonious and prosperous and peaceful Zion a vision of the future toward which they struggled.

Today Christians read these powerful texts from Isaiah especially during Advent, a season of hope and of a turning toward the future. Again, the message they proclaim is a double-edged one. They can serve as an indictment and judgment on the present in proclaiming in forceful terms what *should* be the shape of our present society. These same texts can also function to hold out hope and a promise of what is possible to those who struggle for a more just and peaceful order.

ISAIAH'S FIRST PERIOD OF MINISTRY: THE SYRO-EPHRAIMITE CRISIS OF 735 B.C.E.

The collection of Isaiah's oracles headed by the account of his vocation narrative and gathered into Isaiah 6:1-8:18 forms the nucleus around which eventually the whole collection in Isaiah 1-12 was gathered. This nucleus is referred to by scholars variously as Isaiah's "Memoirs" or "Testimony," "The Book of Signs," or "The Book of Immanuel." It appears to have a precise historical setting, the Syro-Ephraimite Crisis of 735 B.C.E.

The background for this war was the growing strength of Assyria and the obvious intent of its leaders to expand their imperial rule westward to the

Mediterranean ports. In particular, they were eyeing the lucrative trade routes passing through the Syro-Palestinian corridor. To halt the Assyrian advance, the smaller city-states and kingdoms in this region joined together under the leadership of the northern kingdom of Israel and its king, Pekah (737-732 B.C.E.), and the kingdom of Damascus in Syria, headed by the Aramean king, Rezin.

The southern kingdom of Judah, however, was a weak link in this otherwise united front. Ahaz, King of Judah (732-715 B.C.E.), refused to join the alliance. Ahaz apparently felt that Judah was far enough away geographically from Assyria and from the coastal ports and trade routes that interested Assyria's rulers. Rezin and Pekah did not trust Ahaz, however. They feared that if Ahaz did not join the revolt, he could be pressured by Assyria to attack the coalition from the rear. Thus Pekah and Rezin prepared to mount an invasion of Judah either to force Ahaz into joining them or to remove him from the throne and put a more cooperative ruler in his place.

It is in the context of this threatened attack on Jerusalem by Pekah and Rezin that Isaiah encountered Ahaz while Ahaz was inspecting the work taking place on Jerusalem's defenses. Isaiah brought with him his son, who bore the symbolic name Shear-jashub, "A remnant shall return," and he announced the imminent birth of another whose name will be, again symbolically, Immanuel ("God is/will be with us"). Isaiah knew that Ahaz had three possible courses of action: (1) he could accede to the pressure Pekah and Rezin were bringing to bear on him and join the anti-Assyrian effort; (2) he could submit to Assyrian suzerainty, assume vassalship, and thus be assured of protection not only from Assyrian attack but also of Assyria's help against the threatened invasion by Pekah and Rezin; and (3) he could continue to hold a neutral course, not involving Judah in any foreign alliances, either against Assyria or with Assyria. Isaiah counseled, indeed commanded, Ahaz to choose the third option. Judah was covenanted with Yahweh and with Yahweh alone. Any other course of action—alliance with Pekah and Rezin, or submission to Assyria—would betray a lack of trust in Yahweh. Further, it would demonstrate a futile and prideful desire to try to gain some advantage by joining in the international power politics of the day.

The dramatic confrontation between Isaiah and Ahaz is described in chapters 7 and 8. Isaiah urges Ahaz to continue on the neutral course and trust in Yahweh as his covenant suzerain. Pekah and Rezin's alliance against him does not pose a threat: "It shall not stand, and it shall not come to pass" (Is 7:7). Both Israel and Damascus will eventually fall before the Assyrian onslaught:

Before the child knows how to call his father or mother by name, the wealth of Damascus and the spoil of Samaria shall be carried off by the king of Assyria (Is 8:4).

But if Ahaz joins the political power game, Assyria, like the flooding waters of the River Euphrates, will inundate and sweep away Ahaz and Judah along with Damascus and the northern kingdom of Israel:

> Therefore the LORD raises against them
>   the waters of the River, great and mighty
>   [the king of Assyria and all his power].
> It shall rise above all its channels,
>   and overflow all its banks;
> It shall pass into Judah, and flood it all throughout:
>   up to the neck it shall reach;
> It shall spread its wings
>   the full width of your land, Immanuel! (Is 8:7-8)

Ahaz must trust in Yahweh alone (*ta'amīnū*, "Unless you believe"), or he and Judah will surely fall (*lō tē'amēnū*, "you shall not stand"). Isaiah makes this promise, playing on the different meanings of the Hebrew root *'mn* "to believe, trust, stand firm" (Is 7:9).

Unfortunately Ahaz did not heed the command of Isaiah, speaking, as he claimed, in God's name. Out of fear and a lack of trust, he called on Assyria's aid and in the process submitted to Assyrian vassalship. This included installing Assyrian idols and rites in Yahweh's Temple in Jerusalem. By this action Ahaz implied that Assyrian might and pride, symbolized in its idols, were more powerful and more to be trusted than Israel's own god, Yahweh. He failed to be convinced that Isaiah's counsel was correct.

This illustrates what we said above about the breadth of Isaiah's vision. Isaiah was able to discern the lack of faith and trust in the heart of Ahaz, king of Judah. This lack of faith and trust found its counterpart and repercussions in the lack of insight and consequent error on the level of the relationship between peoples and nations. The two arenas are not sealed off from one another and governed by separate dynamics and codes of conduct and ethics. The same loving and merciful God is involved in and influencing both.

Isaiah's disappointment and apprehension at the results of Ahaz's failure to heed his prophecies are seen in Isaiah's command to his disciples to write down and seal up his words for future generations. They will read and understand that Isaiah indeed had spoken accurately. Isaiah then withdrew from public life until a second active period of involvement during the reign of Ahaz's son and successor, Hezekiah (715-686 B.C.E.). He returned in connection with the punitive invasion of Judah and siege of Jerusalem by the Assyrian king, Sennacherib (704-681 B.C.E.).

THE SENNACHERIB INVASION AND CRISIS, 705-701 B.C.E.

Hezekiah seems to have gradually reversed the pro-Assyrian policies of his father, Ahaz. At first he acted unobtrusively through cultic reforms, such as downplaying or removing the Assyrian elements his father had accepted into the Jerusalem Temple and ritual at the time of the submission to Assyria. Hezekiah enhanced and gave greater emphasis and attention to the centrality and worship of Yahweh. The intervening years had seen the fall of the northern kingdom of Israel to Assyria (722 B.C.E.), the destruction of its capital Samaria, and the incorporation of the northern kingdom's territory into the empire as an Assyrian province. The favorable attention of the Deuteronomistic historians to Hezekiah (see 2 Kgs 18-20) may be accounted for by Hezekiah's welcoming of the Deuteronomic reform elements fleeing from the collapse of the northern kingdom.

The anti-Assyrian policies of Hezekiah took a more serious and decisive turn, however, after the death of the Assyrian king Sargon II (721-705 B.C.E.). This event seems to have caused temporary confusion among the Assyrian leadership. Hezekiah seized on the opportunity and became the leader of a revolt by Syro-Palestinian states against Assyrian suzerainty. In this move he was opposed by Isaiah, who again saw it as a vain and prideful attempt at power politics. Instead of trust in foreign alliances and political intrigues, Isaiah again counseled a quiet and firm trust in Yahweh and a continuing loyalty to the covenant with Israel's *unique* suzerain: "In returning and rest you shall be saved; in quietness and trust shall be your strength" (Is 30:15).

Many of the oracles of Isaiah gathered in chapters 28-32 appear to come from this period of the Sennacherib Crisis (705-701 B.C.E.). Hezekiah foolishly believed that he could somehow gain freedom from Assyrian rule during the interregnum between the death of Sargon II and the accession of Sennacherib. Two of Assyria's enemies, Babylon to Assyria's southeast and Egypt to the southwest, fomented the rebellion against Assyria and promised help to the rebels (see the story of the delegation from the Babylonian king Merodach-baladan in Isaiah 39). Isaiah denounced these intrigues:

Woe to those who go down to Egypt for help,
who depend on horses;

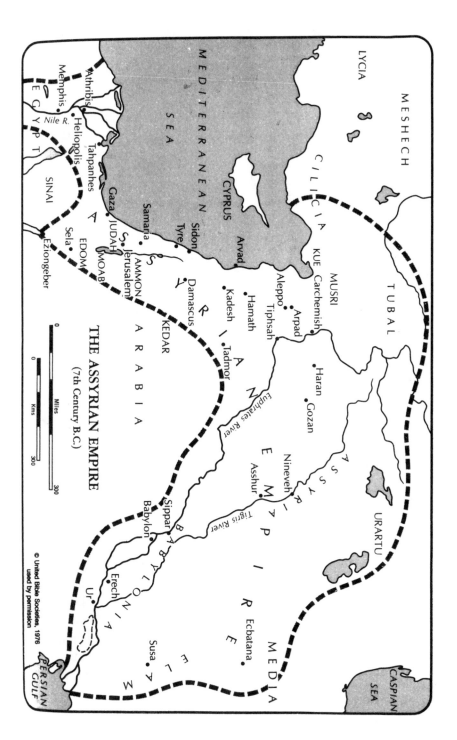

THE ASSYRIAN EMPIRE
(7th Century B.C.)

© United Bible Societies, 1976
used by permission

Who put their trust in chariots because of their number,
and in horsemen because of their combined power,
But look not to the Holy One of Israel
nor seek the LORD! (Is 31:1)

Isaiah, in fact, called the pact with Egypt a "covenant with death" (Is 28:15). Isaiah's reading of the situation proved correct. The promised support from Egypt and Babylon failed to materialize. The revolt was crushed by the new Assyrian king, Sennacherib. In 701 B.C.E. Judah itself was invaded and devastated. The vivid picture of the capture and destruction of Judah's second largest city, Lachish, can be seen today in the wall reliefs from Sennacherib's palace on display at the British Museum in London. It is also preserved in the archeological remains from the city of Lachish itself, which clearly testify to the terrible destruction and loss of life. Jerusalem alone, it seems, escaped destruction for some reason. Perhaps Sennacherib was worried about events back in Mesopotamia, dynastic problems, or concerns about Babylon. In any case he lifted the siege on Jerusalem and withdrew without attacking the city, but only after exacting a huge tribute.

Again, the breadth of Isaiah's vision had proven true. He had been able to see and bring together the affairs of state and international politics on the one hand, and the motives and movements of the human heart on the other, and to recognize in which direction the call of God's Spirit should have led.

ISAIAH AND THE "HOLY ONE" OF ISRAEL

We have examined the account of Isaiah's call to prophecy as an example both of the genre of the call narrative and of what it represents in expressing the prophet's overwhelming encounter with the deity. Isaiah's call speaks of a profound experience of God as the "Holy One." His vision of Yahweh as king seated upon "a high and lofty throne" includes the song of the seraphim with its threefold repetition, "Holy, holy, holy is Yahweh, God of the (heavenly) armies." Such a threefold repetition signifies in Hebrew the superlative, that is, Yahweh is "the holiest." Yahweh is the one "set apart"; this is Isaiah's way of conceptualizing and expressing his sense of God's transcendence. God, for Isaiah, embodies that element in human life and human history which is beyond human control or manipulation. It is an unseen yet benevolent and powerful presence; it represents, among other things, the accumulation of Israel's experience as a people. Their history reflects their constant struggle to discover those key elements necessary in building and preserving a community and society characterized by justice and harmony and providing a satisfying and productive life for *all* its members.

This sense of Yahweh's "holiness" pervaded Isaiah's oracles; his favorite designation for the deity was "the Holy One of Israel." The phrase captures something of the nature of the God whom he encountered in that overwhelming experience of his call. This manner of speaking about the deity as "the Holy One of Israel" was continued by those in Isaiah's circle or school over the next two hundred years as the traditions associated with this figure in Israel's history were meditated on and added to by others.

THE ISAIAH TRADITION AND THE BOOK OF ISAIAH

We have focused in this chapter on texts from Isaiah 1-39 that relate to the life and preaching of the eighth-century prophet, the "historical Isaiah." A later chapter (20) will look more closely at Isaiah 40-55, a collection of poems stemming from the so-called "Second Isaiah" (or Deutero-Isaiah), a sixth-century successor to the eighth-century prophet.

Despite the fact that the book was composed over the course of some four centuries (eighth to fifth centuries B.C.E.), scholars have recently begun

Prisoners, handcuffed together, are escorted by Assyrian guards, while another is executed. Relief from the palace of Sennacharib, Nineveh 690 B.C.E.

to pay more attention to the literary and thematic links among the various parts of the book. This approach better highlights the overall unity of the book. Thus, it has become more clear that the book of Isaiah as a whole, chapters 1-66, constitutes a single literary entity. Over the centuries, the collection of prophecies associated with the Isaiah tradition underwent revision and expansion. The book probably reached its final form in the time of Ezra and Nehemiah, in the fifth century B.C.E.

A number of links among the various sections of the book reinforce its basic unity. For example, catchwords connect chapter 1 and chapters 65 and 66. Such a repetition of words constitutes an inclusion or "envelope figure," a set of brackets at the beginning and end to bind the whole book together (for example, "ask" and "seek" in 1:12, 17 and 65:1; "sacrifice" in 1:11 and 65:3; 66:3). Other links include the portrayal of Babylon as a symbol of a world power arrayed against Yahweh in both earlier and later sections (for example, in chapters 14 and 47). Finally, the themes of "justice" (*mishpat*) and "righteousness" (*zedaqa*) permeate the entire text.

The book, taken as a whole, divides into two halves, chapters 1-33 and chapters 34-66. The first half looks ahead to judgment and eventual restoration. The second half announces that the judgment has ended and restoration has begun. In this sense, a continuity has been maintained from the "historical Isaiah" and his preaching in the eighth century through to the final compilation of traditions and teachings of his successors in the fifth century. Isaiah of the eighth century was a prophet announcing a message of salvation. It is this perspective that motivated and determined the growth of the book through to its completion.

The words of the "historical Isaiah" preserved in the text form a link with the past. But for those words to continue their relevance and their ability to speak to new groups and new generations, they needed revision and reformulation. Awareness and study of this traditioning process can be liberating. It frees us from focusing too closely on a fixed text from the past. It invites us to continue that same process of reinterpreting and rediscovering the liberating message of God's love and God's will for justice anew in every generation.

REVIEW QUESTIONS

1. Give three indications of the importance of Isaiah both as a prophet and as a person.

2. Describe the historical context within which Isaiah's prophetic career took place.

3. Discuss the character of Isaiah's poetry. Give an example of his use of irony and of the breadth of vision revealed in his poetry.

4. Why is there an unrelenting sense of doom and disaster at the heart of Isaiah's message?

5. How does Isaiah differ from Amos and Hosea in his choice of language and imagery to express his message? What was the source and background of Isaiah's language and imagery?

6. What are the contrasting roles of the utopian elements in Isaiah's poetry? Could they play a similar role for us today?

7. How do scholars characterize the material in Isaiah 6:1-8:18? Describe the historical setting of these texts.

8. What were the three options open to King Ahaz of Judah in the face of the "Syro-Ephraimite Crisis" of 735 B.C.E.? Which option did Isaiah advise, and why? Which option did Ahaz finally choose, and what did that choice reveal about Ahaz?

9. Describe the developments on the international scene that resulted in the "Sennacherib Crisis" of 705-701 B.C.E. What policy did King Hezekiah of Judah pursue in the face of this crisis? Why was Isaiah critical of this policy?

10. What was Isaiah's favorite designation for God? Why?

11. Describe some of the indications of the literary unity of the Book of Isaiah.

12. How can a study of the traditioning process that produced the Book of Isaiah be liberating?

18

Jeremiah

Suggested Bible Readings: Jeremiah 1-3; 7; 11; 15; 18-20; 26-33; 52

INTRODUCTION

The second major collection in the Latter Prophets is the group of prophetic materials gathered under the name of the prophet Jeremiah. As with the Book of Isaiah, both the book's length (fifty-two chapters) and the forty or more years attributed to Jeremiah's ministry (ca. 627-587/582 B.C.E.) testify to the stature and influence of this prophet. This was true not only for his own day but for the later generations who collected, reworked, expanded, and handed on to future generations his oracles and sermons and the record of his activity.

The opening words of the book identify Jeremiah as a member of a priestly family from the village of Anathoth in the territory of Benjamin (Jer 1:1). Anathoth is only two miles north of Jerusalem and, although Jeremiah continued to have connections with his family and home village (see Jer 32), most of what is recorded in the book about his preaching and activity takes place in Jerusalem. His prophetic career was located for the most part in this capital of the southern kingdom of Judah, and he was intimately involved in the events that led to the destruction of that kingdom and that city. But Jeremiah's roots are clearly in the north. His home village is in the territory of the northern tribe of Benjamin. Also, indications are that the priestly line into which he was born was a northern one. It may even trace back to Abiathar (see 1 Kgs 2:26-27), a descendant of Eli, who was the priest at the old northern shrine of the tribal confederation days at Shiloh (1 Sm 1-4).

Jeremiah's preaching stresses typical northern motifs such as the Exodus and Mosaic covenant traditions:

Speak to the men of Judah and to the citizens of Jerusalem, saying to them: Thus says the LORD, the God of Israel: Cursed be the man who does not observe the terms of this covenant, which I enjoined upon your fathers the day I brought them up out of the land of Egypt, that iron foundry, saying: Listen to my voice and do all that I command you (Jer 11:2-4; see also 2:5-8).

Little or nothing is heard of Zion/Jerusalem theology or the promises to the house of David such as we find in Jeremiah's predecessor Isaiah. However, scholars have demonstrated the obvious influence of the great northern prophet Hosea in Jeremiah. There appear to be connections between Jeremiah and the Deuteronomic reform movement too, although how much of that evidence comes from later Deuteronomic reworking of Jeremian material is difficult to tell.

Jeremiah, like other prophets, has left us a call narrative, an account of the encounter with God that resulted in his prophetic vocation. This call narrative is found at the very beginning of the book, in chapter 1, and takes the form of a conversation between the young Jeremiah and Yahweh. The conversation begins with the words of Yahweh commissioning Jeremiah as a prophet (v. 5). It continues with objections on Jeremiah's part (v. 6), followed by reassurance from Yahweh (v. 7). Then comes Yahweh's description of the formidable task Jeremiah is commanded to undertake:

> See, I place my words in your mouth!
> This day I set you
> over nations and over kingdoms,
> To root up and to tear down,
> to destroy and to demolish,
> to build and to plant (Jer 1:9-10).

The overwhelming nature of this encounter and the powerful reassurance and sense of mission it gave Jeremiah was necessary to sustain him through the long years of opposition. So strong was this opposition that at times it tempted Jeremiah to discouragement and apparently caused him great personal suffering. But from this encounter with God, as well as from the traditions he had inherited from preceding prophets, especially Hosea, came a deep sense of God's love and mercy and care for his people. The marriage imagery found in Jeremiah had its origins with Hosea and had been continued and developed by later prophets. Jeremiah used it effectively as well. Despite its unfortunate chauvinist character in casting Israel in the role of the "faithless wife," this imagery nevertheless adds emotional depth and coloring to the language and vocabulary about Israel's God. Jeremiah 2:2-3 provides a good example (see also Jer 3:12, 19-20):

Go, cry out this message for Jerusalem to hear!
I remember the devotion of your youth,
    how you loved me as a bride,
Following me in the desert,
    in a land unsown.
Sacred to the LORD was Israel,
    the first fruits of his harvest.

This kind of language strengthened and gave credibility to Jeremiah's words of hope, which have so nourished and sustained the faith of future generations.

THE HISTORICAL BACKGROUND TO JEREMIAH'S PROPHETIC CAREER

Jeremiah's call to prophecy came, as he tells us in Jeremiah 1:2, in the thirteenth year of the reign of Josiah, king of Judah, that is, in 627/626 B.C.E. These years saw the precipitous decline of Assyria on the international scene and, within Judah, the Deuteronomic reform, promoted and supported by King Josiah. Josiah's reign and the reform movement were cut short, however, by Josiah's unexpected death in battle in 609 B.C.E. Josiah had been able to rule with some degree of independence from the weakened Assyria. But his death came at the beginning of a tug-of-war over the Syro-Palestinian corridor between Egypt and the newly emerging Mesopotamian empire ruled by Babylon.

Josiah's immediate successor, his son Jehoahaz, was removed by the Egyptians after only one month on the throne. They put in Jehoahaz's place his elder brother Jehoiakim, who remained loyal to Egypt for the next four years. By this time it was becoming obvious that Babylon would soon overshadow Egypt and become the dominant force on the Asian mainland. (See map on page 227.) The most prudent course appeared to be to accept, at least nominally, Babylonian suzerainty. But Jehoiakim and his party and many in the ruling classes were intent on maintaining "independence at all costs." Thus, Jehoiakim revolted at the first sign of weakness on Babylon's part. Between his revolt and the arrival of the punitive expedition from Babylon, Jehoiakim died (assassinated?) and his son, Jehoiachin, assumed the throne.

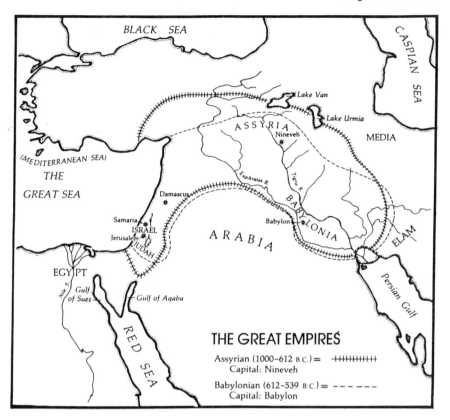

BLACK SEA

CASPIAN SEA

Lake Van

Lake Urmia

A S S Y R I A
Nineveh

MEDIA

(MEDITERRANEAN SEA)

THE

GREAT SEA

Damascus

Euphrates R.

Tigris R.

B A B Y L O N I A

Samaria
ISRAEL
Jerusalem
JUDAH

A R A B I A

Babylon

ELAM

EGYPT

Nile R.

Gulf
of Suez

Gulf of Aqaba

Persian Gulf

RED SEA

THE GREAT EMPIRES

Assyrian (1000–612 B.C.) = ++++++++++
Capital: Nineveh

Babylonian (612–539 B.C.) = – – – – – –
Capital: Babylon

The Babylonians took Jehoiachin prisoner and led him off in chains to Babylon, along with a number of his court officials. The Babylonians put Josiah's third son, Zedekiah, on the throne. But Zedekiah also was determined to follow a policy of independence. He too revolted, counting on help from Egypt that never materialized. This time the Babylonians were determined to eliminate any further basis for trouble or revolt so close to their sensitive border area with Egypt. Thus the sons of Zedekiah were executed and Jerusalem with its royal palace and Temple were put to the torch. Zedekiah himself was blinded and led off to prison in Babylon.

The northern kingdom of Israel with its capital at Samaria had been brought to an end 135 years earlier (722 B.C.E.) by the armies of Assyria. Now the days of the monarchy in Israel came to a definitive end with the demise of Judah, Jerusalem, and the line of David at the hands of the Babylonians in July of 587 B.C.E. This date represents in many ways a watershed in biblical history. From this point on, if the people of Israel were to survive, they could no longer be associated with any *political* state. The next two generations were to see a shift in their way of life and basis for identity.

These were the calamitous times through which Jeremiah lived and prophesied. His preaching represented a continuing opposition to the national leadership's policy of "independence at all costs." He helped lay the foundation for the rebirth beyond the Exile of his people as "Jews" under a new form as a religious cultural community identified as "Judaism."

JEREMIAH'S MESSAGE

Jeremiah experienced his call to prophecy in 627 B.C.E. There is some possibility that he engaged in prophetic activity and preaching during the days of King Josiah and the Deuteronomic reform (622-609 B.C.E.). However, Jeremiah seems to have emerged as a significant and forceful voice only after the death of Josiah and the ensuing collapse of the Deuteronomic reform movement. The ominous nature of his words and warnings are captured in the two visions he reports in chapter 1. In the first of these visions (vv. 11-12) Yahweh shows him an almond tree in blossom:

> The word of the LORD came to me with the question: What do you see, Jeremiah? "I see a branch of the watching-tree," I replied.

The almond tree's white flowers are among the first heralds of spring in Palestine. These small flowers appear as hundreds of eyes covering the tree, wide open as if watching for other signs of the imminent change of season. Hence, the name of the tree in Hebrew is *shaqēd,* "the watcher." Yahweh shows the tree in bloom to Jeremiah, and when Jeremiah pronounces its name, *shaqēd,* God responds, "Well have you seen, for I am watching [*shōqēd*] to fulfill my word" (v. 12).

Even more ominous, the next vision reveals a pot set on a hot fire, boiling over, its contents spilling toward the south. When Jeremiah describes what he sees, Yahweh says,

> And from the north, said the LORD to me, evil will boil over upon all who dwell in the land.

> Lo, I am summoning
> all the kingdoms of the north, says the LORD;

> Each king shall come and set up his throne
>> at the gateways of Jerusalem,
> Opposite her walls all around
>> and opposite all the cities of Judah (1:14-15).

Judah and Jerusalem's fate was sealed because its king and ruling classes refused to listen to Jeremiah as he spoke the words he believed came from Yahweh himself. Jeremiah's overwhelming encounter with God gave him courage, confidence, and a sense of mission. Further, he was rooted in the village and countryside and thus more aware of the sources of Israel's strength and identity as a people and community. This enabled him to discern the fundamental errors in the policies of the king and ruling classes. They were intent on a foreign policy aimed at securing independence from foreign suzerainty at all costs. To pursue this policy the king and ruling classes needed to mount and finance militarizing efforts. This need served to justify their harsh repression of the majority of the people and their exploitation of agricultural surpluses to finance these efforts and, no doubt, to finance their opulent lifestyle as well. Jeremiah indicted Jehoiakim for his failure to continue his father Josiah's social reforms. He also condemned the king's ambitious building program, including a sumptuous new palace:

> Woe to him who builds his house on wrong,
>> his terraces on injustice;
> Who works his neighbor without pay,
>> and gives him no wages.
> Who says, "I will build myself a spacious house,
>> with airy rooms,"
> Who cuts out windows for it,
>> panels it with cedar,
>> and paints it with vermilion.
> Must you prove your rank among kings
>> by competing with them in cedar? . . .

Therefore, thus says the LORD concerning Jehoiakim, son of Josiah, king of Judah:

> They shall not lament him,
>> "Alas! my brother"; "Alas! my sister."
> They shall not lament him,
>> "Alas, LORD! alas, Majesty!"

> The burial of an ass shall he be given,
> dragged forth and cast out
> beyond the gates of Jerusalem (Jer 22:13-15, 18-19).

Jeremiah counsels submission to Babylon instead of this "independence at all costs" policy. Such a policy brought with it militarizing efforts and accompanying repression and exploitation of Judah's inhabitants by the king and ruling elite. Submission to Babylon would mean loss of independence, but even that independence was a precarious and fragile one at best. However, in Jeremiah's judgment, submission to Babylon would mitigate the injustice and suffering the majority of Israelites were undergoing and provide the opportunity to continue the social reforms begun earlier under Josiah. So convinced was Jeremiah of the correctness of this judgment that he denounced again and again the foolishness and blindness of the ruling elite's policies. He unrelentingly predicted doom and devastation for Judah and Jerusalem if they continued on their course.

Jeremiah could see that part of the problem lay in a blind and foolish faith in the theology of the royal court. It clung to the dogma of the inviolability of Jerusalem. This notion of Jerusalem's inviolability had its basis in the promises associated with the permanence of the Davidic dynasty and especially in the promise of Yahweh's permanent presence in the Temple in Jerusalem. Jeremiah attacked this latter notion as a false and superstitious dogma, when divorced from the accompanying covenant demands of justice and right living. We have two accounts (chapters 7 and 26) of Jeremiah's famous Temple sermon in which he attempts to demolish this false hope and in the process almost loses his life. The account in chapter 7 makes clear the superstitious way in which many interpreted God's promise of presence among his people:

> The following message came to Jeremiah from the LORD: Stand at the gate of the house of the LORD, and there proclaim this message: Hear the word of the LORD, all you of Judah who enter these gates to worship the LORD! Thus says the LORD of hosts, the God of Israel: Reform your ways and your deeds, so that I may remain with you in this place. Put not your trust in the deceitful words: "This is the temple of the LORD! The temple of the LORD! The temple of the LORD!" . . .
>
> But here you are, putting your trust in deceitful words to your own loss! Are you to steal and murder, commit adultery and perjury, burn incense to Baal, go after strange gods that you know not, and yet come to stand before me in this house which bears my name, and say: "We are safe; we can commit all these abominations again"? Has this

house which bears my name become in your eyes a den of thieves? I too see what is being done, says the LORD (Jer 7:1-4, 8-11).

Chapter 26 repeats this incident, and includes the reaction of some of Jeremiah's audience, especially some among the leadership of Judah. They call for Jeremiah's execution as a traitor:

> When Jeremiah finished speaking all that the LORD bade him speak to all the people, the priests and prophets laid hold of him, crying, "You must be put to death!" (Jer 26:8)

THE QUESTION OF TRUE AND FALSE PROPHECY

One of the most well-known episodes in the life of Jeremiah is his confrontation with his fellow prophet Hananiah, son of Azzur, from Gibeon (Jer 27-28). The episode raises a crucial question about discerning between the "true" prophet and the "false" prophet. As both Henri Mottu and Norman Gottwald demonstrate, however, it is not so much the abstract question of truth *vs.* falsehood, as if the conundrum could be solved by purely intellectual criteria alone. It is, above all, a question of point of view and of differing class-based perspectives on the same situation. These differing points of view result not only in different evaluations of the situation. These differing vantage points also determine different programs of *action* for confronting the situation.

The episode begins with Jeremiah donning a wooden yoke. He announces, not only to Judah and to its king, but also to the neighboring nations, that it is Yahweh's will that they all come under the yoke of Nebuchadnezzar, king of Babylon. If they do not submit, the result will be destruction and suffering for their people:

> Thus says the LORD of hosts, the God of Israel: . . . Now I have given all these lands into the hand of Nebuchadnezzar, king of Babylon, my servant; even the beasts of the field I have given him for his use. All nations shall serve him and his son and his grandson, until the time of his land, too, shall come. Then it in turn will serve great nations and mighty kings. Meanwhile, if any nation or kingdom will not serve Nebuchadnezzar, king of Babylon, or will not bend its neck under the yoke of the king of Babylon, I will punish that nation with the sword, famine, and pestilence, says the LORD, until I give them into his hand (Jer 27:4, 6-8).

Hananiah, however, contradicts Jeremiah and announces what he claims is the *true* word of Yahweh:

> "Thus says the LORD of hosts, the God of Israel: 'I will break the yoke of the king of Babylon. Within two years I will restore to this place all the vessels of the temple of the LORD which Nebuchadnezzar, king of Babylon took away from this place to Babylon. And I will bring back to this place Jeconiah, son of Jehoiakim, king of Judah, and all the exiles of Judah who went to Babylon,' says the LORD, 'for I will break the yoke of the king of Babylon' " (Jer 28:2-4).

Thus Hananiah predicts that within two years all those who were taken into exile by Nebuchadnezzar will be freed and will return home. To demonstrate in a dramatic and *visual* way that Yahweh will *break* the yoke Nebuchadnezzar has laid on Judah, Hananiah removes the wooden yoke from Jeremiah's shoulders and breaks it in two. Jeremiah counters by replacing the wooden yoke with a yoke of iron. Jeremiah then denounces Hananiah's words as "a lie," and he foretells the imminent death of Hananiah:

> To the prophet Hananiah Jeremiah said: Hear this, Hananiah! The LORD has not sent you, and you have raised false confidence in this people. For this, says the LORD, I will dispatch you from the face of the earth; this very year you shall die, because you have preached rebellion against the LORD (Jer 28:15-16).

Hananiah was reading the situation from the point of view of the king and ruling elite. Their policy of "independence at all costs" reflected their interests. In order to remain in power and continue to enjoy their comfortable, even luxurious lifestyle, Judah had to continue its militaristic efforts and seek to preserve its independence from foreign rule. The words of Hananiah reflected this perspective and that desire.

Jeremiah, on the contrary, viewed the situation through the eyes of the majority of his fellow citizens. If Judah continued its militaristic efforts and pursued the policy of "independence at all costs," the social and economic reforms undertaken by Josiah would stay on the back burner. Further, the suffering and plight of the ordinary Judaite would persist and probably grow worse. For one thing, there would most likely be additions to the burden of taxes and forced labor for the ordinary citizen to support the military adventures of the king and ruling classes and to pay for their luxurious lifestyle. Second, the inevitable invasions and war would affect above all the populace of the countryside. Their crops and cattle would become the object of seizure and destruction by the clashing armies. From Jeremiah's perspective, and that of the *ruled* class, submission to Babylon offered the possibility of peace and the opportunity to turn their energies and attention to implementing the much-needed economic and social reforms.

One can see from this analysis how far from the abstract, other-worldly, and individualistic are the words and teachings of prophets like Jeremiah. They are rooted in and grow out of the conflicts and struggles within the society and community over basic everyday issues of economics and politics. Issues like this are ultimately issues of life or death both for the individual and for the society as a whole. Jeremiah demonstrated keen insight into the situation. His single-minded sense of commitment to and mission from Yahweh, and his experience of and awareness of the ideals of a just and life-giving community gave his words and his preaching their clarity and power.

But the situation deteriorated and the leadership stubbornly persisted in their policy. Jeremiah realized that his calls for repentance, for a "turning around" of the fundamental attitudes and goals on the part of the leadership, were futile. His prophecies begin to take on an ever more insistent note of doom for Judah and Jerusalem. The point of no return had been reached. The end of the monarchy and the end of the city of Jerusalem with its Temple and its cult were inevitable. Whatever the future held for his people, it would be a future without those institutions.

In a demonstration that his actions corresponded with his words, Jeremiah took part in the short-lived attempt to create that future in Judah itself. He joined the community that gathered around the Babylonian-appointed Judaite administration of Gedaliah. This administration replaced the exiled king and his court (Jer 40:7-12). Gedaliah was soon assassinated by the anti-Babylonian faction, and Jeremiah was dragged off to Egypt where he finished out his days. But in his clear-sighted vision and insistence on the inevitability of Jerusalem's downfall and the demise of the monarchy and the Temple, he provided in advance an explanation of the trauma of the Exile. That his words proved to be so accurate helped guarantee their preservation for future generations. These would not only continue to learn from his words. They would also find in them a basis for hope on which to build for the future.

THE JEREMIAN TRADITION

It has become commonplace among biblical scholars to speak of the three types of material we find in the Book of Jeremiah: (1) the shorter prophetic oracles in poetry; (2) the longer passages of prophecy in prose; and (3) the biographical narratives. Almost all agree that the shorter pieces and poetry most likely represent the *ipsissima verba,* that is, Jeremiah's own words spoken in prophecy. Later, possibly with collaboration of Jeremiah himself, the core ideas and elements of these shorter poetic oracles were elaborated and developed, most likely for catechetical and teaching purposes, in the Exilic and post-Exilic communities. This would be, in part, the source of the longer prose versions of Jeremiah's prophecies and preaching. A good example of the contrast between the two can be seen in the famous Temple sermon preserved in two versions. The shorter poetic one appears in the context of the narrative in chapter 7. The longer prose sermon is found in chapter 26. Finally, the third type of material, the biographical narratives, may have been composed to give us a sense of what kind of reactions and response his preaching provoked.

The question of Jeremiah's relationship with the Deuteronomic reform movement under King Josiah is a difficult one. Jeremiah was certainly aware of the movement and probably began his prophetic career during it. But there is disagreement among scholars as to whether he supported it, opposed it, or remained neutral toward it. Two things seem sure, however. First, his activity and influence as a prophet increased following the death of Josiah and the stalling of the reform movement. Second, Deuteronomistic circles, or at least circles influenced by the Deuteronomistic outlook, were principally responsible for collecting, developing, and handing on the Jeremian tradition. Thus much of what comes to us from Jeremiah we find in Deuteronomistic dress.

JEREMIAH'S "CONFESSIONS"

Among the most well-known passages of the Book of Jeremiah are the so-called Confessions. These moving poems follow the pattern of the traditional Lament or Song of Supplication known from the large number of similar prayers in the Psalter and elsewhere. The passages usually identified as examples of the prophet's Confessions include Jeremiah 11:18-23; 12:1-6; 15:10-12, 15-21; 17:14-18; 18:18-23; and 20:7-18. The last cited passage, from chapter 20, is perhaps one of the more well-known:

> You duped me, O LORD, and I let myself be duped;
>   you were too strong for me, and you triumphed.
> All the day I am an object of laughter;
>   everyone mocks me.
> Whenever I speak, I must cry out,
>   violence and outrage is my message;

> The word of the LORD has brought me
>   derision and reproach all the day.
> I say to myself, I will not mention him,
>   I will speak in his name no more.
> But then it becomes like a fire burning in my heart
>   imprisoned in my bones;
> I grow weary holding it in,
>   I cannot endure it.
> Yes, I hear the whisperings of many:
>   "Terror on every side!
>   Denounce! let us denounce him!"
> All those who were friends
>   are on the watch for any misstep of mine.
> "Perhaps he will be trapped; then we can prevail,
>   and take our vengeance on him" (Jer 20:7-10).

Because of the fixed and traditional nature of much of the language of these songs, it is difficult to say how far they go in revealing the "real" Jeremiah. Nonetheless, a consensus seems to be emerging among scholars that these Confessions give us at least some sense of the character and struggle of this great human being and prophet as he faced almost overwhelming opposition, rejection, and persecution by Judah's leadership and the abuse and ridicule of so many of his contemporaries. Though some of the language may be stereotypical and exaggerated, nevertheless these poems can remind us of the enormity of the task and challenge Jeremiah faced. The example of his courage despite these odds provided a source of strength and hope for the Jewish people in Exile and beyond.

THE BASIS FOR HOPE IN JEREMIAH

The bulk of Jeremiah's activity and words as a prophet occurred before the destruction of Judah and Jerusalem and thus before the onset of the Babylonian Exile. His main focus was the possibility and then the inevitability of doom and destruction. The end will surely come; after a certain point has been passed, there is no turning back. Whatever hopeful elements there were in his message during his lifetime were to a large degree overshadowed by this principal focus on the inevitable end. Whatever the future would bring would come only *after* that inevitable end.

But there were hopeful elements, which were seized upon, expanded, and developed by future generations. Interspersed among the prophecies of warning and doom are clear and moving passages that open out onto a hopeful future. Three of these more hopeful elements were emphasized and developed in the Jeremian tradition. They include Jeremiah's "Letter to the Exiles" (Jer 29:1-14), and the story of his redemption of family property in Anathoth (Jer 32), and the oracles on the new covenant (Jer 30-31).

In the "Letter to the Exiles," Jeremiah advises those who have been carried off to captivity in Babylon to accept their condition quietly for the time being:

> Build houses to dwell in; plant gardens, and eat their fruits. Take wives and beget sons and daughters (Jer 29:5-6).

Jeremiah advises submission for the moment, but he holds out the hope that the next generation will again enjoy freedom and restoration:

> Thus says the LORD: Only after seventy years have elapsed for Babylon will I visit you and fulfill for you my promise to bring you back to this place (Jer 29:10).

In a second passage that includes some basis of hope for the future Jeremiah takes advantage of the offer by a kinsman in Anathoth to redeem a plot of ancestral land. Jeremiah's action here is taken against the background of the imminent end of the kingdom and the confusion that would bring. Thus Jeremiah's redemption of the ancestral property demonstrates his profound hope based on God's promise that beyond the end there will be new possibilities and a new beginning:

> Thus says the LORD of hosts, the God of Israel: Take these deeds, both the sealed and the open deed of purchase, and put them in an earthen jar, so that they can be kept there a long time. For thus says the LORD of hosts, the God of Israel: Houses and fields shall again be bought in this land (Jer 32:14-15).

The third and perhaps most well-known passage containing glimmers of hope for a future beyond the impending disaster is the collection of oracles in chapter 31. They foretell the establishment of a new covenant between Yahweh and his people:

> The days are coming, says the LORD, when I will make a new covenant with the house of Israel and the house of Judah. It will not be like the covenant I made with their fathers the day I took them by the hand to lead them forth from the land of Egypt; for they broke my

covenant, and I had to show myself their master, says the LORD. But this is the covenant which I will make with the house of Israel after those days, says the LORD. I will place my law within them, and write it upon their hearts; I will be their God, and they shall be my people. No longer will they have need to teach their friends and kinsmen how to know the LORD. All, from the least to the greatest, shall know me, says the LORD, for I will forgive their evildoing and remember their sin no more (Jer 31:31-34).

The clear and firm sense of hope in these oracles is probably a result of an Exilic reworking and expansion of the Jeremian oracles. They presuppose an end to the former more external instruction typical of the Temple context and pre-Exilic community. They present a radical new vision of a Torah founded on a profound conversion of heart and based on a thoroughly internalized desire and commitment to the vision and ideals of a community and society built on justice and love. This kind of thought and expression takes seriously the people of Israel's new situation without land and Temple and helps prepare the way for them to rebuild their communal life on a new basis.

REVIEW QUESTIONS

1. Describe briefly Jeremiah's background and the location and context of his prophetic career.

2. Discuss briefly Jeremiah's "call narrative" and the lasting effect it had on him.

3. Describe the historical background of Jeremiah's prophetic career. Why is July of 587 B.C.E. so significant in this context?

4. What were the two "visions" of Jeremiah described in chapter 1? What was their significance?

5. What foreign policy did Judah's kings and ruling elite pursue during this period? Why did Jeremiah speak out against it?

6. How did the notion of Jerusalem's inviolability arise? What was Jeremiah's attitude toward this notion?

7. Describe briefly the confrontation between Jeremiah and Hananiah. What was the crucial question this confrontation raised?

8. From what point of view did Hananiah assess the political situation? How did that point of view affect his advice?

9. From what point of view did Jeremiah assess the political situation? How did that point of view affect his advice?

10. Describe briefly each of the three types of material found in the Book of Jeremiah.

11. What was Jeremiah's relationship with the Deuteronomic reform movement? What two things, at least, seem certain about that relationship?

12. What can Jeremiah's Confessions reveal to us about this great prophet? Why do we need to exercise a certain caution in drawing conclusions about Jeremiah from them?

13. Give three examples of hopeful elements in Jeremiah's message. What role did they play for later generations?

PART VI

THE EXILE
AND
THE RESTORATION

19

The Destruction of Jerusalem, the Exile, and the Prophet Ezekiel

Suggested Bible Readings: 2 Kings 17; 24-25; Lamentations 1-2; Ezekiel 1-5; 8-12; 14; 16; 18; 23-24; 33-34; 36-37; 43; 47

INTRODUCTION

The destruction of Jerusalem by Nebuchadnezzar's armies in 587 B.C.E. marks a dramatic turning point in Old Testament history. For six hundred years this community had enjoyed a degree of autonomy and a sense of control over its own history and future. All of that came to an abrupt and brutal end with a finality that stunned and shattered this people and threatened to send them down the path of historical oblivion. But somehow they managed, over the next two or three generations, to pick up the pieces from the disaster and to rebuild and revitalize their community and establish a new basis for their life and identity. This was due in no small part to the earlier prophets, such as Amos, Hosea, Isaiah, and Jeremiah, and to the Deuteronomistic historians. Their words of warning and threats of doom had provided an explanation in advance for the debacle. The people and especially their leadership had refused to follow the conditions and ideals of the vision for human life and society embodied in their covenant and in their loyalty to their God, Yahweh. This refusal had brought the calamity on them and their children. Survival and renewal would come only with a recommitment to those ideals and conditions.

Appropriate to the dramatic shifts in the life and identity of this people during this period is also a change in the way of speaking about them. During the earlier period of relative autonomy and self-determination, we continually referred to this people as Israel and Israelites. These terms designated (a) all the members of this people who professed loyalty to the one God, Yahweh, and adherence to the covenant that formed the basis of their life together as a people; (b) the citizens of the northern kingdom, Israel, with its capital at Samaria (in contrast to Judaites or Judeans, the citizens of the southern kingdom of Judah). From 587 B.C.E., however, with the end of their political autonomy and degree of self-determination, we refer to these people as Jews and to the religio-cultural community that eventually formed as Judaism.

With the end of six hundred years of autonomy also came an end to their sense of being able to determine their own history. No longer were they in a position to "make" history as a people or to assert a degree of direct control over events and decisions. This probably accounts for the end also of significant history writing on their part. The writing of history, or at least "history-like" literature, which had flourished during the previous six hundred years, came to an end. Consequently, our sources for reconstructing the history and events of this and following periods are quite meager and fragmented. The Jews continued to produce literature of various kinds and genres. Except for a burst of history writing, however, during the brief period of independence under the Maccabees and Hasmoneans in 140-63 B.C.E., no further significant history writing was forthcoming.

THE DESTRUCTION OF JERUSALEM
AND THE DEVASTATION OF JUDAH

The Babylonian king Nebuchadnezzar had responded in a rather lenient manner in his suppression of the earlier revolt of 597 B.C.E. After the surrender of Jerusalem the Judean king Jehoiachin was taken into exile in Babylon along with a large group of government officials. But the monarchy and kingdom were allowed to continue under the administration of Zedekiah, Josiah's son and Jehoiachin's uncle. However, nationalist elements within the governing circles misread this soft stance of the Babylonians and fomented a new revolt. This time the Babylonians showed no mercy. After the walls of Jerusalem were breached and the city taken in July of 587 B.C.E., the Babylonian army was allowed to loot the city. A few weeks later Nebuchadnezzar ordered its razing. Thus the Temple of Solomon, the royal palace, and the main residential quarters were put to the torch and the city walls were pulled down:

On the seventh day of the fifth month . . . Nebuzaradan, captain of the bodyguard, came to Jerusalem as the representative of the king of Babylon. He burned the house of the LORD, the palace of the king, and all the houses of Jerusalem; every large building was destroyed by fire. Then the Chaldean troops who were with the captain of the guard tore down the walls that surrounded Jerusalem (2 Kgs 25:8-10; see also Jer 52:12-14).

The people were forced to flee, were led into exile (2 Kgs 25:11; Jer 52:15), or were executed (2 Kgs 25:18-21; Jer 52:24-27).

Archeological evidence also bears eloquent testimony to the havoc wrought upon the rest of Judah by the Babylonian armies at the same time. It seems that every fortified town or city was destroyed. The economic infra-structure of the land—its agriculture, commerce, and industry—was severely crippled if not totally wiped out. The population, at least initially, was sig-nificantly depleted. Many were killed in battle or subsequently seized and executed; large numbers undoubtedly perished from disease or starvation; many simply fled the country. One deportation of the nobility and leading citizens had already taken place in 597 B.C.E., with the removal of King

A relief from Tiglath-Pilesar's palace at his capital, Nimrud, depicts the capture of the city of Ashtoreth-Karnaim in Gilead, annexed together with Galilee in 733-732 B.C.E., and the procession of deportees.

Jehoiachin to Babylon. Now, in 587 B.C.E., Nebuchadnezzar forced a second group from among the upper classes to resettle in Babylon. A third deportation took place in 582 B.C.E. The figures given in Jeremiah 52 and 1 Kings 24 indicate that the exiles from these three deportations totaled some twenty thousand. In other words, life in Judah as an organized society suffered a major disruption. If life was once again to flourish in the land, a complete rebuilding and reorganization would have to take place. That would come, but only in fits and starts, and not for another two generations.

ISRAEL IN EXILE

Scholars usually refer to the period from 587-539 B.C.E. as the Exile or Babylonian Captivity. In one sense this designation is accurate. The bulk of Israel's leadership, those not killed or executed in the revolt of 587 B.C.E., was transplanted to Babylon. And it would be from among this leadership—the royal family, the nobility, bureaucrats, priests, Temple personnel, merchants, and artisans—that the impetus, support, and direction for the rebuilding of Jewish life and community would come.

However, the term Exile is potentially misleading if not deceptive in the sense that it gives the impression of a major movement of most if not all of the surviving Judean population to Babylon. In fact, a significant number remained, although they represented mainly the workers, poorer artisans, and minor officials in the city and the farmers and sheepherders of the surrounding countryside. It is probably more accurate to speak of these deportations as one more step in the dispersal of the Jewish community. This dispersal had begun almost 150 years earlier in the deportations to Mesopotamia and the scattering of the population of the northern kingdom of Israel by the Assyrian invasion and destruction of 722 B.C.E. (2 Kgs 15:29). It is this phenomenon of *dispersal* that needs to be highlighted as much as if not more than *exile*.

As far back as 722 B.C.E. and the destruction of the northern kingdom, groups of Jews had been transplanted to or had fled to other parts of the ancient world. Although some eventually lost their identity as members of the covenant community and were assimilated with the local populations, others held firm to that identity and began to form communities of Israelites on foreign soil (see Is 11:11-16; Jer 44:1). A good number of these communities continued contact and communication with the homeland in Jerusalem and Judah.

With the transplanting of a large group of Jews into or near Babylon by the deportations of 597-582 B.C.E., a Jewish community was established there that continued until modern times. Likewise, those Jews already in Egypt were joined by others fleeing the invasions and destruction of Judah, for example, the group who finally brought the prophet Jeremiah with them to Egypt (Jer 43:1-7). Many also fled to neighboring lands such as Phoenicia, Edom, and Moab. Although some of them undoubtedly returned once the fighting was over, others settled into these new environments.

After 587 B.C.E. the *majority* of the Jewish people lived in communities *outside* Judah and Jerusalem. The Babylonian invasion and destruction thus represents a major step in a process which had already begun earlier, a dispersal of Jews into communities throughout the known world. They would eventually look to Jerusalem for direction and view it as a symbolic center, but otherwise they became active and influential participants in the life and society of the lands where they had settled.

THE SITUATION IN THE MAJOR CENTERS OF JUDAISM, 587-539 B.C.E.

Judah and Jerusalem

Life did continue in Judah, despite the hardships and difficulties it now involved. The major cities and fortified centers suffered massive damage, but a number of smaller, unfortified towns and villages remained relatively unharmed. Administration of the territory of Judah, initially under the pro-Babylonian Jewish leader Gedaliah, was moved to the territory of Benjamin with its ancient shrine at Mizpah, immediately north of Jerusalem. Poorer farmers and landless peasants and workers took over the larger estates left vacant by landowners and officials who had been exiled to Babylon.

The ancient shrine and sacred rock in Jerusalem where Solomon's Temple had stood continued to be an object of pilgrimage where sacrifices were offered on the altar.

Two things in particular are worth noting about the community that continued to inhabit the land. First, now that the monarchy had disappeared, the village- and family-based networks of cooperation and support were able to reemerge and strengthen themselves. These systems of organization and identity became an important part of the foundation upon which Jewish life and community would be rebuilt. Second, religious and literary activity did not come to an end. The Book of Lamentations and some of the Jeremian and other prophetic traditions in circulation emerged from this milieu. Some scholars also argue that the final editing of the Deuteronomistic History took place here rather than in Babylon.

Thus life continued in Judah, and important developments for Judaism's future took place even though the leadership had been transferred temporarily to Babylon. The two centers remained in active communication, with mutual influence and interchange. But the main impetus, support, and direction for the reestablishment of Judah and especially Jerusalem as the center would come from Babylon and the leaders of the Jewish community now in residence there.

Babylon

We have no direct evidence of the living arrangements and conditions of the Jewish exiles in Babylon. Estimates based on the biblical evidence put the number at around twenty thousand. But these twenty thousand included the bulk of the ruling classes and important families of Judah and Jerusalem. They may have been settled in isolated or abandoned areas that needed rebuilding and development.

Two factors facilitated the maintenance of their identity. First, they were allowed to live together in families and communities. Second, the presence of the deposed king and his family provided a visible symbol for their separate peoplehood and a basis for hope for an eventual restoration.

These exiles in Babylon apparently took Jeremiah's advice seriously to "build houses and live in them; plant gardens and eat their produce; take wives and have sons and daughters . . . seek the welfare of the city where I have sent you into exile" (Jer 29:5-7). The use of Aramaic became widespread, as well as the employment of the square Aramaic script for writing. Records from later in the Persian Period (for example, the Murasha tablets, 455-403 B.C.E.) testify to an active involvement in the economic life of the country by the Jews.

Thus the Jews settled and apparently prospered, eventually providing important officials in the Persian court. When the opportunity to reestablish Jerusalem and Judah once again as the center for Judaism arose, the impetus, support, and direction would come principally from these communities in Babylon. Although most of them would not take part in the actual rebuilding and refounding, they would provide money and would influence the Persian authorities to allow and to assist in the task. Some from their own number would journey to Jerusalem to settle and to direct the restoration.

Egypt

Direct evidence of Jewish presence in Egypt is provided by a cache of papyri found at Elephantine, an island near the First Cataract of the Nile

River in Upper Egypt. A colony of Jewish mercenaries originally in the employ of Persia settled there, built a temple, and carried on a correspondence with the Jewish community in Jerusalem (late fifth century B.C.E.; see *ANET,* pp. 491-92, 548-49).

There is no direct evidence of other Jews in Egypt at this period. But groups such as those who had fled to the Delta Region carrying the prophet Jeremiah with them (Jer 43:1-7) probably formed nuclei around which the rapid growth of the Jewish communities would later take place. During the Hellenistic period these communities would become the major centers of the Jewish world.

THE PROPHET EZEKIEL

Ezekiel's Character and Accomplishments

Israel managed to survive the catastrophe of 587 B.C.E. and emerge as a humbled and renewed community. The people preserved a firm continuity with their past history and traditions, but not without major changes and transformations. That they were able to survive at all was due not only to the vitality of those traditions and their experience of confronting and coping with adversity as a community. It was also because of singularly gifted and creative individuals such as the prophet Ezekiel. Ezekiel and others like him were able, in dialogue with their traditions, in discussion, and often in dialectic with their contemporaries, to lay a new foundation for the future.

Ezekiel was a priest and prophet who had apparently been a member of the Temple personnel in Jerusalem prior to its destruction. He was taken prisoner in the capture of the city by Nebuchadnezzar's army in 597 B.C.E. He journeyed to Babylon along with the young king, Jehoiachin, and other members of the ruling classes in the first of the three major deportations (597 B.C.E., 587 B.C.E., and 582 B.C.E.). He was obviously a very sensitive and creative individual for whom the events of his time, especially the destruction of Jerusalem and its Temple, were horrifying and profoundly disconcerting and disorienting experiences. He attempted to understand and come to grips with these experiences and to bring his fellow Jews to an awareness of their true import and implications. His attempts resulted sometimes in what appear to be unusual, even bizarre prophetic actions on his part. For example, it is reported that he lay immobile on his side for 390 days as a symbol of the lengthy period of exile ahead:

You shall lie on your left side, while I place the sins of the house of Israel upon you. As many days as you lie thus, you shall bear their sins. For the years of their sins I allot you the same number of days, three hundred and ninety, during which you shall bear the sins of the house of Israel. When you finish this, you are to lie down again, but on your right side, and bear the sins of the house of Judah forty days; one day for each year I have allotted you (Ez 4:4-6).

Ezekiel also refused to mourn over the death of his wife because his personal loss was so insignificant in comparison with the loss his people were about to endure in the destruction of Jerusalem:

Thus the word of the LORD came to me: Son of man, by a sudden blow I am taking away from you the delight of your eyes, but do not mourn or weep or shed any tears. Groan in silence, make no lament for the dead, bind on your turban, put your sandals on your feet, do not cover your beard, and do not eat the customary bread. That evening my wife died, and the next morning I did as I had been commanded. . . . Thus says the Lord GOD: I will now desecrate my sanctuary, the stronghold of your pride, the delight of your eyes, the desire of your soul. The sons and daughters you left behind shall fall by the sword. Ezekiel shall be a sign for you: all that he did you shall do when it happens. Thus you shall know that I am the LORD (Ez 24:15-18, 21, 24).

Ezekiel's attempts to grasp and cope with the loss and disorientation of this time also resulted in the powerful and imaginative poetry and images that make up the bulk of the book which has come down to us under his name.

The seemingly exotic nature of some of his images and prophecies, for example, in his call narrative (Ez 1-3), along with the apparently extreme character of some of his prophetic actions, have caused commentators in the past to conclude that Ezekiel was suffering from some form of mental illness. More important, perhaps, is the need to recognize the centrality and the impact of the event that stands at the center of Ezekiel's book—the destruction of Jerusalem—and the extremity of the crisis it provoked for Ezekiel and for his people. At one stroke, that which had appeared to be at the heart of their identity as a people—the holy city of Jerusalem, its Temple and rich cultic traditions, and the Davidic kingship—had been brought to an end. The effort even to grasp what had happened, much less begin to understand and express the implications and begin to pick up the pieces and rebuild, was staggering. The challenge and the task Ezekiel faced, in all its dimensions—intellectual, psychological, emotional, theological, institutional—were enormous. Put into this wider context, the language and actions of Ezekiel do not seem quite as exaggerated as they might appear at first reading. Rather, his accomplishments and those of his circle of disciples and collaborators, as well as the wider community of which he was a part, inspire admiration and respect. Both Ezekiel and his audience had been for the most part members of the privileged classes. Now they found themselves classless, defeated, and largely deprived of the material, moral, psychological, and spiritual resources upon which they had depended in the past. The challenge was not only to survive, but also to lay the groundwork for the future without abandoning their past roots.

Ezekiel's Doctrine and Work

The Structure of the Book

The Book of the Prophet Ezekiel revolves around the central event of the destruction of Jerusalem and its Temple. After the narrative of Ezekiel's call to prophecy in chapters 1-3, a series of prophetic signs and oracles announcing and warning about the imminent fall of the city continues through chapter 24. The judgmental character of these oracles and signs is unrelenting. Like his predecessor Jeremiah, whom Ezekiel may even have heard preaching in person before his deportation, Ezekiel leaves no doubt about the inescapability of Yahweh's judgment on Judah and Jerusalem. There will be no escaping. Their fate has been sealed. Ezekiel leaves no room for hope that the city is not doomed and that the end is not near. Chapter 24 also contains the notice that the siege of Jerusalem had begun and that Ezekiel would remain speechless until the siege ends with the city's destruction:

> As for you, son of man, truly, on the day I take away from them their bulwark, their glorious joy, the delight of their eyes, the desire of their soul, the pride of their hearts, their sons and daughters, that day the fugitive will come to you, that you may hear it for yourself; that day your mouth shall be opened and you shall be dumb no longer. Thus you shall be a sign to them, and they shall know that I am the LORD (Ez 24:25-27).

This focus on Jerusalem and Judah is interrupted by a long series of oracles pronounced against seven foreign nations (Ez 25-32), with the bulk of attention going to Tyre and Egypt. The judgment announced for these neighboring nations prepares the way for the announcement of Jerusalem's judgment and fate. Chapter 33 brings us back to the focus on Jerusalem. The news of the city's fall is brought to Ezekiel in Babylon:

An engraving by Gustave Doré of Ezekiel's vision of the valley of dry bones: "And he said unto me, Son of man, can these bones live? And I answered, O LORD God, thou knowest . . ." (Ezekiel 37:3).

On the fifth day of the tenth month, in the twelfth year of our exile, the fugitive came to me from Jerusalem and said, "The city is taken!" (Ez 33:21).

Ezekiel regains his speech and from this point on the tone of the oracles becomes decidedly more comforting and hopeful. These later chapters include the promise of a new leadership (Ez 34) and a "new heart" and "new spirit" (Ez 36) paralleling Jeremiah's new covenant:

For I will take you away from among the nations, gather you from all the foreign lands, and bring you back to your own land. I will sprinkle clean water upon you to cleanse you from all your impurities, and from all your idols I will cleanse you. I will give you a new heart and place a new spirit within you, taking from your bodies your stony hearts and giving you natural hearts. I will put my spirit within you and make you live by my statutes, careful to observe my decrees. You shall live in the land I gave to your fathers; you shall be my people, and I will be your God (Ez 36:24-28).

Finally, chapters 40-48 describe Ezekiel's vision and plan for a new temple.

Ezekiel's Call to Prophecy

The Book of Ezekiel begins with Ezekiel's call narrative. It has many affinities with those of other prophets, such as Isaiah (Is 6) and Jeremiah (Jer 1), but it is much longer and more elaborate, taking up three whole chapters. As in the other prophetic call narratives, Ezekiel is suddenly caught up into the midst of the heavenly court in the presence of the Great King. Ezekiel attempts to give us some sense of the overpowering nature of this experience in his description of the majestic scene of which he found himself a part. His language draws on the imagery of mythology and cult, which had deep roots in the older Canaanite traditions to which Israel was heir. But it also includes Babylonian imagery and motifs taken from the environment in which this exiled community now dwelled, for example, the descriptions of the "four living creatures" that attended Yahweh's chariot-throne:

As I looked, a stormwind came from the North, a huge cloud with flashing fire [enveloped in brightness], from the midst of which [the midst of the fire] something gleamed like electrum. Within it were

The gate of the city of Gezer built by Solomon, discovered at archaeological excavations. It matches exactly the design of the eastern gate of Solomon's Temple, which still stood in the lifetime of Ezekiel and which the prophet described so meticulously in his celebrated vision.

figures resembling four living creatures that looked like this: their form was human, but each had four faces and four wings, and their legs went straight down; the soles of their feet were round. They sparkled with a gleam like burning bronze.

Their faces were like this: each of the four had the face of a man, but on the right side was the face of a lion, and on the left side the face of an ox, and finally, each had the face of an eagle (Ez 1:4-7, 10).

Ezekiel's description of this vision is colorful and majestic, and the reader or listener is almost overwhelmed by the wealth of elaborate and confusing detail. The ultimate effect is a powerful impression of the transcendence of Israel's God, an impression which comes across in two ways. First, the almost incomprehensible majesty of God's appearance is felt in the description itself, which seems just beyond the ability actually to visualize. Second, implicit in this first vision of God's glory by the river Chebar in Babylon is the realization that Israel's God is not tied to a particular place such as Judah or the Temple in Jerusalem. Here God appears to Ezekiel in the land of his exile, in Babylon. God's rule and God's power extend throughout the universe. They transcend time and place and thus God's glory can manifest itself even here in this foreign land. Even in this strange country, far from Jerusalem and its Temple, God is close to his people, to judge those who have sinned and to protect those who have remained faithful.

Ezekiel's threefold repetition of this vision of God's glory is one of the devices that serve to unify the book. The first and most elaborate description of the vision takes up the first three chapters. The vision occurs again in chapters 8-11, in which Ezekiel finds himself transported back to Jerusalem. There he witnesses God's actual abandonment of the Temple and the city preparatory to its destruction:

Then the glory of the LORD left the threshold of the temple and rested upon the cherubim. These lifted their wings, and I saw them rise from the earth, the wheels rising along with them. . . . Then the cherubim lifted their wings, and the wheels went along with them, while up above them was the glory of the God of Israel. And the glory of the LORD rose from the city and took a stand on the mountain which is to the east of the city (Ez 10:18-19; 11:22-23).

Finally, the vision returns a third time toward the end of the book as part of Ezekiel's vision of the new Temple in Jerusalem. Here the hope-filled promise contained in the vision of a restored Temple includes the promise also of a return of God's glory to that Temple so that God may once again dwell in it in the midst of his people:

The vision was like that which I had seen when he came to destroy the city, and like that which I had seen by the river Chebar. I fell prone as the glory of the LORD entered the temple by way of the gate which faces the east, but the spirit lifted me up and brought me to the inner court. And I saw that the temple was filled with the glory of the LORD (43:3-5).

Ezekiel and the Prophetic Tradition

Ezekiel was obviously immersed in Israel's older prophetic traditions. He drew on them—borrowing, expanding, and transforming themes, motifs, and images. Two examples serve to illustrate this link with earlier prophets. The first is the motif of "the spirit," which inspires and guides the prophet. Again and again there is mention of "the spirit" in Ezekiel: "the spirit" guiding the fiery chariot upon which God was enthroned (Ez 1-3); "the spirit" that would "enter" Ezekiel, which would "stand him up" or "lift him up" and command him to speak (see Ez 2:2; 3:12, 14, 24).

This emphasis on the role and power of "the spirit of Yahweh" in the prophetic vocation links Ezekiel with Israel's oldest prophetic traditions going back to Moses and Joshua ("Now Joshua, son of Nun, was filled with the spirit of wisdom, since Moses had laid his hands upon him" [Dt 34:9; see also Nm 11:16-30]), Samuel (for example, 1 Sm 29:20), and Elijah and Elisha (for example, 2 Kgs 2:9, 15).

A second example of Ezekiel's links with Israel's prophetic tradition is his use of marriage imagery as a means of expressing the relationship between Yahweh and Israel. In this he draws upon the earlier use of this theme by Hosea and Jeremiah, which he expands and allegorizes (Ez 16, 23). In both of these cases, however, "the wife" is depicted as an unfaithful woman, an adulteress. Her unfaithfulness symbolizes the the unfaithfulness of the people of Israel (Ez 16) and the cities of Jerusalem and Samaria (Ez 23) to their covenant with Yahweh. In his use of the marriage metaphor in this way, Ezekiel typifies the bias and prejudice of the patriarchal society and culture of the Ancient Near East, including Israel, of which he was a part.

Ezekiel and the Task of Rebuilding

Ezekiel's work as a prophet involved not only his preaching and transforming of Israel's traditions for the community as a whole. His word and his work were intended to touch the lives of individuals and reform their conduct as well (see Ez 3:17-21; 14:1-11; 18; 22:1-16; 33:1-9). Ezekiel echoes Jeremiah's emphasis on personal responsibility for one's actions before God:

> Thus the word of the LORD came to me: Son of man, what is the meaning of this proverb that you recite in the land of Israel:
>
> "Fathers have eaten green grapes,
> thus their children's teeth are on edge"?

As I live, says the Lord GOD: I swear that there shall no longer be anyone among you who will repeat this proverb in Israel (Ez 18:1-3; cf. Jer 31:29-30).

Individual repentance and conversion are important not because there is the possibility that such will divert the judgment already pronounced against Judah and Jerusalem. Rather, Ezekiel's work of bringing individuals to repentance and conversion through his preaching, instruction, and example, will begin to build the new community by preparing its individual members to take part in that rebuilding. Leaving behind the pride and pretensions associated with a political state, this community will find a new identity as a people. They will draw on their older traditions with their roots in the village and family structures of a community of equals. This community will center on the family, pledging mutual support and protection, and humble loyalty to the demands of their covenant with their unique sovereign, Yahweh.

REVIEW QUESTIONS

1. Why is the destruction of Jerusalem by the Babylonians in 587 B.C.E. referred to as a watershed event?

2. What is the difference between an Israelite and a Jew?

3. Why did the writing of history, or at least "history-like" literature, come to an end with the destruction of Jerusalem in 587 B.C.E.?

4. Describe the extent of the devastation effected upon Judah and Jerusalem by the Babylonians.

5. Why is the term *Exile* both appropriate and not appropriate in referring to the period from 587 B.C.E. to 539 B.C.E.?

6. Describe the situation of the Jewish people remaining in Judah and Jerusalem from 587 B.C.E. to 539 B.C.E.

7. Describe briefly the situation of the Jewish people in exile in Babylon.

8. Who was Ezekiel? How might one account for the unusual and seemingly exotic nature of some of his images, prophecies, and prophetic actions?

9. Discuss some of the characteristics of Ezekiel's call narrative.

10. What are some of Ezekiel's links with Israel's older prophetic traditions?

11. How is individual repentance and conversion related to the rebuilding of the community of Jews as whole?

20

Second Isaiah (Is 40-55)

Suggested Bible Readings: Isaiah 40-45; 49-55

THE HISTORICAL CONTEXT AND ITS RELATIONSHIP TO THE REST OF THE BOOK

We mentioned above in our discussion of the prophet Isaiah that a circle of collaborators and disciples had gathered around him during his lifetime and had initiated a tradition or school, which continued long after his death. The latter part of the Book of Isaiah (Is 40-66), is a good example of the work of such a school. Isaiah 40-55 in particular has been recognized by a growing number of scholars since the end of the last century as the work of a member of the Isaiah school living some 150 years after the "historical" Isaiah.

This section of Isaiah, even though it continues some of the ideas of the eighth century Isaiah, has a unity and coherence all its own. The literary style and vocabulary is quite distinct from the earlier chapters, and the concerns, context, and historical setting are clearly different. Thus scholars are generally agreed that chapters 40-55 come from the hand of a poet-theologian who stood in the tradition of the "historical" Isaiah but who addressed a message of comfort and hope to the Jews of the Exile in Babylon sometime between 550 and 539 B.C.E. We do not know this prophet's name; consequently, the author of these chapters is referred to as Deutero-Isaiah or Second Isaiah.

The final ten chapters of the book (Is 56-66) stem from an even later time, the post-Exilic period or Restoration, after 539 B.C.E. Again, the author (or authors) is anonymous. This section picks up themes and images from the poetry of Second Isaiah and develops them, addressing the concerns and the challenges of rebuilding a Jewish presence and community in Jerusalem and Judah. The poet (or poets) responsible for these chapters has been designated Trito-Isaiah or "Third Isaiah." We will focus on the work of the Second Isaiah.

The prophet Jeremiah had advised the exiles in Babylon to settle down for a long stay: "Build houses to dwell in; plant gardens and eat their fruits" (Jer 29:5). It was not long, however, before tumultuous changes on the international level heralded drastic changes in the lives of these exiles. The Babylonian Empire, which had reached its zenith under Nebuchadnezzar, moved into a rapid decline with the short and troubled reigns of his three successors. Finally, the last ruler, Nabonidus, managed to alienate the powerful priestly class and population of Babylon itself by his downgrading of the status of Babylon's patron deity, Marduk.

On the wider horizon, around 550 B.C.E., Cyrus the Persian appeared, ruler of a small kingdom within the empire of the Medes, the rival power to the north and east of Babylon (see map on p. 227). By a series of adroit diplomatic moves and military victories, Cyrus was successful in seizing control of the Median Empire and was soon in a position to fall heir to Babylon and to the remnants of Babylon's dominion as well.

It was during this period, from the rise of Cyrus around 550 B.C.E. to his ultimate capture of the city of Babylon itself in 539 B.C.E., that the Second Isaiah addressed the Jews of the Exile with words of comfort and hope. The tumultuous changes on the international political scene were obviously disconcerting to this people in their precarious and vulnerable situation as exiles and strangers in a foreign land. But the impending changes also held out the possibility of changes for the better, indeed even the hope of restoration and return to their homeland after the long years in exile.

THE SHAPE AND STYLE OF SECOND ISAIAH

There is unity and continuity in the material of Isaiah 40-55. Above all, the energy of the poetry is such that the words and literary forms are barely able to control and contain the enthusiasm and intensity of the writer. The prophet appears so excited by the prospects for the future of the exiles, which the unforeseen changes on the political scene have raised, that the poetry seems to burst the bonds of the literary forms adapted by the author. Norman Gottwald refers to the document's " 'controlled hysteria' which arrests and taxes us with its emotional intensity and its intellectual breadth."

The poet in Second Isaiah makes use of and adapts a number of literary forms drawn from Israel's cultic and literary traditions, including the "oracle of salvation":

> But you, Israel, my servant,
> > Jacob, whom I have chosen,
> > offspring of Abraham, my friend—. . .
> Fear not, I am with you;
> > be not dismayed; I am your God.
> I will strengthen, and help you,
> > and uphold you with my right hand of justice.
> > (Is 41:8, 10; see also 43:1-7; 44:1-5; 54:4-6)

Other literary forms this poet adapts include the "proclamation of salvation" (see Is 41:17-20; 42:14-17; 43:16-21; 49:7-12; 51:1-8; 54:11-17) and the "hymn of praise" or "eschatological hymn":

> Sing to the LORD a new song,
> > his praise from the end of the earth:
> Let the sea and what fills it resound,
> > the coastlands, and those who dwell in them.
> Let the steppe and its cities cry out,
> > the villages where Kedar dwells;
> Let the inhabitants of Sela exult,
> > and shout from the top of the mountains.
> Let them give glory to the LORD,
> > and utter his praise in the coastlands (Is 42:10-12; see
> > > also 44:23; 45:8; 48:20-21; 49:13; 52:7-10; 54:1-3).

Fifty or more formal "units" have been identified and isolated in these sixteen chapters. But no consensus has been reached among scholars as to how these individual units relate to each other in the architecture of the whole work. The repetition and weaving together of themes, images, and vocabulary serve to unify the entire composition. But a more complete grasp of how the formal unity has been achieved seems just beyond reach. Some scholars claim that these fifty or more units have been grouped together into complexes unified by various literary devices. These scholars argue for a clear extended development of ideas and motifs throughout the whole work. Others hold that there is no overall unity, that the fifty or more separate units are simply strung together like pearls on a string. Finally, there are those who propose that the work represents a series of repetitions

Scroll of the Book of Isaiah.

The Isaiah scroll from Qumran. One of the first finds at Qumran in 1947, this scroll, dating from around 100 B.C.E., contains the complete text of the Book of Isaiah. Collection and editing of the prophet's writings began in earnest during and following the Babylonian Exile.

and reformulations of key themes and ideas recomposed and proclaimed on successive separate occasions.

THE PURPOSE OF SECOND ISAIAH

One purpose which may be inferred from the style and form of Second Isaiah's poetry is the attempt of the prophet to mediate conflicts and disputes within the Exilic community. The ambiguity and elusiveness of the poetry, which skillfully weaves together the various motifs and ideas, may have been a way of reconciling and bringing together clashing points of view on how the community should prepare for and respond to the evolving political situation.

Along with this effort to mediate and reconcile was the more fundamental task of preparing the community for the future. The situation for the exiles was without doubt about to change. The chaotic events on the international scene were already having an effect on the local scene. What the future would bring was not at all clear. There was anxiety and conflict about how to respond to these developments. Second Isaiah wrote to bring a message of comfort and reassurance and above all a message of hope to this uncertain and vulnerable people.

THE MESSAGE OF SECOND ISAIAH

Comfort and Reassurance

To calm the anxieties and fears of his people in the face of the turbulent changes that had taken place and that were continuing to take place, Second Isaiah proclaimed a message of hope and reassurance and comfort. This small community had already endured the trauma and humiliation of the destruction of its homeland in the previous generation. Now exiled and strangers in a foreign land, the people were at the mercy of those who ruled and dominated them. The events on the international scene seemed sure to bring about important changes, changes over which they would have little or no control. Those changes could mean a turn for the better for the exiles; they could also mean a turn for the worse. Was there any reason to hope that it might even bring an opportunity for some to return to their homeland and begin to restore and rebuild? Above all, how should they respond to the developments already taking place around them? What were their options and how could they know what practical choices to make? Should they continue to support the Babylonian regime? Should they begin to cooperate with those groups undermining it and preparing the way for Cyrus and his Persian army? Or should they try to remain neutral?

It was to respond to these anxieties, to counter their sense of vulnerability and powerlessness, and to bring assurance of comfort and hope that Second Isaiah preached. It is remarkable that, in contrast to his predecessor of 150 years earlier, these sixteen chapters contain not a word of judgment or condemnation for Israel. Rather, from the opening words, the message is one of solace and reassurance:

> Comfort, give comfort to my people,
>   says your God.
> Speak tenderly to Jerusalem, and proclaim to her
>   that her service is at an end,
>   her guilt is expiated;
> Indeed, she has received from the hand of the LORD
>   double for all her sins (Is 40:1-2).

One key element in Second Isaiah's message of reassurance to the exiles is the hope the prophet holds out for a return to the homeland and the opportunity to rebuild and restore the community there. His strategy in expressing and legitimating this hope is to reach back to the central element in Israel's traditions, the Exodus from Egypt. The poet presents the journey home to Judah and Jerusalem as a New Exodus, a new act of deliverance by Yahweh of his people from bondage:

> Thus says the LORD,
>   who opens a way in the sea
>   and a path in the mighty waters,
> Who leads out chariots and horsemen,
>   a powerful army,
> Till they lie prostrate together, never to rise,
>   snuffed out and quenched like a wick.
> Remember not the events of the past,
>   the things of long ago consider not;
> See, I am doing something new!
>   Now it springs forth, do you not perceive it?
> In the desert I make a way,
>   in the wasteland, rivers (Is 43:16-19).

This reuse and transformation of the Exodus theme is not a purely abstract and allegorical one, however. It is put into concrete terms that respond directly to the experience and fears and possibly real sufferings the exiles were undergoing. Yahweh had responded to the powerlessness and cry of their ancestors in Egypt. He had provided them, whether on their journey or at last in the Promised Land, with fresh, life-giving water (Is 41:17-18; 55:1-2), food (Is 49:9-10; 55:1-2), guidance (Is 42:16), prosperity, and fruitfulness both of field and offspring:

> Though you were waste and desolate,
>   a land of ruins,
> Now you shall be too small for your inhabitants. . . .
> You shall ask yourself:
>   "Who has borne me these?
> I was bereft and barren
>   [exiled and repudiated];
>   who has reared them?
> I was left all alone;
>   where then do these come from? (Is 49:19, 21;
>   see also 51:3; 55:10-11)

He had given them strength and victory in battle (Is 41:10-13; 54:14-17). So now Yahweh is coming once again in an even more wonderful and powerful way to renew his saving actions on behalf of his people and set them free from their imprisonment:

> Thus says the LORD:
> In a time of favor I answer you,
>   on the day of salvation I help you,
> To restore the land
>   and allot the desolate heritages,
> Saying to the prisoners: Come out!
> To those in darkness: Show yourselves!. . .
> Sing out, O heavens, and rejoice, O earth,
>   break forth into song, you mountains,
> For the LORD comforts his people
>   and shows mercy to his afflicted (Is 49:8-9, 13;
>   see also 43:14-15).

Strategy for Reconciliation

There also arises the question of how these returning exiles would be received by those Jews who had not gone into exile and who still lived in and around Jerusalem. What kind of welcome could the returnees expect, these former members of the leadership class and their offspring—nobles, prophets, priests, bureaucrats, artisans? Were these not the very groups whose misconduct and disloyalty to the covenant had brought down the disaster and destruction upon Jerusalem and Judah? The book of Lamentations contains a stinging indictment of such individuals:

> In Zion the LORD has made
>   feast and sabbath to be forgotten;
> He has scorned in fierce wrath
>   both king and priest. . . .
> Your prophets had for you
>   false and specious visions;
> They did not lay bare your guilt,
>   to avert your fate:
> They beheld for you in vision
>   false and misleading portents. (Lam 2:6, 14)

> Because of the sins of her prophets
>   and the crimes of her priests,

> Who shed blood in her midst
>> the blood of the just!. . .
> The LORD himself has dispersed them,
>> he regards them no more;
> He does not receive the priests with favor,
>> nor show kindness to elders. (Lam 4:13, 16)

Carol Newsom has discerned Second Isaiah's strategy. The prophet's work avoids references to the previous status of these returning exiles—princes, priests, prophets, elders. Instead he seems purposefully to stress kinship language—children, sons and daughters. In this way the prophet prepares the way for reconciliation and reunion with their brothers and sisters in the homeland. Jerusalem, personified as "Mother Zion," is suprised by the appearance of these returning children who have been born to her during her time of sorrow:

> But Zion said: "The LORD has forsaken me;
>> my LORD has forgotten me."
> Look about and see,
>> they are all gathering and coming to you. . . .
> Though you were waste and desolate,
>> a land of ruins,
> Now you shall be too small for your inhabitants. . . .
> The children whom you had lost
>> shall yet say to you,
> "This place is too small for me
>> make room for me to live in. . . ."
> Thus says the Lord GOD:
> See, I will lift up my hand to the nations,
>> and raise my signal to the peoples;
> They shall bring your sons in their arms,
>> and your daughters shall be carried on their shoulders."
>>>> (Isa 49:14, 18-20, 22)

Together, both those who had gone into exile and those who remained in Judah constitute members of a single family, children of a common mother, Zion (Jerusalem). Tension and conflict will arise over questions of leadership, land, and the proper strategy for dealing with imperial powers. But the prophet emphasizes their common bonds and fundamental unity as Yahweh's chosen people.

Creative Redemption

One of the elements in the poetry of Second Isaiah that gives it such power and appeal is the tension the prophet builds by weaving together in a remarkable way the dual themes of creation and redemption. Yahweh's cosmic rule as Creator is linked to and juxtaposed with Yahweh's guidance and direction of human history. This can be seen especially in the presentation of the return to Jerusalem not only as a New Exodus, a reenactment of the deliverance from Egypt, but as an event linked with creation itself. It is as if this action of liberation were an intimate and constitutive part of the very fabric of the universe and linked to its emergence and meaning and completeness. God crowns creation in the act of liberation, once from Egypt, and now, even more wonderfully, in the liberation from Babylon.

This linking of creation, Exodus, and re-creation/New Exodus, is caught up in a remarkable passage in which the rescue of Israel from the Egyptians at the sea is pictured in cosmic terms as Yahweh's defeat of the dragon of the chaotic deep (Rahab). This rescue from Egypt foreshadowed the renewed act of creation/liberation in the deliverance of Israel from Babylon:

> Awake, awake, put on strength,
>   O arm of the LORD!
> Awake as in the days of old,
>   in ages long ago!
> Was it not you who crushed Rahab,
>   you who pierced the dragon?
> Was it not you who dried up the sea,
>   the waters of the great deep,
> Who made the depths of the sea into a way
>   for the redeemed to pass over?
> Those whom the LORD has ransomed will return
>   and enter Zion singing,
>   crowned with everlasting joy;
> They will meet with joy and gladness,
>   sorrow and mourning will flee (Is 51:9-11).

The Servant of Yahweh

One of the most well-known and intriguing aspects of Second Isaiah is the figure of the Servant of Yahweh and the four "Servant Songs" put on his lips (Is 42:1-4; 49:1-6; 50:4-9; 52:13-53:12). Christians are especially familiar with this figure and these songs because of the New Testament's identification of the Servant with Jesus.

The identity of the Servant and his role in the overall scheme of Second Isaiah's prophecy has been a continuing object of discussion among scholars. Is he a historical individual or is he meant to be a representative figure for Israel as a whole? If he was a historical figure, with whom is he supposed to be identified: Moses, Jeremiah, King Jehoiachin, or possibly Second Isaiah himself?

Recent studies have tended to see the Servant as an actual historical figure, possibly the prophet himself. Whoever he might be, his experience reflects in concrete personal terms the suffering, hope, and triumph of the people as a whole. However, the concrete personal experience of the Servant is rooted in the actual historical experience of the political and social tensions and conflicts of the Exilic community, tensions and conflicts in which the Servant played a role as both participant and victim.

In his exhortations to the Exilic community, the prophet presented the figure of Cyrus, recently appeared on the international political scene, as a potential liberator, unknowingly chosen and destined by Yahweh to fulfill that role:

> Thus says the LORD to his anointed, Cyrus,
>> whose right hand I grasp,
> Subduing nations before him,
>> and making kings run in his service,
> Opening doors before him
>> and leaving the gates unbarred. . . .
> For the sake of Jacob, my servant,
>> of Israel, my chosen one,
> I have called you by your name,
>> giving you a title, though you knew me not.
>> (Is 45:1, 4; see also 44:28)

Such language was dangerous. It could have aroused the suspicion and eventual reprisal on the part of the community's Babylonian captors.

The prophet may have taken care in the actual delivery of his oracles not to mention Cyrus directly, but only in coded form understandable to his Jewish audience. Nevertheless, there were undoubtedly pro-Babylonian elements within the Exilic community—Jews who had won positions of trust and responsibility in the Babylonian administration. They would have been threatened by the prophet's anti-Babylonian/pro-Persian rhetoric, seeing

their own interests endangered by an end to Babylonian rule. The persecution and trials of the Servant figure would then reflect the actual
historical experience of the prophet, arrested and imprisoned by the
Babylonians with the collaboration of the pro-Babylonian Jews. His suffering and eventual release and rescue are described and celebrated in
the Fourth Servant Song (Is 52:13-53:12). In this interpretation the song
would be seen as a typical song of thanksgiving, such as those from the
Psalter.

> He was spurned and avoided by men,
> a man of suffering, accustomed to infirmity,
> One of those from whom men hide their faces,
> spurned, and we held him in no esteem. . . .
> Though he was harshly treated, he submitted
> and opened not his mouth;
> Like a lamb led to the slaughter
> or a sheep before the shearers,
> he was silent and opened not his mouth.
> Oppressed and condemned, he was taken away,
> and who would have thought any more of his
> destiny? . . .
> Because of his affliction.
> he shall see the light in fullness of days;
> Through his suffering, my servant shall justify many,
> and their guilt he shall bear.
> Therefore I will give him his portion among the great,
> and he shall divide the spoils with the mighty.
>   (Is 53:3, 7-8, 11-12)

Such a scenario admittedly is hypothetical. But it does have the merit of
helping one imagine what may indeed have been the concrete situation of
struggle and conflict involving real social and political issues, with all their
complexity and ambiguity, in which these remarkable prophetic texts had
their origin.

The Servant Language in the New Testament

The figure of the Servant of Yahweh and the texts associated with him,
especially the Fourth Servant Song in Isaiah 52:13-53:12, are familiar to
readers of the New Testament. The early Christians identified the Servant
figure with Christ (for example, Acts 8:26-40). The history of Christian

exegesis has tended to follow the lead of the New Testament itself in reading these texts from Isaiah as directly predictive of Christ and his passion and resurrection.

A serious drawback to this approach lies in the loss of the meaning these texts had in their own context of the Exilic community and the experiences of that community which they embody. A more satisfying approach is to recognize the key role these texts played in providing Jesus with a model for understanding his own identity and mission. These Servant Songs supplied him with a traditional language and imagery through which he could express that identity and mission. This parallel between Jesus and the Servant is imbedded in the oldest strata of the New Testament and may well look to Jesus himself.

This language and imagery was rooted in the history and traditions of Jesus' people. Further, the Servant figure of Second Isaiah provided the lens and the language with which the earliest Christian community, following the lead of Jesus, could view and describe his person and mission. This approach, first of all, avoids flattening out the biblical text to a one-dimensional, prediction-fulfillment interpretation. Second, it respects the integrity of both sets of texts and the historical experiences that lie behind them. Finally, it provides a way of understanding the relationship between the Old and New Testaments more sensitive to the dynamic role that tradition and religious language play in shaping, handing on, and expressing a faith community's experience.

TWO IMPORTANT LESSONS FROM SECOND ISAIAH

New Testament Use of Old Testament Texts

The description above of how Jesus and the New Testament communities adopted and made use of the Servant of Yahweh passages from Isaiah offers a good example for the hermeneutic employed in general in the New Testament. On the surface it seems as if the New Testament writers read the Old Testament almost exclusively through "Christological lenses." By examining the process at work in greater depth, one can discover how a community takes traditional language and imagery and adapts and reuses it to put into words its own experience and reflections on that experience. A community with an oral and written tradition—such as the early Christians had in the Jewish Scriptures—is thereby able to make sense of its experience in a way that links it with its past. It also enables them to clarify and legitimate their interpretation and grasp of a sometimes disconcerting and not wholly comprehensible present.

Thus, for example, the shameful and horrifying death of Jesus as a common criminal in the crucifixion finds at least the beginning of an explanation and legitimation in the texts concerning the Servant of Yahweh in Second Isaiah. We could go on to give other examples of this reuse of the words and images of the Jewish Scriptures. The early Christians and their contemporary Jewish counterparts, for example, the Essene Community at Qumran, made use especially of prophetic texts and the Psalms. However, enough has been said here to indicate that the superficial and oversimplified prophecy-fulfillment model for understanding the relationship between the Old and the New Testament is no longer an adequate one.

Vicarious Suffering

A second important element in the Servant figure, one which has more obvious relevance today, is the notion of vicarious suffering, that is, that one innocent individual could take upon himself or herself the suffering of others. The Servant of Yahweh is explicitly depicted as assuming that role, especially in the Fourth Servant Song:

> Yet it was our infirmities that he bore,
>   our sufferings that he endured,
> While we thought of him as stricken,
>   as one smitten by God and afflicted.
> But he was pierced for our offenses,
>   crushed for our sins;
> Upon him was the chastisement that makes us whole,
>   by his stripes we were healed.
> We had all gone astray like sheep,
>   each following his own way;
> But the LORD laid upon him
>   the guilt of us all (Is 53:4-6).

Similar ideas are echoed in the Book of Job, which may be contemporaneous with Second Isaiah (for example, compare Job 42:8, 10 and Isaiah 53:10-12). Such reflections would not be surprising in the context of the bewilderment and suffering of the Exile experience. These texts provided an important element for the development of post-Exilic Jewish piety, for example, among the Essenes at Qumran and by Jesus and the early Christians.

REVIEW QUESTIONS

1. What is the historical context usually assigned for Isaiah 40-55? What is the relationship of these chapters to the rest of the Book of Isaiah?

2. Why does Gottwald speak of "controlled hysteria" when referring to the style of the poetry of Second Isaiah? What are some of the possibilities for describing the shape and structure of these chapters?

3. Discuss two of the purposes Second Isaiah seemed to have had in mind.

4. Why does the sense of comfort and reassurance hold such a central place in the poetry of these chapters?

5. What role does the theme of the Exodus play in these chapters? How does Second Isaiah reuse and transform the theme?

6. Describe Second Isaiah's "strategy for reconciliation" between Jews returning from Exile in Babylon and those living in Jerusalem and Judah.

7. Discuss the notion of creative redemption in Second Isaiah and its role in these chapters.

8. Who is "the Servant of Yahweh"? Why is this figure important for Christians who read the Old Testament?

9. Describe one possible historical scenario that would provide a context and background for the Servant and his experience.

10. How did Jesus and the early Christians use the Servant-language and Servant-figure found in Second Isaiah?

21

The Reestablishment of a Jewish Community in Jerusalem and Judah

Suggested Bible Readings: Genesis 1:1-2:4; 5:1-32; 11:10-27, 31-32; Leviticus 16; 19; Ezra 1; 3-10; Nehemiah 1-2; 4:1-7:4; 8-10; 13; Haggai 1-2; Zechariah 1-8

INTRODUCTION

The fall of the Babylonian empire to the Persians under Cyrus provided the opportunity for the reestablishment of the Jewish community in Judah and Jerusalem. The popular picture of a wholesale displacement of all or most of the Jews in Babylon back to Jerusalem and Judah is a mistaken one, however. In fact, most of the Jews in Babylon had been born there and had never seen Jerusalem. They were well-established and content where they were, and although they would support the reestablishment with help, encouragement, and monetary donations, the majority were not that interested in actually taking part in the return.

In contrast to the Babylonians and Assyrians, the Persians did not employ the practice of deportation and/or resettlement of conquered peoples as a way of demoralizing and inhibiting rebellion and revolt. Instead, the Persians allowed a fair degree of self-rule and encouraged and fostered local customs and religious practices. Indigenous leadership, both civil and religious, was coopted by the Persian authorities to handle a good bit of the day-to-day administration of a conquered territory. These local indigenous leaders found it to their advantage to cooperate and collaborate with the Persian administrators to ensure the Persians' continued support and protection for their rule and position.

The monumental staircase leading to the Audience Hall of the palace built by Persian king Darius I. The Jews lived under Persian rule during the first part of the post-Exilic period (538-333 B.C.E.).

The Persian dominance encompassed a vast territory, the largest empire heretofore in the ancient world. At its greatest dimension under Cyrus's second successor, Darius I, it extended from the Indus Valley in India on the east to Egypt in the west, and north to the threshold of Europe and Greece. To rule this sprawling territory the Persians allowed a significant degree of local autonomy. But they kept tight control by installing Mede and Persian administrators over the larger regions called *satrapies* and by establishing a speedy and effective communication system. Their complex but efficient administration of this vast empire lasted for over two hundred years, until the coming of Alexander the Great in 333 B.C.E.

As part of the Persian policy of granting a degree of local autonomy to conquered peoples, Cyrus issued a decree allowing the reestablishment of the Jewish community in Judah and Jerusalem and the rebuilding of the Temple to Yahweh. Although there is no surviving Persian record of the decree, two versions of it are preserved in the Book of Ezra. The first, in Ezra 1:2-4, is probably the text of the proclamation in Hebrew for the Jews themselves throughout the empire. This proclamation gives permission to return to Jerusalem and rebuild the Temple to any Jew who wishes to do so. It also allows for those who are willing to support the undertaking to contribute gold and silver. A second version of Cyrus' decree

The cylinder of Cyrus found in Babylon in 1879 proclaims in cuneiform the restoration of the temples (538 B.C.E.). It recalls the decree of Cyrus concerning the rebuilding of the Temple at Jerusalem: "The LORD the God of Heaven, has given me all the kingdoms of the earth, and he has charged me to build him a house at Jerusalem, which is in Judah." (Ezra 1:2).

(Ezr 6:3-5) may represent the king's own memorandum preserved in Aramaic in the Persian archives. The decree provides a contribution from the royal treasury to subsidize the rebuilding of the Temple. It also allows for the return to that rebuilt Temple of the gold and silver vessels brought as booty to Babylon from the sack of Jerusalem by Nebuchadnezzar in 587 B.C.E.

THE FOUR STAGES OF THE RETURN AND REESTABLISHMENT

It was to the advantage of the Persian central administration to have a friendly and cooperative local rule in a strategically important place such as Palestine, located at the distant western end of the empire. Thus the Persians gave constant and generous support to the indigenous local leadership, although they split the responsibilities between a civil officer (governor) and a religious one (high priest). The direction and impetus for the restoration of Jewish life and community came principally from the outside, from Babylonian and Persian Jews who contributed both monetary assistance and leaders.

The reestablishment occurred slowly, in stages, and only with difficulty. The Jews were given autonomy initially over only a small area, the city of Jerusalem itself and a surrounding territory equivalent to about twenty-five square miles. One of the obstacles they faced was the condition of the land. It had never fully recovered from the devastation of the Babylonian invasion and destruction of two generations earlier. Only slowly was the socio-economic infrastructure restored. A second obstacle consisted in the inevitable friction between the Jews returning from Babylon and those already inhabiting the land. Those already inhabiting the land were the children and grandchildren of the Jews who had survived the Babylonian war but had not fled or been exiled. The Jews arriving from Babylon were descendants of exiled Jews who had been, for the most part, from among the noble, landowning, and merchant classes. Some of the returning Jews may have laid claim to ancestral properties, and many of them probably enjoyed the advantages and privileges of Persian backing. In addition, their understanding of the Yahwist faith had developed in a different direction from that of the Jews who had remained in Judah. Some of these latter no doubt subscribed to the form of Yahwism practiced by the descendants of the northern kingdom of Israel, who were now known as Samaritans. Thus, besides the rebuilding of the economy, the economic and religio-cultural values among the various groups of Jews had to be negotiated and accommodated as the reestablishment and reunification of the community gradually took place.

The reestablishment of the Jews returning from Babylon came about in four stages. The first stage involved a group of Exilic Jews led by Sheshbazzar. He may have been one of King Jehoiachin's sons, since he is called a "prince of Judah":

> Then the family heads of Judah and Benjamin and the priests and Levites — everyone, that is, whom God had inspired to do so — prepared to go up to build the house of the LORD in Jerusalem. All their neighbors gave them help in every way, with silver, gold, goods, and cattle, and with many precious gifts besides all their free-will offerings. King Cyrus, too, had the utensils of the house of the LORD brought forth which Nebuchadnezzar had taken away from Jerusalem and placed in the house of his god. Cyrus, king of Persia, had them brought forth by the treasurer Mithredath, and counted out to Sheshbazzar, the prince of Judah (Ezr 1:5-8; see also 5:13-15).

The returning exiles were sent out from Babylon in 538 B.C.E., shortly after the decree of Cyrus. It is not clear how many Jews were involved, and the purpose of the group may have been to study the situation and lay some of the groundwork for future missions.

The second stage involved a large group of Exilic Jews who immigrated to Judah in 520 B.C.E (Ezr 2:2-70; Neh 7:7-72). The Persians designated Zerubbabel as the civil officer and Joshua as high priest. One of the first projects undertaken by the new arrivals was the rebuilding of the Temple in Jerusalem:

> Then the prophets Haggai and Zechariah, son of Iddo, began to prophesy to the Jews in Judah and Jerusalem in the name of the God of

Israel. Thereupon Zerubbabel, son of Shealtiel, and Joshua, son of Jozadak, began again to build the house of God in Jerusalem, with the prophets of God giving them support (Ezr 5:1-2; see further, 5:3-12; Hg 1:2-2:9; Zec 4:9).

The rebuilding had progressed enough by March of 515 B.C.E. that the new structure could be dedicated and a regular conduct of the restored cult be carried out. This restoration of the Temple and of a regular sacrificial ritual had a strong symbolic effect for the Jewish community not only in Judah but throughout the Mediterranean world. Many of the Jews lived far from Judah and Jerusalem. But now they had a common center toward which they could look, a point of reference, and a symbol of a rebuilding that held out hopes for future growth and further reestablishment.

But Jerusalem remained unfortified, and Judah was still a long way from the restoration of the economic and administrative infrastructure that would allow it once again to become prosperous. The necessary diligence and commitment in observing and carrying out the demands of the Temple cult were also apparently lacking. Thus the Persian court named Nehemiah as governor in 445 B.C.E. and sent him with an entourage of soldiers and other Jewish officials plus the necessary authority and resources to set matters aright. Nehemiah's main tasks were to rebuild and fortify the walls of Jerusalem, to repopulate it by transferring people in from the countryside, and to reform the Temple worship:

I prayed to God and then answered the king (Artaxerxes): "If it please the king, and if your servant is deserving of your favor, send me to Judah, to the city of my ancestors' graves, to rebuild it" . . . I asked the king further: "If it please the king, let letters be given to me for the governors of West-of-Euphrates, that they may afford me safe-conduct till I arrive in Judah; also a letter for Asaph, the keeper of the royal park, that he may give me wood for timbering the gates of the temple-citadel and for the city wall and for the house that I shall occupy." The king granted my requests, for the favoring hand of my God was upon me. I then proceeded to the governors of West-of-Euphrates and presented the king's letters to them. The king also sent with me army officers and cavalry (Neh 2:4-5, 7-9).

The mission of Ezra represents the fourth and final stage about which we know anything in the reestablishment of Jewish life and community in Judah. There is confusion concerning the chronological relationship of Ezra's mission with that of Nehemiah. But it seems probable that Ezra followed Nehemiah sometime in the late fifth century (between 458 and 398 B.C.E). Ezra was a member of a Jewish priestly family and a scribe or secretary in the Persian court. He led a group of about five thousand Exilic Jews to Judah, and his chief assignment seems to have been the official proclamation and establishment of the Jewish Law or Torah as the fundamental law of the land. This law or Torah was the one which had developed among the Exilic Jewish community and which they had come to accept as authoritative. Nehemiah 8 describes the solemn assembly in the square before the Water Gate in Jerusalem where the proclamation ceremony took place:

> Now when the seventh month came, the whole people gathered as one man in the open space before the Water Gate, and they called upon Ezra the scribe to bring forth the book of the law of Moses which the LORD prescribed for Israel. On the first day of the seventh month, therefore, Ezra the priest brought the law before the assembly, which consisted of men, women, and those children old enough to understand. Standing at one end of the open place that was before the Water Gate he read out of the book from daybreak until midday, in the presence of the men, the women, and the children old enough to understand; and all the people listened attentively to the book of the law (Neh 8:1-3).

Scholars generally identify the Book of the Law of Moses from which Ezra read as some form of our present Pentateuch, either a nearly completed version of it or some part of it such as the Holiness Code (Lv 17-26). The events associated with the missions of Nehemiah and Ezra are sketchy and confused. Very little else is known of the life and activities of the now restored Jewish community in Judah and Jerusalem, especially for most of the fourth century B.C.E. It is only after 333 B.C.E. when Alexander the Great appears on the scene that records, both biblical and non-biblical, are once again available.

THE PRIESTLY WRITER AND THE COMPLETION OF THE PENTATEUCH

With the fall of Jerusalem and the end of the Davidic dynasty in Judah, one of the principal groups that emerged to replace the monarchy in the leadership of the Jewish community was the priests. They were not a homogeneous group but from various lines or families. They included some, like

Jeremiah, who traced their origins to northern priestly groups who had moved south after the destruction of the northern kingdom of Israel. Rivalry and competition among these groups during the monarchy must have been somewhat vigorous since control of the Jerusalem Temple apparatus brought with it wealth and status.

One of these priestly lines, which claimed descent from Moses' brother, Aaron, managed to emerge as the privileged and favored one within the Jewish community during and after the Exile. It seems to have reached something of a compromise with other priestly groups by allowing them the status of Levites with the right to take some of the secondary roles in the restored Temple ritual. It is to this Aaronid priestly line that we owe not only the *P* source of the Pentateuch, but also the creation of the Pentateuch that we have today. This *P* source clearly contains materials reaching back as far as the days of the tribal confederation, although the present form of the *P* source is Exilic or post-Exilic. Since no traces of the *P* source or even its influence appear until Exilic and post-Exilic times, we can assume that this group did not have an important or influential role during the monarchy; other rival priestly lines were in favor. Many among those rival priestly lines who were in favor and thus controlled the Temple and its worship and revenues when Jerusalem fell to the Babylonians were likely killed or scattered. This opened the way for the secondary priestly groups such as the Aaronid line to fill the vacuum.

With their entry into position and influence also came the impetus to consolidate and legitimate that position by casting their traditions into a more formal document. This was similar to what the Yahwist and Elohist had done for their traditions centuries earlier. The traditions of the Aaronid priestly group consisted in collections of laws and customs, some narrative materials, and above all, ritual prescriptions for the ordering of the cult. A document using sources like these would lay the basis for a revitalized and renewed community centered and ordered principally around the Temple and the cult.

An examination of the Priestly source makes this emphasis on *order* clear. It divides history beginning with creation down to Moses into eleven phases, each signaled by the formula "these are the generations of. . . ." Thus it gives us the genealogies for which the *P* source is so well known: the heavens and the earth (Gn 2:4a); Adam (Gn 5:1a); Noah (Gn 6:9); Noah's sons, Shem, Ham, and Japheth (Gn 10:1); Shem (Gn 10:22); Terah (Gn 11:27); Ishmael (Gn 25:12); Isaac (Gn 25:19); Esau (Gn 36:1, 9); Jacob (Gn 37:2); Moses and Aaron (Nm 3:1).

The balance and symmetry in the *P* account of creation in the first chapter of Genesis also serve as excellent examples of that concern for order.

The six days of creation form three pairs in which the works done on each of the first three days serve as a preparation for the works done on each of the last three days. Thus the light created on the first day (Gn 1:3-5) prepared for the creation of the "greater light" (sun), the "lesser light" (moon), and the stars on the fourth day (Gn 1:14-19). Similarly, the seas and sky of the second day (Gn 1:6-8) provide the habitat for the fish and the birds brought into being on the fifth day (Gn 1:20-23). The dry land and vegetation of the third day (Gn 1:9-13) give setting and sustenance for the animal life and the humans created on the sixth day (Gn 1:24-31). Finally, the seventh day is the sabbath, when even God rests from work (Gn 2:1-3). The Priestly source goes so far as to anchor the ritual regulations of Israel in the very structure of the cosmos itself. Thus, for example, to observe the sabbath is not just a customary ritual or arbitrary law; it becomes a way of putting oneself in touch with and in harmony with the way the universe itself operates.

Although there are other ways of reconstructing the process by which our present Pentateuch reached its final form, we will present here the one which seems most plausible to us. This reconstruction sees the *P* document as having been written by one or more members of the Aaronid priesthood in the Exile. It was either this document itself that the priest Ezra brought to Jerusalem from Persia/Babylon and read before the assembled Jewish community (Neh 8), or it was the *P* document already combined with the *JE* epic traditions. In other words, right around the time of Ezra, either before he arrived in Jerusalem or shortly thereafter, the *P* document, a product of Ezra's priestly circle, was combined with the *JE* narrative epic. Eventually the Book of Deuteronomy would be detached from its place as the introduction to the Deuteronomistic History and added on at the end of this combined *JEP* complex (Genesis-Exodus-Leviticus-Numbers).

This process of combining the various legal and narrative traditions into our final Pentateuch did not come about spontaneously or without good reason. There were a number of religious, social, and political factors at work. First of all there was the realization that, if the Jewish community was to survive the demise of the monarchy, it must reinterpret and reformulate its traditions in such a way as to keep its contact with the past and at the same time build a new foundation for the future. The question of how this should be done was not just a theoretical one. The harsh realities of life in the Exilic and post-Exilic times both in Babylon and in Judah and the struggles of various groups and interests within the community were both important contributing factors. The concrete situation and the differing agenda within the community would determine how the laying of the new foundation would take place and who would have the deciding word within that refounded community.

The answer to who would have the say in the refounded community is given by the Pentateuch itself. The obviously controlling tradition is that of the priestly group, which indicates that they had emerged as the chief decision-makers and guides by the end of the Exile and into the post-Exilic period. They created a literary work that was to serve as the self-expression of that refounded community's identity as well as provide the guidelines for its life in the future.

But in the process, the priestly group had to take into account the demands and interests of other groups also contending for leadership, or at least for a voice and for recognition within the community. Thus the priestly group made use of the document embodying their traditions as the controlling frame and principal source (what we have come to call *P*). This they combined with two of the other major complexes of traditions looked upon by other groups as important for the identity and guidance of the new community. These other two major complexes were the *JE* epic narrative and, eventually, the Law Code of the Book of Deuteronomy. These four complexes of tradition, the Yahwist (*J*) and Elohist (*E*), which had already integrated into a unified narrative some 150 years earlier, the Priestly (*P*), and the Deuteronomist (*D*), represented the values, viewpoints, and traditions of the diverse groups within the community. The skillful weaving together of these four complexes resulted not in a neutral and colorless melange. Rather, this process produced a new and genial document which incorporated the best of each tradition, but in a way balanced by, modified by, and in tension with each and all of the others. The *P* tradition is clearly the controlling one, and not only in its role as frame for the others. The sheer bulk of its legal materials dominates and almost overshadows the rest. The result is that the future direction for the identity and life of the community is clear. It will be centered around the restored Temple and its sacrificial ritual, and it will be guided by the priests. The significant presence of the *JE* epic narrative, however, modified and limited to a degree the strong priestly tone of the final product. And despite this strong priestly tone in the Genesis through Numbers complex, the final word eventually went to the Deuteronomic circles, with the appending of the Book of Deuteronomy at the end of the now completed Pentateuch.

THE PENTATEUCH AND THE DEUTERONOMISTIC HISTORY

We have already seen that another major document of the Jewish community predated the completed Pentateuch. This was the Deuteronomistic History, written after the death of king Josiah (after 609 B.C.E.) just before the Exile, and revised during the Exile itself (see above, chap. 11). Our present Book of Deuteronomy originally stood at the head of this document to serve as its introduction. How did the Book of Deuteronomy end up at its present place as the conclusion of the Pentateuch instead? The answer seems to lie in the politics of the restoration process of Jewish life and community in Judah and Jerusalem after the Exile.

In allowing a degree of autonomy and self-rule to their subjugated peoples, the Persians were careful to see that each had an appropriate body of law, civil and/or religious, to govern its internal affairs and ensure order. The logical choice for the newly reestablished Jewish community was either the Pentateuch, completed as far as the Genesis-through-Numbers complex, or the Deuteronomistic History. It did not take much reflection to realize that the Deuteronomistic History, despite the impressive collection of law at its head, would not serve. Its nationalistic tone and its promotion of David and the monarchy under David's descendants would be seen by the Persian officials as possible inspiration for independence and rebellion.

The choice thus fell to the Genesis-through-Numbers complex. However, they also wanted to give a place to the important collection of laws in the Book of Deuteronomy and accommodate those groups and interests within the community who especially valued it. Thus the book was detached from its place at the head of the Deuteronomistic History and edited into its present final position in the now completed Pentateuch. This editing was done, in a somewhat awkward way, by placing the announcement of Moses' impending death toward the end of the Book of Numbers (Nm 27:12-14). The editors then put the words of Deuteronomy on Moses' lips as his last "testament" to his people and added the account of his actual death and burial at the conclusion of this last testament in chapter 34 of Deuteronomy.

CONCLUSION

The community of Jews who emerged from the Exile needed a new focus, a new identity, if they were to survive the loss of their national identity and independence with the demise of the state. This survival meant a degree of cooperation and collaboration with the succession of imperial powers who dominated the Ancient Near East in the following years ahead—Persia, Greece, Rome. This new focus and identity were significantly shaped by the dominant group in this period, the priests. Their influence in stamping the newly formulated foundational document for that community, the Pentateuch or Torah, gave the life of this community a strongly religious and cultic shape, especially with its emphasis on law, ritual, and regulation.

The outward life of the Jews now took on a definite and identifiable character that clearly set them apart from others. The mark of the covenant with God "in the flesh," that is, circumcision, the strict observance of the sabbath, the various dietary laws and regulations, all now served more and more to distinguish the faithful Jew as a member of God's people. A new kind of piety also emerged. Knowing that it had been the violation of the covenant law that had finally brought on the disaster of 587 B.C.E., a new zeal in the observance of the covenant law began to be nourished. As well, a reading and study of that law, both in public gathering and in private, and a focus on its written form, above all in the Pentateuch itself, moved more and more to the center of Jewish life and practice.

At the same time, the production of this document acted as something of a catalyst to crystallize and put into written form other traditional materials. Around this same time the collecting and editing of the prophetic texts began in earnest. Thus within a century or two, the Pentateuch was complemented by "the Prophets." This prophetic corpus included the Former Prophets or Deuteronomistic History, and the Latter Prophets or prophetic books containing the collected and edited oracles of prophets from the pre-Exilic through early post-Exilic periods. "The Law and the Prophets" would soon be spoken of in a single breath as together forming the foundation of Jewish life. The Jews were now becoming increasingly a "people of the Book."

REVIEW QUESTIONS

1. Discuss briefly how the government and leadership's policies of the Persian Empire affected the course of Jewish history.

2. Describe the four stages in the return and reestablishment of a Jewish community in Jerusalem and Judah.

3. Who were Nehemiah and Ezra? What role did they play in the return and reestablishment of a Jewish community in Jerusalem and Judah?

4. What were some of the obstacles faced by the Jewish community in the process of the restoration of Jewish life in Jerusalem and Judah?

5. Discuss the origin and character of the Priestly source in the Pentateuch.

6. Describe one way of reconstructing the process by which the Pentateuch reached its final form during this period.

7. What "politics" caused the Book of Deuteronomy to end up at its present place as the conclusion of the Pentateuch?

8. Which group emerged as the leaders of the Jewish community in the post-Exilic period? What effect did the emergence of that particular group have on the identity and character of that community?

9. Why can we say from this point on that the Jews were "a people of the Book"?

PART VII

THE WRITINGS

22

The Psalms

Suggested Bible Readings: Genesis 49; Exodus 15; Numbers 23-24; Deuteron-omy 32; 1 Samuel 1; Joel 1-2; 1 Chronicles 25; 2 Chronicles 5-7; Psalms 4; 17; 20; 21; 22; 23; 51; 103; 104; 105; 116; 117; 136; 149

INTRODUCTION

A reading and study of the Psalms in the context of an introduction to the Old Testament contributes to a fuller understanding of the Old Testament in a number of ways. For one thing, the various themes, traditions, persons, events, and values come together as a whole and are integrated and celebrated in a community context of prayer and worship. In their origin these prayer poems were composed for and used in Israel's public worship, first at the various shrines throughout the country and later in Solomon's and then Zerubbabel's Temple. In the Psalter we have something of a summary and distillation of the whole of the Old Testament in the context of prayer and worship. As these songs were written down in a more formal style and eventually collected into our present Psalter, they also became the object of private prayer and meditation. From a human word addressing God they gradually assumed the form also of God's word addressing humans.

Another side of the life of ancient Israel which these texts provide for us is a sense of the devotion and piety of its people. Israel's history is filled with men and women who are presented as models of piety and loyalty to Yahweh: Abraham, Hannah (the mother of Samuel), David, Josiah, Judith, Tobit, and others. The Psalms offer us indirectly an idea of the piety and devotion aspired to by the Israelites or Jews in imitation of these heroes and models.

As we shall see, almost one-third of the Psalms fall into the category of the "Individual Lament" or "Song of Supplication," that is, prayer to God for deliverance by one who is in distress. These songs express this people's confidence and trust and love for Yahweh. They put us in touch with the emotions and sentiments which inspired and supported and provided this people with the necessary motivation in their struggle to build a community and society according to the vision that was their heritage.

Finally, these songs give us insight into Israel's idea of the nature and character of Yahweh, the God whom Israel worshipped. We see this in the titles used to talk to and talk about that God: Creator, Redeemer, Shepherd, Rock of Refuge, Light, Shield, Savior. We see it in the attributes ascribed to Yahweh: kind, loving, merciful, just, generous, forgiving, all-powerful, strong. We see it in the actions and events by which Yahweh touched the lives of this people, both as individuals and as a community: he led us out of Egypt, he saved us from our foes, he gives food to the hungry, he heals all our wounds, he guards and protects us.

HEBREW POETRY

The Psalter is a collection of prayer-poems, that is, prayers written in a rhythmic and structured language that has its own characteristics and diction. Every language makes some distinction between speech that functions principally for communication of ideas or information or narration (prose) and speech of a more studied and formal kind (poetry). A quick glance through the Old Testament reveals that one-third of it is of this second kind. Passages of the Pentateuch (for example Genesis 49, Exodus 15, Numbers 23 and 24, Deuteronomy 32 and 33), much of the Prophets, and almost the whole of Job, Proverbs, and the Psalter are in poetry.

The study of the Bible's poetry has advanced significantly in recent years. These advances are largely due to the discovery by archeologists of numerous texts with examples of poetry from Mesopotamia, Egypt, and especially ancient Canaan. One characteristic of Hebrew poetry, however, has been explicitly recognized and studied for over two hundred years: parallelism. The parallelistic nature of Hebrew poetry was first pointed out and defined by Anglican bishop Robert Lowth in a series of lectures delivered at Oxford University in 1753. Among other things, Lowth noted that the lines of poetry in Hebrew are usually divided into two, and sometimes three, segments. In about half of these segmented lines of poetry, the second segment echoes or repeats the thought of the first segment. Lowth referred to this phenomenon as "synonymous parallelism."

Present Division into Five "Books"

Introduction to the Psalter — Psalm 1
Book I   — Psalms 2-41
Book II   — Psalms 42-72
Book III   — Psalms 73-89
Book IV   — Psalms 90-106
Book V   — Psalms 107-150
(Conclusion—Psalm 150)

Traces of Earlier Collections

Book I—Davidic Psalms (Psalms 3-41).
Books II and III—The "Elohist Psalter," so named because it uses the generic name for God (Elohim) which has been systematically substituted throughout these Psalms for the proper name, Yahweh (Psalms 42-89).
Books IV and V—The "Yahwist Psalter" (Psalms 90-150).
Most of the Individual Laments are in Books I and II.
Most of the Hymns of Praise are in Books III and V.

Numbering of the Psalms in the Hebrew Bible versus numbering in the Septuagint (and Latin Vulgate) Bible

Hebrew	Septuagint and Latin Vulgate
1 to 8	1 to 8
9	9:1-21
10	9:22-39
11 to 113	10 to 112
114	113:1-8
115	113:9-26
116:1-9	114
116:10-19	115
117 to 146	116 to 145
147:1-11	146
147:12-20	147
148 to 150	148 to 150

> Not according to our sins does he deal with us,
>> nor does he requite us according to our crimes.
>>> (Ps 103:10; see also Pss 6:2; 9:19)

In this example the phrase, "does he requite," repeats in different words the phrase in the first segment, "does he deal." The word "us" occurs in both segments. And "according to our crimes" in the second half echoes the phrase "according to our sins" in the first half.

In many of the other poetic lines, the second segment balances the first by filling out or completing its thought in what Lowth described as "synthetic parallelism."

> Depart from me, all evildoers,
>> for the LORD has heard the sound of my weeping.
>>> (Ps 6:9)

> Look toward me and have pity on me,
>> for I am alone and afflicted (Ps 25:16).

> He led them forth laden with silver and gold,
>> with not a weakling among their tribes (Ps 105:37).

Scholars are coming to recognize that the first term, "synonymous parallelism," is something of a misnomer, because the second segment is often not, in fact, synonymous with the first segment. That is, it does not simply repeat the idea or expression of the first segment using different words. Rather, the second segment almost invariably heightens, intensifies, clarifies, focuses, or expands on the first segment. This is most obvious when numbers are involved. The number in the second segment is almost always significantly higher in value than the number in the first segment:

> If Cain is avenged sevenfold,
>> then Lamech seventy-sevenfold (Gn 4:24).

> Saul has slain his thousands,
>> and David his ten thousands (1 Sm 18:7).

> Three things are too wonderful for me,
>> yes, four I cannot understand (Prv 30:18).

Proverbs 3:10 is an example of intensification between the two segments taking place:

Then will your barns be filled with grain,
with new wine your vats will overflow.

The granaries will be full. The wine vats will not just be full; they will be so filled that they will be overflowing. Jeremiah 7:34 presents instances of focusing and making the abstract concrete:

In the cities of Judah and in the streets of Jerusalem I will silence the cry of joy, the cry of gladness, the voice of the bridegroom and the voice of the bride, for the land will be turned to rubble.

In the first line of verse 34, the poet focuses. He moves from the larger geographical area, "the cities of Judah," to a small space within it, "the streets of Jerusalem." In the second verse, the abstract terms "gladness" and "joy" from the first verse are made concrete. It is not just gladness and joy in general; it is the gladness and joy of the bridegroom and bride that will be silenced.

The use of parallelism is just one example of the complexity and subtlety of Hebrew poetry, but it is the one most readily identified and transferable in translation. Awareness of it as we read or study or pray the Psalms should remind us that we are not dealing with a primitive and spontaneous form of expression. Rather, we are faced with sophisticated and often elegant poetry, part of an artistic tradition and culture already hundreds of years old when these songs were written, the artistic tradition of ancient Canaan reaching back into the middle and early second millennium B.C.E.

THE LITURGICAL ORIGIN OF THE PSALMS

Because the Psalms are presented to us in a book, a book which in turn is part of the Sacred Scriptures, the tendency has been to assume that they are texts to be read and meditated on. This, in fact, is the origin and purpose of the present Book of Psalms or Psalter. Its editors were intent on creating a literary work, not simply a collection of liturgical texts. The focus in this post-Exilic period was on the written word as the medium of revelation, especially now that prophecy for all practical purposes had ceased. Thus they set out to create a book among the other books which were on their way to becoming, finally, Sacred Scripture. The words by which Israel had spoken to God through these prayers in the public worship were now in the process of becoming God's word to Israel, God speaking to us in human words.

Early in the twentieth century, however, scholars came to the conclusion that the Psalms were not originally composed to be read, either to others or to oneself in private prayer and meditation. Rather, the Psalms have their origin in and their most comprehensible setting in the public worship of ancient Israel. Only later were these poem-prayers written down, collected, and finally edited into book form for more private use. Thus, to understand the Psalms properly, we need to begin with their liturgical origin.

The person chiefly responsible for this breakthrough was the German scholar Hermann Gunkel, whose major work on the Psalms appeared in 1926. Gunkel had developed the method of "form criticism" in dealing with biblical texts, and that method worked particularly well in the study of the Psalms. In surveying a large number of texts, Gunkel found that he could identify certain recurring patterns. In other words, a certain group of texts, perhaps not at first sight related, were found to be examples of the same literary form or genre; that is, all the texts in that group contain the same set of recurring elements. For example, he found that a number of the Psalms, although often using different words and images, all begin with a short invitation to praise or bless God. They continue with a lengthy explanation of why God is worthy of that praise, and conclude with a short repetition of the initial invitation to praise. Gunkel called these Psalms "Hymns" or "Songs of Praise."

Applying this insight to the 150 poems in the Psalter, Gunkel discovered that he was able to group them into five predominant types or literary forms, plus a number of less common types or forms. Each exemplar of the form exhibited the presence of a nearly identical pattern; that is, certain elements almost invariably recurred in each of the Psalms of one particular type. For the Psalter the five predominant types or forms were: (1) Hymns or Songs of Praise; (2) Individual Laments or Songs of Supplication; (3) Individual Thanksgiving Songs; (4) Communal Laments; and (5) Royal Psalms. Some of the less common types include Communal Thanksgiving Songs (for example, Psalms 65, 67, 118), Blessings (Psalms 128, 133, 134), Wisdom Poetry (Psalms 32, 73, 119), and Entrance and Processional Liturgies (Psalms 15, 24, 68, 132).

From study of the forms or recurring speech patterns he had identified in the Psalter, Gunkel came to the conclusion that these forms or speech patterns had their origin and most comprehensible life setting in Israel's public worship. Sigmund Mowinckel, a Norwegian scholar, built on Gunkel's work. In his major work on the Psalms, published in 1951, Mowinckel demonstrated convincingly not only that the Psalm forms had their life-setting in Israel's liturgy. He showed that most of the Psalms in our present Psalter were originally composed for and used in public worship.

THE PSALM FORMS

The Hymn or Song of Praise

The Hymn or Song of Praise almost invariably contains three elements: (1) an invitation, (2) a body, and (3) a conclusion. The Hymn usually begins with an invitation, a brief exhortation to praise or bless God:

> Praise the LORD, all you nations;
> glorify him, all your peoples! (Ps 117:1).

> Sing to the LORD a new song
> of praise in the assembly of the faithful.
> Let Israel be glad in their maker,
> let the children of Zion rejoice in their king.
> (Ps 149:1-2)

The body of the Hymn comprises the bulk of the song and develops the reasons or motives for praising God. These motives could include God's "wondrous works" in Israel's history:

> Who smote the Egyptians in their first-born,
> for his mercy endures forever;
> And brought out Israel from their midst,
> for his mercy endures forever.
> (Ps 136:10-11; see also Pss 78, 105, 106)

Or the body of the Psalm could focus on God's power in nature and creation:

> You fixed the earth upon its foundation,
> not to be moved forever;
> With the ocean, as with a garment, you covered it;
> above the mountains the waters stood.
> (Ps 104:5-6; see also Pss 29; 148)

The Psalm could list God's attributes, such as holiness (Ps 99:3), majesty (Ps 145:5), kindness and loyalty (Ps 117:2). Psalm 103 provides a good example of such a list:

> Merciful and gracious is the LORD,
> slow to anger and abounding in kindness (Ps 103:8).

A brief call to praise or bless God, often a repetition of the opening invitation, usually comprises the Hymn's conclusion:

> Bless the LORD, O my soul;
>> and all my being, bless his holy name.
> Bless the LORD, O my soul,
>> and forget not all his benefits. . . .
> Bless the LORD, all his works,
>> everywhere in his domain.
> Bless the LORD, O my soul!
>> (Ps 103:1-2, 22; see also Ps 136:1-3, 26)

Norman Gottwald lists the following as Hymns or Songs of Praise: Psalms 8; 19:1-6; 29; 33; 95:1-7c; 100; 103; 104; 111; 113; 114; 117; 135; 145-150.

The Individual Lament or Song of Supplication

The most common form among the Psalms, comprising almost one-third of the songs in the Psalter, is the Individual Lament or Song of Supplication. What the massive presence of this particular form might indicate about the situation and struggles in ancient Israel's social and economic life will be explored below. It does correspond to the human tendency to turn to God for help and rescue in moments of trouble and distress. Ordinarily, examples of this form contain five elements. To list or describe these five elements, we refer to the classic example of this form, Psalm 22, the Psalm which the gospel traditions put on the lips of Jesus as he hung dying on the cross (Mt 27:46; Mk 15:34). The Individual Lament normally begins with a short *invocation,* which is often urgent and forceful:

> My God, my God, why have you forsaken me,
>> far from my prayer, from the words of my cry?
> O my God, I cry out by day, and you answer not;
>> by night, and there is no relief for me (Ps 22:2-3).

In the *complaint* the psalmist describes the situation of distress, usually in quite vivid terms:

> But I am a worm, not a man;
>> the scorn of men, despised by the people.
> All who see me scoff at me;
>> they mock me with parted lips, they wag their heads:

"He relied on the LORD; let him deliver him,
  let him rescue him, if he loves him."
        (vv. 7-9; see also vv. 13-19)

The language, however, is for the most part vague, employing many stereotyped images. There are very few concrete or specific references that could help identify a specific individual or situation. The vagueness and generality of the language leaves the Psalm open to use by any number of individuals. This lack of concrete or specific references may also have been a strategy to protect the one praying the Psalm from retaliation by his or her persecutors.

In the *supplication* the psalmist voices the actual plea for rescue:

Be not far from me, for I am in distress;
  be near, for I have no one to help me.
        (v. 12; see also vv. 20-22)

Ordinarily the Lament includes a *motive* expressing trust and indicating why the psalmist expects God to hear and respond to the prayer:

You have been my guide since I was first formed,
  my security at my mother's breast.
To you I was committed at birth,
  from my mother's womb you are my God.
        (vv. 10-11; see also vv. 4-6)

Usually toward the end of the Psalm a dramatic shift in tone occurs. It moves from fervent pleas for rescue to the fifth element, proclamation of confidence or *praise and thanksgiving* that the prayer has been or will be heard and answered:

"You who fear the LORD, praise him;
  all you descendants of Jacob, give glory to him;
  revere him, all you descendants of Israel!
For he has not spurned nor disdained
  the wretched man in his misery,
Nor did he turn his face away from him,
  but when he cried out to him, he heard him."
        (vv. 24-25; see also vv. 23, 26-32)

It appears likely that a pause preceded this final element during which a priest or temple prophet uttered an oracle or blessing. The supplicant was assured that God has acknowledged the petition and that it will be granted. Thus the mood changes abruptly from one of supplication and complaint to one of confidence and even joyful praise and thanksgiving.

The story of Hannah, the mother of Samuel, in 1 Samuel 1 offers a good example of such a scenario. Hannah comes to the shrine of Yahweh at Shiloh with her husband Elkanah for the annual celebration of the Feast of Tabernacles. She approaches the temple or holy place where the Ark of the Covenant was kept and offers up her prayer for the Lord to deliver her from her barrenness:

> In her bitterness she prayed to the LORD, weeping copiously, and she made a vow, promising: "O LORD of hosts, if you look with pity on the misery of your handmaid, if you remember me and do not forget me, if you give your handmaid a male child, I will give him to the LORD for as long as he lives; neither wine nor liquor shall he drink, and no razor shall ever touch his head" (1 Sm 1:10-11).

Hannah engages in a brief exchange with Eli, the attendant priest, who at first mistakes her distraught condition for drunkenness. Hannah then receives a reply from Eli, a kind of priestly "oracle," assuring her that Yahweh will grant her petition: "Go in peace, and may the God of Israel grant you what you have asked of him" (v. 17). The text goes on, "She went to her quarters, ate and drank with her husband, and no longer appeared downcast" (v. 18).

Sometimes in the Individual Lament, the supplicant protests innocence if he or she has a sense of being unjustly punished for a sin (Ps 17:26). Some Individual Laments, on the other hand, contain humble and moving acknowledgments of sin and requests for pardon. The well-known and often prayed Psalm 51 offers an example of this latter type, as do the other six so-called Penitential Psalms of Christian tradition (Pss 6, 32, 38, 102, 130, 143).

Norman Gottwald includes these Psalms in his List of Individual Laments or Songs of Supplication: Pss 3, 5, 6, 7, 9-10, 13, 17, 22, 25, 26, 28, 31, 35, 36, 39, 40, 42-43, 51, 54, 55, 56, 57, 59, 61, 63, 64, 69, 70, 71, 77, 86, 88, 94, 102, 109, 130, 140, 141, 142, 143.

The Individual Thanksgiving Song

Balancing or corresponding to the Laments of the Individual are the Individual Thanksgiving Songs. In these, the individual gives thanks and praise to God for a favor granted or for deliverance from some distress or harmful situation. These could include a dangerous illness or oppression or persecution. The *introduction* of the Individual Thanksgiving Song announces the theme:

> I will give thanks to you, O LORD, with all my heart,
>   [for you have heard the words of my mouth;]
>   in the presence of the angels I will sing your praise.
>   (Ps 138:1)

The *body* of the Song recounts the specific reasons for gratitude and contains: (1) a description of the situation of distress, usually using vague and stereotyped language, as in the Individual Lament; (2) the cry to God for help; and (3) an affirmation that the deliverance was the work of God. Psalm 116 provides a good example of the *body* of a Thanksgiving Psalm with all three of these elements:

> The cords of death encompassed me;
>   the snares of the nether world seized upon me;
>   I fell into distress and sorrow,
> And I called upon the name of the LORD,
>   "O LORD, save my life!". . .
> Return, O my soul, to your tranquillity,
>   for the LORD has been good to you.
> For he has freed my soul from death,
>   my eyes from tears, my feet from stumbling.
>   (Ps 116:3-4, 7-8)

The *conclusion* briefly repeats the initial expression of thanksgiving and praise (see Ps 30:13).

Even though these Psalms bear the name *Individual* Thanksgiving Songs, this does not mean that they were recited alone or in solitude. They originally functioned as a text for the prayer of an individual in a communal context. The setting was the local shrine or, later, the Temple in Jerusalem. The individual wishing to offer this act of thanksgiving came with a group of relatives and/or friends. In their presence he or she would sing or have sung or recited this prayer, often accompanied by a sacrifice or a libation. This could be a cup of costly wine or oil poured out upon the altar, as described in Psalm 116:

> How shall I make return to the LORD
>   for all the good he has done for me?
> The cup of salvation I will take up,
>   and I will call upon the name of the LORD; . . .
> To you will I offer sacrifice of thanksgiving,
>   and I will call upon the name of the LORD.

> ˙ My vows to the LORD I will pay
>> in the presence of all his people (Ps 116:12-13; 17-18).

Gottwald includes in this form Psalms 30, 32, 34, 41, 52, 66, 92, 116, 138.

The Communal Lament

Another frequent form found in the Psalter is the Communal Lament. Its structure follows closely that of the Individual Lament or Song of Supplication. It almost invariably contains at least the cry for help, the description of distress, and the expression of certainty of being heard. In these, the situation of distress is sometimes a little more specific and concrete than in the Individual Lament. Further, it is characterized by the specifically communal nature of the trouble, for example, the threat of an enemy invasion, famine, or socio-economic oppression. The first two chapters of the Book of Joel describe communal distress caused by a locust plague. The response of the community to this threat takes, among other things, the form of a public ceremony of fast and prayer by which the community calls on Yahweh for deliverance:

> Gird yourselves and weep, O priests!
>> wail, O ministers of the altar!
> Come, spend the night in sackcloth,
>> O ministers of my God! . . .
> Proclaim a fast,
>> call an assembly;
> Gather the elders,
>> all who dwell in the land,
> Into the house of the LORD, your God,
>> and cry to the LORD! (Jl 1:13-14).

Further examples of the Communal Lament include Psalms 12, 44, 58, 60, 74, 79, 83, 85, 89, 90, 108, 123, 126, 137, 144.

Royal Psalms

The fifth major category in the Psalter, according to Gunkel, consists of the Royal Psalms. This category does not constitute a special genre or form as such but brings together those Psalms which are obviously associated in some direct way with the king. It thus includes Individual Laments (Ps 144:1-11) and Individual Thanksgiving Songs (Ps 18) intended for recital by or for the king. The Psalter also preserves the texts from ceremonial liturgies for the king. Psalm 20 apparently represents a prayer for the king before going out to battle:

> May we shout for joy at your victory
>   and raise the standards in the name of our God.
> The LORD grant all your requests! . . .
> O LORD, grant victory to the king,
>   and answer us when we call upon you (vv. 6, 10).

Psalm 45 is a marriage song for a royal wedding. A number of the Royal Psalms seem in some way associated with the king's coronation and/or the yearly anniversary celebration of his accession to the throne:

> O LORD, in your strength the king is glad;
>   in your victory how greatly he rejoices! . . .
> For you welcomed him with goodly blessings,
>   you placed on his head a crown of pure gold.
> He asked life of you; you gave him length of days forever
>   and ever (Ps 21:2, 4-5; see also Pss 2; 72; 110).

Minor Categories

Finally there are a number of minor categories in the Psalter, and mixed types which combine the elements of two or more common forms. One minor type, which includes only a few Psalms but Psalms that are well known and popular, is the Psalm of Confidence. This category is minor not only because it contains only a few Psalms but also because it is dependent on and derived from a major category, the Individual Lament.

One of the elements usually present in the Individual Lament described above is the *motive,* in which the supplicant expresses confidence and trust that God will answer the individual's plea. This element evolved into a distinct genre and became the basis of a prayer on its own, one in which the individual elaborates and develops the theme of confidence and trust in God:

> Know that the LORD does wonders for his faithful one;
>   the LORD will hear me when I call upon him. . . .
> You put gladness into my heart,
>   more than when grain and wine abound.
> As soon as I lie down, I fall peacefully asleep,
>   for you alone, O LORD,
>   bring security to my dwelling (Ps 4:4, 8-9).

Besides the popular Psalm 23 ("The Lord is my Shepherd"), which also falls into this category, other Songs of Confidence include Psalms 11, 16, 27, 62, 121, 131.

Some of the other minor types in the Psalter according to Gottwald, are Entrance and Processional Liturgies (Pss 15, 24, 68, 118, 132), Blessings (Pss 128, 133, 134), and Wisdom and Torah Psalms (Pss 1, 19, 37, 49, 73, 91, 112, 119, 127, 139).

THE SHAPE OF THE PSALTER

Our discussion thus far has focused on individual psalms. We have stressed the importance of identifying their form as a helpful guide to understanding and interpretation. This approach recognizes the origin of the psalms as liturgical songs composed for use in public worship in shrine, temple, and synagogue.

The last fifteen years have witnessed a new direction in psalm research, however. Scholars have shifted their attention from a focus on individual psalms to a study of the Psalter as a whole. Previously, there was a tendency to think of the Psalter as simply a haphazard collection of hymns, not unlike our modern hymnals. Apart from some evidence that it was a "collection of collections," no unifying principle was necessarily at work.

Recent work on the Psalter has uncovered clear principles of organization. It is not simply a collection or compilation of liturgical texts but has a unity intentionally greater than the sum of its parts. This intentionality appears right at the beginning, in the choice of the first two psalms. Psalm 1 represents not so much a song as it does an invitation to reflection and prayer. The psalm prefaces what are presumably written texts to be read and pondered, and declares "happy" the one who "meditates on his (the Lord's) law day and night" (v.2).

Psalm 2 in its turn announces the theme of kingship, which the final psalms of Books II and III (Pss 72 and 89, respectively) will echo. But this emphasis on human kingship in this first part of the Psalter concludes on a sad note. Psalm 89 focuses initially on God's covenant with David. Then it moves on to an account of God's rejection of the covenant with David (vv. 39-46) and concludes with the anguished plea and prayer of the Davidic descendants. See for example, verses 47 and 50:

> How long, O Lord? Will you hide yourself forever?
>> Will your wrath burn like fire? . . .
> Where are your ancient favors, O Lord,
>> which you pledged to David by your faithfulness?

By contrast, Books IV (Pss 90-106) and V (Pss 107-150) sound a new note—Yahweh's kingship, as opposed to rule by any human king. This, of course, reflects the period after the exile, when Israel had no king but Yahweh. The "shape" of the Psalter thus reflects a movement from Davidic monarchy, through the demise of the monarchy and the exile, into a new era and a new understanding of Israel's relationship with Yahweh as its unique king.

Other recent studies have highlighted the work of other editors who have had a hand in earlier and later stages of the growth of the Psalter. Besides the theme of kingship, the influence of Israel's wisdom writers and the promoters of Torah piety (see Pss 1 and 119, for example) can also be discerned.

THE SOCIO-HISTORIC SETTING OF THE PSALMS

We remarked above on the massive presence of the Individual Lament in the Psalter, comprising almost one-third of the Psalms preserved therein. What factors in Israelite society help to illuminate and explain this great emphasis on personal distress and suffering? Disease, threat from enemies, loss of property, the prosperity and success of the wicked—these are only a sampling of the generalized situations of distress from which these psalmists cry out to God for deliverance.

We have seen in our survey of the history of the monarchy the systematic attack on the socio-economic order of tribal Israel by the royal establishment in cooperation with the increasingly wealthy merchant class and landed aristocracy. The centralized tributary economy promoted by the kings threatened to subvert and destroy Israel's village-based communitarian economy. The result of this systematic attack was the impoverishment and suffering of the majority of Israel's population. This development within Israelite society was one of the principal subjects of the preaching of the prophets. A few tentative reform movements, such as that under King Hezekiah and that of King Josiah and the Deuteronomic circles, attempted to roll back this process.

The egalitarian thrust of the tribal communitarian economy held out the ideal of equal access to the resources and means of production by all members of the covenant community. For the vast majority of Israelite families that meant the possession of a plot of land and a dwelling place, as well as control over their surplus production. These rights were institutionally protected by the provisions of Israel's covenant in a series of mutual aid measures. One family or clan experiencing difficulty would be helped over the "rough spots" by gifts or low-interest/interest-free loans. Redemption from debt bondage was also guaranteed and freedom from excessive taxation and forced labor was supposed to be the result of a decentralized political system.

All of these arrangements fundamental to the tribal community of Yahweh were threatened by the introduction of the monarchy. Heavy taxation and forced labor imposed by the increasingly powerful and centralizing royal bureaucracy undermined the independence of the small extended family units. Many of these extended family units eventually lost their ancestral properties either by government confiscation or failed mortgages. The increasingly wealthy and powerful merchant and landowning classes, supported by the royal establishment, furthered the creation of large landed estates. This was effected by the accumulation of these small ancestral plots, which they seized by both legal and illegal means. The land was turned from the growing of subsistence crops, especially grains, to the cultivation of vineyards and olive groves for the production of wine and oil for export.

The subsequent suffering and distress of large segments of the Israelite populace is vividly described and denounced by the whole series of prophets whose oracles and preaching have been preserved for us. Obviously this may also be what lies in the background of the complaints and distress given such forceful and poignant voice in these Individual Laments.

Previous interpretation and use of these Psalms tended to emphasize the personal psychological aspects of this suffering and failed to take account of the larger socio-economic context which was often the source of that suffering. Depression and anxiety would inevitably follow the loss of one's source of livelihood, and disease would accompany the resultant poverty with its poor diet, harsh working conditions, and so forth. These situations fit both the descriptions of distress in these Psalms and the socio-economic developments in Israel and Judah during the years of the monarchy. Attention to this wider societal context puts us in clearer touch with the source of the suffering from which this large body of literature pleads for deliverance. It adds depth and new dimension to our understanding of these powerful prayers. It also renders them more meaningful in the larger context of our worship and prayer as a faith community in today's world in which we find so many similar situations.

A good example of this is the adaptation of Psalms by the Nicaraguan poet Ernesto Cardenal. He paraphrases a number of the Psalms, inserting terms and images from a modern Central American context with its economic and political oppression and suffering. The result not only brings the Psalm form to life by making some of the generalized and stereotypical language concrete. It also helps the reader imagine the analogous situations from which an ancient Israelite would have cried out for help and deliverance from God. Note Cardenal's paraphrase of Psalm 22:

My God my God why have you abandoned me?
I am only a mockery of a man
            a disgrace to the people
They ridicule me in all their newspapers

Armored tanks surround me
I am at machine gun point
encircled by barbed wire
            by electrified barbed wire
All day long they call my name from the rolls
They tattooed a number on me
They have photographed me among the barbed wire
all of my bones can be counted as in an X-ray
They have stripped me of all identity
They have brought me naked to the gas chamber
and divided among them my clothes and my shoes

I cry out begging for morphine and no one hears
I cry out in the straightjacket
I cry out all night in the asylum of mad men
in the ward of the terminal patients
in the quarantine of the contagiously sick
in the halls of the old people's home
I squirm in my own sweat in the psychiatric clinic
I suffocate in the oxygen tent
I weep in the police station
in the army stockade
    in the torture chamber
        in the orphanage
I am contaminated with radioactivity
    and fearing infection no one comes near me

Yet will I speak of you to my brothers
I will praise you in the meetings of our people
My hymns will resound in the midst of this great people
The poor will sit down to banquet
Our people will celebrate a great feast
This new generation soon to be born.

Finally, the important role of the Temple and cult in all this needs to be pointed out. The liturgy provided a place where these grievances and complaints could be aired. The role of the priests may not have been such a neutral one as one might suppose. They also had responsibility for proclamation of and defense of the Torah. These traditional covenant laws served as protection for these grieving and persecuted individuals as well as indictments of their oppressors.

The priesthood, then, was in a position to give a hearing through the public liturgy of the Temple to the complaints of the violation of that covenant law. They may also have been able to play a role in alleviating some of the abuses and resulting suffering. The anonymity of the language of the Individual Laments would have served to protect the complaining individuals from retaliation by their persecutors or exploiters.

Today, the church and its public worship can also function to provide a place and context in which the protest and longings for liberation from oppression and misery can come to expression. When the social and political mechanisms for voicing dissent are suppressed or stifled, that dissent can find an outlet and airing through religious language and ritual.

REVIEW QUESTIONS

1. How can a reading and study of the Book of Psalms contribute to a fuller understanding of the Old Testament?

2. Describe and discuss the use of "parallelism" in Hebrew poetry.

3. Why can we say that the Book of Psalms contains both "the words by which Israel spoke to God" and "the words by which God spoke to Israel"?

4. In what setting or context did the Psalm forms, as well as many (if not most) of the Psalms themselves, develop? Explain.

5. What contributions did Hermann Gunkel and Sigmund Mowinckel make that are important for understanding the way we approach a study of the Psalms today?

6. Describe the structure of the Hymn or Song of Praise.

7. Describe the structure of the Individual Lament or Song of Supplication.

8. Describe the structure of the Individual Thanksgiving Song.

9. Why are some of the Psalms referred to as Royal Psalms?

10. How might the new emphasis on the Psalter as a book in itself and not just a haphazard collection affect our understanding and interpretation of individual psalms?

11. Relate the wider socio-economic context of Israel (both northern and southern kingdoms) during the period of the monarchy to the great emphasis on prayer for deliverance from suffering found in the Psalter.

23

Wisdom in Israel

THE DEVELOPMENT AND BACKGROUND
OF ISRAELITE WISDOM

Introduction

In addition to the most basic struggles of securing food, drink, and shelter, family and community expend great energy on rearing and educating the new generation. Even from the most primitive times the older parenting generation focuses much attention on equipping the new generation with the knowledge and skills to cope with life in the "world." But the shape of this world into which the young are being introduced is a relatively arbitrary one. It is the world already evaluated, formed, and determined by their parents and by previous generations. That world and the means of dealing with its challenges and problems are presented to the young as if it were *the* world, objectified and unchangeable. It is *that* world and the means of coping with it that the young are brought to internalize and make their own.

In ancient Israel this primary process of education or socialization took place, as in many societies, within the family and clan. It represents the principal origin and source for Israel's wisdom tradition. This process has as its purpose assisting the individual to cope with life and the world—the physical world of nature and its demands, the social world of other human beings, and the religious world, that is, our relationship with God. Another way of describing it would be to discuss more concretely the role of wisdom literature in the formation of moral character. William P. Brown has written about this approach to understanding the purpose of Israel's wisdom writings. Each of the books in its own way offers a normative profile of a well-rounded, happy, integrated individual who is at peace with himself, with his fellow human beings, and with God. And each of the wisdom works offers its own description of how one achieves such a state of contentment and satisfaction.

The Origins of the Scribal School

As the statist system of societal organization developed in the late fourth and early third millennia in the Ancient Near East, one of the institutions which evolved out of the needs of a centralized and bureaucratic power structure was the scribal school. This scribal school provided training first of all in the most fundamental skill for an ancient bureaucrat, that of reading and writing. And because of the complex and cumbersome nature of the

A statue of an Egyptian scribe from the time of the Fifth Dynasty (second half of the third millennium B.C.E.), which was discovered at Sakkarah in Egypt. Wisdom literature first appeared in Egypt.

first writing systems, Mesopotamian cuneiform and Egyptian hieroglyph-ics, it was a skill that demanded long hours of schooling and practice.

Besides writing, the school inculcated the fundamentals of administration as well as a kind of "survival ethic" for security and for successful maneu-vering within the royal establishment. It was on that royal establishment that the members of those scribal schools depended for their livelihoods and for the life and welfare of their families. And they were well aware of how often their lives were at the mercy of the whims of autocratic rulers. Thus the earliest products of these schools, both in Mesopotamia and Egypt, tended to stress a strongly pragmatic, opportunist, and uniformist attitude. A good example of this attitude can be seen in the Egyptian text, "The Instruction of the Vizier Ptah-Hotep," which dates from the middle of the third millennium (ca. 2450 B.C.E.):

> If thou art one of those sitting at the table of one greater than thyself, take what he may give, when it is set before thy nose. Thou shouldst gaze at what is before thee. Do not pierce him with many stares. . . . Let thy face be cast down until he addresses thee, and thou shouldst speak (only) when he addresses thee. Laugh after he laughs, and it will be very pleasing to his heart and what thou mayest do will be pleasing to the heart (*ANET*, p. 412).

Despite the generally pragmatic and success-oriented tone, these texts often demonstrate considerable psychological insight. This insight resulted from the keen method of observation and evaluation in which these men were trained. We see this insight, for example, in the following passage from that same Egyptian "Instruction":

> If thou art one to whom petition is made, be calm as thou listenest to the petitioner's speech. Do not rebuff him before he has swept out his body or before he has said that for which he came. A petitioner likes attention to his words better than the fulfilling of that for which he came. . . . It is not (necessary) that everything about which he has petitioned *should* come to pass, (but) a good hearing is a soothing of the heart (*ANET*, p. 413).

Besides the production of administrative documents and instructional texts, these scribal schools soon became the context for literary activity in the higher cultural sense. Thus, in addition to administrative, commercial, and diplomatic correspondence, they also composed and copied literary works: collections of proverbs and fables, epics, myths, early history-like material such as the chronicles of kings' deeds. In reflective pieces they addressed some of the more perennial human issues such as the question of innocent suffering, the meaning of life, and human mortality. Here we see the ancestors of the biblical Wisdom books of Job and Qoheleth, both of which address similar themes.

A good example of the literature these schools produced is the famous Epic of Gilgamesh, composed shortly before or after 2000 B.C.E. This great achievement of ancient Mesopotamian culture tells the story of an early Mesopotamian king, Gilgamesh of Uruk. Early in the story his bosom companion, Enkidu, is killed by the jealousy of a goddess. Gilgamesh is overwhelmed by his friend's death and by his confrontation with the realization of his own mortality. Thus, the rest of the epic is taken up with Gilgamesh's search for the secret of immortality. His search would end in failure, not a despairing and anguished failure but a resigned and peaceful acceptance of human fate. The words of Sidaru, the ale-wife (supplier of drink) to the gods, sum up the message:

> Gilgamesh, whither rovest thou?
> The life thou pursuest thou shalt not find.
> When the gods created mankind,
> Death for mankind they set aside,
> Life in their own hands retaining.
> Thou, Gilgamesh, let full be thy belly,
> Make thou merry by day and by night.
> Of each day make thou a feast of rejoicing,
> Day and night dance thou and play!
> Let thy garments be sparkling fresh,
> Thy head be washed; bathe thou in water.
> Pay heed to the little one who holds fast thy hand,
> Let thy spouse delight in thy bosom!
> For this is the task of (mankind)! (*ANET,* p. 90).

Works that dealt with innocent suffering and death in a more explicitly speculative and questioning way emerged both in Egypt and Mesopotamia. Note these lines from the Mesopotamian work, "Man and his God," a Sumerian version of the Job motif, which dates from around 2000 B.C.E. They contain a prayer for deliverance of a righteous man who is bewildered by a series of misfortunes:

> My companion says not a true word to me,
> My friend gives the lie to my righteous word.

> The man of deceit has *conspired* against me,
> (And) you, my god, do not thwart him. . . .
> I, the wise, why am I bound to the ignorant youths?
> I, the discerning, why am I counted among the ignorant?
> Food is all about, (yet) my food is hunger,
> On the day shares were allotted to all, my allotted
>   share was suffering. . . .
> My god, the day shines bright over the land, for me the
>   day is black. . . .
> Tears, lament, anguish, and depression are lodged within me,
> Suffering overwhelms me like one who does (nothing but)
>   weep (*ANET,* p. 590).

The following lines from an Egyptian work entitled "A Dispute Over Suicide" (ca. 2000 B.C.E.) represent an example of similar sentiments from the other end of the fertile crescent. In this text the speaker weighs the pros and cons of suicide as a means of escaping the turmoil of the time:

> Death is in my sight today
>   Like the odor of myrrh
>   Like sitting under an awning on a breezy day. . . .
> Death is in my sight today
>   Like the longing of a man to see his house (again),
>   After he has spent many years held in captivity.
>   (*ANET,* p. 407)

Thus we see that the kinds of texts we associate with wisdom thinking tended to take one of two directions. One direction was the more pragmatic and optimistic one represented by the first Egyptian work quoted above, "The Instruction of the Vizier Ptah-Hotep." Implicit in such texts is a confidence that the human mind, by dutifully following the instruction of the wisdom teacher, can gain insight into the mystery and meaning of the world. That insight can provide us in turn with the knowledge and skill needed to live a happy and successful life. The Book of Proverbs is the Hebrew example of this particular current.

Another direction, more speculative and questioning, does not take such a straightforward approach. It tends to emphasize the skeptical and tentative mode of inquiry. The Egyptian work "A Dispute Over Suicide" is of this type. The Books of Job and Ecclesiastes are the Old Testament's examples of this wing of the wisdom movement in the Ancient Near East.

Allied to the royal establishment or often even an extension of it was the administrative apparatus of the local temple, which usually included its own group of scribes. These were responsible not only for the administrative documents keeping track of the temple's often vast land holdings and commercial interests. They also provided the ritual and mythic texts necessary for the smooth functioning of an invariably lavish cult.

The Royal Scribal School in Israel

When Israel made the fateful step across the line from the decentralized organization of the tribal confederacy to the increasingly centralized and authoritarian monarchical state under David, the need arose for scribes for the new administrative apparatus. David undoubtedly inherited a group of scribes from the ruling establishment of the newly conquered city-state of Jerusalem. But with a full-fledged kingdom emerging during the later years of his reign and into that of Solomon, the need for a bureaucratic apparatus and the attendant scribes quickly outstripped the resources at hand. It seems that early in his reign David, and also Solomon, turned to Egypt for help. In building their administrative structures they followed Egyptian models and imported Egyptian scribes to staff these structures as well as to train native candidates. It is probably within these first circles of court scribes that we could locate, for example, the author of one of Israel's first self-conscious works of religious literature, the Yahwist epic. Some of the first psalm compositions would have come from among the scribes attached to Solomon's Temple.

Within these scribal circles flourished a cultivation of "wisdom." This represented an attitude and approach to life which stressed careful and patient observation of nature, of human society, and of the relations between God, human beings, and the world. This wisdom attitude or approach attempted to locate, or even impose to a certain degree, *order* or *an order* within and among these various spheres. The purpose of this search for order, and the attempt to impose an order through linguistic and conceptual tools, was not simply to satisfy curiosity or seek knowledge for its own sake. The purpose was primarily pragmatic. Once order has been discerned, those who are wise can comport themselves accordingly, ordering their own lives and making decisions in ways best adapted to achieve well-being and success.

This, of course, was also the alleged goal of the education effort within the family and clan. It also seems that certain individuals even outside the royal and Temple scribal circles achieved a reputation for wisdom. They were sought out for their advice and counsel, such as the "wise woman" from Tekoa who assists Joab:

> When Joab, son of Zeruiah, observed how the king felt toward Absalom, he sent to Tekoa and brought from there a gifted [wise] woman, to whom he said: "Put on mourning apparel and do not anoint yourself with oil. . . . Then go to the king and speak to him in this manner." And Joab instructed her what to say (2 Sm 14:1-3).

Thus wisdom came to be recognized as an important component of Israel's religion and culture, on par with prophecy and the priestly "torah" (instruction about divine law later embodied in the Pentateuch). This is witnessed by the remark in Jeremiah 18:18: "Come," they said, "let us contrive a plot against Jeremiah. It will not mean the loss of instruction from the priests, nor of counsel from the wise, nor of messages from the prophets."

The members of these scribal schools belonged to the upper classes. This "social location" gave them advantages not enjoyed by the majority in Israelite society. As members of this elite minority, their writings often reflect satisfaction with the status quo. Thus, works such as the Book of Proverbs are characterized by an optimistic attitude about the possibilities of success and happiness if one learns to be wise. But these scribes also belonged to the people of Israel in covenant with Yahweh, and this larger context made its impact. For example, implicit in their view of the world was the realization that it was not necessarily fixed and eternal. Its origin and continued existence depended on Yahweh, its Creator. Yahweh was always there to intervene and to initiate change whenever ethical or moral disorder appeared. Consequently, we hear dissenting voices among the wise, such as Job and Qoheleth. They felt free to raise questions and challenge the accepted consensus on what represented wise thought and wise action, implicitly demanding that a more just and wise order prevail.

Scribal Circles after the Exile

Parts of the Book of Proverbs seem to be the only actual wisdom texts that have come down to us from these royal scribal schools. As members of the royal establishment, many of the scribes who survived the destruction of Jerusalem in 587 B.C.E. would have been taken into exile by the Babylonians. Thus the context within which wisdom flourished and was cultivated in the Exilic and post-Exilic periods is unknown. The movement undoubtedly continued in some form or other, since it is from the Exile or post-Exilic periods that the literature generally associated with this movement stems: Job (possibly Exilic, or post-Exilic), Proverbs (most likely post-Exilic), and Qoheleth (most likely post-Exilic).

One context in which wisdom teaching continued would have been among court scribes carried into exile by the Babylonians. The Persian administrative structure of the restored province of Judah in post-Exilic times would also have employed native Jewish scribes. It also seems probable that the Deuteronomic circles in the late monarchy and afterward, counted scribes trained in wisdom among their members. Such groups would have been responsible for the two editions of the Deuteronomistic History. Later in the post-Exilic period, these Deuteronomic circles with their wisdom-trained scribes were linked with the Priestly circles who produced the Pentateuch. Among these Priestly circles scribes were also present. Note that Ezra the priest is identified as a scribe or secretary in the Persian court:

> Ezra had set his heart on the study and practice of the law of the LORD and on teaching statutes and ordinances in Israel.
>
> This is a copy of the rescript which King Artaxerxes gave to Ezra the priest-scribe, the scribe of the text of the LORD's commandments and statutes for Israel (Ezr 7:10-11).

Together, the Deuteronomic and Priestly circles of Exilic and post-Exilic times continued the process which led eventually to the creation of the Hebrew Bible. They produced and eventually brought together its first two major components, the Torah or Law (the Pentateuch) and the Prophets (the Former Prophets or Deuteronomistic History, and the Latter Prophets or prophetic texts themselves).

During this same period a major shift took place in the mode of Israel's more formal theological reflection. That shift involved the merging of wisdom and reflection on the Law or Torah. The Torah came to be identified with wisdom. In other words, the Torah came to be regarded as the very embodiment of wisdom, wisdom with a divine source, that is, wisdom as revealed by God himself. Thus the energies of the wisdom-trained scribes were now focused on the Law and its study and exposition. Wisdom in this post-Exilic period accordingly took on a strongly religious tone.

This forms the background and context for a work such as the Book of Sirach. He was a scribe whose study of the Law and whose teaching activity led him to compose his own Wisdom book around 180 B.C.E. This work did not find its way into the Hebrew canon, but it is included among the so-called Deuterocanonical books. In it the Law or Torah is clearly identified as revealed wisdom:

> Wisdom sings her own praises,
> before her own people she proclaims her glory. . . .

> "From the mouth of the Most High I came forth,
> and mistlike covered the earth. . . .
> He who eats of me will hunger still,
> he who drinks of me will thirst for more;
> He who obeys me will not be put to shame,
> he who serves me will never fail."
> All this is true of the book of the Most High's covenant,
> the law which Moses commanded us
> as an inheritance for the community of Jacob.
> It overflows, like the Pishon, with wisdom—
> like the Tigris in the days of the new fruits.
> (Sir 24:1, 3, 20-23)

The Book of Sirach represents a merger of wisdom-type reflection and the focus on the written Word of God in the Law and the Prophets. It is in a direct line with the rabbinic Pharisaism, which eventually came to dominate Jewish life and thought in New Testament times. This tradition continues, especially among the Orthodox Jews, down to our own day.

THE FORMS OF HEBREW WISDOM

The Proverb

Perhaps the most characteristic literary form found in biblical wisdom literature is the *mashal,* the "proverb." The Hebrew word *mashal,* however, includes a broader spectrum than the English proverb, which usually refers to a single line or sentence-saying: "Birds of a feather flock together"; "A new broom sweeps clean"; "Don't count your chickens before they're hatched." The Hebrew word *mashal* means, literally, "a comparison" and is related to the verbal stem *m šl,* "to rule." It thus provides a "rule" or "paradigm" for understanding and encompasses a number of literary forms, all of which attempt to gain insight into a situation by comparison or analogy. It would include, therefore, the parable and the allegory.

Outside the Old Testament books usually called Wisdom books as such (for example, Job, Proverbs, Ecclesiastes) are found a number of popular or folk proverbs. These sayings are usually short and in a single line, for example, "From the wicked comes forth wickedness" (1 Sm 24:13; see also 1 Sm 10:11; 1 Kgs 20:11; Ez 16:44). The literary proverb, however, found in these Wisdom books has a more formal and structured character. It is usually in poetic form and follows the traditional pattern of Hebrew verse. That is, it contains a single line broken into two (sometimes three) parallel segments. In addition, it is marked by its conciseness of expression, and it frequently employs ellipsis, wordplay, and humor:

> The laborer's appetite labors for him,
>> for his mouth urges him on (Prv 16:26).

> The door turns on its hinges,
>> the sluggard, on his bed! (Prv 26:14).

> One who is full, tramples on virgin honey;
>> but to the man who is hungry, any bitter thing is sweet (Prv 27:7).

The Book of Proverbs and two of the Deuterocanonical works, the Book of Sirach and the Wisdom of Solomon, contain collections of hundreds of these more formal literary proverbs. But the Books of Job and Qoheleth include a number of them as well.

The Liberating Potential of Proverb and Parable

One gains insight into the analytical potential of the proverb by examining more closely its expanded form in the parable. Nathan's parable told to David in 2 Samuel 12:1-7 represents an unusually clear example, as do many of the parables of Jesus in the New Testament. In both cases, that of Jesus and that of Nathan, the prophet has "borrowed" a wisdom form by expanding the proverb/comparison into a parable-story.

One can see how such comparison stories can function effectively as "consciousness-raising" in the case of Jesus's story about the Good Samaritan. The lawyer asks Jesus, "Who is my neighbor?" Jesus' answer is in the form of the parable-story. The story compares the responses of three different individuals (priest, levite, Samaritan) to the plight of the man who fell victim to the robbers. The priest and the levite ignore the man in distress. The Samaritan comes to his rescue. We need only to imagine ourselves as the wounded man along the roadside to know what response was demanded by the situation.

The parable would have overturned the expectations and prejudices of Jesus' day. It functioned critically to expose the pride and hypocrisy of the priest and levite. But the parable also plays a constructive role in highlighting the Samaritan's attitude of compassion and care. This demonstrates how a parable can act to liberate the listener from an unjust, unfair, or "foolish" set of expectations and attitudes by positing another just, fair, and wise set.

Other Forms or Genres

Other forms or genres employed by the wisdom writers in the Ancient Near East include forms which only appear once or twice in the Old Testament, such as the riddle (see Jgs 14:10-18) and the fable (Jgs 9:8-15). More frequent is the hymn, a genre borrowed from the cultic context but used as a vehicle for wisdom material. A good example would be this hymn, which the Woman Wisdom sings in praise of herself:

> I, Wisdom, dwell with experience;
>> and judicious knowledge I attain. . . .
> Pride, arrogance, the evil way,
>> and the perverse mouth I hate.
> Mine are counsel and advice;
>> Mine is strength; I am understanding.
> By me kings reign,
>> and lawgivers establish justice;
> By me princes govern,
>> and nobles; all the rulers of the earth.
> Those who love me I also love,
>> and those who seek me find me.
> With me are riches and honor,
>> enduring wealth and prosperity (Prv 8:12-18;
>>> see also Jb 28; Prv 1:20-33).

In the confession or autobiographical narrative the speaker gives advice or makes an observation supposedly based on his own personal experience:

> I passed by the field of the sluggard;
>> by the vineyard of the man without sense;
> And behold! it was all overgrown with thistles;
>> its surface was covered with nettles. . . .
> And as I gazed at it, I reflected;
>> I saw and learned the lesson:
> A little sleep, a little slumber,
>> a little folding of the arms to rest—
> Then will poverty come upon you like a highwayman,
>> and want like an armed man (Prv 24:30-34;
>>> see also Prv 4:6-9; Qoh 1:12-2:26).

The onomasticon or name list represents an early attempt at systematizing and ordering knowledge by listing all known members of a particular category. A good example can be found in the catalogue of precious stones in Job 28:15-19. This partial list gives an idea of the rich store of forms or genres on which Israel's wisdom writers could draw.

REVIEW QUESTIONS

1. What two sources or contexts fed into Israel's wisdom movement?

2. Describe the institution in the Ancient Near East which served as the context for the development of the more formal wisdom movement and which produced the first wisdom literature.

3. Discuss briefly the two directions wisdom thinking tended to take both in Israel and in the wider Ancient Near East.

4. When and by whom were scribal schools established in ancient Israel?

5. Discuss briefly the wisdom attitude or approach to life. Why could one say that its purpose was primarily pragmatic?

6. Describe the shift in the mode of formal theological reflection which took place during post-Exilic times regarding wisdom and the Law.

7. What is the meaning of the Hebrew word *mashal?* How is its meaning broader than simply "proverb"?

8. Describe how the parable that Nathan told to King David in 2 Samuel 12:1-7 functioned both critically and constructively.

9. Choose a parable of Jesus from the Gospels and discuss how it is both critical and constructive.

24

The Wisdom Writings: Proverbs, Job, Ecclesiastes, Sirach, and the Book of Wisdom

Suggested Bible Readings: Job 1-7; 29-31; 38-42; Proverbs 1-3; 8-11; 30-31; Ecclesiastes 1-4; 11-12; Sirach 1-3; 24; 44-50; Wisdom of Solomon 1-11; 16-19

THE BOOK OF PROVERBS

Proverbs 10:1-31:9 consists of six proverb "collections," that is, series of proverbs of one or a few verses simply listed one after the other. By contrast, the opening nine chapters contain more extensive "discourses" and form the elaborate prologue to the book as a whole. Central to this prologue is the figure of "Woman Wisdom," a remarkable literary personification who claims to have been God's companion and helper in the creation of the cosmos. The short poem, "Praise of the Capable Woman" (31:10-31) concludes the book. The two collections entitled "Proverbs of Solomon" (chaps. 10-21, 25-29) form the heart of the book and probably contain material generated by the royal scribal school during the period of the monarchy. Although at first sight these collections seem to contain a series of one-line proverbs simply strung together, a closer examination reveals grouping by catchwords and common themes. There is, moreover, good evidence that some chapters contain more elaborate "proverb poems," in which the single proverbs have been woven into a longer literary unity (for example, chap. 25).

The collection in two chapters 22:17-24:22 entitled "The Sayings of the Wise" has close affinities and parallels with an early first millennium Egyptian work known as "The Instruction of Amen-Em-Ope." A number

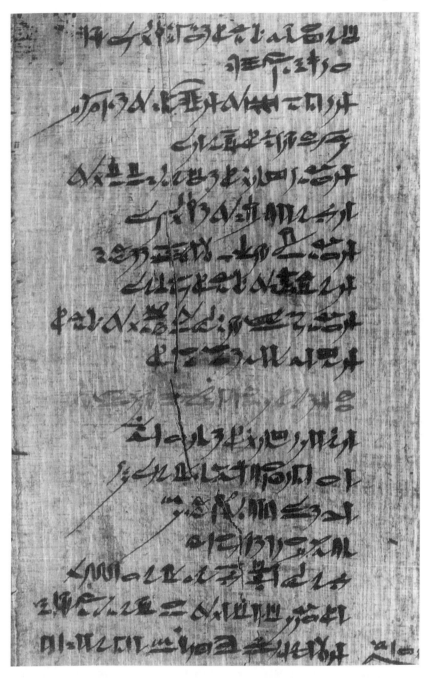

An Egyptian papyrus scroll containing the "Wisdom of Amen-Em-Ope."
Chapters 22:17 to 24:22 of the Book of Proverbs contain material borrowed
from this Egyptian work.

of scholars hold that the Israelite sage used the Egyptian work as his model and adapted some of its content to his Israelite milieu. Compare these two passages, one from Proverbs and the other from Amen-Em-Ope:

> Toil not to gain wealth,
>   cease to be concerned about it;
> While your glance flits to it, it is gone!
>   for assuredly it grows wings,
>   like the eagle that flies toward the heaven (Prv 23:4-5).

> Cast not thy heart in pursuit of riches . . .
> Place not thy heart upon externals. . . .
> If riches are brought to thee by robbery,
> They will not spend the night with thee;
> At daybreak they are not in thy house:
> Their places may be seen, but they are not.
> . . . they have made themselves wings like geese
> And are flown away to the heavens (*ANET,* p. 422).

Finally, titles indicate three other shorter collections, "More Sayings of the Wise" (24:23-34), "The Sayings of Agur" (chap. 30), and "The Sayings of Lemuel" (31:1-9), which round out and complete the contents. Although the book itself stems from the post-Exilic period, it most likely preserves materials from the pre-Exilic or monarchic era, such as the two so-called Solomonic Collections (chaps. 10-21, 25-29).

There is much in the Book of Proverbs that places it squarely within the wider and older current of the Ancient Near Eastern wisdom movement. However, there are also numerous indications that the sages of ancient Israel were marked by the context of Yahwist religion, which leavened the society and world-view within which they lived. For example, one might expect that the bulk of the proverbs dealing with riches and poverty would affirm the presumed truism that poor and rich receive what they deserve: the poor are poor because they are lazy or stupid while the rich are successful because of their diligence, hard work, and intelligence.

A closer examination of the Book of Proverbs reveals, however, that a significant majority of the texts concerning poverty and riches exhibit a concern for a just social order. A number of passages chronicle the often dishonest and oppressive means by which the wealthy gain their riches at the expense and suffering of those who now find themselves poor and the victims of injustice (for example, Prv 15:16, 17, 25, 27;

16:8, 11, 16, 19, 29; 17:1, 2, 5, 23, 26; 20:10, 23; 21:6). Further, the sages' injunctions that those who are wise should demonstrate kindness and generosity toward the poor could in many cases not be simply an exhortation to altruism. It could represent the sages' attempts to reinforce and promote the traditional networks of mutual aid toward those suffering misfortune among the families and clans of Israel, as enjoined by the covenant laws and customs (cf. Prv 14:21, 31; 18:5; 19:17; 21:13, 26; 22:1, 2, 9, 16).

We noted above that the figure of Woman Wisdom holds a central place in the prologue (chaps. 1-9), and that the book concludes with the poem "In Praise of the Capable Woman" (chap. 31). Some scholars have argued recently that this prominence of feminine imagery in Proverbs both reflects and legitimates the expanded role that women played in the post-Exilic period. During this period a dramatic shift had taken place in the Israelite community from a society organized around a king and his centralized bureaucracy to a more family- and household-oriented one. Within the public sphere that dominated Israelite identity and self-consciousness during the period of the monarchic state, men were the dominant, almost exclusive actors. In contrast, the woman's role as wife and mother held a much more central and important place in the private sphere, the family and household. Thus with the shift to the household as the center of societal life and identity after the demise of the monarchy, the status and influence of woman increased. This enhanced prominence and authority of woman in Israel is both symbolized and legitimated by the prominence of feminine imagery in this post-Exilic book. Woman Wisdom is the partner of God in the creation of the cosmos (Prv 8). She is God's "voice" speaking and inviting human beings through the order and harmony of creation (Prv 9:1-6).

This prominence of women in the post-Exilic Israelite community through their place in the newly important household/family context contrasts with the new "public" center of the reemergent Israelite community after the Exile, the Temple. Here the all-male priesthood dominated, and one of the central aspects of the Law Codes promoted by the priestly groups were the "pollution" laws, which stigmatized the processes of menstruation and birth as "unclean." This reinforced the marginalization of women from the public and cultic spheres. Differing interests and agenda thus characterize these two exemplars of the community's religious literature, the Priestly legislation of the Pentateuch and the Book of Proverbs. The former tends to marginalize women while the latter enhances their place and role. This contrast may reflect the conflicts and tensions within that post-Exilic community.

THE BOOK OF JOB

The Book of Job, one of the great works of world literature, represents the more speculative and questioning current in Israelite and Ancient Near Eastern wisdom. In the opening and closing sections (Jb 1:1-2:13; 42:7-17) the author retells an ancient tale about a virtuous and well-respected man who loses family, fortune, and finally health in a series of unexpected and inexplicable disasters. But the retelling of this tale serves as the starting point for discussing a series of questions and issues in a creative and provocative way. Central to a number of these questions and issues is the problem of innocent suffering, of which Job himself is obviously a prime example.

The issue of innocent suffering is raised and formulated in a clear and forceful way with Job's case, and the bulk of the book, chapters 3-37, is taken up with a debate or disputation between Job and three friends (and a fourth who appears unannounced in chapters 32-37) about this and related matters. The friends represent the rigid and dogmatic positions of supposedly traditional wisdom that there cannot be anything such as "innocent" suffering. Action inevitably receives its due: good will be rewarded and evil punished. If someone experiences suffering, it must be because he or she has sinned. Job suffers, therefore he must be guilty:

> Reflect now, what innocent person perishes?
>   Since when are the upright destroyed?
> As I see it, those who plow for mischief
>   and sow trouble, reap the same.
> By the breath of God they perish,
>   and by the blast of his wrath they are consumed.
>   (Jb 4:7-9)

Job protests their simplistic and mechanically rigid response and points to his own case as disproving their position. He is innocent, yet he suffers. Why?

Job holds his ground for a single, fundamental reason: the assertions of his friends are inconsistent with his own experience. "For Job, to hold fast to his own integrity means to insist on the authority of his own experience, even when it seems to be contradicted by what all the world knows to be true" (See Carol Newsom, "Job," p. 133). The book, in its own way, authenticates the crucial role of personal experience in the critique of received tradition.

Job gradually enlarges his argument to include other examples where the friends' assertions are contradicted. He begins to call into question God himself and God's just government of the cosmos. Job accuses God of afflicting him cruelly and without reason and challenges God to appear and defend himself:

> I will carry my flesh between my teeth,
>   and take my life in my hand.
> Slay me though he might, I will wait for him;
>   I will defend my conduct before him. . . .
> Behold, I have prepared my case,
>   I know that I am in the right. . . .
> What are my faults and my sins?
>   My misdeeds and my sins make known to me!
> Why do you hide your face
>   and consider me your enemy?
> Will you harass a wind-driven leaf,
>   or pursue a withered straw? (Jb 13:14-15, 18, 23-25)

Job's friends are horrified at this apparent blasphemy. But God eventually does appear and speaks to Job "from out of the whirlwind," a traditional context for divine-human encounter. God does not answer Job's questions or give any explanations. Instead, God challenges Job about Job's ability to understand and govern the universe:

> Who is this that obscures divine plans with words of
>   ignorance?
> Gird up your loins now, like a man;
>   I will question you, and you tell me the answers! . . .
> Have you comprehended the breadth of the earth?
>   Tell me, if you know all:
> Which is the way to the dwelling place of light,
>   and where is the abode of darkness,
> That you may take them to their boundaries
>   and set them on their homeward paths?
> You know, because you were born before them,
>   and the number of your years is great!
>   (Jb 38:2-3, 18-21)

These ironic questions and challenges in the "Yahweh Speeches" (chaps. 38-41) reduce Job to silence. Job finally admits that he had spoken about things he did not really understand; he is satisfied that God has answered his challenge and appeared:

> I have dealt with great things that I do not understand;
>> Things too wonderful for me, which I cannot know.
> I had heard of you by word of mouth,
>> but now my eye has seen you.
> Therefore I disown what I have said,
>> and repent in dust and ashes (Jb 42:3-6).

Though the book raises and discusses a number of key issues, it offers no clear and definitive answers even to the question of innocent suffering. In some ways, it is enough that it establishes the fact clearly and forcefully that there *is* innocent suffering. No simple and straightforward solution is possible. One cannot just explain it away with smug formulas and prepackaged answers.

Implicit in the discussion as well is the issue of theological language or "God-talk." Is it possible for the human mind, with human words and concepts, to "explain" God and God's actions? The Book of Job provides a clear negative to this question. In so doing, the work affirms divine freedom and preserves the ultimate mystery that inevitably separates the transcendant Creator from mortal creatures.

THE BOOK OF ECCLESIASTES (QOHELETH)

This relatively short wisdom book stems from the third or fourth century B.C.E. The author's name in Hebrew, Qoheleth, is actually a title. It does not mean "the preacher," as some modern translations render it. The Hebrew root *qahal,* from which the word comes, means "to gather, assemble." The title could thus be characterizing the author as an "assembler" (of students, of listeners) or "collector" (of wisdom sayings). Also, like King Solomon, he gathered great wealth and wisdom (see chapter 1 and 2), and in his book he seeks to collect some sense and meaning out of his life and experience. The Greek name in the Septuagint, "Ecclesiastes," is simply a translation of the Hebrew *Qoheleth.*

Above, in chapter 23, we mentioned the Mesopotamian Epic of Gilgamesh and the hero's futile search for immortality. The discovery of the opening lines of this ancient classic had shed new light on the epic's literary form and, indirectly, on the literary form of Qoheleth. The newly found introductory portion depicts Gilgamesh as an old and wise king. In the story that follows, he recounts his many experiences and the wisdom he has derived from his life. This "prologue" effectively turns Gilgamesh the warrior into Gilgamesh the sage. This fuller version of the Gilgamesh epic has implications for the Book of Qoheleth and its genre or literary form. Chapters 1 and 2 of the book also present its author as a great king whose wide experience provides the basis of the sage advice that he imparts in chapters 3 through 12. Thus, a learned and experienced king dominates both works, Gilgamesh and Qoheleth. Both show strong influence of the literary form of a "royal testament" or autobiography.

The book's tone or outlook is one of almost unrelenting skepticism. Like the Book of Job, Qoheleth belongs within the more speculative, questioning current of the Ancient Near Eastern and Hebrew wisdom movements. His questioning is aimed at anyone who would attempt to affirm any absolute values in this life, including possessions, fame, success, pleasure, or even wisdom itself.

The refrain, "Vanity of vanities, says Qoheleth, vanity of vanities! All things are vanity!" (Eccl 1:2; 12:8), begins and ends the book and is repeated at key points throughout. The Hebrew word *hebel,* which older translations render "vanity," has the sense of "emptiness, futility, absurdity": "I have seen all things that are done under the sun, and behold, all is vanity and a chase after wind" (Eccl 1:14; 2:11, 17, 26; 4:4, 16; etc.). Everything in human life is subject to change, to qualification, to loss: "What profit has man from all the labor which he toils at under the sun?" (Eccl 1:3). The answer is in the negative: no absolute profit or gain is possible. Even if some temporary profit or gain is achieved, it will ultimately be cancelled out by the great leveler, death:

> The wise man has eyes in his head,
>> but the fool walks in darkness.

> Yet I knew that one lot befalls both of them. So I said to myself, if the fool's lot is to befall me also, why then should I be wise? Where is the profit for me? And I concluded in my heart that this too is vanity (Eccl 2:14-15; see also 3:19-20).

Wisdom has an advantage over foolishness, but it is only a qualified advantage. It has no absolute value in and of itself.

Many commentators locate Qoheleth in the third century B.C.E., that is, when Judah was under the heel of the Hellenistic kingdom of the Ptolemies ruling from Egypt. These Hellenistic kings were highly efficient in their exploitation of the land. They established an elaborate and oppressive administration composed of both foreign bureaucrats and native Jewish ones to extract heavy taxes and forced labor from the populace:

> If you see oppression of the poor, and violation of rights and justice in the realm, do not be shocked by the fact, for the high official has

another higher than he watching him and above these are higher still (Eccl 5:7).

These bureaucrats fostered the creation of larger estates. They ruthlessly foreclosed on mortgages. Some would even make use of illegal means such as extortion or the bribing of judges. In this way they were able to seize the traditional small family land holdings and merge them into more extensive properties. These large estates were cultivated by the now dis-possessed Jews who worked as tenant farmers or day laborers. Agriculture was also directed more and more toward the production of crops for export rather than subsistence products to feed the majority of the people. In the face of this political and economic situation under an oppressive foreign rule, the average Jew certainly would have felt a sense of powerlessness and inability to change things for the better.

Qoheleth does not confront the unjust and oppressive rule of these Hel-lenistic kings directly. Rather there is a sense in which his work functions in an indirect, indeed subversive way. It undermines the intellectual foun-dations, the so-called "wisdom," of this Hellenistic monetary economy, which was wreaking such havoc in the lives of his fellow Jews.

Commentators have noted the "commercial" character of Qoheleth's lan-guage and his obvious fascination with numbers. Again and again come words dealing with profit and loss, surplus and deficit, wages, poverty, and wealth. All activity in the kingdom ruled by the Ptolemys was oriented toward eco-nomic profit and productivity.

Qoheleth seems to take up this language of commerce purposely in order to subvert the mindset that it presupposes. Such an approach to life pridefully presumes that humans can acquire some sense of security and control by the amassing of riches. In chapter 7, however, we find Qoheleth coopting a bookkeeping metaphor to express his frustration and inability to find answers to his searching questions:

"See, this is what I learned," says Qoheleth, "adding one to one to reach the total, which my mind has sought repeatedly, but I have not found" (vv. 27-28; my translation).

Again, in 4:6, Qoheleth shows how mathematics, from a wisdom perspec-tive, is an imprecise science:

Better is one handful with tranquility
than two with toil and a chase after wind!

In this case, "one" is in fact "more than" or better than "two." "More" quantity does not necessarily mean "more" quality.

The economic and political situation seems to have affected even Qoheleth's understanding of God. For Qoheleth, God is remote and uncommunicative, and we cannot hope to understand much less affect God's governance of the world:

> He [God] has made everything appropriate in its time, and has put the timeless into their hearts, without men's ever discovering, from beginning to end, the work which God has done (Eccl 3:11; see also 8:16-17).

Qoheleth's honest and blunt appraisal of the human condition provides a healthy corrective to the occasionally excessive self-assurance of, for example, passages in the Book of Proverbs. The latter sometimes gives the impression that the possession of wisdom is an infallible guarantee to happiness and success. But Qoheleth's radical skepticism is tempered by the "imperative of joy." For despite the circumscribed nature of human beings' ability to affect or change the world in which they live, that world ultimately is good. It has been created by a God who, though remote and uncommunicative, is good and gives good things to his creatures, bringing some joy and contentment into their lives. Thus Qoheleth's advice in the last analysis is to accept the good God wills to give. To accept it and rejoice in it is to respect and honor the Creator from whom it comes:

> There is nothing better for man than to eat and drink and provide himself with good things by his labors. Even this, I realized, is from the hand of God. For who can eat or drink apart from him? For to whatever man he sees fit he gives wisdom and knowledge and joy (Eccl 2:24-26; see also 3:12-13; 5:18-20).

THE BOOK OF SIRACH
(ECCLESIASTICUS OR BEN SIRA)

The wider canon of the Greek-speaking Jews in Alexandria (also known as the Septuagint) contains two wisdom works which the Jewish rabbis in Palestine did not include in the Hebrew Bible when they finalized its contents toward the end of the first century C.E. These are the Book of Sirach (also called the Book of Ben Sira or Ecclesiasticus) and the Book of Wisdom (or Wisdom of Solomon). We will take a brief look at both of these works. With regard to the first of these books, Sirach, the reason for its exclusion by the rabbis from the Hebrew Bible was its author's lack of belief in the resurrection of the just. Martin Luther was influenced by these rabbis' decision and segregated Sirach into an appendix to his German translation of the Bible, along with other so-called "apocryphal works." But the book continues to enjoy a prominent place in the Roman Catholic and Greek Orthodox canons. Most Protestant churches follow Martin Luther's lead and do not accept Sirach as canonical, though it is valued as instructive and edifying.

Sirach is the only book of the Old Testament in which the author gives us his name, "Jesus, son of Eleazar, son of Sirach (=Hebrew *ben Sira*)" (50:27). He was a well-educated Jew who worked in some form of government service for most of his life. After work and/or after retirement he operated a private school for the sons of wealthy families in Jerusalem (see 51:23).

Ben Sira compiled his book possibly from class notes and other materials he had composed or collected. He wrote it in Hebrew around 180 B.C.E. But it has come down to us in the form of the Greek translation made by his grandson around 130 B.C.E. for the Greek-speaking Jewish community of Alexandria in Egypt. Since the end of the nineteenth century, a number of manuscripts have been found containing sections of the work in its original Hebrew.

As we shall see in the next chapter, this period of Jewish history witnessed the domination and exploitation of the Jewish people under Hellenistic kings. By their predatory economic measures to siphon off the wealth and resources of their subject peoples, these rulers threatened to sabotage and undermine the traditional networks of family and kinship ties among the Jews. Ben Sira countered this threat by building and fostering ties within families and among friends and community through his teachings. Chapter 6:5-17 represents a good example in which he develops Proverbs' teaching on friendship. Sirach commends wholesome friendships, grounded in the friends' common commitment to Israel's covenant Lord. Note, for example, vv. 14-17:

> A faithful friend is a sturdy shelter;
> > he who finds one finds a treasure.
> A faithful friend is beyond price,
> > no sum can balance his worth.
> A faithful friend is a life-saving remedy,
> > such as he who fears God finds;
> For he who fears God behaves accordingly,
> > and his friend will be like himself.

Further, Ben Sira emphasized compassion and respect for the poor, and he insists on the obligation to support and help them (see, for example, 3:29-30; 4:1-6, 8-10).

Ben Sira also had to contend with a second challenge, the attraction of the Greek culture and way of life, especially to young Jews. There was danger that they would abandon their people's traditions and beliefs. Ben Sira responded by reaffirming the value, relevance, and truth of the Jewish religion. In addition, he made use of Greek materials and resources in composing his book and thus demonstrated to the Jews of his day that the best of foreign thought need not represent a danger to their faith. He recasts what he borrows into a form that is thoroughly Jewish and compatible with earlier Jewish tradition.

One particular value of reading and studying Sirach comes from the light it sheds on the role of Jesus as a sage. Comparison of Ben Sira and his teaching with Jesus reveals striking similarities. In Ben Sira, the various streams of the biblical tradition were beginning to overlap. Although he was a sage, he claimed to speak with prophetic authority. Ben Sira's wisdom ultimately came from God, a revealed wisdom and renewed prophetic word.

Jesus appears to be a continuation and development of this understanding of the role and activity of the sage. His parables and counsels walk a fine line between wisdom teaching based on observation and reflection on the one hand ("the birds of the air . . . the lilies of the field" [Mt 6:26, 28]), and revealed wisdom and prophecy on the other (see Mt 11:25-30).

THE BOOK OF WISDOM
(WISDOM OF SOLOMON)

The Book of Wisdom, or Wisdom of Solomon, is a second work which the Roman Catholic and Greek Orthodox canons include, but which most Protestant Bibles list among the "apocrypha." Its author lived in Alexandria, the major Mediterranean port city in Egypt. He wrote his work in Greek for the large Greek-speaking Jewish community there, shortly after the beginning of Roman rule in 28 B.C.E. He probably taught in one of the many synagogues in the city, and his book demonstrates the profound knowledge he possessed of both Jewish and Greek culture and learning. He combines some of the best elements of Greek literary style with an eager desire to share his enthusiasm and love of the ancient faith of his people.

The author directs his work toward his young Jewish students to counteract the threat which the attraction of Greek culture and learning constituted to their beliefs. The Jews were in a minority and were threatened by the hostility of non-Jews. The resulting defection of many of their members served as a source of discouragement as well. The author shows that one can be open to Greek ways and still remain a faithful Jew. The book thus represents an example of resistance to the pressures of the dominant culture.

James M. Reese divides the Book of Wisdom into four major blocks of text. Part I (1:1-6:11+ 6:17-21), the "Book of Eschatology," describes the final goal of the righteous and their persecutors, "the ungodly." It is in this first part that the author puts forward the astounding claim that "righteousness is immortal" (1:15). He assures his readers that, even if their loyalty to God and God's covenant results in their death, their union in love with their God will continue beyond the grave. He does not address the question of how such a thing is possible. He simply makes the statement based on his own profound experience of love and union with God; for example, in 5:15-16:

> But the just live forever,
>> and in the LORD is their recompense,
>> and the thought of them is with the Most High.
> Therefore they shall receive the splendid crown,
>> the beauteous diadem, from the hand of the LORD—
> For he shall shelter them with his right hand,
>> and protect them with his arm.

Part II (6:12-16 + 6:22-10:21) focuses on the Wisdom Woman and her place in God's plan for the world. Love of wisdom and union with the Wisdom Woman constitute the means for attaining to union with God himself. To be with the Wisdom Woman means to be with God. See, for example, Wis 8:1-3, 13:

> Indeed, she reaches from end to end mightily
>> and governs all things well.
> Her I loved and sought after from my youth;
>> I sought to take her for my bride
>> and was enamored of her beauty.
> She adds to nobility the splendor of companionship with
>>> God;
>> even the LORD of all loved her. . . .
> For her sake I should have immortality
>> and leave to those after me an everlasting memory.

Part III (11:15-16:1) exposes the folly of idolatry and the harm that it has done to human beings. But the author reserves his harshest words for the Egyptians, who descriminate against and persecute his people. They worshipped not only material images but animals, especially such repulsive creatures as snakes:

> And besides, they worship the most loathesome beasts—
>> for compared as to folly, these are worse than the rest.
> Nor for their looks are they good or desirable beasts,
>> but they have escaped both the approval of God and
>> his blessing (Wis 15:18-19).

Part IV (11:1-14 + 16:2-19:22) contains a meditation or reflection on the Exodus story. In this section, the author asserts the unity of God's activity: creation and salvation are both acomplished by means of wisdom. In *creating* the cosmos by means of wisdom, God brought order out of the primeval chaos. In *saving* Israel in the Exodus by means of wisdom, God brings a just order out of the ethical chaos of injustice. The Exodus thus represents the model or paradigm for the way in which God intervenes to save the persecuted and oppressed. He newly fashions his created world into a means for saving his people:

> For all creation, in its several kinds, was being made over
>> anew,
>> serving its natural laws,
>> that your children might be preserved unharmed.
> The cloud overshadowed their camp;
>> and out of what had before been water, dry land was
>> seen emerging:
> Out of the Red Sea an unimpeded road,
>> and a grassy plain out of the mighty flood.
> Over this crossed the whole nation sheltered by your hand,
>> after they beheld stupendous wonders.
> For they ranged about like horses,
>> and bounded about like lambs,
>> praising you, O Lord! their deliverer (Wis 19:6-9).

REVIEW QUESTIONS

1. Describe briefly the structure and contents of the Book of Proverbs.

2. What are some of the indications in the Book of Proverbs of the leavening effect of the Yahwist religion on the society of ancient Israel?

3. Discuss the prominence of feminine imagery in the Book of Proverbs. What might this reflect about the role of women in post-Exilic Judaism?

4. Describe the structure and contents of the Book of Job.

5. How could Job's critique of "common sense" or received tradition on the basis of personal experience prove important, for example, for minority groups in winning recognition for the validity and value of their way of life?

6. What point does the Book of Job make about theological language or "God-talk"?

7. What does the name "Qoheleth" mean?

8. At whom is the almost unrelenting skepticism of Qoheleth's questioning aimed throughout his book?

9. What is Qoheleth's response to the oppressive rule of the Hellenistic kings and their emphasis on economic profit and productivity?

10. What tends to temper Qoheleth's radical skepticism?

11. When was the Book of Sirach written, and by whom? Describe the historical context.

12. Why is the Book of Sirach found in only some Bibles?

13. What are two of the challenges which the author of Sirach was responding to?

14. What special value does the study of Sirach have for understanding better the New Testament?

15. Where and when was the Book of Wisdom written?

16. What seems to be the author's reason or reasons for composing his work?

17. Describe the author of Wisdom's notion of "immortality."

25

Daniel and the Apocalyptic Literature

Suggested Bible Readings: Daniel 1-3; 6-7; 10-12; 1 Maccabees 1-4

HISTORICAL BACKGROUND

The rule of the Persians over Judah and Jerusalem came to an end with the arrival of the armies of Alexander the Great in 333 B.C.E. Alexander's father, Philip of Macedon, had managed to impose Macedonian rule over the Greek mainland heretofore divided into rival Greek city-states. Philip had also developed military tactics characterized by a strict discipline. This discipline, along with carefully planned and organized maneuvers, put his troops at a distinct advantage over less organized, though often more numerous, foes. Alexander followed up the momentum of his father's successes in Greece by crossing the Hellespont into Asia and challenging the vast empire of the Persians in 334 B.C.E. In eight short years he was at the borders of India, having seized control of the Persian Empire and extended its boundaries. The Ancient Near East from the Nile to the Indus Valley was now under the domination of the Greeks.

The high priest in Jerusalem acknowledged Greek rule on behalf of Judah in 333 B.C.E. Alexander accepted the Persian policy of permitting a degree of autonomy to the local population. Thus the administrative structure in Jerusalem and Judah established under the Persians continued to exercise a large degree of control over local affairs. Nonetheless, the impact of Hellenistic culture and politics on Judaism had major consequences both for the internal order and shape of the community as well as for the forms the expression its Yahwistic faith would take. (The noun and adjective, Hellenism and Hellenistic, refer to Greek culture as it manifested itself in the context of the Ancient Near East.)

At the same time as the armies of Alexander were sweeping across the ancient world, the aggressive militarism of the Greeks served to set the stage for an unparalleled expansion of Greek commercial enterprises. Alexander the Great is often credited with a dream of spreading the benefits and advances of Greek culture to other peoples of his time. In fact, Greek culture, philosophy, and religion provided powerful ideological tools both for justifying and for effecting the subjugation and exploitation of the conquered nations. The Greeks had "proven" the superiority of their culture by their success on the battlefield; their vast empire was forged by brute force. Greek culture and Greek ways thus held out a powerful attraction to the population under Greek rule. Throughout the empire, including Palestine, Greek cities were founded and peopled by Greek veterans and traders.

A marble bust of Alexander the Great, founder of the Hellenistic Empire (c. 350-400 C.E.).

One of the key questions facing the Jews during these years was their stance toward the Greek political domination but also toward the attempt by their Greek rulers to impose a Greek cultural and intellectual domination as well. There were undoubted benefits for Jewish culture in contacts with this Greek or Hellenistic culture, as its Near Eastern manifestation is called. However, because of the privileged position this Hellenistic culture held in the social, economic, and political structures, there was clear danger that Judaism could be absorbed and its basic character distorted or lost.

The question facing the Jews was not a purely theoretical one, or a matter of opinion or tastes. Both as individuals and as a community Jews were faced with choices and decisions that affected the shape and future of their culture. They also had to deal with concrete questions about who would exercise authority and control within their own community. The Hellenistic rulers would naturally favor those individuals and parties more open to Hellenism.

The eventual prominence of Jews more open to Hellenism under the high priests Jason in 174 B.C.E. and Menelaus in 171 B.C.E. provoked a backlash which led to the Maccabean revolt in 167 B.C.E. and a short-lived independent Jewish state. This state survived until the arrival of the Romans in 63 B.C.E. The backlash against the Hellenizing Jewish rulers was a determining factor in the option for a clear arm's-length attitude toward Hellenism by the large majority of Jews. It also provided the occasion for a strong reaffirmation of the Mosaic law as the fundamental force and guide for Jewish life and identity.

These last two hundred years of the Old Testament period provide the context for the final works included in the Hebrew canon and the Deuterocanon of some Christians. These include the two Books of Maccabees, which were written in Greek and recount the events and conflicts of the Maccabean revolt against Hellenistic rule. Also, there is the work of the Jewish scribe Jesus Ben Sira and the Book of Wisdom. The former was composed around 180 B.C.E. in Jerusalem and the latter was written sometime after 28 B.C.E. in the Egyptian city of Alexandria. We examined these two works above in chapter 24. Finally, there is the Book of Daniel, written in Hebrew and Aramaic in the year 165 B.C.E. It belongs to a type of literature known as apocalyptic, which requires its own introduction.

THE NATURE OF APOCALYPTIC LITERATURE

The apocalyptic movement emerged as a way of thinking or mind set, and as literature, early in the second century B.C.E., and lasted into the third century C.E. It combines elements of both the prophetic and the wisdom movements, although the major forerunner appears to be prophecy. Readers of the Bible are familiar with this form or genre of literature both from the Book of Daniel in the Old Testament and from the Book of Revelation in the New Testament. Included, as well, are some sections of the Exilic and post-Exilic prophets such as Ezekiel 38-39 and Zechariah 9-14, a few passages of the gospels (for example, Mark 13), and a number of late Jewish and Jewish-Christian works (such as the Book of Enoch, 2 Baruch, 4 Ezra, the Assumption of Moses). Although the latter were not accepted into all final Christian canons, they were especially popular in early Christian communities, and we owe their preservation to this popularity among these groups.

Apocalypse comes from the Greek word meaning "unveiling," "disclosure," "revelation." The revelation is given either through a vision or through a report from some otherworldly mediator, usually an angel. The one receiving the revelation is most often a famous personage from the past, for example, Enoch (Gn 5:21-24) or Abraham. In the case of the Book of Daniel the recipient recalls a venerated figure from ancient days who is named along with Job and Noah in Ezekiel 14:

> Or if I were to send pestilence into the land, pouring out upon it my blood-thirsty fury, cutting off from it man and beast, even if Noah, Daniel, and Job were in it, as I live, says the Lord GOD, I swear that they could save neither son nor daughter; they would save only themselves by their virtue (Ez 14:19-20; see also v. 14).

The content of the revelation could be temporal; that is, it could involve the past or especially the present and the future. It usually points toward the imminent end of this present world. Further, it provides signs, especially cosmic upheavals to herald those final days, and announces the salvation or judgment to be effected when the new age dawns.

Besides the temporal content, the revelation might include a spatial element, that is, a journey through heavenly realms (or through the netherworld), for it is especially from the heavenly realms that the future course of history on earth is determined. Note, for example, chapter 7 of Daniel and especially Daniel 11:36: "What is determined must take place." The apocalypse usually concludes with an exhortation to the faithful to remain steadfast, to watch carefully for signs of the imminent end, and to wait with confidence and hope for the salvation that will be theirs in the new age about to dawn.

The heart of the apocalyptic world-view, to put it simply, is a profound disillusionment with the present order, a sense of powerlessness to effect any changes for the better, and a conviction that this worthless age is about to end. This radical pessimism about present history combines with a radical optimism based on the belief in the new age about to erupt and in the power of God to bring about that new age and establish God's kingdom. In biblical terms, the vision of that final triumph of God's saints is reported, for example, in Daniel 12:

> "At that time there shall arise
>   Michael, the great prince,
>   guardian of your people;
> It shall be a time unsurpassed in distress
>   since nations began until that time.
> At that time your people shall escape,
>   everyone who is found written in the book.
> Many of those who sleep
>   in the dust of the earth shall awake;
> Some shall live forever,
>   others shall be an everlasting horror and disgrace.
> But the wise shall shine brightly
>   like the splendor of the firmament,
> And those who lead the many to justice
>   shall be like the stars forever" (Dn 12:1-3; see also
>   Dn 7:13, 26-27; and Rv 21-22).

THE BOOK OF DANIEL

Historical Background

During this post-Exilic period the Jews were under the imperial domination of the succession of empires that ruled the Ancient Near East—Babylonian, Persian, Hellenistic, Roman. Having lost the sense of being able to control their own history and determine their own future, they consequently developed a negative view of the present order. This would be especially true if they found that history and that order oppressive and hostile to their interests.

Such was the case in particular under the Hellenistic kings known as the Ptolemies, who dominated Palestine from their capital in Egypt from 301 to 198 B.C.E. The Ptolemies' harsh and exploitative government of the land led the inhabitants to welcome the new rule, in 198 B.C.E., by the Seleucid Hellenistic kings centered in Antioch. Soon, however, financial pressures on the Seleucid king Antiochus IV Epiphanes moved him to initiate new political and cultural policies designed to increase his control over the population and enable him to exact even more taxes. These policies included the attempt to Hellenize the Jewish religion. New laws prohibited a number of traditional Jewish practices, for example, circumcision, the observance of the sabbath, Temple sacrifice, and the avoidance of certain foods such as pork.

When many Jews resisted what they saw as the virtual abolition and destruction of their faith, a fierce persecution broke out. This eventually led to a revolt by the Jews under the elderly priest Mattathias and then under his sons. These were eventually tagged with the epithet "Maccabees" from the nickname of one of the brothers, Judas Maccabee, that is, Judas "the Hammerer." The revolt, however, split the Jewish community. Some Jews supported the Seleucid kings and were in favor of adopting some of the more attractive and advantageous elements of Hellenistic culture. Among these were probably those Jews who held positions in the province's administration or were involved in trade and commerce and found Hellenistic rule advantageous to their enterprises. The majority of the rural population, however, continued to suffer under exploitative tax burdens and at the mercy of land-grabbing Greeks and Jews. The population in the rural countryside lent strong support to the attempt to throw off the yoke of foreign domination. It is in the context of this persecution by the Seleucid king Antiochus IV Epiphanes that many scholars locate the writing of the Book of Daniel, most likely in the year 165 B.C.E.

The Book of Daniel

The Book of Daniel is divided into two major parts, chapters 1-6 and chapters 7-12. In the Greek Septuagint version two additional chapters (13-14) contain further stories about the book's protagonist, Daniel. These include, among others, the well-known tale about Daniel's vindication of the falsely accused Susannah.

The first part of the book recounts a number of stories about a young Jew named Daniel at the time of the Babylonian Exile. The episode concerning God's rescue of Daniel from the lion's den, for example, is contained in chapter 6. Daniel pursues a successful career as a bureaucrat and official in the service successively of the Babylonian and then the Persian courts. His ability and achievement are credited particularly to his piety and faithful observance of the Jewish Law. The stories thus seem to have their origin as models for those Jews for whom the Exile opened up opportunities, for instance, through service in the administrations and governments of foreign rulers:

> He [King Nebuchadnezzar] advanced Daniel to a high post, gave him
> many generous presents, made him ruler of the whole province of

Babylon and chief prefect over all the wise men of Babylon. At Daniel's request the king made Shadrach, Meshach, and Abednego administrators of the province of Babylon, while Daniel himself remained at the king's court (Dn 2:48-49; see also Dn 5:29; 6:1-3, 29).

At the same time there are cautions and warnings implicit in the description of these rulers about the potential dangers and the ambiguity of the Jews' position. For these foreign rulers were easily given to arrogance and brutality and could at times act harshly and arbitrarily:

At this the king became violently angry and ordered all the wise men of Babylon to be put to death. When the decree was issued that the wise men should be slain, Daniel and his companions were also sought out (Dn 3:4-5; see also Dn 2:12-13; 3:19-23; 5:2-4; 6:13).

These stories about young Daniel and his companions may stem from the Babylonian Exile and its aftermath. But in their present form in the Book of Daniel they have been reworked and used to provide a well-known personage of the past to be the recipient of the revelatory visions in the second part of the work, chapters 7-12.

Through the symbolic medium of visions and dreams, chapters 7-12 review the history of the post-Exilic period down to the time of the actual composition of the book in 165 B.C.E. Daniel, the subject of these dreams and visions, "foresees" this history and its events from his perspective in the fifth and early fourth centuries B.C.E. The purpose of this review of recent history through the eyes of a figure of the past serves to underline the apocalyptic notion of the determined nature of that history. What has happened and is presently happening has come about because God determined it beforehand. Thus all the events of that history, including the present time of tribulation and suffering, were willed by a beneficent and all-powerful God, who guides the course of world events in accord with his providential designs.

Those providential designs include the final triumph of God's kingdom and power in the age to come and the ultimate vindication of his holy people, that is, those Jews who remain steadfast and faithful to him. Thus the book concludes with a prediction of the end of Antiochus IV Epiphanes' persecution of the Jews and Antiochus' own death. There is also a veiled reference to the end of this present world with the arrival of the world to come (Dn 12:1-3). Those who remain faithful will participate in the triumph of God's power; and those who die in the persecutions because of their loyalty to God will rise from the dead to share also in the establishment of God's kingdom.

The stories about Daniel and other pious Jews in chapters 1-6 and Daniel's "review" of post-Exilic history in chapters 7-12 affirm in no uncertain terms the absolute power of God over the events of the world's history. They underline God's providential determination and guidance of that history. That providential guidance includes God's benevolent protection of his pious and loyal servants and their ultimate participation in the triumph of his kingdom in the new age. This new era is about to break in upon an unsuspecting world. Thus, even though the book's final predictions about the imminent arrival of God's final victory proved inaccurate, its ringing affirmation of God's power and benevolent protection of his people assured it a place in the canon.

APOCALYPTIC AS A BACKGROUND TO THE NEW TESTAMENT

This discussion of the Book of Daniel as an example of the emerging apocalyptic movement within Judaism offers us a bridge to the New Testament. Just around the time when Daniel was written, or shortly thereafter, a group of about fifty Jews gathered under the leadership of an anonymous figure known to us only by his title, "The Teacher of Righteousness" or, perhaps more accurately, "the Righteous Teacher." This small group, together with its leader, retreated into the barren wilderness region of Judea east of Jerusalem. There the group established a settlement on a promontory overlooking the Dead Sea at the site of an eighth century B.C.E. Judean border fort. Today that site is known as Khirbet Qumran, or "The Ruin of Qumran."

The group who settled at Qumran represented a branch of the *Hasidean* party, the "loyal" or "faithful" ones who strongly opposed any compromise with or accommodation to Greek ways. The particular group of Hasideans that settled at Qumran were known to their contemporaries and to later history as Essenes (from the Aramaic form of *Hasidean*). The community at Qumran flourished during the final century and a half B.C.E. and into the first century of the Common Era until the year 70 C.E. At that point it was destroyed by the Roman army during that army's suppression of the First Jewish Revolt (66-70 C.E.).

The discovery, beginning in 1947, of the Dead Sea community's library in the caves surrounding the settlement's ruins included the discovery also of copies of their community rule as well as scripture commentaries by its members. It is evident from these works and from other literature produced or preserved by the group that its community life and organization was shaped and thoroughly leavened by the apocalyptic mind set. The members understood themselves as the "faithful remnant" who rejected the decadent present order, doomed as it was to an imminent and catastrophic end. They had retreated into the wilderness to found a community faithful to the Law of Moses in every detail and to watch for signs that would announce the definitive inbreaking of God's power. This definitive intervention by God would bring to a finish the present age and inaugurate God's kingdom.

The mind set and literature of this and other contemporary Jewish groups had an obvious impact on Jesus and the early Christians. The preaching of Jesus, his expression and mode of thought, evidences the strong influence of the apocalyptic movement. The literature of the New Testament cannot be understood properly unless seen against the background of this contemporary Jewish apocalyptic thought and expression.

There was a decisive difference, however, between the Qumran Essenes and the New Testament Christians. The Essenes saw themselves as the

Some of the eleven caves in cliffs around the ruins of the Essene monastery at Qumran in which scrolls and fragments of writings of the Essene community were found.

specially chosen community who gathered to watch for signs and hold themselves in readiness for God's decisive inbreaking into history to inaugurate the new age. For the early Christians, that decisive inbreaking had already occurred in the person and life of Jesus Christ. In his death and resurrection that end time had already begun and the Christian community saw itself as the community of the new age. That new age had been initiated by Jesus' proclamation of its arrival in his person and in his announcement of its presence. Its definitive establishment, for the New Testament Christians, awaited Jesus' imminent return in glory.

REVIEW QUESTIONS

1. What do we mean by Hellenism?

2. What was the principal question facing the Jewish community vis-à-vis Hellenism at this time? Why was this not a purely theoretical question?

3. What stance toward Hellenism finally prevailed as the dominant one among the Jews as a result of the Maccabean revolt in 167 B.C.E.? What effect did this stance have on the future shape of Jewish life and identity?

4. Describe briefly some of the canonical and Deutero-canonical literature produced during these final two centuries of the Old Testament period.

5. What does the word *apocalypse* mean?

6. Discuss the sources and some of the characteristics of the apocalyptic movement, mind set, and literature. What notion lies at the heart of the apocalyptic world-view?

7. Describe the historical background of the Book of Daniel.

8. Describe the contents and purpose of the two parts of the Book of Daniel: chapters 1-6, and chapters 7-12.

9. How is an understanding of the apocalyptic movement and mind set important for an understanding of Jesus and the early Christian movement?

10. What was the decisive difference between the Qumran Essenes and the New Testament Christians?

26

Some Conclusions

THE OLD TESTAMENT: A LIBERATION PERSPECTIVE

Coming to the end of our look at the Old Testament from a liberation perspective, we might ask the question: What does a liberation perspective bring to the reading of the Old Testament? How does it differ from other, more traditional approaches to the text?

The Bible and Today's World

In Chapter 1 we saw the role which the Bible can and does play in a variety of settings in today's world—in politics, in the church, in the university, in popular culture. In each case, not only the particularity of the setting but, perhaps more importantly, the "social location" of the person in that setting were key factors in the kinds of questions asked. People in different settings, with differing economic and political commitments, have a variety of reasons for reading the Bible and thus it speaks to them in such diverse ways. The first of these settings we described, for example, was the political arena where questions of public policy and debate over the shape and character of the community and society take place. In our culture, appeal to the Bible is made to advance and justify decisions and directions.

The Hermeneutic of Suspicion

A closer look at the biblical text, as in the preceding chapters, demonstrates whence comes this easy affinity between the Bible and politics. In accord with our description of a liberation perspective in Chapter 1, we have tried consistently to apply a hermeneutic of suspicion to the text. And we have discovered, among other things, that the Bible and politics walk hand in hand so easily today because much of the material of the Bible emerged in response to what we might term today political issues. These include questions of tension and conflict-resolution within a village-based extended family, or politics on a national scale involving a king and his foreign policy. Conflict-resolution strategies within a village-based extended family appear in the story of Abraham and Lot's parting of the ways in Genesis 13, discussed in Chapter 4. When the shepherds of Abraham and Lot begin to quarrel over the use of the well-water, the two negotiate and agree to separate. Each settled and made use of the pasturage and water resources in different parts of the land. The story may represent not only a memory but may also be meant to serve as an example for conflict-resolution strategies for the extended families and clans who comprised the pre-monarchic tribal confederation. The story also involves issues of property rights and the vital access to cultivable land and to supplies of fresh water. These must have been of great concern to the earlier groups who joined together in that federation. The people of Israel saw their God as intimately concerned about and involved in all such questions.

In Chapter 17 we dealt with the "Immanuel" prophecy of Isaiah (Is 7:13). Isaiah confronts King Ahaz of Judah over the latter's decision to make an alliance with imperial Assyria: "Unless you trust in Yahweh alone (*ta'amī-nū*)"—that is, form no alliances with any king other than Israel's proper sovereign, Yahweh—"you (and Judah) will surely fall (*lō' tē'amēnū*)." The imminent birth of a male child to be named Immanuel, constituted a sign both of the truthfulness of the prophecy and a confirmation of its content: God's promise of presence and protection (*'immanu-'ēl*, "God is/will be with us") is and should be more meaningful than any promises from an Assyrian emperor.

Again, the hermeneutic of suspicion employed by scholars sympathetic to women's concerns reveals not only the patriarchal structure of society in the ancient world. It also exposes the patriarchal bias of those who assembled the text (for example, Genesis 12-50). There is some evidence of the unusually prominent role of women in the pre-monarchic tribal confederation. But our discussion above in Chapter 4 shows that only by "reading between the lines" of the present text can this unusual prominence of women be brought clearly into focus. Close attention to the women who play roles in these stories reveals that they function mainly as actors in stories about their husbands and sons. Nonetheless Sarah, Hagar, Rebekah, Rachel, Tamar, and others, clearly demonstrate initiative, strength of will, intelligence and wisdom, self-possession, and an unusual degree of independence in their actions and in their dealings with the men.

The prominent role of the Priestly class in the last stages in the formation of the Pentateuch could serve as a final example of the use of the hermeneutic of suspicion. The controlling hand of the Priestly group in these last stages during the Exile and post-Exilic periods ensured that the future direction for the identity and life of the Jewish community would be centered around the restored Temple and its sacrificial ritual. In such a context, the Temple priesthood thus assured itself of a prominent and decisive role in the life and governance of that community.

The Hermeneutical Privilege of the Poor

The so-called hermeneutical privilege of the poor served as a second interpretive tool in our liberation approach to the biblical text. The importance—indeed centrality—of this tool becomes understandable when we remember the decisive role the Exodus played in Israel's own story. The experience of that small group of slaves, at the very bottom of Egyptian society, was later seen by Israel as the central moment and source which gave meaning and purpose to their life as a people. The Scriptures themselves seem to suggest, then, that we should read the Bible and its history "from the bottom," that is, from the underside, through the eyes of the powerless and the poor, from the point of view of the oppressed. Consequently, we should not be surprised we are discovering today that those who find themselves "at the bottom" can experience and express such extraordinary affinity with and insight into the Bible's message.

We have tried to demonstrate in our various discussions how useful this perspective, this option for the poor, can be for approaching and understanding the biblical text. Again and again we have seen how important this approach proved to be for gaining access to the sense and substance of a whole variety of passages. It certainly proved to be the case with regard to the prophets. Amos (Chapter 16) served as a particularly prominent example of the usefulness of this hermeneutical tool. The passion and devastating directness of his prophetic condemnations arose from his first-hand experience of the destructive pressures and deep suffering his people were undergoing as a result of the injustices carried out by the elite ruling classes. Amos viewed the situation in his society through the eyes of these suffering poor. His encounter with the God of Israel, who stood by the poor and defended and protected them, empowered him to speak out forcefully on their behalf.

In Chapter 22 on the Psalms, we noted the massive presence of the Individual Laments, or Songs of Supplication, in the Psalter. Previous interpretation and use of these psalms tended to focus on the personal psychological aspects of the suffering that produced these psalms. But these interpreters failed to take into account the larger socio-economic context which was often the source of that suffering. By employing the hermeneutical tool of viewing Israelite society through the eyes of the poor, the number of Individual Laments needs no further explanation. The suffering to which they give witness arises from the poverty and exploitation experienced by the majority of the people in that society.

Liberation and Israel's God

A liberation perspective with its hermeneutic of suspicion and hermeneutical privilege of the poor has thrown new light on the God addressed by these prayers of the Psalter and revealed in the pages of the Bible. This God is a God of the poor and the oppressed. It has often been stressed in the past that the God of the Bible is revealed principally in the events and in the unfolding of the people's history. Our approach in these preceding pages has amply demonstrated the character of that history. Again and again it has been a story of struggle for liberation from oppression, exploitation, and injustice. Again and again the God of the Old Testament is recognized as one who has taken sides in that struggle—the side of the poor and the exploited. This should not be surprising when we remember the experience and story that gave birth to this people and that lies at the heart of the Old Testament—the Exodus. This God first spoke and was manifested in the lives and history of these people as the one who stood by them in their suffering and who acted on their behalf in delivering them from the slavery of Egypt.

God formed them into a new and "unique" or "chosen" people inasmuch as their community—in its political, economic, social, and religious character—was unique in the ancient world. Other groups like them, smaller or larger, may have existed for a time. The vision of a community ordered above all toward justice and cooperation corresponds to the deepest dreams and hopes of almost every human being. But Israel alone survived the pressures and vicissitudes of history. They have left a record and a living tradition, a diverse community of believers in that vision who continue to honor and worship Israel's God and who continue the struggle on their own behalf and on behalf of others for a more just and more peaceful world.

Liberation and Covenant

Viewing the pervasive theme of covenant in the Old Testament from this liberation perspective has added new depth and dimension to it. We have seen above in Chapter 8 and again in Chapters 10 and 11 how the people who first formed Israel's tribal confederation created and developed an instrument usually identified by the word covenant. Later reflection and theologizing, for example, in the New Testament and in Christian tradition, have elaborated and given depth, color, and dimension to the covenant theme. It has been broadened and deepened to include personal, spiritual, and existential dimensions. However, these spiritual and personal applications have taken such a prominent place in Christian thought that they have tended to obscure the social and political aspects of this key notion of covenant. But even a cursory examination of the texts dealing with covenant reveals that it was not seen as primarily concerned with religious matters such as worship and ritual. Rather, it was the great charter that served as the organizational foundation of Israel's distinctive society. Its commandments and stipulations encompassed the whole complex of life in ancient Israel, regulating political, economic, and social relations as well as the religious dimension.

Thus the biblical notion of covenant is only incompletely understood when it is examined solely in its religious aspects. To appreciate it fully requires attention to the other dimensions to which these religious aspects were intimately connected and from which they took their particular shape and concrete expression. Only through fidelity to all the provisions of this covenant would Israel continue to prosper and possess the land; violation of any of the provisions would bring about the eventual dissolution and disappearance of Israel as the unique and distinctive society that it was.

We saw in Chapter 11 how the covenant with their God touched every aspect the lives of the people. It involved economic questions affecting ownership, sale of land, debt repayment; questions of political organization such as the limits on the rights of the king in monarchic times; social questions such as care of the poor, the disadvantaged, the aged. All of Israel's life was seen in the light of the covenant with its unique and sovereign God.

Our liberation perspective has rewarded us with a recouping of this wider function and meaning of covenant. It has made clearer the challenge to us who continue to profess loyalty to that tradition of covenant. We ignore to our own peril the social, economic, and political demands which such loyalty implies.

LIBERATION AND LIFE

We noted above the close relationship between the Bible and politics. This facile "hand-in-hand" arises from the very nature of the biblical text itself. It is so often, as we have seen again and again, the product of social and ideological struggle. The text's gaps and silences and inner contradictions often reflect the confrontations and triumphs of opposed groups, or at least the tensions or uneasy harmony between or among them.

In reading and interpreting the Bible we must take account of this, and not only because the nature and origin of the text itself demand it. As we noted in Chapter 10, the Bible claims that it is within the unfolding of the history of this people that the will, indeed the very face of God is revealed. Their centuries-long story of struggle and liberation and their checkered journey of faithfulness and infidelity, of loyalty and betrayal, act as a model and paradigm of how we can recognize God as present in our own life and history.

When we speak of the Bible in this context, we mean the *whole* Bible, including the New Testament. Contrary to popular notions, the New Testament does not mark a break with the "materialistic" ethos of the Old. A number of recent commentators have demonstrated convincingly how central to the life and preaching of Jesus were economic, political, and social issues, as well as religious ones. This was true also for the first Christian communities, those responsible for the development of the traditions and for the texts preserved in the New Testament. For example, in *The Liberation of Christmas,* Richard Horsley highlights the importance of political and economic liberation, which the Infancy Narratives of Luke and Matthew proclaim:

> The infancy narratives are about liberation. The birth of the Christ-child means that God has inaugurated the long-awaited deliverance of the people of Israel from their enemies. More precisely, God has begun to free the people from domination and exploitation by the imperial ruler and from their own rulers, particularly the tyrannical king. The people's liberation evokes brutal repression and involves suffering, but the dominant tone is one of relief and excitement as the people respond readily to God's initiative (p. 155).

To read and interpret the Bible from a liberation perspective, then, is no mere academic exercise. As we follow the trails it opens up into the text, we cannot help but feel drawn into the questions and struggles and confrontations we discover. We find ourselves readily taking sides in an issue or debate. And when we step back to assess our walk through the text, we often realize how strongly our own social location and political convictions have influenced our choice of stance or response to the text.

One of the strategies we used in the preceding pages was that of reimagining the context out of which these stories grew. We described at least plausible situations which the elements of the story or text could reflect. More often than not, the theological point became clear, that is, the insight into the way in which the people saw God present and active. At that point we could easily have taken the step into an analogous situation today. In most cases we refrained from taking that step, although at times we suggested it in the questions at the end of each chapter. However, as we close our discussion of the Old Testament from a liberation perspective, we would like to pick up a few of those threads and indicate where and how they might be followed.

The Bible and Contemporary Socio-economic Issues

The story of the parting of Abraham and Lot in Genesis 13 involved issues of property rights and the vital access to cultivable land and to supplies of fresh water. Such concerns must have been central to the lives of the groups who joined together to form the tribal confederation. Indeed, the affirmation by the tradition of God's involvement in this question underlines its importance: the promise of land and the divine sanction of the right of possession and of access to its fruits are central, for example, to the covenant language of Genesis 13, 15, and 28:

> The LORD said to Abram: "Look about you, and from where you are, gaze to the north and south, east and west; all the land that you see I will give to you and your descendants forever. . . . Set forth and walk about in this land, through its length and breadth, for to you I will give it" (Gn 13:14-15, 17).

It is only a small step from Abraham and Lot's world of 3,500 or so years ago into our own day and age. In so many areas of our world—for example, Brazil, Guatemala, India, and other places—similar questions of the vital access to cultivable land and control of the fruits of its cultivation continue to be concerns. More often than not it involved the question of life and death itself.

From reading between the lines of the text of Genesis 12-50, we noted also the unusual prominence of women in these stories, despite the patriarchal structure of the society and the bias of those who put the text together. Sarah, Hagar, Rebekah, Rachel, and others, clearly demonstrate initiative and a degree of independence. Again, the step is only a short one from this second millennium B.C.E. context into our own. Around the world women are beginning to achieve varying degrees of self-consciousness. This leads to demands and actions on behalf of their rights and their access to full participation in the decision-making processes of their societies.

The hermeneutic of suspicion also allowed us to uncover some of the political and socio-economic issues at stake in the Priestly class's central role in the final stages of the formation of the Pentateuch. By their decisive involvement in the way in which Israel's story and traditions were definitively recorded, they insured a prominent role for themselves in the social, economic, and political life of the restored post-Exilic community. We do not have to go far in contemporary history, or even beyond this morning's newspaper, for similar examples of the manipulation of a society's history, traditions, language, or religious ritual for social, political, or economic purposes.

Finally, we highlighted above the larger socio-economic context of the poverty and exploitation of a major portion of the population in ancient Israel. Such a situation of poverty and exploitation offers a plausible explanation for the massive presence of the Individual Lament psalms in the Psalter. The cries of these suffering poor in ancient Israel for deliverance and rescue are echoed by millions of voices in our world today. Consciousness of this connection can only bring new depth and meaning to our own understanding and use of these same prayers today.

The Bible and Decision-making

In Chapter 20 we offered an imaginative reconstruction of one possible scenario for the origin of the Servant Songs of Second Isaiah (Is 40-55). This reconstruction presumes that the Servant stands for the prophet himself, and the experiences of the Servant as described in the Servant Songs represent events in the prophet's own life.

In his preaching to the Exilic community the prophet heralds the Persian leader Cyrus as a potential liberator. Yahweh has chosen and destined Cyrus to fulfill that role, even though Cyrus is unaware of that fact. However, the prophet dare not speak openly and explicitly of this impending triumph of Cyrus and his army lest he appear as a traitor and Persian agent to the Jews' Babylonian captors. Despite his coded language, however, the prophet is betrayed by members of his own community who resent his pro-Persian/anti-Babylonian stance. These members of the Jewish community hold important positions in the Babylonian administration and see in the prophet a threat to their own status and interests. The sufferings of the Servant thus reflect the experience of the prophet himself, arrested and imprisoned by the Babylonian authorities with the collaboration of these pro-Babylonian Jews. Those sufferings and possibly also the prophet's eventual martyrdom are described in the fourth and last of the Servant Songs (Is 52:13-53:12).

This reconstruction allows us a glimpse of the tensions and conflicts which must have been a part of life within the Exilic community. The prophet played a role both as participant and victim in these tensions and conflicts. His courageous decision to bring the message of hope and comfort to his people earned him imprisonment and suffering.

Questions about the ambiguity and uncertainty surrounding the prophet's decision could be raised. Was he right in speaking out? Did he really have to take the risk that he did? Christians or any individuals who take a stance in regard to questions of right and fairness and justice cannot escape similar ambiguity and uncertainty today. But our liberation perspective has demonstrated that we cannot avoid making decisions or taking sides even when the issues appear to be basically political, economic, or social, rather than primarily religious ones. The humility and fidelity of a figure like the Servant of the Lord, this prophet of the Exile, serve as a model and inspiration. He was willing to accept the uncertainty and suffering his stand involved. New Testament scholars tell us that the Servant was a model also for Jesus in his life and ministry; the Servant, and Jesus himself, still serve as models for us today.

The Bible and Human Liberation

We begin this final section simply by reiterating a point made in the closing paragraphs of Chapter 1 and again in Chapter 10. We have seen that the story of the Bible is, at its heart, the story of a people striving to achieve and maintain a life-giving community. It embodies the record of their belief that their God was present and active in the midst of that struggle. Indeed, this God was revealed as one who stands with and defends them in that struggle. If such is the case, it follows that the easiest way into this text, the way that best puts us in touch with its dynamics and fundamental concerns, is through the eyes of those who today are themselves involved in similar struggles.

In other words, our liberation perspective has demonstrated that the Bible itself provides its own key for interpretation: it is best read and understood in the context of the struggle for liberation. This fact serves as a challenge to those not directly involved to examine the reality of their solidarity with those who are involved in the struggle for more just and fair arrangements in the world's economic order. The struggle for liberation also includes the concern for women's full access to and participation in the decision-making processes of their societies, for an end to the exclusion of any human being on the basis of sex, race, religious or political convictions, age, or mental, physical or emotional/psychological handicaps.

I lived and taught in a seminary in South India for almost nine years. I cannot help but be aware of the enormous challenges the Indian people face. So many of these challenges are tied to economic questions, especially about the justice of the present ordering of the world economy. Present economic arrangements mandate that the majority of the human race go without the basic necessities of adequate food, clothing, and shelter, and even more, the necessities of the spirit—access to education, recreation, and enjoyment of the beauties of divine and human creativity. Almost every human being on this planet is caught up in this economic order, usually either supporting and benefiting from it or suffering from its consequences. Our liberation perspective suggests that we cannot read the Bible, with its call to take the side of the poor and the exploited, and yet ignore the unfairness and injustice of these present economic arrangements and the political, social, and religious structures that so often exist mainly to keep those arrangements in place.

REVIEW QUESTIONS

1. From among the various Old Testament texts in the preceding pages, choose one (e.g., the stories about Samson in the Book of Judges) and apply a "hermeneutic of suspicion" to it.

2. How can we take a short step with that text from the biblical world of two thousand or more years ago into our world or even our own lives and context today?

3. Choose a passage from the New Testament (such as the Beatitudes in Chapter 5 of Matthew's Gospel) and apply a hermeneutic of suspicion to it. Again, how can we take a short step with that passage from the world of Jesus and the first Christians into our own twenty-first-century context?

4. Discuss the hermeneutical privilege of the poor in connection with a passage from the wisdom literature of the Old Testament (Proverbs, Job, Ecclesiastes, the Wisdom of Ben Sira, the Wisdom of Solomon). How can we move with that text from the world of the Israelite sages to the world of today?

5. Choose a passage from the Johannine literature (Gospel of John, Epistles of John, the Apocalypse) and discuss it in the light of the hermeneutical privilege of the poor. How can we move with that passage into a twenty-first-century context?

Bibliography

1. THE BIBLE IN THE MODERN WORLD

Brueggemann, Walter. *Theology of the Old Testament: Testimony, Dispute, Advocacy.* Minneapolis, Minn.: Fortress Press, 1997.

Coote, Robert B., and Mary P. Coote. *Power, Politics, and the Making of the Bible.* Minneapolis, Minn.: Fortress Press, 1990.

Cormie, Lee. "The Hermeneutical Privilege of the Oppressed: Liberation Theologies, Biblical Faith, and Marxist Sociology of Knowledge." *Catholic Theological Society of America, Proceedings* 32 (1978): 155-81.

———. "Revolutions in Reading the Bible." In *The Bible and the Politics of Exegesis,* edited by Peggy Day, David Jobling, and Gerald Sheppard. New York: Pilgrim Press, 1991.

Felder, Cain Hope. *Troubling Biblical Waters: Race, Class, and Family.* The Bishop Henry McNeal Turner Studies in North American Black Religion 3. Maryknoll, N.Y.: Orbis Books, 1989.

Fitzmyer, Joseph A. *The Biblical Commission's Document "The Interpretation of the Bible in the Church": Text and Commentary.* Subsidia Biblica 18. Rome: Pontifical Biblical Institute, 1995.

Gottwald, Norman K. "Angles of Vision on the Hebrew Bible." Chap. 1 in *The Hebrew Bible: A Socio-Literary Introduction.* Philadelphia: Fortress Press, 1985.

———. "Sociology (Ancient Israel)." In *The Anchor Bible Dictionary,* edited by David Noel Freedman, 6:79-89. New York: Doubleday, 1992.

Gutiérrez, Gustavo. "Theology from the Underside of History." Chap. 7 in *The Power of the Poor in History: Selected Writings.* Maryknoll, N.Y.: Orbis Books, 1983.

———. *A Theology of Liberation: History, Politics, and Salvation.* Rev. ed. Maryknoll, N.Y.: Orbis Books, 1988.

Hope, Marjorie, and James Young. *The South African Churches in a Revolutionary Situation.* Maryknoll, N.Y.: Orbis Books, 1981.

Matthews, Victor H., and Don C. Benjamin. *Social World of Ancient Israel 1250-587 B.C.E.* Peabody, Mass.: Hendrickson, 1993.

Mesters, Carlos. *Defenseless Flower: A New Reading of the Bible.* Maryknoll, N.Y.: Orbis Books; London: Catholic Institute for International Relations, 1989.

———. *God, Where Are You? Rediscovering the Bible.* Maryknoll, N.Y.: Orbis Books, 1995.

———. "The Use of the Bible in Christian Communities of the Common People." In *The Challenge of Basic Christian Communities: Papers from the International Ecumenical Congress of Theology, February 20-March 2, 1980, São Paulo, Brazil,* edited by Sergio Torres and John Eagleson, 197-210. Maryknoll, N.Y.: Orbis Books, 1981.

Newsom, Carol A., and Sharon H. Ringe, eds. *The Women's Bible Commentary.* London: SPCK, 1992.

Schüssler Fiorenza, Elisabeth. *Bread Not Stone: The Challenge of Feminist Biblical Interpretation.* Boston: Beacon Press, 1984.

———. ed. *Searching the Scriptures: A Feminist Introduction: A Feminist Commentary.* 2 vols. New York: Crossroad, 1993, 1994.

Sugirtharaja, Rasiah S. *Asian Biblical Hermeneutics and Postcolonialism: Contesting the Interpretations.* The Biblical Seminar 64. Sheffield: Sheffield Academic Press, 1999.

———. ed. *Voices from the Margin: Interpreting the Bible in the Third World.* New ed. Maryknoll, N.Y.: Orbis Books, 1995.

2. A MODERN LOOK AT BIBLICAL TIMES

Baly, Denis. *Basic Biblical Geography.* Philadelphia: Fortress Press, 1987.

Biblical Archaeologist 56/1 (March 1993). Special issue, "Celebrating and Examining W. F. Albright."

Biggs, Robert D. "Ebla Texts." In *The Anchor Bible Dictionary,* edited by David Noel Freedman, 2:263-70, New York: Doubleday, 1992.

Brown, Raymond E. "Our New Approach to the Bible." In *New Testament Essays,* 3-16. Milwaukee: Bruce, 1965.

———. *Recent Discoveries and the Biblical World.* Wilmington, Del.: Michael Glazier, 1983.

Coogan, Michael D. *Stories from Ancient Canaan.* Philadelphia: Fortress Press, 1978.

Craigie, Peter C. *Ugarit and the Old Testament.* Grand Rapids, Mich.: Eerdmans, 1983.

Dever, William G. "Archaeology, Syro-Palestinian and Biblical." In *The Anchor Bible Dictionary,* edited by David Noel Freedman, 1:354-67. New York: Doubleday, 1992.

"Dogmatic Constitution on Divine Revelation (*Dei Verbum*)." In *Vatican Council II: The Conciliar and Post Conciliar Documents,* edited by Austin Flannery, 750-65. Northcourt, N.J.: Costello, 1975.

Gottwald, Norman K. "The World of the Hebrew Bible." Chap. 2 in *The Hebrew Bible: A Socio-Literary Introduction.* Philadelphia: Fortress Press, 1985.

Kealy, John (Sean). *Our Changing Bible.* Denville, N.J.: Dimension Books, 1977.

LaFay, Howard, "Ebla: Spendor of an Unknown Empire." *National Geographic* 154/6 (December 1978), 730-59.

Lance, H. Darrell. *The Old Testament and the Archaeologist.* Guides to Biblical Scholarship, Old Testament Series. Philadelphia: Fortress Press, 1986.

Miller, J. Maxwell. "Archaeology and the Bible." In *The International Bible Commentary: A Catholic and Ecumenical Commentary for the Twenty-First Century,* edited by William R. Farmer, 203-11. Collegeville, Minn.: Liturgical Press, 1998.

Parker, Simon B., ed. *Ugaritic Narrative Poetry.* Writings from the Ancient World Series 9. Atlanta: Scholars Press, 1997.

Pettinato, Giovanni. *Ebla: A New Look at History.* Baltimore and London: Johns Hopkins University Press, 1991.

Reading the Past: Ancient Writing from Cuneiform to the Alphabet. Introduced by J. T. Hooker. Berkeley and Los Angeles: University of California Press, 1990.

Senner, Wayne M., ed. *The Origins of Writing.* Lincoln and London: University of Nebraska Press, 1989.

3. THE HISTORICAL BACKGROUND
OF THE ANCIENT NEAR EAST

Braidwood, Robert J. *Prehistoric Men.* 8th ed. Glenview, Ill.: Scott, Foresman, 1975.

Bright, John. "The Ancient Orient before ca. 2000 B.C." and "The World of Israel's Origins." Prologue and chap. 1 in *A History of Israel.* 3d ed. Philadelphia: Westminster, 1981.

Frankfort, H., et al. *Before Philosophy: The Intellectual Adventure of Ancient Man.* Harmondsworth: Penguin, 1949.

Gottwald, Norman K. "The World of the Hebrew Bible." Chap. 2 in *The Hebrew Bible: A Socio-Literary Introduction.* Philadelphia: Fortress Press, 1985.

Hallo, William W., and William Kelly Simpson. *The Ancient Near East: A History.* New York: Harcourt Brace Jovanovich, 1971.

———. *Origins: The Ancient Near Eastern Background of Some Modern Western Institutions.* Studies in the History and Culture of the Ancient Near East 6. Leiden: Brill, 1996.

Kramer, Samuel Noah. *History Begins at Sumer: Thirty-Nine Firsts in Man's Recorded History.* Philadelphia: University of Pennsylvania Press, 1981.

Matthews, Victor H., and Don C. Benjamin. *Old Testament Parallels: Laws and Stories from the Ancient Near East.* Fully rev. and exp. ed. New York/Mahwah, N.J.: Paulist Press, 1997.

Miller, J. Maxwell, and John H. Hayes. "The Setting." Chap. 1 in *A History of Ancient Israel and Judah.* Philadelphia: Westminster, 1986.

Oates, David, and Joan Oates. *The Rise of Civilization.* The Making of the Past. Lausanne: Elsevier/Phaidon, 1976.

Wilson, John A. *The Culture of Ancient Egypt.* 2d ed. Chicago: University of Chicago Press, 1956.

4. THE ANCESTORS OF ISRAEL

Bright, John. "The Patriarchs." Chap. 2 in *A History of Israel.* 3d ed. Philadelphia: Westminster, 1981.

Brueggemann, Walter. *The Land.* Overtures to Biblical Theology. Philadelphia: Fortress Press, 1977.

Callaway, Joseph A. "A Visit with Ahilud: A Revealing Look at Village Life When Israel First Settled the Promised Land." *Biblical Archaeology Review* 9 (1983), 42-53.

Ceresko, Anthony R. "Potsherds and Pioneers: Recent Research on the Origins of Israel." *Indian Theological Studies* 34 (1997), 5-22.

Dever, William J., and W. Malcolm Clark. "The Patriarchal Traditions." Chap. 2 in *Israelite and Judean History,* edited by John H. Hayes and J. Maxwell Miller. London: SCM Press, 1977.

———. "Ceramics, Ethnicity, and the Question of Israel's Origins." *Biblical Archaeologist* 58 (1995), 200-213.

Dresner, Samuel. "Rachel and Leah: Sibling Tragedy or Triumph of Pity and Compassion." *Bible Review* 6 (1990), 22-27, 40-42.

Exum, J. Cheryl. "The Mothers of Israel: The Patriarchal Narratives from a Feminist Perspective." *Bible Review* 2 (1986), 60-67.

Gottwald, Norman K. "Traditions about the Fathers and Mothers of Israel." Chap. 4 in *The Hebrew Bible: A Socio-Literary Introduction.* Philadelphia: Fortress Press, 1985.

———. *The Tribes of Yahweh: A Sociology of the Religion of Liberated Israel 1250-1050 B.C.E.* Maryknoll, N.Y.: Orbis Books, 1979.

Halpern, Baruch. "Settlement of Canaan." In *The Anchor Bible Dictionary,* edited by David Noel Freedman, 6:1120-43. New York: Doubleday, 1992.

Hayes, John H. "The History of the Study of Israelite and Judean History." Chap. 1 in *Israelite and Judean History,* edited by John H. Hayes and J. Maxwell Miller. London: SCM Press, 1977.

Mendenhall, George E. "The Hebrew Conquest of Palestine." *Biblical Archaeologist* 25 (1962), 66-87. In *Biblical Archaeologist Reader* 3, edited by Edward F. Campbell and David N. Freedman, 100-120. Garden City, N.Y.: Doubleday Image, 1970.

Meyers, Carol L. "The Family in Early Israel." In *Families in Ancient Israel,* by Leo Perdue, et al., 1-47. The Family, Religion, and Culture. Louisville, Ky.: Westminster John Knox Press, 1997.

———. "Procreation, Production and Protection: Male-Female Balance in Early Israel." *Journal of the American Academy of Religion* 51 (1983), 569-93.

Nelson, Richard D. "The Historical Context." Chap. 2 in *The Historical Books.* Interpreting Biblical Texts. Nashville, Tenn.: Abingdon Press, 1998.

5. THE DOCUMENTARY HYPOTHESIS

Blenkinsopp, Joseph. *The Pentateuch: An Introduction to the First Five Books of the Bible.* Anchor Bible Reference Library. New York: Doubleday, 1992.

Childs, Brevard S. "Introduction to the Pentateuch." Chap. 5 in *Introduction to the Old Testament as Scripture.* Philadelphia: Fortress Press, 1979.

Gottwald, Norman K. Parts 2 and 3 in *The Tribes of Yahweh: A Sociology of the Religion of Liberated Israel 1250-1050 B.C.E.* Maryknoll, N.Y.: Orbis Books, 1979.

Guinan, Michael D. *The Pentateuch.* Message of Biblical Spirituality 1. Collegeville, Minn.: Liturgical Press, 1990.

Habel, Norman. *Literary Criticism of the Old Testament.* Guides to Biblical Scholarship, Old Testament Series. Philadelphia: Fortress Press, 1971.

Hayes, John H. "The Historical-Critical Approach to the Old Testament." Chaps. 3 and 5 in *An Introduction to Old Testament Study.* Nashville, Tenn.: Abingdon Press, 1979.

Murphy, Roland E. *Responses to 101 Questions on the Biblical Torah: Reflections on the Pentateuch.* New York/Mahwah N.J.: Paulist Press, 1996.

Noth, Martin. *A History of Pentateuchal Traditions,* introduction by Bernhard W. Anderson. Englewood Cliffs, N.J.: Prentice-Hall, 1972.

Rast, Walter. *Tradition History and the Old Testament.* Guides to Biblical Scholarship, Old Testament Series. Philadelphia: Fortress Press, 1972.

Vawter, Bruce. *On Genesis: A New Reading.* Garden City, N.Y.: Doubleday, 1977.

6. THE FOUR SOURCES

Brueggemann, Walter, and Hans Walter Wolff, *The Vitality of Old Testament Traditions.* 2d ed. Atlanta: John Knox, 1982.

Coote, Robert B. *In the Beginning: Creation and the Priestly History.* Minneapolis, Minn.: Fortress Press, 1991.

———. *In Defense of Revolution: The Elohist History.* Minneapolis, Minn.: Fortress Press, 1991.

Coote, Robert B., and David Robert Ord. *The Bible's First History.* Philadelphia: Fortress Press, 1989.

Ellis, Peter F. *The Men and Message of the Old Testament.* 3d ed. Collegeville, Minn.: Liturgical Press, 1975. (Note the "Color Outline" of sources of the Pentateuch, 58-73.)

———. *The Yahwist: The Bible's First Theologian.* Notre Dame, Ind.: Fides, 1968.

Fretheim, Terence E. *The Pentateuch.* Interpreting Biblical Texts. Nashville, Tenn.: Abingdon Press, 1996.

Friedman, Richard E. "Torah (Pentateuch)." In *The Anchor Bible Dictionary,* edited by David Noel Freedman, 6:605-22. New York: Doubleday, 1992.

Gottwald, Norman K. "On the Sources for Israel's Premonarchic History." Prologue to Part II in *The Hebrew Bible: A Socio-Literary Introduction.* Philadelphia: Fortress Press, 1985.

Laffey, Alice L. *The Pentateuch: A Liberation-Critical Reading.* Minneapolis, Minn.: Fortress Press, 1998.

Vawter, Bruce. *On Genesis: A New Reading.* Garden City, N.Y.: Doubleday, 1977.

7. THE EXODUS

Bruggemann, Walter. "The Book of Exodus: Introduction, Commentary, Reflections." In *New Interpreter's Bible,* edited by Leander E. Keck, et al., 1:675-981. Nashville, Tenn.: Abingdon Press, 1996.

Childs, Brevard S. *The Book of Exodus: A Critical Theological Commentary.* Philadelphia: Westminster, 1974.

———. "Exodus." Chap. 7 in *Introduction to the Old Testament as Scripture.* Philadelphia: Fortress Press, 1979.

Cross, Frank Moore. *Canaanite Myth and Hebrew Epic: Essays in the History of the Religion of Israel.* Cambridge: Harvard University, 1973. See 121-44.

Fretheim, Terence E. *Exodus.* Interpretation. Louisville, Ky.: Westminster John Knox Press, 1991.

Gottwald, Norman K. "Traditions about Moses: Exodus, Covenant, and Lawgiving." Chap. 5 in *The Hebrew Bible: A Socio-Literary Introduction.* Philadelphia: Fortress Press, 1985.

Hyatt, J. Philip. *Exodus.* Rev. ed. New Century Bible Commentary. Grand Rapids, Mich.: Eerdmans, 1980.

Pixley, George V. *On Exodus: A Liberation Perspective.* Maryknoll, N.Y.: Orbis Books, 1987.

Sarna, Nahum M. "Exodus, Book of." In *The Anchor Bible Dictionary,* edited by David Noel Freedman, 2:689-700. New York: Doubleday, 1992.

———. *Exploring Exodus: The Heritage of Biblical Israel.* New York: Schocken Books,1986.

8. COVENANT

Ancient Near Eastern Texts Relating to the Old Testament, with Supplement (ANET). Edited by James B. Pritchard. 3d ed. Princeton, N.J.: Princeton University Press, 1969.

Cross, Frank Moore. "Kinship and Covenant in Ancient Israel." In *From Epic to Canon: History and Literature in Ancient Israel.* Baltimore: Johns Hopkins University Press, 1998.

Dumbrell, William J. *Covenant and Creation: An Old Testament Covenant Theology.* Exeter, U.K.: Paternoster Press, 1984.

Gottwald, Norman K. "Traditions about Moses: Exodus, Covenant, and Lawgiving." Chap. 5 in *The Hebrew Bible: A Socio-Literary Introduction.* Philadelphia: Fortress Press, 1985.

Hillers, Delbert R. *Covenant: The History of a Biblical Idea.* Seminars in the History of Ideas. Baltimore: Johns Hopkins University, 1969.

McCarthy, Dennis J. *Old Testament Covenant: A Survey of Current Opinions.* Atlanta: John Knox, 1972.

———. *Treaty and Covenant: A Study in Form in the Ancient Oriental Documents and in the Old Testament.* 2d ed. Analecta Biblica 21A. Rome: Pontifical Biblical Institute, 1978.

Mendenhall, George E. *Law and Covenant in Israel and in the Ancient Near East.* Pittsburgh: Biblical Colloquium, 1955.

Mendenhall, George E., and Gary A. Herion. "Covenant." In *The Anchor Bible Dictionary,* edited by David Noel Freedman, 1:1179-1202. New York: Doubleday, 1992.

Shanks, Hershel. "God as Divine Kinsman." *Biblical Archaeology Review* 25/4 (July-August 1999), 32-33, 60.

9. THE "CONQUEST" OF CANAAN

Albertz, Rainer. *A History of Israelite Religion*, translated by John Bowden. Louisville, Ky.: Westminster/John Knox Press, 1994, p. 76.

Albright, William F. *From the Stone Age to Christianity: Monotheism and the Historical Process.* 2d ed. Garden City, N.Y.: Doubleday, 1957.

Bright, John. "Exodus and Conquest: The Formation of the People of Israel." Chap. 3 in *A History of Israel.* 3d ed. Philadelphia: Westminster, 1981.

Callaway, Joseph A. "A Visit with Ahilud: A Revealing Look at Village Life When Israel First Settled the Promised Land." *Biblical Archaeology Review* 9 (1983), 42-53.

Ceresko, Anthony R. "Potsherds and Pioneers: Recent Research on the Origins of Israel." *Indian Theological Studies* 34 (1997), 5-22.

Dever, William G. "Ceramics, Ethnicity, and the Question of Israel's Origins." *Biblical Archaeologist* 58 (1995), 200-213.

———. *Recent Archaeological Discoveries and Biblical Research.* Seattle and London: University of Washington Press, 1990.

Gnuse, Robert. "Israelite Settlement of Canaan: A Peaceful Internal Process." *Biblical Theology Bulletin* 21 (1991): 56-66, 109-17.

Gottwald, Norman K. "Models of the Israelite Settlement in Canaan." Part 5 in *The Tribes of Yahweh: A Sociology of the Religion of Liberated Israel 1250-1050 B.C.E.* Maryknoll, N.Y.: Orbis Books, 1979.

Halpern. Baruch. "Settlement of Canaan." In *The Anchor Bible Dictionary,* edited by David Noel Freedman, 5:1120-43. New York: Doubleday, 1992.

Levy, Thomas E., ed. *The Archaeology of Society in the Holy Land.* New York: Facts on File, 1995.

McDermott, John J. *What Are They Saying about the Formation of Israel?* New York/Mahwah, N. J.: Paulist Press, 1998.

McNutt, Paula. *Reconstructing the Society of Ancient Israel.* Library of Ancient Israel. Louisville, Ky.: Westminster John Knox Press; London: SPCK, 1999.

Mendenhall, George E. "The Hebrew Conquest of Palestine." *Biblical Archaeologist* 25 (1962), 66-87. In *Biblical Archaeologist Reader* 3, edited by Edward F. Campbell and David N. Freedman, 100-120. Garden City, N.Y.: Doubleday Image, 1970.

Miller, J. Maxwell. "The Israelite Occupation of Canaan." Chap. 6 in *Israelite and Judean History,* edited by John H. Hayes and J. Maxwell Miller. London: SCM, 1977.

Miller, J. Maxwell and John H. Hayes. "The Question of Origins." Chap. 2 in *A History of Ancient Israel and Judah.* Philadelphia: Westminster, 1986.

Nelson, Richard D. "The Historical Context." Chap. 2 in *The Historical Books.* Interpreting Biblical Texts. Nashville, Tenn.: Abingdon Press, 1998.

Noth, Martin. *The History of Israel: Biblical History.* 2d ed. London: Adam and Charles Black, 1959.

Stager, Lawrence E. "The Archaeology of the Family in Ancient Israel." *Bulletin of the American Schools of Oriental Research* 260 (Fall/November 1985), 1-35.

Trible, Phyllis. "Bringing Miriam out of the Shadows." *Bible Review* 5 (1989), 14-25, 34.

Walsh, J. P. M. *The Mighty from Their Thrones: Power in the Biblical Tradition.* Overtures to Biblical Theology. Philadelphia: Fortress Press,1987.

10. ISRAEL IN THE PERIOD OF THE JUDGES

Ackerman, Susan. *Under Every Green Tree: Popular Religion in Sixth-Century Judah.* Harvard Semitic Monographs 46. Atlanta: Scholars Press, 1992.

Albertz, Rainer. "The History of Israelite Religion in the Period before the State." Part 2 in *A History of Israelite Religion in the Old Testament Period,* 1: 23-103. London: SCM, 1994.

Bird, Phyllis A. "Israelite Religion and the Faith of Israel's Daughters: Reflections on Gender and Religious Definition." In *The Bible and the Politics of Exegesis,* edited by Peggy Day, David Jobling, and Gerald Sheppard, 97-108. New York: Pilgrim Press, 1991.

Bloch-Smith, Elizabeth, and Beth Alpert Nakhai. "A Landscape Comes to Life: The Iron I Period." *Near Eastern Archaeology* 62 (1999), 62-92, 101-127.

Ceresko, Anthony R. "The Challenge of the Tenth Commandment." *Compass: A Jesuit Journal* 6 (1988), 47.

Chaney, Marvin L. "Ancient Palestinian Peasant Movements and the Formation of Premonarchic Israel." In *Palestine in Transition: The Emergence of Ancient Israel,* edited by David Noel Freedman and David F. Graf, 39-90. The Social World of Biblical Antiquity Series 2. Sheffield: Almond Press, 1983.

———. "You Shall Not Covet Your Neighbor's House." *Pacific Theological Review* 15 (Winter 1982), 3-13.

Dever, William G. "Archaeology and the Religions of Israel." *Bulletin of the American Schools of Oriental Research* 301 (1996), 83-90.

Finkelstein, Israel. *The Archaeology of the Settlement of Israel.* Jerusalem: Israel Exploration Society, 1988.

Gnuse, Robert K. "Holy History in the Hebrew Scriptures and the Ancient World: Beyond the Present Debate." *Biblical Theology Bulletin* 17 (1987), 127-36.

Gottwald, Norman K. "Traditions about Intertribal Israel's Rise to Power in Canaan." Chap. 6 in *The Hebrew Bible: A Socio-Literary Introduction.* Philadelphia: Fortress Press, 1985.

———. Parts 6-10 in *Tribes of Yahweh: A Sociology of the Religion of Liberated Israel 1250-1050 B.C.E.* Maryknoll, N.Y.: Orbis Books, 1979.

Hayes, John H., and J. Maxwell Miller, eds. "The Period of the Judges and the Rise of the Monarchy." Chap. 5 in *Israelite and Judean History,* edited by John H. Hayes and J. Maxwell Miller. London: SCM, 1977.

Hopkins, David C. *The Highlands of Canaan: Agricultural Life in the Early Iron Age.* Social World of Biblical Antiquity 3. Sheffield: Almond Press, 1985.

Keel, Othmar, and Christopher Uehlinger. *Gods, Goddesses, and Images of God.* Minneapolis, Minn.: Fortress Press, 1998.

Kennedy, James M. "The Social Background of Early Israel's Rejection of Cultic Images: A Proposal." *Biblical Theology Bulletin* 17 (1987), 138-44.

McKenzie, John L. *The World of the Judges.* Englewood Cliffs, N.J.: Prentice-Hall, 1966.

Mendenhall, George E. *The Tenth Generation: The Origins of the Biblical Tradition.* Baltimore and London: Johns Hopkins University Press, 1973.

Meyers, Carol L. " 'To Her Mother's House': Considering a Counterpart to the Israelite *Bet 'ab.*" In *The Bible and the Politics of Exegesis,* edited by Peggy Day, David Jobling, and Gerald Sheppard, 39-51. New York: Pilgrim Press, 1991.

Miller, J. Maxwell. *The Old Testament and the Historian.* Guides to Biblical Scholarship, Old Testament Series. Philadelphia: Fortress Press, 1976.

Miller, J. Maxwell, and John H. Hayes. "Before Any King Ruled in Israel." Chap. 3 in *A History of Ancient Israel and Judah.* Philadelphia: Westminster, 1986.

Shanks, Hershel. *The Rise of Ancient Israel.* Washington D.C.: Biblical Archaeology Society, 1992.

Smith, Mark S. *The Early History of God: Yahweh and the Other Deities in Ancient Israel.* New York: Harper & Row, 1991.

Toorn, Karel van der. *From Her Cradle to Her Grave: The Role of Religion in the Life of the Israelite and Babylonian Woman.* The Biblical Seminar 23. Sheffield: JSOT Press, 1994.

Zevit, Ziony. *The Religions of Ancient Israel: A Synthesis of Parallelistic Approaches.* London: Cassell, 1999.

11. THE BOOK OF DEUTERONOMY
AND THE DEUTERONOMISTIC HISTORY

Childs, Brevard S. "Deuteronomy." Chap. 10 in *Introduction to the Old Testament as Scripture.* Philadelphia: Fortress Press, 1979.

Christensen, Duane L., ed. *A Song of Power and the Power of Song: Essays on the Book of Deuteronomy.* Sources for Biblical and Theological Study. Winona Lake, Ind.: Eisenbrauns, 1993.

Clifford, Richard. *Deuteronomy, Excursus on Covenant and Law.* Old Testament Message, vol. 4. Wilmington, Del.: Michael Glazier, 1982.

Doorly, William J. *Obsession with Justice: The Story of the Deuteronomists.* New York/Mahwah, N.J.: Paulist Press, 1994.

Freedman, David Noel. "Deuteronomic History." In *Interpreter's Dictionary of the Bible, Supplementary Volume,* edited by Keith Crim, 226-28. Nashville, Tenn.: Abingdon Press, 1976.

Fretheim, Terence E. *Deuteronomic History.* Nashville, Tenn.: Abingdon Press, 1983.

Hoppe, Leslie L. *Deuteronomy.* Collegeville Bible Commentary. Old Testament, vol. 6. Collegeville, Minn.: Liturgical Press, 1985.

Mayes, A. D. H. *Deuteronomy.* New Century Bible Commentary. Grand Rapids, Mich.: Eerdmans, 1981.

McCarter, P. Kyle. "The Deuteronomistic History." In *1 Samuel: A New Translation with Introduction and Commentary.* Anchor Bible, 8:12-17. Garden City, N.Y.: Doubleday, 1980.

Miller, Patrick D. *Deuteronomy.* Interpretation. Louisville, Ky.: John Knox Press, 1990.

Nelson, Richard D. *The Double Redaction of the Deuteronomistic History.* Journal for the Study of the Old Testament Supplement Series 18. Sheffield: JSOT Press, 1981.

———. *Joshua: A Commentary.* Old Testament Library. Louisville, Ky.: Westminster John Knox Press, 1997.

Noth, Martin. *The Deuteronomistic History.* Journal for the Study of the Old Testament Supplement Series 15. Sheffield: JSOT Press, 1981.

Phipps, William E. "A Woman Was the First to Declare Scripture Holy." *Bible Review* 6 (1990), 14-15, 44.

Polzin, Robert. *Moses and the Deuteronomist: A Literary Study of the Deuteronomic History.* Part One: *Deuteronomy, Joshua, Judges.* Indiana Studies in Biblical Literature. Bloomington and Indianapolis: Indiana University Press, 1993.

Weinfeld, Moshe. *Deuteronomy and the Deuteronomic School.* Oxford: Clarendon Press, 1972.

Wolff, Hans Walter. "The Kerygma of the Deuteronomic Historical Work." Chap. 5 in *The Vitality of Old Testament Traditions,* edited by Walter Brueggemann and H. W. Wolff. Atlanta: John Knox, 1975.

12. THE PHILISTINES AND SAUL

Bright, John. *A History of Israel.* 3d ed. Philadelphia: Westminster, 1981. See pages 184-85.

Coote, Robert B., and Keith W. Whitelam. *The Emergence of Early Israel in Historical Perspective.* Sheffield: Almond Press, 1987.

Dothan, Trude. "What Do We Know about the Philistines?" *Biblical Archeology Review* 8/4 (July/August 1982), 20-44.

———. *The Philistines and Their Material Culture.* New Haven, Conn., and London: Yale University Press; Jerusalem: Israel Exploration Society, 1982.

———. "The Philistines." *The Anchor Bible Dictionary,* edited by David Noel Freedman, 5:322-33. New York: Doubleday, 1992.

Dothan, Trude, and Moshe Dothan. *People of the Sea: The Search for the Philistines.* New York: Macmillan, 1992.

Fine, John V. A. *The Ancient Greeks: A Critical History.* Cambridge: Harvard University, 1983. See pages 12-17.

Flanagan, James W. "Chiefs in Israel." *Journal for the Study of the Old Testament* 20 (1981), 47-73.

Frick, Frank S. *The Formation of the State in Ancient Israel: A Survey of Models and Theories.* Sheffield: Almond Press, 1985.

Gitin, Seymour, Amihai Mazar, and Ephraim Stern. *Mediterranean Peoples in Transition: Thirteenth to Early Tenth Centuries B.C.E. (In Honor of Professor Trude Dothan).* Jerusalem: Israel Exploration Society, 1998.

Gunn, D. M. *The Fate of King Saul.* Sheffield: JSOT Press, 1980.

Humphreys, W. Lee. "From Tragic Hero to Villain: A Study of the Figure of Saul and the Development of 1 Samuel." *Journal for the Study of the Old Testament* 22 (1982), 95-117.

————. *The Tragic Vision and the Hebrew Tradition.* Overtures to Biblical Theology 18. Philadelphia: Fortress Press, 1985.

Mayes, A. D. H. "The Reign of Saul." Chap. 5 in *Israelite and Judean History,* edited by John H. Hayes and J. Maxwell Miller. London: SCM Press, 1977.

Miller, J. Maxwell, and John H. Hayes. "The Early Israelite Monarchy." Chap. 4 in *A History of Ancient Israel and Judah.* Philadelphia: Westminster, 1986.

13. FROM CHIEFTAIN TO KING

Bright, John. *A History of Israel.* 3d ed. Philadelphia: Westminster, 1981. See pages 195-228.

Brueggemann, Walter. *David's Truth in Israel's Imagination and Memory.* Philadelphia: Fortress Press, 1985.

Conroy, Charles. *1-2 Samuel, 1-2 Kings, Excursus on Davidic Dynasty and Holy City Zion.* Old Testament Message vol. 6. Wilmington, Del.: Michael Glazier, 1983.

Finkelstein, Israel. "The Emergence of the Monarchy in Israel: The Environmental and Socio-economic Aspects." *Journal for the Study of the Old Testament* 44 (1989), 43-74.

————. "State Formation in Israel and Judah: A Contrast in Context, a Contrast in Trajectory." *Near Eastern Archaeology* 62 (1999), 35-52.

Flanagan, James W. *David's Social Drama: A Hologram of Israel's Early Iron Age.* Journal for the Study of the Old Testament Supplement Series 73. Sheffield: Almond Press, 1988.

Gottwald, Norman K. "Traditions about the United Kingdom." Chap. 7 in *The Hebrew Bible: A Socio-Literary Introduction.* Philadelphia: Fortress Press, 1985.

Gunn, David M. *The Story of King David: Genre and Interpretation.* Journal for the Study of the Old Testament Supplement Series 6. Sheffield: JSOT Press, 1978.

Humphreys, W. Lee. "The Davidic and Zion Traditions." Part 1, chap. 2 in *Crisis and Story: Introduction to the Old Testament.* 2d ed. Mountain View, Calif.: Mayfield, 1990.

Maly, Eugene H. *The World of David and Solomon.* Englewood Cliffs, N.J.: Prentice-Hall, 1966.

Miller, J. Maxwell, and John H. Hayes, "David, King of Jerusalem" and "The Reign of Solomon." Chaps. 5 and 6 in *A History of Ancient Israel and Judah.* Philadelphia: Westminster, 1986.

Noth, Martin. "The Transition to the Development of Political Power." Part 2, chap. 2 in *The History of Israel: Biblical History.* 2d ed. London; Adam and Charles Black, 1959.

Ollenberger, Ben C. *Zion, the City of the Great King: A Theological Symbol of the Jerusalem Cult.* Journal for the Study of the Old Testament Supplement Series 41. Sheffield: JSOT Press, 1987.

Seow, C. L. *Myth, Drama, and the Politics of David's Dance.* Harvard Semitic Monographs 44. Atlanta: Scholars Press, 1989.

Soggin, J. Alberto. "The Davidic-Solomonic Kingdom." Chap. 6 in *Israelite and Judean History,* edited by John H. Hayes and J. Maxwell Miller. London: SCM Press, 1977.

14. THE DIVIDED MONARCHY

Albertz, Rainer. "The History of Israelite Religion during the Monarchy." Part 3 in *A History of Israelite Religion in the Old Testament Period,* 1:105-242. London: SCM, 1994.

Bright, John. Chaps. 6, 7, and 8 in *A History of Israel.* 3d ed. Philadelphia: Westminster, 1981.

Donner, Herbert. "The Separate States of Israel and Judah." Chap. 7 in *Israelite and Judean History,* edited by John H. Hayes and J. Maxwell Miller. London: SCM Press, 1977.

Doorly, William J. *The Religion of Israel: A Short History.* New York/Mahwah, N.J.: Paulist Press, 1997.

Gottwald, Norman K. "Traditions about the Northern Kingdom" and "Traditions about the Southern Kingdom." Chaps. 8 and 9 in *The Hebrew Bible: A Socio-Literary Introduction.* Philadelphia: Fortress Press, 1985.

Lambert, Frith. "The Tribe/State Paradox in the Old Testament." *Scandanavian Journal of the Old Testament* 8 (1994), 20-44.

Miller, J. Maxwell, and John H. Hayes. Chaps. 7-12 in *A History of Ancient Israel and Judah.* Philadelphia: Westminster, 1986.

Nakanose, Shigeyuki. *Josiah's Passover: Sociology and the Liberating Bible.* Maryknoll, N.Y.: Orbis Books, 1993.

Nelson, Richard D. *The Historical Books.* Interpreting Biblical Texts. Nashville, Tenn.: Abingdon Press, 1998.

Noth, Martin. "The Coexistence of the Separate Kingdoms of Judah and Israel." Part 2, chap. 3 in *The History of Israel: Biblical History.* 2d ed. London: Adam and Charles Black, 1959.

Pixley, Jorge. *Biblical Israel: A People's History.* Minneapolis, Minn.: Fortress Press, 1992.

Soggin, J. Alberto. "The Divided Kingdom." Part 3 in *An Introduction to the History of Israel and Judah.* 2d rev. and updated ed. London: SCM, 1993.

15. THE ORIGINS AND DEFINITION OF PROPHECY

Albright, William F. *Samuel and the Beginnings of the Prophetic Movement.* The Goldensen Lecture for 1961. Cincinnati: Hebrew Union College Press, 1961.

Barton, John. "Prophecy: Postexilic Hebrew Prophecy." In *The Anchor Bible Dictionary,* edited by David Noel Freedman, 5:489-95. New York: Doubleday, 1992.

Blenkinsopp, Joseph. *A History of Prophecy in Israel from the Settlement in the Land to the Hellenistic Period.* Rev. and enl. ed. Louisville, Ky.: Westminster John Knox Press, 1996.

Fleming, Daniel E. "The Etymological Origins of the Hebrew *nabi':* The One Who Invokes God." *Catholic Biblical Quarterly* 55 (1993), 217-24.

Gordon, Robert P., ed. *This Place Is Too Small for Us: The Israelite Prophets in Recent Scholarship.* Sources for Biblical and Theological Study 5. Winona Lake, Ind.: Eisenbrauns, 1995.

Gottwald, Norman K. *All the Kingdoms of the Earth: Israelite Prophecy and International Relations in the Ancient Near East.* New York: Harper & Row, 1964.

———. "From Tribal Existence to Empire: The Socio-Historical Context for the Rise of the Hebrew Prophets." Chap. 1 in *God and Capitalism: A Prophetic Critique of Market Economy,* edited by J. M. Thomas and V. Visick. Madison, Wisconsin: A-R Editions 1991, 11-29.

———. *The Hebrew Bible: A Socio-Literary Introduction.* Philadelphia: Fortress Press, 1985.

Heschel, Abraham. *The Prophets.* 2 vols. New York: Harper & Row, 1962.

Holladay, John S. "Assyrian Statecraft and Prophets of Israel." *Harvard Theological Review* 63 (1970), 39-51.

Huffman, Herbert B. "Prophecy: Ancient Near Eastern Prophecy." In *The Anchor Bible Dictionary,* edited by David Noel Freedman, 5:477-82. New York: Doubleday, 1992.

———. "Prophecy in the Ancient Near East." *Interpreter's Dictionary of the Bible, Supplementary Volume,* edited by Keith Krim, 697-700. Nashville, Tenn.: Abingdon Press, 1976.

Koch, Klaus. *The Prophets.* 2 vols. Philadelphia: Fortress Press, 1982-83.

Lewis, I. M. *Ecstatic Religion: An Anthropological Study of Spirit Possession and Shamanism.* Baltimore: Penguin Books, 1971.

———. *Religion in Context: Cults and Charisma.* Cambridge: Cambridge University Press, 1986.

Lindblom, Johannes. *Prophecy in Ancient Israel.* New York: Oxford University Press, 1962.

Matthews, Victor H., and Don C. Benjamin. *Social World of Ancient Israel 1250-587 B.C.E.* Peabody, Mass.: Hendrickson, 1993, p.212.

Overholt, Thomas W. *Channels of Prophecy: The Social Dynamics of Prophetic Activity.* Minneapolis, Minn.: Fortress Press, 1989.

———. *Cultural Anthropology and the Old Testament.* Guides to Biblical Scholarship, Old Testament Series. Minneapolis, Minn.: Fortress Press: 1996.

Rabe, Virgil W. "The Origins of Prophecy." *Bulletin of the American Schools of Oriental Research* 221 (1976), 125-28.

Rendtorff, Rolf. *The Old Testament: An Introduction.* Philadelphia: Fortress Press, 1986. See pages 112-24.

Schmitt, John J. "Prophecy: Preexilic Hebrew Prophecy." In *The Anchor Bible Dictionary,* edited by David Noel Freedman, 5:482-89. New York: Doubleday, 1992.

Scott, R. B. Y. *The Relevance of the Prophets.* New York: Macmillan, 1967.

West, James King. "Thus Says the Lord: Prophecy in Israel." Chap. 4, part 1 in *Introduction to the Old Testament: "Hear, O Israel."* 2d ed. New York: Macmillan, 1981.

Westermann, Claus. *Prophetic Oracles of Salvation in the Old Testament.* Edinburgh: T. and T. Clark, 1991.

Wilson, Robert R. *Prophecy and Society in Ancient Israel.* Philadelphia: Fortress Press, 1980.

16. THE EIGHTH-CENTURY B.C.E. PROPHETS: AMOS AND HOSEA

Anderson, Bernhard W. *The Eighth Century Prophets: Amos, Hosea, Isaiah, Micah.* Proclamation Commentaries. Philadelphia: Fortress Press, 1978.

Brueggemann, Walter. *Tradition for Crisis: A Study in Hosea.* Richmond: John Knox, 1968.

Childs, Brevard S. "Introduction to the Latter Prophets," "Hosea," and "Amos." Chaps. 16, 20, and 22 in *Introduction to the Old Testament as Scripture.* Philadelphia: Fortress Press, 1979.

Coote, Robert B. *Amos among the Prophets: Composition and Theology.* Philadelphia: Fortress Press, 1981.

Doorly, William J. *Prophet of Justice: Understanding the Book of Amos.* Mahwah, N.J.: Paulist Press, 1989.

———. *Prophet of Love: Understanding the Book of Hosea.* Mahwah, N.J.: Paulist Press, 1991.

Gottwald, Norman K. *The Hebrew Bible: A Socio-Literary Introduction.* Philadelphia: Fortress. Press, 1985. See pages 302-8, 338-42, 353-63.

Hayes, John H. *Amos, the Eighth-Century Prophet: His Times and His Preaching.* Nashville, Tenn.: Abingdon Press, 1988.

Laffey, Alice L. "The Major and Minor Prophets." Part 3 in *An Introduction to the Old Testament: A Feminist Perspective.* Philadelphia: Fortress Press, 1988. See esp. pages 167-71.

Rad, Gerhard von. *The Message of the Prophets.* New York: Harper & Row, 1968.

Rendtorff, Rolf. *The Old Testament: An Introduction.* Philadelphia: Fortress Press, 1986. See pages 215-18, 220-23.

Vawter, Bruce. *Amos, Hosea, Micah: Excursus on Classical Prophecy.* Old Testament Message 7. Wilmington, Del.: Michael Glazier, 1981.

Westermann, Claus. *Basic Forms of Prophetic Speech.* Philadelphia: Fortress Press, 1967.

Wolff, Hans Walter. *Amos the Prophet.* Philadelphia: Fortress Press, 1973.

Yee, Gale A. "The Book of Hosea: Introduction, Commentary, and Reflections." In *New Interpreter's Bible,* 7:195-297. Nashville, Tenn.: Abingdon Press, 1996.

17. ISAIAH

Childs, Brevard S. "Isaiah." Chap. 17 in *Introduction to the Old Testament as Scripture.* Philadelphia: Fortress Press, 1979.

Gottwald, Norman K. *The Hebrew Bible: A Socio-Literary Introduction.* Philadelphia: Fortress Press, 1985. See pages 377-87.

Jensen, Joseph. *Isaiah 1-39.* Old Testament Message 8. Wilmington, Del.: Michael Glazier, 1984.

Melugin, Ray F., and Marvin A. Sweeney, eds. *New Visions of Isaiah.* Journal for the Study of the Old Testament Supplement Series 214. Sheffield: Sheffield Academic Press, 1996.

Rendtorff, Rolf. *The Old Testament: An Introduction.* Philadelphia: Fortress Press, 1986. See pages 188-93.

Sweeney, Marvin A. *Isaiah 1-39, with an Introduction to Prophetic Literature.* The Forms of the Old Testament Literature 16. Grand Rapids, Mich.: Eerdmans, 1996.

18. JEREMIAH

Boadt, Lawrence. *Jeremiah 1-25* and *Jeremiah 26-52.* Old Testament Message 9, 10. Wilmington, Del.: Michael Glazier, 1982, 1983.

Bright, John. *Jeremiah: A New Translation with Introduction and Commentary.* Anchor Bible 21. Garden City, N.Y.: Doubleday, 1965.

Brueggeman, Walter. *A Commentary on Jeremiah: Exile and Homecoming.* Grand Rapids, Mich. and Cambridge, U.K.: Eerdmans, 1998.

Carroll, Robert P. *The Book of Jeremiah: A Commentary.* Old Testament Library. Philadelphia: Westminster Press, 1986.

———. *From Chaos to Covenant: Prophecy in the Book of Jeremiah.* New York: Crossroad, 1981.

Childs, Brevard S. "Jeremiah." Chap. 18 in *Introduction to the Old Testament as Scripture.* Philadelphia: Fortress Press, 1979.

Crenshaw, James L. "A Living Tradition: The Book of Jeremiah in Current Research." *Interpretation* 37 (1983), 117-29.

Gottwald, Norman K. *The Hebrew Bible: A Socio-Literary Introduction.* Philadelphia: Fortress Press, 1985. See pages 395-404.

Holladay, William L. *Jeremiah 1: A Commentary on the Book of the Prophet Jeremiah, Chapters 1-25* and *Jeremiah 2: A Commentary on the Book of the Prophet Jeremiah, Chapters 26-52.* Hermeneia. Philadelphia: Fortress Press, 1986, 1989.

King, Philip J. *Jeremiah: An Archaeological Companion.* Louisville, Ky.: Westminster John Knox Press, 1993.

Laffey, Alice L. "The Major and Minor Prophets." Part 3 in *An Introduction to the Old Testament: A Feminist Perspective.* Philadelphia: Fortress Press, 1988. See pages 144-80, esp. 169, 174-77.

Lundbom, Jack R. "Jeremiah, Book of." In *The Anchor Bible Dictionary,* edited by David Noel Freedman, 3:706-21. New York: Doubleday, 1992.

McKane, William. *A Critical and Exegetical Commentary on Jeremiah.* 2 vols. Edinburgh: T. and T. Clark, 1986, 1996.

Mottu, Henri. "Jeremiah *vs.* Hananiah: Ideology and Truth in Old Testament Prophecy." In *Bible and Liberation: Biblical and Social Hermeneutics,* edited by Norman K. Gottwald and Richard A. Horsley. The Bible and Liberation Series. Maryknoll, N.Y.: Orbis Books, 1993.

Rendtorff, Rolf. *The Old Testament: An Introduction.* Philadelphia: Fortress Press, 1986. See pages 201-7.

19. THE DESTRUCTION OF JERUSALEM, THE EXILE, AND THE PROPHET EZEKIEL

Ackroyd, Peter R. *Exile and Restoration: A Study of Hebrew Thought of the 6th Century B.C.* Philadelphia: Westminster Press, 1968.

Albertz, Rainer. "A History of Israelite Religion in the Exilic Period." Part 4 in *A History of Israelite Religion in The Old Testament Period,* 2:369-436. London: SCM, 1994.

Ancient Near Eastern Texts Relating to the Old Testament, with Supplement (ANET). Edited by James B. Pritchard. 3d ed. Princeton, N.J.: Princeton University Press, 1969. See pages 491-92, 548-49.

Boadt, Lawrence. "Ezekiel, Book of." In *The Anchor Bible Dictionary,* edited by David Noel Freedman, 2:711-22. New York: Doubleday, 1992.

Bright, John. Chaps. 8 and 9 in *A History of Israel.* 3d ed. Philadelphia: Westminster, 1981.

Carroll, Robert P. "Israel, History of (Post-Monarchic Period)." In *The Anchor Bible Dictionary,* edited by David Noel Freedman, 3:567-76. New York: Doubleday, 1992.

Childs, Brevard S. "Ezekiel." Chap. 19 in *Introduction to the Old Testament as Scripture.* Philadelphia: Fortress Press, 1979.

Cody, Aelred. *Ezekiel.* Old Testament Message 11. Wilmington, Del.: Michael Glazier, 1984.

Gottwald, Norman K. *The Hebrew Bible: A Socio-Literary Introduction.* Philadelphia: Fortress Press, 1985. See pages 420-28, 482-92.

Greenberg, Moshe. *Ezekiel 1-20: A New Translation with Introduction and Commentary* and *Ezekiel 21-37: A New Translation with Introduction and Commentary.* Anchor Bible 22 and 22A. Garden City, N.Y.: Doubleday, 1983, 1997.

Klein, Ralph W. *Israel in Exile: A Theological Interpretation.* Overtures to Biblical Theology 6. Philadelphia: Fortress Press, 1979.

Laffey, Alice L. "The Major and Minor Prophets." Part 3 in *An Introduction to the Old Testament: A Feminist Perspective.* Philadelphia: Fortress Press, 1988. See pages 144-80, esp. 169-70, 177-78.

Miller, J. Maxwell, and J. H. Hayes. "The Last Years of the Davidic Kingdom" and "The Period of Babylonian Domination." Chaps. 12 and 13 in *A History of Ancient Israel and Judah.* Philadelphia: Westminster, 1986.

Noth, Martin. "The Age of Assyrian and Babylonian Power." Part 3, chap. 1 in *The History of Israel: Biblical History.* 2d ed. London: Adam and Charles Black, 1959.

Oded, Bustenay. "Judah and the Exile." Chap. 8 in *Israelite and Judean History,* edited by John H. Hayes and J. Maxwell Miller. London: SCM Press, 1977.

Rendtorff, Rolf. *The Old Testament: An Introduction.* Philadelphia: Fortress Press, 1986. See pages 208-14.

Zimmerli, Walther. *Ezekiel.* 2 vols. Hermeneia. Philadelphia: Fortress Press, 1979, 1984.

20. SECOND ISAIAH

Bright, John. Chap. 9 in *A History of Israel.* 3d ed. Philadelphia: Westminster, 1981.

Ceresko, Anthony R. "The Rhetorical Strategy of the Fourth Servant Song (Isaiah 52:13-53:12): Poetry and Exodus/New Exodus." *Catholic Biblical Quarterly* 56 (1994), 42-55.

Childs, Brevard S. "Isaiah." Chap 17 in *Introduction to the Old Testament as Scripture.* Philadelphia: Fortress Press, 1979.

Clifford, Richard J. *Fair-Spoken and Persuading: An Interpretation of Second Isaiah.* Theological Inquiries. Ramsey, N.J.: Paulist Press, 1984.

Gitay, Yehoshua. *Prophecy and Persuasion: A Study of Isaiah 40-48.* Forum Theologiae Linguisticae 14. Bonn: Linguistica Biblica, 1981.

Gottwald, Norman K. *The Hebrew Bible: A Socio-Literary Introduction.* Philadelphia: Fortress Press, 1985. See pages 492-502.

———. "Social Class and Ideology in Isaiah 40-55." In *Ideological Criticism of Biblical Texts,* edited by David Jobling and Tina Pippin, 43-57. *Semeia* 59. Atlanta: Scholars Press, 1992.

Laffey, Alice L. "The Major and the Minor Prophets." Part 3 in *An Introduction to the Old Testament: A Feminist Perspective.* Philadelphia: Fortress Press, 1988. See pages 144-80, esp. 172-74.

Miller, John W. "Prophetic Conflict in Second Isaiah: The Servant Songs in the Light of Their Context." In *Wort, Gebet, Glaube. Walter Eichrodt zum 80. Geburtstag,* edited by J. J. Stamm, 77-85. Abhandlungen zur Theologie des Alten und Neuen Testaments 59. Zurich: Zwingli Verlag, 1970.

Muilenburg, James. "Introduction and Exegesis to Isaiah 40-66." In *The Interpreter's Bible,* vol. 5, edited by G. A. Buttrick, 381-773. Nashville, Tenn.: Abingdon Press, 1956.

Newsom, Carol A. "Response to Norman K. Gottwald, 'Social Class and Ideology in Isaiah 40-55.'" In *Ideological Criticism of Biblical Texts,* edited by David Jobling and Tina Pippin, 73-78. *Semeia* 59. Atlanta: Scholars Press, 1992.

North, Christopher R. *The Suffering Servant in Deutero-Isaiah: An Historical and Critical Study.* London: Oxford University Press, 1964.

Rendtorff, Rolf. *The Old Testament: An Introduction.* Philadelphia: Fortress Press, 1986. See pages 193-96.

Scullion, John. *Isaiah 40-66.* Old Testament Message 12. Wilmington, Del.: Michael Glazier, 1982.

Stuhlmueller, Carroll. *Creative Redemption in Deutero-Isaiah.* Analecta Biblica 43. Rome: Pontifical Biblical Institute, 1970.

21. THE REESTABLISHMENT OF A JEWISH COMMUNITY IN JERUSALEM AND JUDAH

Ackroyd, Peter R. *Exile and Restoration: A Study of Hebrew Thought of the Sixth Century B.C.* Philadelphia: Westminster, 1968.

———. "The History of Israel in the Exilic and Post-Exilic Periods." In *Tradition and Interpretation: Essays by Members of the Society for Old Testament Studies,* edited by G. W. Anderson, 328-50. Oxford: Clarendon Press, 1979.

Albertz, Rainer. "A History of Israelite Religion in the Post-Exilic Period." Part 5 in *A History of Israelite Religion in the Old Testament Period,* 2:437-597. London: SCM, 1994.

Blenkinsopp, Joseph. *Ezra-Nehemiah. A Commentary.* Old Testament Library. London: SCM, 1989.

———. *Prophecy and Canon.* Notre Dame, Ind.: University of Notre Dame Press, 1977.

Bright, John. Chap. 9 in *A History of Israel.* 3d ed. Philadelphia: Westminster, 1981.

Gottwald, Norman K. *The Hebrew Bible: A Socio-Literary Introduction.* Philadelphia: Fortress Press, 1985. See pages 428-39.

Grabbe, Lester L. *Ezra-Nehemiah.* Old Testament Readings. London: Routledge, 1998.

Levine, Baruch. "Priestly Writers." *Interpreter's Dictionary of the Bible, Supplementary Volume,* edited by Keith Krim, 683-87. Nashville, Tenn.: Abingdon Press 1976.

Miller, J. Maxwell, and John H. Hayes. "The Era of the Persian Empire." Chap. 14 in *A History of Ancient Israel and Judah.* Philadelphia: Westminster, 1986.

Myers, J. N. *The World of the Restoration.* Englewood Cliffs, N.J.: Prentice-Hall, 1968.

Noth, Martin. "The Rule of the Persians and Macedonians." Part 3, chap. 1 in *The History of Israel: Biblical History.* 2d ed. London: Adam and Charles Black, 1959.

Rendtorff, Rolf. *The Old Testament: An Introduction.* Philadelphia: Fortress Press, 1986. See pages 55-76.

Soggin, J. Alberto. "Under the Empires of East and West." Part 4 in *An Introduction to the History of Israel and Judah.* 2d rev. and updated ed. London: SCM, 1993.

Widengren, Georg. "The Persian Period." Chap. 9 in *Israelite and Judean History,* edited by John H. Hayes and J. Maxwell Miller. London: SCM Press, 1977.

22. THE PSALMS

Alter, Robert. *The Art of Biblical Poetry.* New York: Basic Books, 1985.

Anderson, Bernhard W. *Out of the Depths: The Psalms Speak to Us Today.* Rev. ed. Philadelphia: Westminster, 1982.

Berlin, Adele. *The Dynamics of Biblical Parallelism.* Bloomington, Ind.: Indiana University Press, 1985.

———. "Introduction to Hebrew Poetry." In *New Interpreter's Bible,* edited by Leander E. Keck, 4:301-15. Nashville, Tenn.: Abingdon Press, 1996.

———. "Parallelism." In *The Anchor Bible Dictionary,* edited by David Noel Freedman, 5:155-62. New York: Doubleday, 1992.

Brenner, Athalya, and Carole Fontaine, eds. *Wisdom and Psalms.* A Feminist Companion to the Bible (Second Series). Sheffield: Sheffield Academic Press, 1998.

Brueggemann, Walter. *Israel's Praise: Doxology against Idolatry and Ideology.* Philadelphia: Fortress Press, 1988.

———. *The Message of the Psalms: A Theological Commentary.* Augsburg Old Testament Studies. Minneapolis, Minn.: Augsburg Press, 1984.

Cardenal, Ernesto. *Psalms of Struggle and Liberation.* New York: Herder and Herder, 1971, pages 35-36.

Ceresko, Anthony R. "The Sage in the Psalms." In *The Sage in Israel and the Ancient Near East,* edited by John G. Gammie and Leo J. Perdue, 217-30. Winona Lake, Ind.: Eisenbrauns, 1990.

Childs, Brevard S. "The Psalms." Chap. 22 In *Introduction to the Old Testament as Scripture*. Philadelphia: Fortress Press, 1979.

Craghan, John F. *The Psalms: Prayers for the Ups, Downs and In-Betweens of Life: A Literary-Experiential Approach*. Background Books 2. Wilmington, Del.: Michael Glazier, 1985.

Dahood, Mitchell J. *Psalms*. 3 vols. Anchor Bible 16, 17, 17A. Garden City, N.Y.: Doubleday, 1966-70.

Gerstenberger, Erhard S. *Psalms, Part I with an Introduction to Cultic Poetry*. The Forms of the Old Testament Literature 14. Grand Rapids, Mich.: Eerdmans, 1988.

Gottwald, Norman. *The Hebrew Bible: A Socio-Literary Introduction*. Philadelphia: Fortress Press, 1985. See pages 525-41.

Gunkel, Hermann. *The Psalms: A Form-Critical Introduction*. Facet Books, Biblical Series 19. Philadelphia: Fortress Press, 1967.

Guthrie, Harvey H. *Theology as Thanksgiving: From Israel's Psalms to the Church's Eucharist*. New York: Seabury, 1981.

Kraus, Hans-Joachim. *Psalms 1-59: A Commentary* and *Psalms 60-150: A Commentary*. Minneapolis, Minn.: Augsburg, 1988, 1989.

Kugel, James L. *The Idea of Biblical Poetry: Parallelism and Its History*. New Haven, Conn.: Yale University Press, 1981.

McCann, J. Clinton, "The Book of Psalms: Introduction, Commentary, and Reflections." In *New Interpreter's Bible,* edited by Leander E. Keck, et al., 4:639-1280. Nashville, Tenn.: Abingdon Press, 1996.

———. ed. *The Shape and Shaping of the Psalter*. Journal for the Study of the Old Testament Supplement Series 159. Sheffield: JSOT Press, 1993.

Mowinckel, Sigmund. *The Psalms in Israel's Worship*. 2 vols. Oxford: Basil Blackwell, 1962.

Murphy, Roland E. *The Psalms, Job*. Proclamation Commentaries. Philadelphia: Fortress Press, 1977.

Pleins, J. David. *The Psalms: Songs of Tragedy, Hope, and Justice*. Bible and Liberation Series. Maryknoll, N.Y.: Orbis Books, 1993.

Rendtorff, Rolf. *The Old Testament: An Introduction*. Philadelphia: Fortress Press, 1986. See pages 246-50.

Sabourin, Leopold. *The Psalms: Their Origin and Meaning*. Enl. and updated ed. New York: Alba House, 1974.

Smith, Mark S. *Psalms: The Divine Journey*. Mahwah, N.J.: Paulist Press, 1987.

Weiser, Artur. *The Psalms: A Commentary*. Old Testament Library. Philadelphia: Westminster, 1962.

Westermann, Claus. *Praise and Lament in the Psalms*. Atlanta: John Knox Press, 1981.

Wilson, Gerald E. *The Editing of the Hebrew Psalter*. Society of Biblical Literature Dissertation Series 76. Chico, Calif.: Scholars Press, 1985.

23. WISDOM IN ISRAEL

Ancient Near Eastern Texts Relating to the Old Testament, with Supplement (ANET). Edited by James B. Pritchard. 3d ed. Princeton, N.J.: Princeton University Press, 1969.

Bergant, Dianne. *Israel's Wisdom Literature: A Liberation-Critical Reading*. Minneapolis, Minn.: Fortress Press, 1997.

Berry, Donald K. *An Introduction to Wisdom and Poetry of the Old Testament.* Nashville, Tenn.: Broadman and Holman, 1995.

Boadt, Lawrence. *Wisdom Literature and Proverbs.* Collegeville, Minn.: Liturgical Press, 1984.

Brown, William P. *Character in Crisis: A Fresh Approach to the Wisdom Literature of the Old Testament.* Grand Rapids, Mich., and Cambridge, U.K.: Eerdmans, 1996.

Brueggemann, Walter. *In Man We Trust: The Neglected Side of Biblical Faith.* Atlanta: John Knox, 1972.

Ceresko, Anthony R. *Introduction to Old Testament Wisdom: A Spirituality for Liberation.* Maryknoll, N.Y.: Orbis Books, 1999.

Clifford, Richard J. *The Wisdom Literature.* Interpreting Biblical Texts. Nashville, Tenn.: Abingdon Press, 1998.

Cox, Dermot. *Introduction to the Sapiential Books and Proverbs.* Old Testament Message 18. Wilmington, Del.: Michael Glazier, 1982.

Crenshaw, James L. *Education in Ancient Israel: Across the Deadening Silence.* Anchor Bible Reference Library. New York: Doubleday, 1998.

———. *Old Testament Wisdom: An Introduction* (revised and enlarged). Louisville, Ky.: Westminster/John Knox Press, 1998.

———. "Wisdom." In *Old Testament Form Criticism,* edited by John H. Hayes, 225-64. San Antonio: Trinity University, 1974.

———. ed. *Studies in Ancient Israelite Wisdom.* New York: Ktav, 1976.

Gammie, John G., and Leo G. Perdue, eds. *The Sage in Israel and the Ancient Near East.* Winona Lake, Ind.; Eisenbrauns, 1990.

Gottwald, Norman K. *The Hebrew Bible: A Socio-Literary Introduction.* Philadelphia: Fortress Press, 1985. See pages 563-71.

Hill, R. Charles. *Wisdom's Many Faces.* A Michael Glazier Book. Collegeville, Minn.: Liturgical Press, 1996.

Laffey, Alice L. *An Introduction to the Old Testament: A Feminist Perspective.* Philadelphia: Fortress Press, 1988. See pages 181-219.

Murphy, Roland E. *The Tree of Life: An Exploration of Biblical Wisdom Literature.* 2d ed. Grand Rapids, Mich., and Cambridge, U.K.: Eerdmans, 1996.

———. "Wisdom and Creation." *Journal of Biblical Literature* 104 (1985), 3-11.

———. *Wisdom Literature: Job, Proverbs, Ruth, Canticles, Ecclesiastes and Esther.* The Forms of the Old Testament Literature 13. Grand Rapids, Mich.: Eerdmans, 1981.

O'Connor, Kathleen M. *The Wisdom Literature.* Message of Biblical Spirituality 5. Wilmington, Del.: Michael Glazier, 1988.

Perdue, Leo G. *Wisdom and Creation: A Theology of Wisdom Literature.* Nashville, Tenn.: Abingdon Press, 1994.

Rad, Gerhard von. *Wisdom in Israel.* Nashville, Tenn.: Abingdon, 1972.

Schams, Christine. *Jewish Scribes in the Second Temple Period.* Journal for the Study of the Old Testament Supplement Series 291. Sheffield: Sheffield Academic Press, 1998

Scott, R. B. Y. *The Way of Wisdom in the Old Testament.* New York: Macmillan, 1971.

24. THE WISDOM WRITINGS

Book of Proverbs

Camp, Claudia. *Wisdom and the Feminine in the Book of Proverbs.* Bible and Literature Series 11. Sheffield: Almond Press, 1985.

Ceresko, Anthony R. Chaps. 7 and 8 in *Introduction to Old Testament Wisdom: A Spirituality for Liberation.* Maryknoll, N.Y.: Orbis Books, 1999.

Childs, Brevard S. "Proverbs." Chap. 35 in *Introduction to the Old Testament as Scripture.* Philadelphia: Fortress Press, 1979.

Clifford, Richard J. *The Book of Proverbs and Our Search for Wisdom.* The Père Marquette Lecture in Theology 1995. Milwaukee: Marquette University Press, 1995.

Cox, Dermot. *Proverbs, with an Introduction to the Sapiential Books.* Old Testament Message 17. Wilmington, Del.: Michael Glazier, 1982.

Crenshaw, James L. "Proverbs, Book of." In *The Anchor Bible Dictionary,* edited by David Noel Freedman, 5:513-20. New York: Doubleday, 1992.

Fontaine, Carol R. "Proverbs." In *The Women's Bible Commentary,* edited by Carol A. Newsom and Sharon H. Ringe, 145-52. London: SPCK, 1992.

Golka, Friedemann W. *The Leopard's Spots: Biblical and African Wisdom in Proverbs.* Edinburgh: T. and T. Clark, 1993.

Gottwald, Norman K. *The Hebrew Bible: A Socio-Literary Introduction.* Philadelphia: Fortress Press, 1985. See pages 571-75.

McKane, William. *Proverbs: A New Approach.* Old Testament Library. Philadelphia: Westminster, 1970.

Murphy, Roland E. "The Kerygma of the Book of Proverbs." *Interpretation* 20 (1966), 3-14.

———. *Proverbs.* Word Biblical Commentary 22. Nashville, Tenn.: Thomas Nelson, 1998.

———. "Wisdom in the Old Testament." In *The Anchor Bible Dictionary,* edited by David Noel Freedman, 6:920-31. New York: Doubleday, 1992.

Rendtorff, Rolf. *The Old Testament: An Introduction.* Philadelphia: Fortress Press, 1986. See pages 255-58.

Scott, R. B. Y. *Proverbs. Ecclesiastes.* Anchor Bible 18. Garden City, N.Y.: Doubleday, 1965.

Van Leeuwen, Raymond C. "The Book of Proverbs." In *New Interpreter's Bible,* edited by Leander E. Keck, et al., 5:17-264. Nashville, Tenn.: Abingdon Press, 1996.

Westermann, Claus. *Roots of Wisdom: The Oldest Proverbs of Israel and Other Peoples.* Louisville, Ky.: Westminster John Knox Press, 1995.

Whybray, R. N. *The Book of Proverbs: A Survey of Modern Study.* History of Biblical Interpretation Series. Leiden: Brill, 1995.

Williams, James G. *Those Who Ponder Proverbs: Aphoristic Thinking and Biblical Literature.* Sheffield: Almond Press, 1981.

Book of Job

Andersen, Francis I. *Job: An Introduction and Commentary.* Tyndale Old Testament Commentaries. Downers Grove, Ill.: Inter-Varsity Press, 1976.

Bergant, Diane. *Job and Ecclesiastes.* Old Testament Message 18. Wilmington, Del.: Michael Glazier, 1982.

Ceresko, Anthony R. Chaps. 9 and 10 in *Introduction to Old Testament Wisdom: A Spirituality for Liberation.* Maryknoll, N.Y.: Orbis Books, 1999.

Childs, Brevard S. "Job." Chap. 34 in *Introduction to the Old Testament as Scripture.* Philadelphia: Fortress Press, 1979.

Crenshaw, James L. "Job, Book of." In *Anchor Bible Dictionary,* edited by David Noel Freedman, 3:858-68. New York: Doubleday, 1992.

Dhorme, Edouard. *A Commentary on the Book of Job.* Nashville, Tenn.: Thomas Nelson, 1984.

Good, Edwin M. *In Turns of Tempest: A Reading of Job.* Stanford, Calif.: Stanford University Press, 1990.

Gordis, Robert. *The Book of Job: Commentary, New Translation and Special Studies.* New York: Ktav, 1978.

Gottwald, Norman K. *The Hebrew Bible: A Socio-Literary Introduction.* Philadelphia: Fortress Press, 1985. See pages 575-79.

Gutiérrez, Gustavo. *On Job: God-Talk and the Suffering of the Innocent.* Maryknoll, N.Y.: Orbis Books, 1987.

Habel, Norman. *Job: A Commentary.* Old Testament Library. Philadelphia: Westminster, 1985.

Hartley, John E. *The Book of Job.* New International Commentary on the Old Testament. Grand Rapids, Mich.: Eerdmans, 1988.

Janzen, J. Gerald. *Job.* Interpretation: A Bible Commentary for Teaching and Preaching. Atlanta: John Knox, 1985.

Murphy, Roland. *The Psalms. Job.* Proclamation Commentaries. Philadelphia: Fortress Press, 1977.

Newsom, Carol A. "The Book of Job." In *New Interpreter's Bible,* edited by Leander E. Keck, et al., 4:317-637. Nashville, Tenn.: Abingdon Press, 1996.

———. "Job." In *The Women's Bible Commentary,* edited by Carol A. Newsom and Sharon H. Ringe, 130-36. London: SPCK, 1992.

Perdue, Leo G. *Wisdom in Revolt: Metaphorical Theology in the Book of Job.* Journal for the Study of the Old Testament Supplement Series 112, Bible and Literature Series 29. Sheffield; Almond Press, 1991.

Pope, Marvin H. *Job: A New Translation with Introduction and Commentary.* 3d ed. Anchor Bible 15. Garden City N.Y.: Doubleday, 1974.

Rendtorff, Rolf. *The Old Testament: An Introduction.* Philadelphia: Fortress Press, 1986. See pages 250-55.

Rowley, H. H. *The Book of Job.* Rev. ed. New Century Bible Commentary. Grand Rapids, Mich. Eerdmans; London: Marshall, Morgan and Scott, 1976.

Vawter, Bruce. *Job and Jonah: Questioning the Hidden God.* Ramsey, N.J.: Paulist Press, 1983.

Book of Ecclesiastes (Qoheleth)

Ancient Near Eastern Texts Relating to the Old Testament, with Supplement (ANET). Edited by James B. Pritchard. 3d ed. Princeton, N.J.: Princeton University Press, 1969.

Ceresko, Anthony R. Chaps 11 and 12 in *Introduction to Old Testament Wisdom: A Spirituality for Liberation.* Maryknoll, N.Y.: Orbis Books, 1999.

Childs, Brevard S. "Ecclesiastes." Chap. 38 in *Introduction to the Old Testament as Scripture.* Philadelphia: Fortress Press, 1979.

Clifford, Richard J. "The Book of Qoheleth (Ecclesiastes)." Chap. 5 in *The Wisdom Literature.* Interpreting Biblical Texts. Nashville, Tenn.: Abingdon Press, 1998.

Crenshaw, James E. *Ecclesiastes.* Old Testament Library. Philadelphia: Westminster, 1988.

———. "Ecclesiastes, Book of." In *The Anchor Bible Dictionary,* edited by David Noel Freedman, 2:271-80. New York: Doubleday, 1992.

Fox, Michael V. *A Time to Tear Down and a Time to Build Up: A Rereading of Ecclesiastes.* Grand Rapids, Michigan: Eerdmans, 1999.

Gordis, Robert. *Koheleth—The Man and His World.* 3d ed. New York: Schocken Books, 1968.

Gottwald, Norman K. *The Hebrew Bible: A Socio-Literary Introduction.* Philadelphia: Fortress Press, 1985. See pages 579-82.

Murphy, Roland E. "Ecclesiastes (Qohelet)." In *Wisdom Literature: Job, Proverbs, Ruth, Canticles, Ecclesiastes, and Esther.* The Forms of the Old Testament Literature 13. Grand Rapids, Mich.: Eerdmans, 1981. See pages 125-50.

———. *Ecclesiastes.* Word Biblical Commentary 23A. Dallas, Tex.: Word Books, 1992.

Rendtorff, Rolf. *The Old Testament: An Introduction.* Philadelphia: Fortress Press, 1986. See pages 265-67.

Seow, Choon-Leong. *Ecclesiastes: A New Translation with Introduction and Commentary.* Anchor Bible 18C. New York: Doubleday, 1997.

Towner, W. Sibley. "The Book of Ecclesiastes." In *New Interpreter's Bible,* edited by Leander E. Keck, et al., 5:256-360. Nashville, Tenn.: Abingdon Press, 1996.

Wright, Addison. "The Riddle of the Sphinx Revisited: Numerical Patterns in the Book of Qoheleth." *Catholic Biblical Quarterly* 42 (1980), 38-51.

Book of Sirach

Albertz, Rainer. "A Prospect on the History of Religion in the Hellenistic Period." Part 6 in *A History of Israelite Religion in the Old Testament Period.* London: SCM, 1994.

Ceresko, Anthony R. "The Liberative Strategy of Ben Sira: The Sage as Prophet." *Toronto Journal of Theology* 13 (1997), 169-85.

———. Chaps. 13 and 14 in *Introduction to Old Testament Wisdom: A Spirituality for Liberation.* Maryknoll, N.Y.: Orbis Books, 1999.

Crenshaw, James L. "The Book of Sirach." In *New Interpreter's Bible,* edited by Leander E. Keck, et al., 5:601-867. Nashville, Tenn.: Abingdon Press, 1996.

Di Lella, Alexander A. "Wisdom of Ben Sira." In *The Anchor Bible Dictionary,* edited by David Noel Freedman, 6:931-45. New York: Doubleday, 1992.

MacKenzie, R. A. F. *Sirach.* Old Testament Message 19. Wilmington, Del.: Michael Glazier, 1983.

O'Connor, Kathleen M. "Sirach and Communion with God." Chap. 6 in *The Wisdom Literature.* Message of Biblical Spirituality 5. Wilmington, Del.: Michael Glazier, 1988.

Skehan, Patrick W., and Alexander A. Di Lella. *The Wisdom of Ben Sira.* New trans. with notes by P. W. Skehan, intro. and comm. by A. A. Di Lella. Anchor Bible 39. New York: Doubleday, 1987.

Witherington, Ben. *Jesus the Sage: The Pilgrimage of Wisdom.* Minneapolis: Fortress Press, 1994.

Book of Wisdom

Ceresko, Anthony R. Chaps. 15 and 16 in *Introduction to Old Testament Wisdom: A Spirituality for Liberation.* Maryknoll, N.Y.: Orbis Books, 1999.

Kolarcik, Michael. "The Book of Wisdom." In *New Interpreter's Bible,* edited by Leander E. Keck, et al., 5:435-600. Nashville, Tenn.: Abingdon Press, 1996.

O'Connor, Kathleen M. "The Wisdom of Solomon and the Fullness of Life." Chap. 7 in *The Wisdom Literature.* Message of Biblical Spirituality 5. Wilmington, Del.: Michael Glazier, 1988.

Reese, James M. *The Book of Wisdom, Song of Songs.* Old Testament Message 20. Wilmington, Del.: Michael Glazier, 1983.

Winston, David. "Solomon, Wisdom of." In *The Anchor Bible Dictionary,* edited by David Noel Freedman, 6:120-27. New York: Doubleday, 1992.

———. *The Wisdom of Solomon: A New Translation with Introduction and Commentary.* Anchor Bible 43. New York: Doubleday, 1979.

Wright, Addison G. "Wisdom." In *New Jerome Biblical Commentary,* edited by Raymond E. Brown, et al., 510-22. Englewood Cliffs, N.J.: Prentice-Hall, 1990.

25. DANIEL AND THE APOCALYPTIC LITERATURE

Bright, John. Part 6, chaps. 11 and 12 in *A History of Israel.* 3d ed. Philadelphia: Westminster, 1981.

Brown, Raymond E., Pheme Perkins, and Anthony J. Saldarini. "Apocrypha; Dead Sea Scrolls; Other Jewish Literature." In *New Jerome Biblical Commentary,* edited by R. E. Brown, et al., 1055-82. Englewood Cliffs, N.J.: Prentice-Hall, 1990.

Childs, Brevard S. "Daniel." Chap. 41 in *Introduction to the Old Testament as Scripture.* Philadelphia: Fortress Press, 1979.

Collins, John J. *1-2 Maccabees, Daniel, Excursus on Apocalyptic Movement.* Old Testament Message 16. Wilmington, Del.: Michael Glazier, 1981.

———. *The Apocalyptic Imagination: An Introduction to the Jewish Apocalyptic Literature.* 2d ed. The Biblical Resource Series. Grand Rapids, Mich.: 1998.

———. *Daniel: A Commentary on the Book of Daniel.* Hermeneia. Minneapolis, Minn.: Fortress Press, 1993.

———. *Daniel, with an Introduction to Jewish Apocalyptic Literature.* The Forms of the Old Testament Literature 20. Grand Rapids, Mich.: Eerdmans, 1984.

Cross, Frank Moore. *The Ancient Library of Qumran.* 3d ed. The Biblical Seminar. Sheffield: Sheffield Academic Press, 1995.

Doran, Robert. "The First Book of Maccabees: Introduction, Commentary, and Reflections" and "The Second Book of Maccabees: Introduction, Commentary, and Reflections." In *New Interpreter's Bible,* edited by Leander E. Keck, et al., 4:1-178, 179-299. Nashville, Tenn.: Abingdon Press, 1996.

Garcia Martinez, Florentino. *The Dead Sea Scrolls Translated: The Qumran Texts in English,* translated by Wilfred G. E. Watson. Leiden: Brill, 1994.

Gaster, Theodor H. *The Dead Sea Scriptures.* In English Translation and Notes. 3d ed. Garden City, N.Y.: Doubleday/Anchor Books, 1976.

Gottwald, Norman K. *The Hebrew Bible: A Socio-Literary Introduction.* Philadelphia: Fortress Press, 1985. See pages 439-56, 582-94.

Hartman, Louis F., and Alexander A. DiLella, *The Book of Daniel: A New Translation with Introduction and Commentary.* Anchor Bible 23. Garden City, N.Y.: Doubleday, 1978.

Hayes, John H. "Daniel and Apocalyptic." Chap. 10 in *An Introduction to Old Testament Study.* Nashville, Tenn.: Abingdon Press, 1979.

Hengel, Martin. *Judaism and Hellenism: Studies in Their Encounter in Palestine during the Early Hellenistic Period.* 2 vols. Philadelphia: Fortress Press, 1974.

Murphy, Frederick J. "Introduction to Apocalyptic Literature." In *New Interpreter's Bible,* edited by Leander E. Keck, et al., 7:1-16. Nashville, Tenn.: Abingdon Press, 1996.

Rendtorff, Rolf. *The Old Testament: An Introduction.* Philadelphia: Fortress Press, 1986. See pages 273-77.

Schafer, Peter. "The Hellenistic and Maccabean Periods." Chap. 10 in *Israelite and Judean History,* edited by John H. Hayes and J. Maxwell Miller. London: SCM, 1977.

Schiffman, Lawrence H. *Reclaiming the Dead Sea Scrolls: The History of Judaism, the Background of Christianity, the Lost Library of Qumran.* Philadelphia and Jerusalem: Jewish Publication Society, 1994.

Shanks, Hershel, ed. *Understanding the Dead Sea Scrolls: A Reader from the Biblical Archaeology Review.* New York: Random House, 1992.

Smith-Christopher, Daniel. "The Book of Daniel: Introduction, Commentary, and Reflections" and "The Additions to Daniel: Introduction, Commentary, and Reflections." In *New Interpreter's Bible,* edited by Leander E. Keck, et al., 7:17-152, 153-94. Nashville, Tenn.: Abingdon Press, 1996.

Vermes, Geza. *The Complete Dead Sea Scrolls in English.* Complete ed. Allen Lane, The Penguin Press, 1997.

26. SOME CONCLUSIONS

Boff, Clodovis, and George V. Pixley. *The Bible, the Church, and the Poor.* Theology and Liberation Series. Maryknoll, N.Y.: Orbis Books, 1989.

Cormie, Lee. "Revolutions in Reading the Bible." In *The Bible and the Politics of Exegesis,* edited by Peggy Day, David Jobling, and Gerald Sheppard. New York: Pilgrim Press, 1991.

Gottwald, Norman K. "Sociohistoric Horizon of the Psalms." *The Hebrew Bible: A Socio-Literary Introduction.* Philadelphia: Fortress Press, 1985. See pages 537-41.

Horsley, Richard A. *The Liberation of Christmas: The Infancy Narratives in Social Context.* New York: Crossroad, 1989.

Miller, John W. "Prophetic Conflict in Second Isaiah: The Servant Songs in the Light of Their Context." In *Wort, Gebet, Glaube. Walter Eichrodt zum 80. Geburtstag,* edited by J. J. Stamm, 77-85. Abhandlungen zur Theologie des Alten und Neuen Testaments 59. Zurich: Zwingli Verlag, 1970.

General Index

Aaron, 105, 190, 277
Aaronid priestly line, 277-78
Abiathar, 151, 157, 224
Abimilech, 53, 110
Abraham: call of, 60; and covenant, 68–69; and Isaac, 46, 70; and land, 52; and Lot, 46–47, 53, 342, 347; and revelation, 334; and Sarah, 54, 75–77; and the strangers, 74–77; as tribal ancestor, 51, 77, 97
Absalom, 157
Adonijah, 157
agriculture, development of, 31–32
Ahab, King, 169–71, 188
Ahaz, King, 174, 209, 211, 216–17, 342
Ahaziah, King, 130
Ahijah of Shiloh, 166
Ahilud (Canaanite villager), 42–43, 100, 104
Akhenaton, Pharaoh, 100
Akkadians, the, 38
Albertz, Rainer, 104
Albright, William F., 20–21, 98
Alexander the Great, 276, 331–32
Amalekites, 146
Amarna Letters, 19–20, 43–44, 100–102
Amaziah, King, 174
Amaziah (priest), 202
Amon, King, 125
Amos: formation of Book of, 198–203; and Hosea, 203–5; impact of, 198; life of, 202; and the poor, 343–44; on ruling elites, 171–73, 199–201; and shift to writing, 188–89; whole people as audience, 197
ancestor theme, 51–52, 65
Antiochus IV Epiphanes, King, 335–37
Aphek, battle of, 141–44
apocalyptic tradition, 331–40
"apochrypha," 326–27
Arameans, 146, 216
archeology: and agriculture, 31–32; and Babylonian conquest, 243; vs. biblical record, 97–98; and history, 20–22; and languages, 18–20; on monarchy, 149–50; and social revolution model, 97–98, 111–12; and village life, 42–43; and women's role, 116–17
Ark of the Covenant, 126, 141–42, 151, 169, 294
Asherah, female deity, 117, 184

Assyrians, the: conquest of Israel, 70–71, 129–30, 166, 173–78; decline of, 226, 228–29; foreign policy of, 189; rise of, 38, 173; and Syro-Ephraimite Crisis, 215–20

Baalism, 112, 167, 170–73, 182, 184
Babylon: capture by Persians, 258; rise of, 175, 218–20; sack of Israel/Judah, 227–33, 241–44
Babylonian Exile: and Book of Daniel, 336–37; and Book of Hosea, 206–7; and Deuteronomist history, 71–72, 134–35; and Deutero-Isaiah, 209–10; Ezekiel in, 247–55; Jehoiachin in, 135, 242–44; Jeremiah and, 233, 235–37, 258; narrative traditions in, 173, 244–45; return from, 203, 262–65, 271–81; scribes in, 310–12
Balaam, 183
Balak, King, 183
Baruch, 197
Base Christian Communities, 10–11, 14
Bathsheba, 195
Benjamin, Don, 187–88
Benjamin, tribe of, 145, 149, 168, 224
Ben Sirah (See, Sirach, Book of)
Bethel: excavations, 99; shrine at, 169, 202
Bible, the: academic study of, 5–12, 58–59, 90, 276–81, 342–43, 347–48; historical–critical approach to, 17–22, 29–39; and liberation theology, 9–16, 341–50; literary qualities, 22, 197, 210–15, 286–89; and modern world, 3–16, 341, 347–48; and politics, 3–4, 345–47; and popular culture, 6–7; present arrangement of, 129–30; Protestant churches and, 58–59, 326, 327; purposes of, 112–19; Roman Catholic Church and, 4–5, 18, 326, 327; and sociology, 7–9, 11–12; Third World readings of, 15–16
"Book of the Law of Moses," 72, 125–26, 276

Callaway, Joseph, 42–43
Canaanites: city-states of, 44–45, 98–101, 105, 111, 138–47, 160; conflicts among, 43–44; and Egypt, 81, 99; Israelites as, 9, 41–56, 64, 106, 151–53; language of, 19, 38; and prophecy, 183–84; religious ideology of, 112; social revolution among, 97–106; strategic importance of, 24–25, 35, 38–39; unity through stories, 64–66

374

Scripture Index